THE ASSESSMENT OF LEARNING
COGNITIVE AND AFFECTIVE

THE ASSESSMENT
OF LEARNING
COGNITIVE AND AFFECTIVE

DAVID A. PA
University of Georgia

D. C. HEATH AND COMPANY
Lexington, Massachusetts   Toronto   London

FOR ALL OF US:

Mary Ann
and Mike, Steve, Jeff, and Karen

PREFACE

This book has a singular purpose: to provide the ever-increasing number of classroom teachers and professional evaluators a practical and efficient set of techniques to aid in evaluating learning outcomes. The essential principles of educational and psychological assessment are articulated, and illustrated with as many concrete examples as is practical. Abbreviated but valid statistical techniques and tables will be described, focusing on their use to improve test analyses and interpretation. Primary attention, however, will be on item and test construction and the development of principles useful in assessing the "cognitive" outcomes of education.

Surveying progress and innovation in education today, one notes a significant omission, involving what educational psychologists have called affective variables. The author's second major intent, then, is to promote awareness of techniques useful in assessing such educational outcomes as attitudes, values, and interests. The humanistic movement in education demands that these kinds of variables be addressed. Certain technical injustices may be perpetrated in the name of simplicity, but one must consider that this book represents many educators' first exposure to affective methods, which have only recently been adapted from other disciplines. Such an emphasis on the assessment of affective outcomes distinguishes this book from the usual educational measurement text.

It is hoped that this book will find an audience in undergraduate and graduate classes studying test construction or evaluative research methods, and that all students of education will find it useful. At both the preservice and in-service stages of professional development, questions involving the specification and measurement of learning outcomes arise. Most undergraduate teacher-training programs are quite deficient in developing measurement competencies. The teacher who has been in the field a few years should find valuable reference and review material here. An attempt has been made to develop generalized principles applicable, on the basis of expert opinion and utility in practice, to a wide range of grades and a variety of subject-matter fields. Finally, the growth of educational evaluation as a field of study, particularly in relation to the assessment of curricula, should stimulate the need for such a book as this.

A philosophy of testing that emphasizes the role of a test in facilitating communication within the learning situation is embedded in a methodological framework referred to as *educational assessment.* By contrast to the denotations and connotations of the terms *measurement* and *evaluation,* assessment concerns itself not only with the inputs and outputs of an instructional system, but also with the transactions within it. A comprehensive approach is desired.

The samples of behavior represented by a test, and our evaluation of them, should communicate meaningful information to both instructor and student. The importance of educational objectives, therefore, cannot be overemphasized, for it is typically by specifying expected outcomes that an instructor can best teach, a student best learn, and both best evaluate rationally. Considerable weight is therefore given to the specification of cognitive and affective variables, and their roles in learning and assessment.

Achievement in school involves progress toward a specified set of educational goals. Historically, these goals have emphasized the development of intellectual skills and abilities in conjunction with the acquisition of information. Information acquisition has, unfortunately, dominated educational curricula. Only within the last several decades have professional educators moved away from the stultifying emphasis on recall of specific facts and information. Where appropriate, efforts have been made in this book to illustrate how higher-order mental abilities, skills, and knowledges can be measured with relative efficiency.

This book represents a complete revision and expansion of a paperback volume (Payne 1968) on educational measurement. Its 18 chapters are divided into six parts. The frame of reference, terms, and applications of educational assessment data are considered in the first chapter. Chapters Two through Four describe the planning process, giving particular attention to the definition of the learning outcomes to be assessed. Various approaches to the development of custom or tailor-made devices are described in detail in Chapters Five through Eight. Methods useful in summarizing and interpreting assessment data are examined in Chapters Nine and Ten. Instrument refinement is covered in Chapters Eleven and Twelve. Criterion-referenced and standardized measures are discussed in Chapters Thirteen through Fifteen. In these chapters the author has excerpted critical comments from test reviews in an attempt to promote a critical evaluative attitude in the reader. The comments are less harsh than they might appear on first reading. Chapter Sixteen deals with observational methods, and Chapter Seventeen with the ever-perplexing problem of marking and reporting. The book concludes with an examination of some of the many issues—legal, ethical, and social—that confront today's professional educational assessor.

Space limitations prohibit full discussion of certain topics. It is hoped that the reader will seek out in the end-of-chapter Suggested Readings examples of how paper-and-pencil items and tests, as well as other measurement approaches, may be used to assess a nearly infinite variety of learning outcomes. Imagination and practice both play significant roles in the development of variations on the assessment methods discussed in the book.

At the beginning of each chapter the student will find a set of Summary Preview Statements highlighting the major points to be discussed. This list should be studied before and after reading the chapter. The statements serve as an introduction and a stimulus for review, and imply instructional objectives.

A number of the author's colleagues have contributed significantly to this project. Several individuals at Syracuse University contributed useful critical comments and ideas to the volume on which this book is based (Payne 1968). Eric Gardner, James Powers, James Diamond, Donald Meyer, Robert Weatherford, and the late Ray Kuhlen read selected chapters and made significant suggestions. Special acknowledgement is made of Bob McMorris of the State University of New York at Albany, who read much of both manuscripts. In addition, Jason Millman of Cornell University, S. David Farr of the State University of New York at Buffalo, and James Terwilliger of the University of Minnesota contributed critical evaluations of the manuscript of this book. The author would also like to acknowledge the significant influence of the writings of Dr. Robert L. Ebel of Michigan State University. Much of what is useful in the book reflects the contributions of these individuals. The author must assume responsibility for errors and misinterpretations.

A heartfelt acknowledgement is made of Mrs. Ada Kornmuller, who typed the initial draft of the first edition, and of Ms. June McClain, who patiently, cheerfully, and professionally translated my chicken scratchings into their present form. Mrs. Ann Stillman and Mr. Lowell Ensey contributed what the author considers excellent statistical, item-construction, and general material on testing. Thanks also go to the several individuals and publishers who permitted the publication of copyrighted materials. Acknowledgement of each is made in the appropriate place in the text.

David A. Payne
May 1973
Athens, Georgia

CONTENTS

III INSTRUMENT DEVELOPMENT

IV SUMMARIZING AND INTERPRETING TEST PERFORMANCES

V INSTRUMENT REFINEMENT

VI OTHER SOURCES AND USES OF ASSESSMENT DATA

AN INSTRUCTOR'S LAMENT

My face is lined, my hair is gray
Though I'm but five and twenty;
I'll tell you how I got this way
My friends, I've been through plenty.

My principal once took a course
In measurement and testing
And since that God-forsaken day,
We've none of us been resting.

Each term begins the same old way,
We give tests diagnostic;
I once believed there was a God,
Now I'm a grim agnostic.

When all the papers have been
   marked
With data tabulated,
They're stored away till Judgment
   Day
Berated, hated, fated.

And then we give Achievement Tests
To find the children's level;
I fear my faith in life now rests
A-shattered with the devil.

We take them home and through the
   night
Work out the correlations,
We seek deficient coefficients
And those obscure relations.

And then without a breathing spell
We test to find IQ's,
Like soldiers shocked by shrieking
   shell
We seek out those M.A.'s.

Each day, each week, each month, we
   test
No matter what the weather,
For teaching there's no time at all
To ever get together.

The Mid-terms come, the Finals too,
And tests with other labels,
We're working now with fevered
   brows
Computing phoney tables.

The end has come, our principal
Now gives the figures study.
His face lights up, he shakes each
   hand,
He even calls me "Buddy."

"In one short term, our children
   gained
Three years," he cries, "that's plenty."
But he forgets to mention us—
His teachers—we've lost twenty.

Author Unknown

I
AN OVERVIEW

1
A PERSPECTIVE ON EDUCATIONAL ASSESSMENT

SUMMARY PREVIEW STATEMENTS

1. The process and results of educational assessment constitute a very powerful force that can be used to improve the effectiveness of teaching-learning situations.

2. The term *educational assessment* refers to the collection and evaluation of data involving inputs to, transactions within, and outputs from an educational system.

3. The diagnosis of learning difficulties and their implications for remedial procedures is one of the major intents of educational assessment.

4. The chief inputs to an educational assessment decision-making system derive from measurement and evaluation procedures.

5. A test is a means of measurement characterized by systematic administration and scoring procedures, formalized objectives, and applications aimed at intra- or interindividual comparisons.

6. Measurement is the process of collecting, quantifying, and ordering information on an individual, attribute, or object.

7. Evaluation is the process of making value judgments about measurement data.

8. Tests may be categorized as standardized, informal (teacher-made), oral, written, mastery, survey, speed, power, verbal, nonverbal, or performance.

9. Measurement data can be used to help:
   a. Select, appraise, and clarify instructional objectives.
   b. Describe and report pupil progress toward, or achievement of, educational objectives.
   c. Plan, direct, and improve learning experiences.

10. The processes of instruction and evaluation are intimately related.

11. The evaluation of curricula represents one major application of educational assessment principles.

12. Educational assessment and evaluation involve the following stages:
    a. Specifying goals and objectives.
    b. Designing the assessment system.
    c. Selecting data-gathering methods.
    d. Collecting relevant data.
    e. Analyzing and summarizing data.
    f. Contrasting data and objectives.
    g. Feeding back results.

13. The movement for accountability in the schools is placing great demands on educational assessment systems.

14. A good measuring instrument should, as a rule, be:
    a. Relevant.
    b. Balanced.
    c. Efficient.
    d. Objective.
    e. Specific.
    f. Appropriately difficult and discriminating.
    g. Reliable.
    h. Fair.
    i. Unspeeded.

15. A relevant measurement contains samples of behavior directly related to the objectives.

16. An educational assessment system should be responsive to relevant cognitive, affective, and psychomotor educational objectives.

17. A balanced measurement must weigh test behaviors in proportion to their actual occurrence.

18. An efficient measurement provides the maximum number of relevant scorable responses per unit of time.

19. The extent to which experts agree on the scorability of a measurement is an indication of its degree of objectivity.

20. Educational measurements should be specifically applicable to the instructional field, area, discipline, or course in which they are used.

21. Item difficulty and discrimination in educational measurements should depend upon the projected use of the results, the level of

student and subject matter, and the nature of students' prior instructional experience.

22. Educational measurements should yield reliable, consistent, and replicatable results.

23. Each student should have a fair opportunity to demonstrate his or her knowledge or skill.

24. Most educational measurements should be unspeeded so that comparable behavior samples can be gathered from all students.

The thoughtful and intelligent application of educational assessment principles and devices can profoundly improve the quality of education. Measurement's primary relevance is, of course, to the activities of student and instructor, but its applicability to administration, curriculum development, counseling, and supervision should not be overlooked.

THE NATURE OF EDUCATIONAL ASSESSMENT

The use of the term *assessment* in this book is similar to Bloom's (1970)[1] description of systematic approaches to the description of relationships between selected task requirements, criterion behaviors, and the environment. The inclusion of the environmental element distinguishes assessment from other tasks and activities, such as measurement and testing, associated with evaluating teaching-learning situations. Assessment concerns itself with the totality of the educational setting, and is the more inclusive term, i.e., it subsumes measurement and evaluation. It focuses not only on the nature of the learner, but also on what is to be learned and how. Stake (1967) has drawn attention to the importance of what he calls the "transactions" of the classroom: the countless interactions between student and teacher, student and instructional material, and student and student that constitute the process of education. In a very real sense, educational assessment is diagnostic in intent. Those with responsibility for overseeing education are concerned not only with the strengths and weaknesses of an individual learner, but also with the effectiveness of the instructional materials and

---

[1] Parenthetical references relate to the bibliography at the end of the book.

curriculum. Indeed, the whole area of curriculum evaluation has recently experienced an intense reawakening (Heath 1969; Forehand 1971; Stufflebeam *et al.* 1971; Provus 1971; Payne 1974).

Educational assessment is difficult to define. English and English (1958) define assessment as "a method of evaluating personality in which an individual, living in a group under partly controlled physical and social conditions, meets and solves a variety of lifelike problems, including stress problems, and is observed and rated. . . ." (p. 44) This statement describes the procedures used by the military to select staff for the Office of Strategic Services (a forerunner of the Central Intelligence Agency) during World War Two (OSS Assessment Staff 1948). This intense process utilized a variety of data-gathering techniques, such as observations, stress interviews, performance measures, group discussions, individual and group tasks, peer ratings, projective techniques, and various kinds of structured tests.

Cronbach (1960) notes three principal features of assessment: (1) the use of a variety of techniques, (2) reliance on observations in structured and unstructured situations, and (3) integration of information. These characteristics and the foregoing definition are readily applicable to a classroom situation. The term *personality* as used above refers to the totality of an individual's characteristics—cognitive, affective, and psychomotor. The classroom setting is social and provides for both structured and unstructured phases. And, finally, problem solving is a major learning task. Obviously, a variety of instruments would be needed to measure the myriad relevant variables. Appraisal of the totality of the student, his environment, and his accomplishments is the objective of educational assessment.

The following statement by Bloom (1970, p. 31) admirably summarizes the process of educational assessment:

> Assessment characteristically begins with an analysis of the criterion and the environment in which the individual lives, learns, and works. It attempts to determine the psychological pressures the environment creates, the roles expected, and the demands and pressures—their hierarchical arrangement, consistency, as well as conflict. It then proceeds to the determination of the kinds of evidence that are appropriate about the individuals who are placed in this environment, such as their relevant strengths and weaknesses, their needs and personality characteristics, their skills and abilities.

THE NATURE AND PLACE OF MEASUREMENT IN ASSESSMENT

The primary component of educational assessment is data collection—specifically, data collection through measurement. Measurement is the backbone of any educational process, as it provides information for decisionmaking. Decisions are made continuously about objectives, materials, the cost effectiveness of the instructional system, student progress, and other similarly important questions.

Educational measurement is a process of gathering data that will provide for a more precise and objective appraisal of learning outcomes than could be accomplished by less formal and systematic procedures. But why be concerned with precision at all? It may be enough to say, with Churchman (1959), that precise information is desirable because it can be applied to a wide variety of problems and decision-making activities.

There are probably as many definitions of measurement as there are tests and testers. Although qualitatively different, all definitions involve the systematic assignment of numerals to objects or events. Such a definition is not sufficient, because it allows enumeration and classification to be considered an aspect of measurement. Measurement is more than counting or sorting. It is the comparison of something with a unit or standard amount or quantity of that same thing, in order to represent the magnitude of the variable being measured. A synonym for measurement might be "quantification," specifically, the quantification of *properties* of objects, not the objects themselves. The alternative to measurement is verbal description; but attempts, however systematic, to describe phenomena verbally tend to be laborious and inefficient, and the results to be rather vague and inexact.

Four major benefits deriving from measurement may be summarized as follows:

Descriptive flexibility. The application of measurement procedures allows us to discriminate between individuals and to describe individual differences.

Assistance in interpretation. We can not only identify and describe individual differences, but can also order individuals with respect to the variable measured, and thereby derive an interpretation based on relative position or performance against a standard.

Identification of patterns. Descriptive flexibility allows for the identification and measurement of individual differences in a number of different behaviors, which may then be interrelated in meaningful ways.

Data reduction. The introduction of metrical terms allows for the application of useful mathematical and statistical procedures to summarize large numbers of observations.

These four characteristics serve to summarize the "why" of measurement. The remainder of this book will address itself to the "what" and "how" of educational measurement.

TESTS, MEASUREMENTS, AND EVALUATION

Words in common parlance often take on new and sometimes esoteric meanings when used by specialists. Such is the case with the terms *test, measurement,* and *evaluation.* As commonly used, they are interchangeable. In an educational assessment situation, however, this can lead to confusion. Within the umbrella category "assessment," *evaluation* is the most inclusive term. It describes a general process for making judgments and decisions. The data used to make evaluations may be quantitative or qualitative. A teacher may draw upon classroom exams, anecdotal materials, scores from standardized tests, and informal observations in arriving at a decision on the promotion of a pupil. Measurement, on the other hand, is concerned with the systematic collection, quantification, and ordering of information. It implies both the process of quantification and the result.

Measurement may take many forms, ranging from the application of very elaborate and complex electronic devices, to paper-and-pencil exams to rating scales or checklists. A test is a particular form of measurement. Implicit in the current usage of the term is the notion of a formal standardized procedure in which the examinee is aware that he is being tested for a particular purpose at a specified time. A test might be defined as a systematic method of gathering data for the purpose of making intra- or interindividual comparisons. It is a sample of behavior.

Tests might further be characterized as (1) *informal* (teacher-made) or *standardized* (specialist-made); (2) *oral* or *written;* (3) *mastery* (of basic knowledge and skills), *survey* (of general achievement), or *diagnostic* (of specific disabilities and deficiencies); (4) *speed* (in responding to items of approximately equal difficulty) or *power* (in responding to items of increasing difficulty, with speed deemphasized); and (5) *verbal, nonverbal,* or *performance* (requiring manipulation of objects). Many other types of classifications are possible, depending upon the needs and philosophy of the developer or user. Because written mastery, survey, and diagnostic tests have, in general, proved to be the most useful in assessing learning outcomes, the emphasis in this book will be on paper-and-pencil tests.

USE OF EDUCATIONAL ASSESSMENT DATA

Most educators agree that measurement and evaluation are integral components of the instructional process. Progress toward the achievement of instructional goals must be periodically evaluated if effective teaching and learning are to be accomplished. It is widely recognized that educational objectives and learning experiences are intimately related. It is less apparent to many that objectives, learning experiences, *and* measurement-evaluation activities are also intimately related. It is the interaction of these three elements in a well-planned program of education that best promotes the desired changes in pupil behavior. The intimate relationship of instruction and assessment activities has been well defined by Dressel (1954, pp. 23–24). His listing of the parallel elements in these two activities illustrates their common objectives:

Instruction	*Evaluation*
1. Instruction is effective to the degree that it leads to desired changes in students.	1. Evaluation is effective to the degree that it provides evidence of the extent of changes in students.
2. New behavior patterns are best learned by students when the inadequacy of present behavior is understood and the significance of the new behavior patterns thereby made clear.	2. Evaluation is most conducive to learning when it provides for and encourages self-evaluation.
3. New behavior patterns can be more efficiently promoted by teachers who recognize the existing behavior patterns of individual students and the reasons for them.	3. Evaluation is conducive to good instruction when it reveals major types of inadequate behavior and the contributory causes.
4. Learning is encouraged by problems and activities that require thought and/or action by each individual student.	4. Evaluation is most significant in learning when it permits and encourages the exercise of individual initiative.
5. Activities that provide the basis for the teaching and learning of specified behavior are also the most suitable for evoking and evaluating the adequacy of that behavior.	5. Activities or exercises developed for the purpose of evaluating specified behavior are also useful in the teaching and learning of that behavior.

After examining in detail the objectives of both activities, Dressel concludes that they do not really differ in methods or materials. They can be differentiated only when evaluating achievement at the close of a period of instruction.

What, then, are the general uses of measurement data in education? Three broad use categories can be defined.

Selecting, Appraising, and Clarifying
Instructional Objectives

Achievement in school involves movement toward a specified set of objectives. When a teacher sits down to develop an instrument for the collection of data to be used in evaluating progress toward these objectives, he is forced by the very nature of the task to define and review his instruction. Ideally, the specification of objectives will be accomplished before instruction begins, and will continue as the curriculum is modified to meet individual student needs. It may even be desirable to administer an achievement test to reveal deficiencies at the beginning of a course of study. The original objectives may then be modified, enlarged upon, or discarded, as decreed by the data.

Determining and Reporting Pupil Achievement of
Educational Objectives

Educational measurement is most frequently used in assessing the level of pupil achievement in school subjects. The application of measurement procedures yields more objective data on achievement than does subjective appraisal. Such information is obviously of critical importance to the student, as it provides him with some perspective on his position relative to acceptable educational standards. These standards may be those of the school, society, or teacher, or they may be his own.

Many other individuals, in addition to the instructor and student, are interested in individual pupil status with respect to learning. School administrators are obviously concerned. College admissions personnel find high-school grades useful in making decisions. Despite the proliferation of national admissions and scholarship testing programs, previous academic performance remains the single best predictor of future performance.

Planning, Directing, and Improving
Learning Experiences

The diagnostic use of measurement data can be extremely helpful. Tests can serve a valuable function by identifying strengths and weaknesses in the achievement of individual pupils or classes. If the teacher and student can identify the areas in which achievement is less than adequate, individual learning efforts and, for that matter, teaching can be directed more efficiently.

In the improvement and facilitation of learning, data on the sequence, continuity, and integration of learning experiences can be of great value. For example, the requisite skills and knowledges for certain courses or units can be identified. The effectiveness of selected instructional practices can also be evaluated. This use of measurement is becoming more important each year with the appearance of new curricula, particularly in science, mathematics, and social studies. This essentially involves the use of tests for research. A teacher might compare the results of a new device or program to previous educational outcomes with the same class, outcomes obtained in control groups, or outcomes commonly obtained by similar classes.

CURRICULUM EVALUATION AS AN EXAMPLE OF EDUCATIONAL ASSESSMENT

Revitalized interest in the teaching-learning process during the past 25 years or so has resulted in a plethora of new curricula. The impetus to curriculum development has come from both subject-matter scholars and educational researchers—from the former because of new knowledge and insights into the structures of the disciplines, and from the latter because of new insights into the relation of the learning process to the organization and presentation of knowledge. The development of any "new" curriculum creates associated problems of evaluation (Payne 1973, 1974). Overall program effectiveness, cost, variables influencing effectiveness, and relevance are a few of the areas in need of assessment. Evaluation is probably of greater concern today than at any time in history due to the massive amount of knowledge that must be transmitted and processed, as well as to the complexity of this knowledge. Evaluative techniques adequate for assessing the effectiveness of small units of material are significantly less satisfactory when applied to larger blocks of information, the learning of which is highly complex and involves prerequisite learnings, sequential behaviors, and perhaps other programs of study. The traditional use of experimental and control groups (as examined by contrasting gross mean achievement scores in a pre-post treatment design study), although generally valuable, tends not to provide sufficiently detailed information upon which to base intelligent decisions about curriculum effectiveness, validity, efficiency, and the like. Guba (1969) has recently lamented the failure of the evaluation designs for a group of recent government research proposals to meet even minimal requirements. The desire or need to compromise evaluation designs results in far too many "no significant differences." Guba notes, for example, that the practitioner seeking information about the success of his program is "inviting interference." This is a situation incompatible with control. If we lack control, experimental designs and methods of data analysis are considerably less applicable. Most applied studies are done in natural settings, and natural educational settings are anything but controlled. But it is in these relatively unstructured and uncontrolled situations that evaluation and decisions must be undertaken. The field of curriculum evaluation is developing in response to the requirements of decision-making.

Curriculum evaluation will play many roles, contingent upon the demands and constraints placed on it. Heath (1969), for example, suggests three broad functions performed by curriculum evaluation:

1. *Improvement of the curriculum during the development phase.* The importance of formative evaluation is emphasized. Strengths and weaknesses of the program or unit can be identified and enhanced or strengthened. As Heath notes, the process is iterative, involving continuous repetition of the tryout-evaluation-redesign cycle.

2. *Facilitation of rational comparison of competing programs.* Although differing objectives pose a large problem, the description and comparison of alternative programs can contribute to rational decisionmaking.

3. *Contribution to the general body of knowledge about effective curriculum design.* Freed from the constraints of formal hypothesis-testing, curriculum evaluators are at liberty to search out principles relating to the interaction of learner, learning, and environment.

A question remains about the ways curriculum evaluation differs from educational assessment, pure research, or the straightforward evaluation of learning. Following is a list of variables that may clarify the emphases unique to curriculum evaluation:

1. *Nature of goals.* The objectives of curriculum evaluation tend to be oriented more to process and behavior than to subject-matter content.

2. *Breadth of objectives.* The objectives of curriculum evaluation involve a greater range of phenomena.

3. *Complexity of outcomes.* Changes in the nature of life and education, and the increased knowledge we now possess about the teaching-learning process, combine to require objectives that are quite complex from the standpoint of cognitive and performance criteria. The interface of cognitive, affective, and psychomotor variables further complicates the process of identifying what must be evaluated.

4. *Focus of total evaluation effort.* There is a definite trend away from the individual learner and toward the total program.

5. *Context of evaluation.* Curriculum evaluation should take place in a naturalistic setting, if possible. It is in the real-life setting, with all its unpredictable contingencies and uncontrolled variables, that education takes place. We must evaluate and make decisions in the setting in which we teach.

The following statement summarizes well the nature of contemporary curriculum evaluation:

Curriculum evaluation can be viewed as a process of collecting and processing data pertaining to an educational program, on the basis of which decision can be made about that program. The data are of two kinds: (1) objective description of goals, environments, personnel, methods and content, and immediate and long range outcomes; and (2) recorded personal judgments of the quality and appropriateness of goals, inputs and outcomes. The data—in both raw and analyzed form—can be used either to delineate and resolve problems in educational programs being developed or to answer absolute and comparative questions about established programs (Taylor and Maguire 1966).

This broad general description allows the final curriculum evaluation plan to take on any form dictated by its requirements. Some illustrative models are described in the following section.

Models for Curriculum Evaluation

It is frequently helpful to formalize a complex process, such as curriculum evaluation, into a model. The model will frequently take the form of some conceptual paradigm, flow chart, or other schematic formulation. Several authorities in the field have proposed such formal models. The value of abstract representations is open to question, but they do help define activities, examine relationships among the components of activities, and point toward possible new applications or research problems. In general, a model will aid in the planning and implementation of curriculum evaluation (Forehand 1971). One major danger of over-reliance on a model is the routinization of what should be an ever-changing process. Such a danger is particularly acute if the evaluation has been well institutionalized.

Table 1.1 compares a representative group of curriculum evaluation models, each of whose major emphases are briefly described. Many educators have made significant contributions to curriculum evaluation and related issues but failed to propose a systematic design, including detailed descriptions or outlines of specific activities. The developers listed in Table 1.1 must have presented a verbally or schematically detailed outline of the elements in each model and a description of a sequence of activities.

Table 1.1 is presented to suggest the nature of the models available. The overlap in approach, content, and methodology is considerable. The specification of instructional objectives plays a central role in nearly all models, as does the selection of a data-gathering instrument. All emphasize feedback and recycling, and all assume that an assessment of needs has been carried out prior to program development. (Of course, models will differ if the questions asked relate to the evaluation of a single curriculum or are comparative in nature.) And, finally, all models emphasize decisionmaking and reflect the biases and intentions of their developers.

TABLE 1.1 Key Emphases of Selected Curriculum Evaluation Models

Model Developer	Key Emphasis	Model Developer	Key Emphasis
Tyler (1942)	Curriculum objectives and evaluation of student progress.	Crane & Abt (1969)	Cost-effectiveness of alternative curriculum materials.
Provus (1971)	Assessment of discrepancy between program performance and standards.	Welch & Walberg (1968)	Improvement of college physics curriculum using change data.
Taylor & Maguire (1966); Metfessel & Michael (1967)	Objectives and involvement of variety of personnel (e.g., layman, professional educator, students, philosophers, psychologists).	Stufflebeam (1968); Klein et al. (1971)	Rational decisionmaking among alternatives by administrator.
		Light & Smith (1970)	Evaluation of national intervention programs through post hoc survey.
NSSSE (1960)	Staff self-study with overview of content, facilities, and procedures.	Stake (1967)	Collection and processing of description and judgment data.

Source: Suggested by a chart developed by Robert E. Stake, Center for Instructional Research and Curriculum Evaluation, University of Illinois, 1969.

Several comments on some of the models are in order. Tyler's (1942) evaluation model is probably the best-known prototype, at least from a historical perspective. His thinking has significantly influenced both evaluation and curriculum for many years. Tyler emphasizes the individual learner. The "discrepancy model" proposed by Provus (1971) involves a highly complex set of criterion questions, and is probably the most detailed model on the list. Taylor and Maguire (1966) and Metfessel and Michael (1967) are unique in their inclusion of a large sample of people concerned with the educational process. Taylor and Maguire, for example, have identified five groups whose opinions should be solicited at various stages of evaluation: spokesmen for the society-at-large, subject-matter experts, teachers, parents, and students. The counsel of these groups is particularly important during the specification of objectives. This approach was used by National Assessment in establishing its objectives. Too many opinions can, of course, have the adverse effect of diluting the product. The model proposed by Stake (1967), with its emphasis on observation and judgment data, is potentially one of the most valuable yet conceived. The school accreditation model (NSSSE, 1960) frequently leaves the staff exhausted and generally does not yield meaningful results. And, finally, the concerns expressed by Light and Smith (1970) are reflected in the evaluations undertaken on behalf of Head Start. The CIPP model (Context-Input-Process-Product) (Stufflebeam 1968) has achieved considerable acceptance among both theoreticians and working evaluators.

In an effort to illustrate the evaluation process, an attempt has been made to depict the usual steps in the process in Figure 1.1. The activities listed are in approximate order in terms of logic and temporal sequence. Application of PERT (Program Evaluation and Review Technique; Cook 1966) and other management techniques can be extremely valuable when implementing an evaluation program such as that suggested by Figure 1.1. As can be seen, only major activities are identified. It is assumed that decisionmaking is taking place within and between steps. Decisions may be of the go–no go variety, relate to the appropriateness of criteria, or focus on information, processing, reporting, and feedback. The development of a climate supportive of evaluation is an important dimension of the entire process. The importance of the evaluator's interpersonal skills, therefore, cannot be underestimated. The sequence of activities in Figure 1.1 is directly applicable to *summative* (end-of-activity) evaluation, and may be undertaken repeatedly during *formative* (in-process) evaluation (Scriven 1967; Bloom, Hastings, and Madaus 1971).

If applied logically, intelligently, and realistically, the process of curriculum evaluation can give rise to decisions that serve significantly to improve the conditions in our schools.

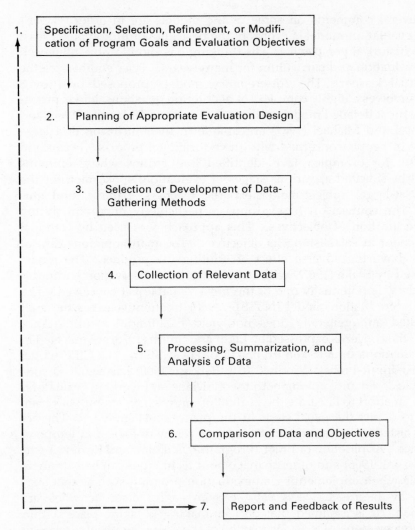

FIGURE 1.1. Overview of Usual Steps in Curriculum Evaluation Process

CONTRIBUTIONS OF EDUCATIONAL ASSESSMENT TO THE ACCOUNTABILITY MOVEMENT

Educational assessment can also make a significant contribution to today's schools in the area of "accountability." Alkin (1972) has defined accountability as "a negotiated relationship in which the participants agree in advance to accept specified rewards and costs on the basis of evaluation findings as to the attainment of specified ends." The key is probably the term *negotiated*, which suggests a dialogue among teachers, parents, administrators, and students. One common type of negotiated relationship is a contract, and the performance contract has already emerged as one of the most frequently used methods of implementing accountability. A performance contract is, basically, an agreement to bring about specified changes in individuals or groups. Criteria are detailed and the level of payment is correlated with performance. Obviously, the measurement of performance is critical. A number of technical problems associated with performance contracts, e.g., regression effects, unreliable gain scores, and so on, have recently been spelled out by Stake (1971). Following is a list (source unknown) of twelve factors in accountability. Each will, at some point during its implementation, require the collection of data to assist in decisionmaking.

Factors in Accountability

1. *Community involvement*: the utilization of members of concerned community groups in appropriate phases of program activity to facilitate: access to community resources; community understanding of objectives, procedures, and accomplishments; and discharge of responsibilities to relevant community client, service, and support groups.

2. *Technical assistance*: the means for providing adequate resources in planning, implementation, operation, and evaluation by drawing upon community, business, industrial, labor, educational, scientific, artistic, social/welfare, and governmental agencies for expertise and services necessary to effective operations.

3. *Needs assessment*: the identification of target-group and situational factors essential to the planning of a relevant program of action.

4. *Change strategies*: the development of effective strategies for systematic change in the educational enterprise and the incorporation of the strategies in program operations.

5. *Management systems*: the adaptation of the systems approach, through such techniques as Management by Objectives, PPBS (Planning-Programming-Budgeting Systems; Hartley 1968), PERT, to educational program management at the local, state, and federal levels.

6. *Performance objectives*: the specification of objectives in a comprehensive, precise manner that indicates measures and means for assessing the degree of attainment of predetermined standards.

7. *Performance budgeting*: the allocation of fiscal resources in accordance with objectives to be realized, rather than objectives or functions to be supported.

8. *Performance contracting*: arrangement for technical assistance in program operations through contracts that condition compensation upon the accomplishment of specified performance objectives.

9. *Staff development*: determination of the nature and extent of staff development needed for the successful implementation of the accountability concept at the local, state, and federal levels, and the design and conduct of indicated development activities.

10. *Comprehensive evaluation*: the establishment of systems of performance control based on the continuous assessment of operational and management processes and resultant products.

11. *Cost effectiveness*: the analysis of unit results obtained in relation to unit resources consumed under alternative approaches to program operation, as a determinant in continued planning.

12. *Program auditing*: a performance control system based upon external reviews conducted by qualified outside technical assistance, designed to verify the results of the evaluation and to assess the appropriateness of evaluation procedures for determining the effectiveness of program operation and management.

Educational assessment can provide useful data in any of these twelve areas. Barro (1970) has suggested that, as the accountability concept takes hold and begins to be implemented, at least two kinds of measures will be needed. First, more comprehensive and accurate pupil performance measures will be required if we are to assess changes in performance validly. Second, methods will have to be developed to estimate the contributions to measured pupil performance of individual teachers, administrators, schools, and districts. Some of the ideas described on pages 11–16 in connection with curriculum evaluation could be applied here. The application of cost-benefit and cost-effectiveness analyses would also be illustrative (Thomas 1969; Alkin 1970). Expansion and refinement of the schools' current systematic collection of educational measurement data must be undertaken. Another issue, because it is both highly technical and new to the schools, poses a much greater challenge: as one develops an assessment system, what are some of the qualities the developer should strive for in selecting or constructing his data-collecting instruments?

THE CHARACTERISTICS OF A QUALITY INSTRUMENT

How does one judge the quality of a classroom test? This question frequently goes unanswered due to (1) lack of knowledge about standards and criteria for evaluation, or (2) lack of effort. If either of these conditions exists, the assessment experience cannot be a meaningful one for student or instructor, both of whom should profit from the experience. The student will profit because the process of preparing for the test will cause him to review and interrelate the material. We might call this learning experience a pretest or motivational effect. Upon com-

pletion of the test, assuming close proximity between the test and knowledge of the results, a posttest or learning effect should be also noted.
The instructor should not only profit from the significant data about
student learning he derives. In constructing a test, a teacher is asked to
summarize the salient elements of his instruction in terms of content,
student behavior, and classroom activity. He then summarizes these
elements in the form of questions to be presented to his students. He is
next, obviously, forced to "think through" his instruction and thus gain
a perspective on his teaching and insight into the organization of the
material that should prove beneficial to himself and his students.

As the teacher constructs a test, what are some of the important
factors that should be considered? Ebel (1965a, pp. 281–307) has provided a very useful summary of ten qualities of a good test:

1. *Relevance.* Relevance is the correspondence between the behavior
required to respond correctly to a test item and the purpose or objective
in writing the item. The test item should be directly related to the
course objectives and actual instruction. When used in conjunction
with educational measurement, relevance must be considered the major
contributor to validity.

2. *Balance.* Balance in a test is the degree to which the proportion of
items testing particular outcomes corresponds to the "ideal" test. The
framework of the test is outlined by a table of specifications.

3. *Efficiency.* Efficiency is defined in terms of the number of responses
per unit of time. Some compromise must be made among available time
for testing, scoring, and relevance.

4. *Objectivity.* For a test question to be considered objective, experts
must agree on the "right" or "best" answer. Objectivity, then, is a
characteristic of the scoring of the test, not of the form (e.g., multiple-
choice, true-false) of the questions.

5. *Specificity.* If subject-matter experts should receive perfect scores,
test-wise but course-naive students should receive near-chance scores,
indicating that course-specific learnings are being measured.

6. *Difficulty.* The test items should be appropriate in difficulty level to
the group being tested. In general, a maximally reliable test is one in
which each item is passed by half of the students.

7. *Discrimination.* The ability of an item to discriminate is generally
indexed by the difference between the proportion of good (or more
knowledgeable) and poor (or less able) students who respond correctly.

8. *Reliability.* Reliability is a complex characteristic, but generally involves consistency of measurement. Consistency of measurement
might be judged in terms of time, items, scorers, examinees, or examiners.

9. *Fairness.* To insure fairness, an instructor should construct and

administer the test in a manner that allows each student an equal chance to demonstrate his knowledge.

10. *Speededness.* To what degree are scores on the test influenced by speed of response? For achievement tests, speed should generally *not* be allowed to play a significant role in determining a score, and sufficient time should generally be allowed for all or most examinees to finish the test.

For the most part, a test constructor or user may evaluate his instrument in light of the foregoing ten factors by careful examination of the test and/or the data it yields. Obviously, consideration should be given these factors before, during, and after test development and administration. The refinement of a test is a continuous and ongoing process.

The characteristics of difficulty and discrimination have greatest relevance if one's intent is to maximize the differences between individuals. If the intent is to assess progress toward a specified set of objectives, they have less applicability in instrument development. See Chapter Thirteen for a clarification of the issues involved in constructing and interpreting criterion-referenced and norm-referenced measures.

Wall and Summerlin (1972) have recently completed an interesting and useful comparative application of Ebel's list of the characteristics of a good measuring instrument. They examine teacher-made and standardized tests in light of each of the ten characteristics. The results of their analyses are as shown in Table 1.2:

TABLE 1.2   Relative Merits of Teacher-Made and Standardized Tests

Characteristic	Teacher-Made	Standardized
Relevance	Measures objectives for the class	Measures achievement for typical classes
Balance	Measures objectives in same proportion as time spent on instruction	Measures a large variety of objectives
Difficulty	Is geared to the group being tested	May vary; usually averages around 50 percent passing for all items
Reliability	Usually not calculated; normally very low but can be as high as standardized tests if carefully planned	Usually high; normally .85 and above
Speededness	Sufficient time is usually given for completion of test	Strict time limits are typical

Source: J. Wall and L. Summerlin, Choosing the right test. *The Science Teacher,* November 1972: 32–36. Reprinted by permission.

TABLE 1.2 (*Continued*)

Characteristic	Teacher-Made	Standardized
Discrimination	Each question helps to differentiate between high- and low-scoring students if differentiation is goal; if testing for mastery this characteristic is meaningless	Attempts to find individual differences between students, with each question contributing to differentiation of those scoring high and low
Specificity	Measures specific learnings	Attempts to measure specific learning
Objectivity	There is agreement among experts on answers to items chosen	Answers have usually been checked by subject-matter experts

OUTLINE OF THE TEST DEVELOPMENT PROCESS

The term *education*, as used throughout this book, is defined as the process of creating behavioral changes. How does this process relate to the construction of a test? How does the testmaker begin to construct his instrument? Presumably, he could simply sit down and begin to write test questions about the material that has been taught. If the instructor is writing the test, the types of questions that easily come to mind will be those that address outcomes high on his list of priorities. If his test is to be a fair one, he will have to examine his test to be sure that content and behavioral applications are covered in the proportion he intends. This is the beginning of a deliberate analytic approach to test-building, whose sequence of steps is approximately as follows:

1. Specify the ultimate goals of the educational process.

2. Derive from these the goals of the portion of the system under study.

3. Specify these goals in terms of expected student behavior. If relevant, specify the acceptable level of successful learning.

4. Determine the relative emphasis or importance of various objectives, their content, and their behaviors.

5. Select or develop situations that will elicit the desired behavior in the appropriate context or environment, assuming the student has learned it.

6. Assemble a sample of such situations which together represent accurately the emphasis on content and behavior previously determined.

7. Provide for the recording of responses in a form that will facilitate scoring but will not so distort the nature of the behavior elicited that it is no longer a true sample or index of the behavior desired.

8. Establish scoring criteria and guides to provide objective and unbiased judgments.

9. Try out the instrument in preliminary form.

10. Revise the sample of situations on the basis of tryout information.

11. Analyze reliability, validity, and score distribution in accordance with the projected use of scores.

12. Develop test norms and a manual, and reproduce and distribute the test.

This sequence of steps describes an idealized process, usually followed in the development of standardized tests. The intent, if not the letter, of the recommendations implicit in the steps should be adhered to in the construction of any custom-made measuring instrument.

Metfessel and Michael (1967) have proposed eight comparable steps for the evaluation of educational programs that may prove of interest to the reader.

The importance of educational objectives in the first stages of test construction cannot be overemphasized. Objectives, ideally in behavioral form, guide and shape the total process.

SUGGESTED READINGS

Anastasi, Anne. *Testing problems in perspective*. Washington: American Council on Education, 1966. A collection of selected pioneer papers presented at the Educational Testing Services Invitational Conference on Testing Problems over several decades.

Bloom, B. S., *et al. Handbook on formative and summative evaluation of student learning*. New York: McGraw-Hill, 1971. An excellent basic source. The last 11 chapters contain measurement applications in selected subject areas.

Bonjean, C. M.; Hill, R. J.; and McLemore, S. D. *Sociological measurement: An inventory of scales and indices*. San Francisco: Chandler, 1967. Many of the data-gathering methods described in this book have useful applications in education and psychological assessment.

Cronbach, L. J. *Essentials of psychological testing*, 3rd ed. New York: Harper and Brothers, 1970. Chapters 1 and 2 are a good introduction to the basic purposes of testing and types of tests available.

Du Bois, P. H. *The history of psychological testing*. Boston: Allyn and Bacon, 1970. A fascinating survey of important events and an introduction to significant people and research.

Ebel, R. L. *Essentials of educational measurement*. Englewood Cliffs, N.J.: Prentice-Hall, 1972. Chapter 13, "How to Judge the Quality of a Classroom Test," describes methods that may be used to evaluate ten major characteristics of an informal test.

Helmstadter, G. C. *Principles of psychological measurement.* New York: Appleton-Century-Crofts, 1964. Chapter 1 presents a succinct overview of the general nature and logic of testing.

Johnson, O. G., and Bommarito, J. W., eds. *Tests and measurements in child development: A handbook.* San Francisco: Jossey-Bass, 1971.

Lake, D. G., Miles, M. B., and Earle, Jr., R. B., eds. *Measuring human behavior.* N.Y.: Teachers College Press, 1973. An extensively annotated listing of measures of social functioning.

Payne, D. A., ed. *Curriculum evaluation: Commentaries on purpose-process-product.* Lexington, Mass.: D. C. Heath, 1974. An integrated collection of theoretical and applied papers in this revitalized area of applied educational assessment.

Payne, D. A., and McMorris, R. F., eds. *Educational and psychological measurement: Contributions to theory and practice*, 2nd ed. Morristown, N.J.: General Learning Press, 1974. A broad perspective on measurement is achieved through articles from a variety of sources on several current issues.

Sciara, F. J., and Jantz, R. K., eds. *Accountability in American education.* Boston: Allyn and Bacon, 1972. An excellent collection of readings covering all aspects of the accountability phenomenon.

Stufflebeam, D. L., *et al. Educational evaluation and decision making.* Itasca, Ill.: Peacock, 1971. An excellent overview of the entire evaluation process, this book describes the development of a complex evaluation system intended to provide information for decisionmaking.

Thorndike, R. L., ed. *Educational measurement,* 2nd ed. Washington: American Council on Education, 1971. The single most comprehensive source on educational measurement, this volume presents recent expert opinion about many topics of concern to the educational assessor. Particularly recommended is Chapter 1, "Educational Measurement for the Seventies."

Tyler, R. W., ed. *Educational evaluation: New roles, new means.* Sixty-Eighth Yearbook of the National Society for the Study of Education. Chicago: University of Chicago Press, 1969.

Whitla, D. K., ed. *Handbook of measurement and assessment in behavioral sciences.* Reading, Mass.: Addison-Wesley, 1968. A collection of topically organized "state of the art" papers by leading authorities.

Wittrock, M. C., and Wiley, D. E., eds. *The evaluation of instruction: Issues and problems.* New York: Holt, Rinehart & Winston, 1970. A collection of highly original symposium papers.

II
PLANNING FOR INSTRUMENT DEVELOPMENT

2

THE NATURE AND SPECIFICATION OF COGNITIVE AND PSYCHO-MOTOR LEARNING OUTCOMES

SUMMARY PREVIEW STATEMENTS[1]

1. The establishment of educational goals and instructional objectives is a time-consuming, important, and often frustrating task.

2. The specification of objectives is probably the single most important step in educational assessment.

3. An educational objective is a statement of desired change in pupil behavior.

4. Objectives may be classified as:
   a. Ultimate or immediate.
   b. General or specific.
   c. Cognitive, affective, or psychomotor.

5. Objectives may be classified at four levels of specificity, depending upon their origin and projected method of application.

6. Objectives are derived from:
   a. Analysis of the needs of individuals and society.
   b. Subject-matter experts.
   c. Professional societies and commissions.
   d. Analyses of the learning process itself.

7. In selecting an instructional objective, one must consider its consistency with the school's educational philosophy and with accepted knowledge and theories of learning and instruction.

8. The teacher needs to be aware that value judgments cannot be avoided in the selection or specification of educational objectives.

---

[1] This chapter is based in part on material from D. R. Krathwohl and D. A. Payne, Defining and assessing educational objectives. In *Educational measurement*, 2nd ed., ed. R. L. Thorndike. (Washington: American Council on Education, 1971), pp. 17–45. Excerpts reprinted by permission of the authors and publisher.

9. The *Taxonomy of Educational Objectives* is a nonsubject-matter hierarchical classification of educational outcomes that are educationally, psychologically, and logically related to each other and to the teaching-learning process.

10. The major categories of the Cognitive Domain in the *Taxonomy of Educational Objectives* are:
    a. Knowledge.
    b. Comprehension.
    c. Application.
    d. Analysis.
    e. Synthesis.
    f. Evaluation.

11. Another useful, and perhaps more theoretically sound, scheme for classifying educational objectives is Gagné's learning hierarchy.

12. Objections to the explicit statement and prespecification of educational objectives focus on:
    a. The likelihood of emphasizing trivial and easily specified behaviors.
    b. Reduced spontaneity and flexibility in the classroom.
    c. The likelihood of overlooking other important outcomes.

13. A good educational objective should:
    a. Deal with actual relevant classroom behaviors.
    b. Be appropriate to the students involved.
    c. Be stated in the form of expected change in individual student behaviors.
    d. Have direct implications for the modification and assessment of behavior.

14. Harrow's *Taxonomy of Psychomotor Objectives* proposes the following six categories:
    a. Reflex movements.
    b. Basic fundamental movements.
    c. Perceptual abilities.
    d. Physical abilities.
    e. Skilled movements.
    f. Nondiscussive communication.

15. Providing students with a list of course objectives can enhance the learning experience.

Educational achievement can be defined as the extent to which specified objectives are accomplished by individual students. In developing methods to measure the extent of achievement, the author believes, the test constructor must posit a detailed set of objectives to guide instrument development. The statement of educational objectives (purpose or goals) in terms of expected pupil changes probably constitutes the single most important element in the development of a sound classroom test. Objectives provide guidelines for both instruction and evaluation. In addition, they serve as standards against which the final validity or relevance of the items and the test will be judged.

An educational objective may be broadly defined as *a statement of desired change in pupil behavior, knowledge, or affect*. Thus, an objective represents a value judgment, and reflects the purposefulness of education. In another sense it represents a normative concept, a standard to be sought by all students. Some teachers rebel at the notion of "setting standards," but who is in a better position than the teacher to make judgments about what students should learn? It is part of the responsibility of a teacher to delineate learning objectives and activities.

An acceptable objective has two components, a "content" element and a "behavioral" element. It is with respect to the behavioral element that most educational objectives are found wanting. As Mager (1962) points out, instructional objectives are frequently couched in such vague, ambiguous terms as "to know," "to appreciate," "to believe," "to have faith in," and the like, which have very little value in the processes determining units of instruction and directing evaluation. A useful set of objectives is couched in terms of expected changes in overt student behavior.

TYPES OF OBJECTIVES

Many systems are available for classifying educational objectives. Dressel (1960), for example, has characterized objectives as (1) achievable or unachievable; (2) explicit or implicit; (3) intrinsic or transcendental; (4) individual or societal; (5) ultimate or immediate; and (6) general or specific. A detailed discussion of the last two types of objectives should help clarify the process of identifying and stating objectives and highlight the importance of objectives in test development.

Ultimate and Immediate Objectives

Ultimate objectives are behaviors ordinarily not observable under classroom conditions. They are important goals of education, but cannot, under normal circumstances, be directly evaluated. Ultimate objectives frequently refer to the projected adult behavior of children and adolescents. Examples of ultimate (broad goal) objectives are sound health habits, intelligent voting behavior, and critical attitudes about literature and the arts.

We must, therefore, approach the evaluation of ultimate objectives by way of immediate or short-range objectives. A teacher would specify a set of immediate objectives measurable under classroom conditions. It is assumed and inferred that accomplishment of the several short-range objectives is directly related to one or more ultimate objectives. Suppose, for example, that an instructor of a graduate-level course in educational tests and measurements adopted the following ultimate objective: "Upon completion of the course, the student will return to his classroom and write better tests." It is not feasible to gather data on the student's accomplishment of this objective. But data on such immediate objectives as recall of specific guidelines for constructing multiple-choice items, comprehension of the concept of reliability, and ability to apply methods of estimating validity can be used as approximate measures of the achievement of the ultimate objective.

General and Specific Objectives

General objectives are similar to ultimate objectives, but often have some comparability over wide grade ranges (e.g., development of reading skills). Specific objectives are usually unique to particular courses, and are stated in terms of expected student behavior. Differences in specific objectives can be traced not only to variations in content but also to relative emphasis on similar objectives across grades or classes. General objectives are useful in providing an overall framework within which the instructional program may be viewed. In addition, they serve as categories or rubrics under which specific objectives may be collected in efficient groupings, which in turn help in the direction of measurement and evaluation efforts.

There is a danger that general objectives may become too global and too influenced by Madison Avenue to be meaningful. Henry Dyer (1967, p. 9) cites the following paragraph from the 1947 report of the President's Commission on Higher Education as an example of "word magic":

> The first goal in education for democracy is the full, rounded, and continuing development of the person. The discovery, training, and utilization of individual talents is of fundamental importance in a free society. To liberate and perfect the intrinsic powers of every citizen is the central purpose of democracy, and its furtherance of individual self-realization is its greatest glory.

As Dyer notes, "it sings to our enthusiasms," but is not couched in terms that permit one to discern when educators have "liberated and perfected the intrinsic powers of a citizen." Nor does this kind of statement help to explain how to calibrate the roundness of his development. But a statement at this level specifying, for instance, that "each student graduating from high school shall, if he desires it, be adequately prepared to enter a vocation" has very concrete implications for vocational education.

Some teachers argue that high-quality instruction can exist without explicit formal statements of the goals of education. This may be true, but assessment cannot be accomplished without a set of operational definitions of instruction. General objectives are usually dictated by community and societal needs, and the teacher is left the task of translating these goals into specific objectives.

It frequently happens that the list of specific objectives for a course of instruction becomes unmanageably long. The breakdown of the instructional program into small but intelligible units has the overriding advantage, however, of greatly facilitating test development. In practice, a compromise between an exhaustive list and a manageable one generally results.

An example of a general objective and related specific objectives will prove helpful at this point:

General Objective: The student will be able to evaluate a test he has constructed and administered.

Specific Objectives: The student will be able to
    a. determine the difficulty level of test items.
    b. determine the discrimination power of items.
    c. relate test items to the educational objectives.
    d. estimate internal consistency reliability.

This list of specific objectives is not exhaustive, but it should be obvious that it would make item-writing a much easier task than would a single general objective.

FOUR LEVELS OF EDUCATIONAL OBJECTIVES

The first and most abstract level of educational objectives consists of the long-term global goals of a complete education or the broad goals toward which a sizable proportion of training—such as college, high school, or elementary school—might strive. Examples of objectives at this level are:

1.   The student shall master the fundamental skills of reading and writing.
2.   The student shall become a citizen who is informed about the major

political issues of the day and who uses this information to act for the betterment of the community.

3. The student shall develop a conscience, a system of morality, and a scale of values.

4. The student shall be prepared to enter a vocation upon graduation from high school, if he wishes.

At the second and more concrete level, global goals are translated into specific behaviors that represent the terminal performance capabilities of students successfully completing an instructional unit, a course, or, in some instances, a sequence of courses.

Applied to pupils completing elementary school, the first general objective might break down into such narrower and more concrete objectives as:

1. The student can name and recognize the letters of the alphabet.

2. The student can write legibly at X words per minute.

3. The student can write a simple letter or paragraph containing no more than Y errors of spelling or punctuation.

4. The student reads with understanding material from simple newspaper stories and books for children.

5. The student adapts reading techniques to a specific purpose (e.g., entertaining himself, finding an item of information, or following an argument).

The third level is characterized by still greater specificity and detail, and provides the guidance needed to develop or choose specific instructional materials. When used, for example, in the development of a linear sequence of programmed instruction, such objectives would describe, at the unit or course level of specificity, a succession of behaviors, each more sophisticated than the preceding one.

For example, the second-level objective that the child be able to name the letters of the alphabet could be translated at the third level into several highly specific objectives describing the child's ability to discriminate between pairs of similar and easily confused letters: the child shall distinguish P from R, O from Q, C from G, and the like. These specific objectives might suggest giving the child practice in recognizing these letters in isolation or choosing between them when presented in pairs.

Third-level objectives can be useful not only to specify instructional materials and experiences but also to guide construction of very discriminating measures of increases in pupil competence. This is the level of measurement used in programs of individualized instruction such as the Oakleaf Project (Cox and Graham 1966), in which the pupil is tested for mastery as he completes each instructional unit. Mastery tests for units of programmed instruction determine whether to recycle the student through the material, direct him to remedial materials, or route him to new material. Thus even the most specific objectives serve the purpose of guiding test construction.

The test items and instructional materials themselves constitute the fourth and most specific level. They describe the situations in which the behaviors to be learned are displayed, and serve as the operational definitions of previous levels of specificity. In some instances, one develops instructional materials, and even test items, before being able to formulate the general objective. This is not to say that teachers do not know what they want to teach, but that they can often assemble materials with particular desired characteristics before being able to verbalize those qualities.

The process of stating objectives is an iterative one; each level helps one understand the levels above and below it. Developments at one level frequently have implications for other levels, and one obtains the most complete understanding—particularly once the major developmental lines have become clear—by working back and forth among the various levels. Thus it is clear that objectives can and must be stated at a variety of levels of specificity, for both testing and curriculum building.

SOURCES OF OBJECTIVES

Objectives at the second or third level are deduced from more abstract objectives by a rational process. Similarly, the formulation of the most abstract objectives is best guided by a rational scheme. Official and semiofficial bodies—namely, the various Presidential commissions on higher education, the American Council on Education, the Educational Policies Commission of the National Education Association, and others—have provided a number of guidelines. For example, the American Council on Education's *A Design for General Education* (1944) presented over 200 objectives, reasonably clearly defined in terms of student behavior and broad descriptive subject-matter content, and grouped under ten broad outcomes.

Many of these efforts have been phrased in such broad descriptive terms as those of the early *Cardinal Principles of Secondary Education* (1918):

1. Good health.
2. Command of fundamental processes.
3. Worthy home membership.
4. Vocational efficiency.
5. Good citizenship.
6. Worthy use of leisure time.
7. Ethical character.

The Educational Policies Commission of the National Education Association has provided one broad socially oriented (1938) and one cognitively oriented (1961) set of objectives:

Social Objectives	*Cognitive Objectives*
1. Self-realization	1. Recalling and imagining
2. Human relationship	2. Classifying and generalizing
3. Economic efficiency	3. Comparing and evaluating
4. Civic responsibility	4. Analyzing and synthesizing
	5. Deducing and inferring

Complete and detailed objectives for elementary schools have been formulated by the Mid-Century Committee on Outcomes in Elementary Education (Kearny 1953), and for the secondary schools by French and others (1957). While neither report provides an overall rationale for the objectives, each represents the combined wisdom of numerous subcommittees and groups. The objectives for elementary education are categorized as (a) knowledge and understandings, (b) skills and competencies, (c) attitudes and interests, and (d) action patterns. These four general categories are related separately to ethical behaviors, standards, and values at one extreme and to quantitative relationships at the other. The secondary-school objectives are classified under the three maturity goals of self-realization, interpersonal relationships, and large-group memberships and leaderships, and in the four behavioral areas of intellectual development, cultural integration, physical and mental health, and economic competence.

Objectives differ according to one's degree of emphasis on the socialization of the individual or on general societal needs. A list of individual-oriented objectives might resemble Havighurst's (1953, pp. 25–41) list of developmental tasks:

1. Learning physical skills necessary for ordinary games.
2. Building wholesome attitudes toward oneself as a growing organism.
3. Learning to get along with age-mates.
4. Developing fundamental skills in reading, writing, and calculating.
5. Developing conscience, morality, and a scale of values.
6. Developing attitudes toward groups and institutions.

A more society-oriented view of education might elicit a set of objectives like Hand, Hoppock, and Zlatchin's (1948, pp. 425–431):

1. To keep the population healthy.
2. To conserve natural resources and use them wisely.
3. To provide opportunity for people to make a living.

4. To enable the population to realize aesthetic and spiritual values.

5. To provide a sufficient body of commonly held beliefs and aspirations to guarantee social integration.

6. To organize and govern in harmony with beliefs and aspirations.

While statements by official bodies and committees and analyses by talented individuals are extremely helpful, in many instances an individual or group wishes to make independent choices or to develop its own objectives. Tyler (1964) has proposed a process for the development and selection of objectives that has proven very effective for first-level objectives and has been used to proceed directly to second-level objectives as well. Tyler names three sources of objectives that should be routinely considered in the process of developing objectives: (a) studies of the needs of the individual in his society, (b) studies of the needs of the society the school must serve, and (c) statements by those trained in specific subject matter about the contributions of their specialty to the area of education under consideration.

CHOICE OF OBJECTIVES

Many more objectives will be proposed by interested parties and derived from first-level objectives than the school will be able to achieve. The final selection of objectives will be dictated in part by the intended function of the school, the assigned role of the portion of the curriculum being developed, a realistic appraisal of what can be accomplished, and the degree of abstraction appropriate to the level of curriculum being developed. Tyler (1964) has discussed two criteria that embody the major considerations in the choice of objectives: (a) the educational philosophy of the person or institution making the selection and (b) the extent to which the objectives are in keeping with psychological realities affecting what can be taught at a given age in the light of the time available and previous learning.

Is the objective consistent with the school's philosophy of education? This criterion engages the values emphasized in a given school situation. Selection will involve such concerns as the school's view of the satisfying and effective life for an individual in our society. What are the most important values? What is the proper relation between the individual and society? What are the proper relations between individuals? Should different kinds of education be provided for different segments of society? Answers to these and similar questions relating to a school's philosophy clearly influence what is ruled out, what is chosen, and what is emphasized.

Is the objective consistent with accepted knowledge and theories about learning, instruction, and the discipline? Theories of learning and instruction will assist in determining whether given objectives are applicable to particular grades or learning sequences. Theory can help keep one realistic about the choice of objectives for short- and long-term emphasis. It can help one to identify appropriate entry behaviors and follow-up behaviors, and to distinguish objectives that are not amenable to teaching from those that are suited to the instructional process.

THE TAXONOMY OF EDUCATIONAL OBJECTIVES

One attempt to provide a framework for the entire panorama of educational objectives is the *Taxonomy of Educational Objectives*, so-called because it is a hierarchical classification scheme. Since the *Taxonomy*'s authors were much concerned with the holistic nature of learning, educational objectives are divided solely for purposes of convenience into three domains—cognitive, affective, and psychomotor. Most of the objectives for conventional courses are in the cognitive and affective domains, and a framework has been developed for each of these (Bloom 1956; Krathwohl, Bloom, and Masia 1964). Tentative frameworks for the psychomotor domain have also been developed (Simpson 1966; Harrow 1972). These frameworks are hierarchical in nature, that is, the lowest level of behavior in the hierarchy is believed to be the least complex, and its achievement is presumed to be the key to successful achievement at the next higher level in the structure.

The structure proposed in the *Taxonomy* is educationally, logically, and psychologically consistent. The *Taxonomy* represents an educational system in that the categories correspond to a teacher's concerns in developing curricula and selecting learning experiences. It is logical because its categories are precisely defined and can be subdivided. It is psychological because it is consistent with current thought in the psychological sciences, although it is not dependent upon any particular theory.

The *Taxonomy* is not a traditional content classification scheme applicable in various subject-matter areas. It represents a set of behavioral goals *per se*, as well as a system for developing goals.

The major reason for developing the *Taxonomy* was to facilitate communication among educational researcher, curriculum developer, and evaluator. The *Taxonomy* has received its widest acceptance among educational testers and evaluators, because of their need for explicit statements of objectives.

The Structure of the Cognitive Domain

The cognitive domain is composed of categories theoretically graded from simple to complex and from concrete to abstract. There is modest research evidence to support its organization (Cox and Wildemann 1970). A synopsis is presented in Table 2.1.

A brief description of the major categories follows:

Knowledge. Recall or recognition in an appropriate context of specific facts, universal principles, methods, process patterns, struc-

TABLE 2.1 Synopsis of the Taxonomy of Educational Objectives: Cognitive Domain

Knowledge

1.00 *Knowledge.* Recall of information
1.10 Knowledge of specifics. Emphasis is on symbols with concrete referents.
    1.11 Knowledge of terminology.
    1.12 Knowledge of specific facts.
1.20 Knowledge of ways and means of dealing with specifics. Includes methods of inquiry, chronological sequences, standards of judgment, patterns of organization within a field.
    1.21 Knowledge of conventions: accepted usage, correct style, etc.
    1.22 Knowledge of trends and sequences.
    1.23 Knowledge of classifications and categories.
    1.24 Knowledge of criteria.
    1.25 Knowledge of methodology for investigating particular problems.
1.30 Knowledge of the universals and abstractions in a field. Patterns and schemes by which phenomena and ideas are organized.
    1.31 Knowledge of principles and generalizations.
    1.32 Knowledge of theories and structures (as a connected body of principles, generalizations, and interrelations).

Intellectual Skills and Abilities

2.00 *Comprehension.* Understanding of material being communicated, without necessarily relating it to other material.
    2.10 Translation. From one set of symbols to another.
    2.20 Interpretation. Summarization or explanation of a communication.
    2.30 Extrapolation. Extension of trends beyond the given data.
3.00 *Application.* The use of abstractions in particular, concrete situations.
4.00 *Analysis.* Breaking a communication into its parts so that organization of ideas is clear.
    4.10 Analysis of elements. E.g., recognizing assumptions.
    4.20 Analysis of relationships. Content or mechanical factors.
    4.30 Analysis of organizational principles. What holds the communication together?
5.00 *Synthesis.* Putting elements into a whole.
    5.10 Production of a unique communication.
    5.20 Production of a plan for operations.
    5.30 Derivation of a set of abstract relations.
6.00 *Evaluation.* Judging the value of material for a given purpose.
    6.10 Judgments in terms of internal evidence. E.g., logical consistency.
    6.20 Judgments in terms of external evidence. E.g., consistency with facts developed elsewhere.

Source: After Cronbach (1960, p. 376).

tures, or settings. Little is required beyond bringing to mind the appropriate material.

Comprehension. The lowest level of what is commonly called "understanding," requiring that the individual be able to paraphrase knowledge accurately, explain or summarize it in his own words, or make logical extensions in terms of implications or corollaries.

Application. The ability to select a given abstraction (idea, rule, procedure, or generalized method) appropriate to a new situation and to apply it correctly.

Analysis. The ability to dissect a communication or concept into its constituent elements in order to illustrate the hierarchy or other internal relation of ideas, show the basis for its organization, and indicate how it conveys its effects.

Synthesis. The arrangement of units or elements of a whole in such a way as to create a new pattern or structure.

Evaluation. Qualitative and quantitative judgment about the extent to which material and methods satisfy criteria determined by the teacher or student.

There have been several attempts to validate the claim of the *Taxonomy* to hierarchical structure, which, if validated, would mean that achievement at a higher level of behavior is dependent upon achievement at a previous level. Ayers (1966); Kropp, Stoker, and Bashaw (1968); Johnson (1966); and Miller (1965) have all obtained empirical evidence that gives at least mild support to the order of the first three categories of the cognitive domain. The order of the more complex categories has largely failed to find support in these studies. All of the investigators encountered problems in developing measures, particularly objective ones, at the most complex end of the continuum. The difficulty of accurately classifying a higher-level item is compounded by the fact that the student's prior experience with the material on which the item is based may have resulted in his learning by rote a problem that would be complex if totally unfamiliar. Such a problem would belong in a lower category, such as Knowledge, for the student who learned it by rote, but would be a measure of more complex behavior for the student who met it afresh.

Illustrative Cognitive Domain Objectives

The following list of objectives should illustrate the flavor of the *Taxonomy*. (Refer to Table 2.1 for the specific classification of each objective.)

1.00 Recall of major facts about particular cultures.

1.25 Knowledge of scientific methods for evaluating health concepts.

2.10 Skill in translating verbal mathematical material into symbolic statements, and vice versa.

3.00 Ability to predict the probable effect of a change in a factor on a biological situation previously at equilibrium.

4.00 Ability to recognize form and pattern in literary and artistic works as a way of understanding their meaning.

4.10 Skill in distinguishing facts from hypotheses.

5.00 Ability to recount a personal experience effectively.

5.20 Ability to plan a unit of instruction for a particular teaching situation.

6.00 Ability to compare a work with the highest known standards in its field, especially other works of recognized excellence.

6.10 Ability to recognize logical fallacies in arguments.

The Usefulness of the Cognitive Domain Taxonomy

The comprehensiveness of the *Taxonomy* has made it useful in determining whether or not a formulated set of objectives includes objectives at all levels appropriate to the curriculum under consideration. The *Taxonomy*, like a periodic table of elements or a check-off shopping list, offers a panorama of possible objectives. In particular, it provides many examples of complex objectives, which are frequently omitted or given insufficient emphasis. An interesting application of the *Taxonomy* in curriculum evaluation has been provided by Charters (1970).

The *Taxonomy* has also been used in the analysis of examinations and teaching practices to compare the emphases in course objectives with those in test questions and instruction (McGuire 1963; Scannell and Stellwagen 1960). As might be expected, the balance between factual knowledge and thinking called for in the statement of objectives frequently fails to be actualized in the examination items or materials of instruction. Heavy emphasis on memorization is indicated by the over-proportionate use of the *Knowledge* category, often outweighing other categories combined. It is not unusual to find that 50 to 90 percent of the total time available is spent on knowledge instruction.

When searching for ideas for a new curriculum, the work of others is frequently most helpful. If one's own work and that of others are both formulated in terms of the *Taxonomy*, comparison is markedly facilitated. Translation of objectives into the *Taxonomy* framework can provide a basis for more precise comparison. Furthermore, where similarities exist, it becomes possible to trade experiences regarding the value of certain learning experiences with more confidence that there is a firm basis for comparison and that the other person's experience is truly relevant.

It is also important to note the implications of the hierarchical nature of the *Taxonomy* for curriculum building. If the foregoing analysis is correct, then a hierarchy of objectives in a given subject-matter area suggests a readiness relationship between those objectives lower and higher in the hierarchy. Thus, the *Taxonomy* may suggest the sequence in which objectives should be pursued in the curriculum.

The *Taxonomy* is intended to assist those operating at the unit and course level. Statement of objectives for smaller units of instruction, such as programmed books used with teaching machines or computers, require a finer category system, such as Gagné's (1965).

Gagné's Learning Hierarchy

Gagné's system, which was used in the curriculum sponsored by the American Association for the Advancement of Science and the National Science Foundation—*Science–A Process Approach*—is a blend of behavioristic and cognitive psychology. It is intended to distinguish between behaviors learned under different conditions. Since it is also a hierarchical scheme, each capability depends on the prior learning of a simpler one. Gagné's categories, in order, are:

Signal learning. Signal learning is the general, diffuse, and emotional reaction that results involuntarily as a learned reaction to certain stimuli. Fear of water or of heights, or a pleasurable feeling on entering an art gallery, are examples of this kind of learning.

Stimulus-response learning. This learning involves a precise skeletal muscle response to a particular complex of stimulation. This form of learning appears, for example, to govern the acquisition of a new vocalization habit by a young child.

Chaining. Chaining results from the sequential connection of two previously learned stimulus-response behaviors. Our language is full of chains of verbal sequences (e.g., horse and buggy). Such acts as starting a car or properly positioning a specimen under a microscope are also chains.

Verbal association. Verbal association is a subvariety of chaining dependent on a verbal code or clue to provide the link between the learned responses in the chain. Gagné gives the example of the French student who uses the word *illuminate* as a code or clue for *allumette*, the French word for match. `

Multiple discrimination. This type of learning occurs when a number of learned chains interfere with one another so that retention of certain individual chains is shortened and forgetting occurs. Multiple discrimination occurs when, for example, a teacher learns to call each of his students by name.

Concept learning. Concept learning requires a response to the abstract properties of stimuli, such as shape, color, position, or number.

Examples of such concepts are up and down, near and far, and right and left.

Principle learning. Learning a principle requires the chaining of two or more concepts. It is exemplified by the acquisition of the "idea" contained in a proposition such as "gases expand when heated."

Problem solving. The chaining of principles into new combinations to fit particular circumstances is the heart of problem solving. Examples include the solution of simple problems, such as the reorganization of an office staff to fit the space available in a new building, or the abstract manipulation of physics principles to derive a new theory.

OBJECTIONS TO EXPLICIT STATEMENTS OF EDUCATIONAL OBJECTIVES

While many consider the explicit formulation of behavioral objectives a very useful approach, that attitude is not universal. Atkin (1968), Eisner (1967), Macdonald and Walfron (1970), and Broudy (1970), among others, have voiced serious objections to the extensive use of behavioral objectives in teaching, evaluation, and curriculum development. A majority of the objections involve fear of creating a lock-step instructional setting and failing to provide for spontaneity and creativity. Admittedly, the possibility of a mechanical approach to instruction exists, but the advantages attendant on the use of explicit statements of goals to clarify intent and assist in the selection of content, behavior to be changed, and instructional materials probably outweigh the disadvantages.

It is imperative that the teacher's instructional intent be communicated to the student. The following anecdote, reported by Yelon and Scott (1970, p. 5), illustrates a possible result of failure to communicate:

> At a parent-teacher conference the teacher complained to Mr. Bird about the foul language of his children. Mr. Bird decided to correct this behavior. At breakfast he asked his oldest son, "What will you have for breakfast?" The boy replied, "Gimme some of those damn cornflakes." Immediately Mr. Bird smashed the boy on the mouth. The boy's chair tumbled over and the boy rolled up against the wall. The father then turned to his second son and politely inquired, "What would you like for breakfast?" The boy hesitated, then said, "I don't know, but I sure as hell don't want any of those damn cornflakes!"

Moral: If you want someone to change his behavior, tell him your goals.

Popham (1969), in a recent monograph on the place of instructional objectives in curriculum evaluation, has summarized eleven major objections to the use of behavioral objectives. He then proceeds to respond to each objection. The following parallel lists (adapted from

Wynn 1973) serve to summarize the pros and cons of behavioral objectives:

Objection to Behavioral Objectives	*Rebuttal to Objection*
1. Trivial behaviors are easiest to operationalize. Really important outcomes will be underemphasized.	1. Explicit objectives more readily focus attention on important goals.
2. Prespecification prevents the teacher from capitalizing on unexpected instructional opportunities.	2. Ends do not necessarily specify means. Serendipity is always welcome.
3. Other types of educational outcomes are also important, e.g., for parents, staff, community.	3. Schools can't do everything. Their primary responsibility is to pupils.
4. Objectively, mechanistically measured behaviors are dehumanizing.	4. The broadened concept of evaluation includes "human" elements.
5. Precise, preplanned behavior is undemocratic.	5. Society knows what it wants. Instruction is naturally undemocratic.
6. Behaviorally described teaching is unnatural and makes unrealistic demands on teachers.	6. Identifying the status quo is different than applauding it.
7. In certain areas, e.g., fine arts and humanities, it is more difficult to measure behaviors.	7. Sure it's tough; but it is still a responsibility.
8. General statements appear more worthwhile to outsiders. Precise goals appear innocuous.	8. We must abandon the ploy of "obfuscation by generality."
9. Measurability implies accountability. Teachers might be judged solely on their ability to produce particular results.	9. Teachers should be held accountable for producing changes.
10. It is more difficult to generate precise objectives than to talk about them in vague terms.	10. We should allocate the necessary resources to accomplish the task.
11. Unanticipated results are often most important. Prespecification may cause inattentiveness.	11. Dramatic unanticipated outcomes cannot be overlooked. Keep your eyes open!

CONSIDERATIONS IN STATING SPECIFIC EDUCATIONAL OBJECTIVES

Two major factors must be considered in constructing statements of educational objectives: content and form. Objectives should be evaluated not only in terms of subject matter (content), but also of the way in which the subject matter is treated (form). These two dimensions are inexorably interrelated, and can significantly influence the utility of objectives, and thus the quality of the resulting test and items. Desirable characteristics of objectives will be discussed in this section.

Content

1.   Objectives should be appropriate in terms of level of difficulty and of prior learning experiences. If the *Taxonomy* were used as a guide, objectives encompassing all six major levels might be stated for a college-level course, but only the first three levels might be adopted for a fifth-grade history course.

2.   Objectives should be "real," in the sense that they describe behaviors the teacher actually intends to act on in the classroom situation. Frequently a teacher will state that he intends to bring about changes in the "attitudes" and "appreciations" of his students, but plan no specific learning experiences to achieve these kinds of objectives. This is not to say that they are not useful or desirable objectives, but that if one adopts an objective one must evaluate progress toward it. Conversely, if an objective is not part of the actual instructional program, one shouldn't evaluate it.

3.   A useful objective will describe both the content and the mental process or behavior required for an appropriate response. A list of objectives should *not* become a "table of contents"—a list of topics to be covered in class. Such a list should describe the overt behavior expected and the content vehicle (e.g., instructional procedure) that will be used to bring about change.

4.   The content of the objectives should be responsive to the needs of both the individual *and* society.

5.   Generally, a variety of behaviors should be stated, since most courses attempt to develop skills other than "recall." Only recently, however, have we made a concerted effort to abandon the stultifying emphasis on the memorization of facts. This seems strange in light of the results of relevant research, which have been available for some time. Tyler (1933), for example, has shown that knowledge of specific information is not a lasting outcome of instruction. On the other hand, the higher-order mental abilities and skills (e.g., application and interpretation) show much greater stability.

Form

1.   Objectives should be stated in the form of expected pupil changes. They should *not* describe teacher activities. If we are to measure and evaluate validly, we must articulate precisely what we expect students to be able to do at the end of a course or unit of instruction.

2.   Objectives should be stated in behavioral or performance terms. The terms used should have the same meaning for student and instructor. Mager (1962) points out that words such as "identify," "differentiate," "solve," "construct," "list," "compare," and "contrast" communicate more precisely and efficiently than does traditional educational terminology. In general, the broad class of words called "action verbs" is preferable. Objectives must be stated operationally if we are to evaluate them adequately.

3.   Objectives should be stated singly. Compound objectives are likely to lead to inconsistent measurement. At the beginning of a course, a teacher may have in mind a particular objective, say, "The student should be able to recall, comprehend, and apply the four major correction-for-guessing formulas." When it comes time to measure the achievement of this objective, any of the three behaviors might be measured. And, those selected may or may not be measured in proportion to the emphasis given them in class. If the resulting test is not responsive to the objectives of instruction, it is invalid for the purpose of determining whether these goals have been accomplished. Another shortcoming of compound objectives is that the easier portions of the objectives may be measured because it is easier to write recall (knowledge) items than application items. Again, the relevance of the test is destroyed.

4.   Objectives should be parsimonious. Statements of instructional goals are easier to work with when trimmed of excess verbiage.

5.   Objectives should be grouped logically, so they make sense in determining units of instruction and evaluation.

Two additional desirable characteristics that are generally overlooked are:

6.   The conditions under which the expected pupil behavior will be observed should be specified. The objective "to be able to solve problems in algebra," though useful, could be improved as follows: "Given a linear algebraic equation with one unknown, the learner must be able to solve for the unknown without the aid of references, tables, or calculating devices" (Mager 1962). Although a little more wordy, the intent of the instructor and the expected student behavior are now clearly identifiable.

7.   If possible, the objective should contain a statement indicating the

criteria for acceptable performance. Criteria might involve time limits or a minimum number of correct responses.

How elaborately should objectives be specified? What degree of refinement is necessary? These questions do not have absolute answers, and require decisions on the part of the teacher-evaluator. Suffice it to say that the more refined the objectives, the easier the task of measurement. Obviously, there is a point of diminishing returns. The list could become so lengthy and involved that it would be unwieldy, confusing, and perhaps negatively reinforcing to the writer. Instructors are encouraged to consider the guidelines listed above in developing a suitable style to express their objectives.

Following are several specific objectives from a course in educational tests and measurements which illustrate many of the points in the foregoing discussion.

The student should be able to:

1. Write a multiple-choice item free of grammatical errors.
2. Correctly classify a set of ten test items in the six major categories of the *Taxonomy of Educational Objectives.*
3. Select the most important rule in constructing matching exercises from a list of positive suggestions.
4. Construct a scoring checklist for an essay item.

BEHAVIORAL COGNITIVE CATEGORIES FOR THE TAXONOMY OF EDUCATIONAL OBJECTIVES

Objectives may be stated, as we have seen, at a variety of levels of abstraction. It is at the second level of abstraction that the *Taxonomy* may find one of its most significant applications. To assist in application at the third level, Metfessel, Michael, and Kirsner (1969) have provided a series of verbal guidelines useful in operationalizing specific levels of the *Taxonomy.* That portion of their guidelines dealing with the cognitive domain is summarized in Table 2.2. Their use of infinitives and direct objects should facilitate the writing of instructional objectives, which, although keyed to the *Taxonomy,* are closer to being behavioral statements.

A SYSTEM FOR DEVELOPING INSTRUCTIONAL OBJECTIVES

Yelon and Scott (1970) have described a system for developing instructional objectives. The major framework for this system is illus-

TABLE 2.2 Instrumentation of the Taxonomy of Educational Objectives: Cognitive Domain

Taxonomy Classification	KEY WORDS	
	Examples of Infinitives	Examples of Direct Objects
1.00 Knowledge		
1.10 Knowledge of Specifics		
1.11 Knowledge of Terminology	to define, to distinguish, to acquire, to identify, to recall, to recognize	vocabulary terms, terminology, meaning(s), definitions, referents, elements
1.12 Knowledge of Specific Facts	to recall, to recognize, to acquire, to identify	facts, factual information, (sources), (names), (dates), (events), (persons), (places), (time periods), properties, examples, phenomena
1.20 Knowledge of Ways and Means of Dealing with Specifics		
1.21 Knowledge of Conventions	to recall, to identify, to recognize, to acquire	form(s), conventions, uses, usage, rules, ways, devices, symbols, representations, style(s), format(s)
1.22 Knowledge of Trends and Sequences	to recall, to recognize, to acquire, to identify	action(s), processes, movement(s), continuity, development(s), trend(s), sequence(s), causes, relationship(s), forces, influences
1.23 Knowledge of Classification and Categories	to recall, to recognize	area(s), type(s), feature(s), class(es), set(s), division(s), arrangement(s), classification(s), category/categories
1.24 Knowledge of Criteria	to recall, to recognize, to acquire, to identify	criteria, basics, elements

Source: W. S. Metfessel, W. B. Michael, and D. A. Kirsner, Instrumentation of Bloom's and Krathwohl's taxonomies for the writing of educational objectives. *Psychology in the Schools* 6 (1969): 227–231. Reprinted by permission of the publisher.

TABLE 2.2 *(Continued)*

	KEY WORDS	
Taxonomy Classification	Examples of Infinitives	Examples of Direct Objects
1.25 Knowledge of Methodology	to recall, to recognize, to acquire, to identify	methods, techniques, approaches, uses, procedures, treatments
1.30 Knowledge of the Universals and Abstractions in a Field		
1.31 Knowledge of Principles and Generalizations	to recall, to recognize, to acquire, to identify	principle(s), generalization(s), proposition(s), fundamentals, laws, principal elements, implication(s)
1.32 Knowledge of Theories and Structures	to recall, to recognize, to acquire, to identify	theories, bases, interrelations, structure(s), organization(s), formulation(s)
2.00 Comprehension		
2.10 Translation	to translate, to transform, to give in own words, to illustrate, to prepare, to read, to represent, to change, to rephrase, to restate	meaning(s), sample(s), definitions, abstractions, representations, words, phrases
2.20 Interpretation	to interpret, to reorder, to rearrange, to differentiate, to distinguish, to make, to draw, to explain, to demonstrate	relevancies, relationships, essentials, aspects, new view(s), qualifications, conclusions, methods, theories, abstractions
2.30 Extrapolation	to estimate, to infer, to conclude, to predict, to differentiate, to determine, to extend, to interpolate	consequences, implications, conclusions, factors, ramifications, meanings, corollaries, effects, probabilities
3.00 Application	to apply, to generalize, to relate, to choose, to develop, to organize, to use, to employ, to transfer, to restructure, to classify	principles, laws, conclusions, effects, methods, theories, abstractions, situations, generalizations, processes, phenomena, procedures
4.00 Analysis		

TABLE 2.2 *(Continued)*

	KEY WORDS	
Taxonomy Classification	*Examples of Infinitives*	*Examples of Direct Objects*
4.10 Analysis of Elements	to distinguish, to detect, to identify, to classify, to discriminate, to recognize, to categorize	elements, hypothesis/hypotheses, conclusions, assumptions, statements (of fact), statements (of intent), arguments, particulars
4.20 Analysis of Relationships	to analyze, to contrast, to compare, to distinguish, to deduce	relationships, interrelations, relevance, relevancies, themes, evidence, fallacies, arguments, cause-effect(s), consistency, consistencies, parts, ideas, assumptions
4.30 Analysis of Organizational Principles	to analyze, to distinguish, to detect, to deduce	form(s), pattern(s), purpose(s), point(s) of view(s), techniques, bias(es), structure(s), theme(s), arrangement(s), organization(s)
5.00 Synthesis		
5.10 Production of a Unique Communication	to write, to tell, to relate, to produce, to constitute, to transmit, to originate, to modify, to document	structure(s), pattern(s), product(s), performance(s), design(s), work(s), communications, effort(s), specifics, composition(s)
5.20 Production of a Plan or Proposed Set of Operations	to propose, to plan, to produce, to design, to modify, to specify	plan(s), objectives, specification(s), schematic(s), operation(s), way(s), solution(s), means.
5.30 Derivation of a Set of Abstract Relations	to produce, to derive, to develop, to combine, to organize, to synthesize, to classify, to deduce, to develop, to formulate, to modify	phenomena, taxonomies, concept(s), scheme(s), theories, relationships, abstractions, generalizations, hypothesis/hypotheses, perceptions, ways, discoveries
6.00 Evaluation		

TABLE 2.2 *(Continued)*

Taxonomy Classification	KEY WORDS	
	Examples of Infinitives	Examples of Direct Objects
6.10 Judgments in Terms of Internal Evidence	to judge, to argue, to validate, to assess, to decide	accuracy/accuracies, consistency/consistencies, fallacies, reliability, flaws, errors, precision, exactness
6.20 Judgments in Terms of External Criteria	to judge, to argue, to consider, to compare, to contrast, to standardize, to appraise	ends, means, efficiency, economy/economies, utility, alternatives, courses of action, standards, theories, generalizations

TABLE 2.3 Checklists to Accompany Figure 2.1 Specifying Criterion Questions Used in Writing Instructional Objectives

Checklist I

1. Is the general goal a broad statement of something desirable and within your subject area?   Yes   No
2. Is the general goal stated in terms of:
   a. Student behavior?   Yes   No
   b. Ends of instruction?   Yes   No
3. Is general goal chosen from dependent variables as stated in the most feasible system modification?   Yes   No

Checklist II

1. Does the description include:
   a. the situation for which the student is being prepared?   Yes   No
   b. the type of performance required in that situation?   Yes   No
   c. the standards usually used to judge the performance in that situation?   Yes   No

Checklist III

1. Is the statement in behavioral terms?   Yes   No
2. Is the stated behavior the closest feasible simulation to the behavior required in the referent situation?   Yes   No

Checklist IV

1. Has one or more of these standards been used in writing the criterion?   Yes   No

Source: Stephen L. Yelon and Roger O. Scott, *A strategy for writing objectives* (Dubuque, Iowa: Kendall/Hunt, 1970). Reprinted by permission of the authors.

TABLE 2.3 *(Continued)*

a. With these characteristics: _____		
b. So quickly that: _____		
1. Exact time?	Yes	No
2. Approximate time?	Yes	No
a. Limits for _____ unit of time.		
c. According to: _____		
1. Performance identical to reference?	Yes	No
2. Performance which approximates characteristics or meaning of reference?	Yes	No
d. So well that: _____		
1. Consequence of product identical in characteristics?	Yes	No
2. Consequence approximates characteristics of product?	Yes	No
2. Is the stated standard the closest approximation to the standard usually used in the referent situation?	Yes	No

Checklist V

1. Are the limit and the standards sufficient:		
a. as prerequisite to learning another performance?	Yes	No
b. as directly prerequisite to performing in the referent situation?	Yes	No
c. to convince you that the performance is stable?	Yes	No

Checklist VI

1. Are the stated conditions the closest feasible simulation to the conditions in the referent situation?	Yes	No
2. Are the conditions those affecting this performance only?	Yes	No

Checklist VII

1. Are all the statements so clear that one or more groups of (a) colleagues, (b) students, or (c) any parent or citizen could look at the objective and the student's performance and would agree whether the student had performed according to the criterion limit under the required conditions?	Yes	No

trated in the flowchart presented in Figure 2.1. As the reader moves through the flowchart, he is referred to a series of checkpoints in Table 2.3, which describe various criteria that must be met if the objectives are to be explicit and sufficiently behavioral. The combined use of the Yelon and Scott (1970) system and the Metfessel, Michael, and Kirsner (1969) list should greatly facilitate the statement of operational instructional objectives.

PSYCHOMOTOR OBJECTIVES

Several attempts have been made to specify the elements of a psychomotor taxonomy. A summary of four of these attempts is presented in Table 2.4. Only the model proposed by Simpson represents

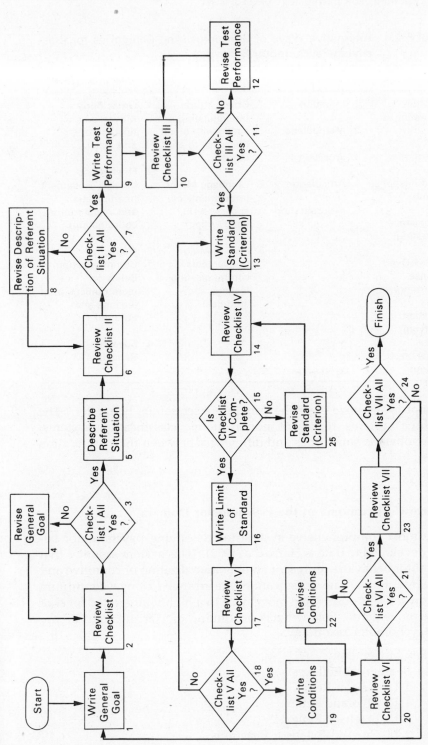

FIGURE 2.1.   Flowchart for a System for Writing Instructional Objectives

Source: Stephen L. Yelon and Roger O. Scott, *A strategy for writing objectives* (Dubuque, Iowa: Kendall/Hunt, 1970).   Reprinted by permission of the authors.

TABLE 2.4 Alternative Ways of Conceptualizing Categories for Classifying Psychomotor Behaviors

Simpson (1966)	Dave (1970)	Ragsdale (1950)	Kibler et al. (1970)
1. Perception (interpreting)	1. Imitation	1. Object Motor (manipulating or acting with direct reference to an object)	1. Gross Body Movements (locomotor and axile)
2. Set (preparing)	2. Manipulation		
	3. Precision		
3. Guided Response (learning)	4. Articulation	2. Language Motor (movements of speech, sight, handwriting)	2. Finely Coordinated Movement (manipulation and visual motor coordination)
4. Mechanism (habituating)	5. Naturalization		
5. Complex Overt Response (performing)		3. Feeling Motor (movements communicating feelings and attitudes)	3. Nonverbal Communication Behavior (communication of feelings and attitude)
6. Adaptation (modifying)			4. Speech Behaviors
7. Origination (creating)			

an attempt to organize the behaviors into a sequential hierarchy. The other three systems represent nontaxonomic classification systems. There are obvious similarities and differences between the classification schemes.

Harrow's Taxonomy of the Psychomotor Domain

The most comprehensive system for classifying psychomotor behaviors developed to date is Harrow's (1972). This system assumes that psychomotor behaviors represent an operationalization of cognitive and affective intentions. The classifications are arranged along a continuum from a low level of observable movement to a highly integrated level of complex movement. Following is an outline of Harrow's (1972, pp. 96–98) psychomotor taxonomy:

1.00 Reflex Movements
 1.10 Segmental Reflexes
  1.11 Flexion Reflex
  1.12 Myotatic Reflex
  1.13 Extensor Reflex
  1.14 Crossed Extensor Reactions

1.20 Intersegmental Reflexes
    1.21 Cooperative Reflex
    1.22 Competitive Reflex
    1.23 Successive Induction
    1.24 Reflex Figure
1.30 Suprasegmental Reflexes
    1.31 Extensor Rigidity
    1.32 Plasticity Reactions
    1.33 Postural Reflexes
        1.331 Supporting Reactions
        1.332 Shifting Reactions
        1.333 Tonic-Attitudinal Reflexes
        1.334 Righting Reaction
        1.335 Grasp Reflex
        1.336 Placing and Hopping Reactions
2.00 Basic-Fundamental Movements
    2.10 Locomotor Movements
    2.20 Non-Locomotor Movements
    2.30 Manipulative Movements
        2.31 Prehension
        2.32 Dexterity
3.00 Perceptual Abilities
    3.10 Kinesthetic Discrimination
        3.11 Body Awareness
            3.111 Bilaterality
            3.112 Laterality
            3.113 Sidedness
            3.114 Balance
        3.12 Body Image
        3.13 Body Relationship to Surrounding Objects in Space
    3.20 Visual Discrimination
        3.21 Visual Acuity
        3.22 Visual Tracking
        3.23 Visual Memory
        3.24 Figure-Ground Differentiation
        3.25 Perceptual Consistency
    3.30 Auditory Discrimination
        3.31 Auditory Acuity
        3.32 Auditory Tracking
        3.33 Auditory Memory
    3.40 Tactile Discrimination
    3.50 Coordinated Abilities
        3.51 Eye-Hand Coordination
        3.52 Eye-Foot Coordination

4.00 Physical Abilities

    4.10 Endurance

        4.11 Muscular Endurance

        4.12 Cardiovascular Endurance

    4.20 Strength

    4.30 Flexibility

    4.40 Agility

        4.41 Change Direction

        4.42 Stops and Starts

        4.43 Reaction-Response Time

        4.44 Dexterity

5.00 Skilled Movements

    5.10 Simple Adaptive Skill

        5.11 Beginner

        5.12 Intermediate

        5.13 Advanced

        5.14 Highly Skilled

    5.20 Compound Adaptive Skill

        5.21 Beginner

        5.22 Intermediate

        5.23 Advanced

        5.24 Highly Skilled

    5.30 Complex Adaptive Skill

        5.31 Beginner

        5.32 Intermediate

        5.33 Advanced

        5.34 Highly Skilled

6.00 Non-Discursive Communication

    6.10 Expressive Movement

        6.11 Posture and Carriage

        6.12 Gestures

        6.13 Facial Expression

    6.20 Interpretive Movement

        6.21 Aesthetic Movement

        6.22 Creative Movement[2]

With regard to her psychomotor taxonomy classifications, Harrow states:

> . . . Acting as a basis for all movement behavior is the first category, reflex movement (1.00), and the second category, basic of funda-

---

mental movement patterns (2.00), is actually the combining of reflex movements into inherent movement patterns. The learner responds involuntarily in the first category and though the movement patterns in the second category are inherent within the learner, he utilizes these patterns during voluntary movement. It is upon these voluntary movement patterns that he builds his skilled movements. The next two categories, perceptual abilities (3.00) and physical abilities (4.00), are further developed through maturation and learning. The learner goes through many learning experiences that sharpen his perceptual abilities, and engages in many activities that increase the quality of his physical abilities. The efficiency and degree of skilled movement attained by any learner is based upon the learner's control of his basic or fundamental movements, the degree of efficiency with which he perceives stimuli, and the level of development he has attained in the fourth category of physical abilities. Once the learner has acquired a skilled movement vocabulary (5.00) he has the necessary tools (an efficient body—an accurate perceptual system—and skilled movement repertoire) for modifying and creating aesthetic movement patterns (6.00) (p. 33).

Illustrative Psychomotor Objectives

Following are selected objectives adapted from Harrow's (1972) psychomotor taxonomy. The reader should refer to the list of categories for specific classifications. Due to the autonomic nature of classification 1.00—Reflex Movements—no objectives need be developed by teachers.

2.10 At the end of the school year, the preschool student will be able to accomplish a two-footed jump beginning with both feet parallel, using the arms for forward thrust and landing with both feet together.

3.40 The student will be able to distinguish between a penny, a nickel, a dime, and a quarter solely by touch 100 percent of the time.

4.20 Upon completion of a six-week training session, the student will have improved his grip strength by at least five pounds as measured by a dynamometer.

5.10 A first-year typing student will be able to type at least thirty words per minute during a five-minute typing test with no more than five errors.

6.20 The student will be able to produce a recognizable rhythmic pattern for at least thirty seconds.

SUGGESTED READINGS

Ahmann, J. S., and M. D. Glock. *Evaluating pupil growth,* 4th ed. Boston: Allyn and Bacon, 1971. See Chapter 2, "Educational Objectives in Evaluation."

Cox, R. C., and Wildemann, Carol E. *Taxonomy of educational objectives: Cognitive domain—an annotated bibliography,* Monograph I. Pittsburgh: Learning Research and Development Center, University of Pittsburgh, 1970.

Furst, E. J. *Constructing evaluation instruments.* New York: Longmans, Green, 1958. Chapters 2 and 3 contain discussions of the sources of educational objectives and problems encountered in defining them.

Gronlund, N. E. *Stating behavioral objectives for classroom instruction.* New York: Macmillan, 1970.

Kapfer, Miriam B., ed. *Behavioral objectives in curriculum development.* Englewood Cliffs, N.J.: Educational Technology Publications, 1971. A collection of 43 selected readings and bibliography from a variety of sources, this is an extremely valuable reference volume.

Kibler, R. J.; Barker, L. L.; and Miles, D. T. *Behavioral objectives and instruction.* Boston: Allyn and Bacon, 1970.

Lindvall, C. M., ed. *Defining educational objectives.* Pittsburgh: University of Pittsburgh Press, 1964.

Mager, R. F. *Preparing objectives for programmed instruction.* San Francisco: Fearon Publishers, 1962. This brief but excellent programmed text provides rationale and procedures for stating operational educational objectives.

Scriven, M. *The methodology of evaluation.* Lafayette, Ind.: Social Science Education Consortium, 1965.

Thomas, R. M. *Judging student progress,* 2nd ed. New York: David McKay, 1960. See Chapter 2, "Stating Goals."

The following references are sources of ideas about what to measure and how educational objectives should be defined.

Bernabei, R., and Leles, S. *Behavioral objectives in curriculum and evaluation.* Dubuque, Iowa: Kendall/Hunt, 1970.

Bloom, B., *et al. Taxonomy of educational objectives, Handbook I: Cognitive domain.* New York: Longmans, Green, 1956.

French, W., *et al. Behavioral goals of general education in high school.* New York: Russell Sage Foundation, 1957.

Kearney, N. C. *Elementary school objectives.* New York: Russell Sage Foundation, 1953.

Krathwohl, D. R., *et al. Taxonomy of educational objectives, Handbook II: Affective domain.* New York: Longmans, Green, 1964.

Following are two sources of comprehensive collections of objectives. Often the teacher finds it easier to *select* than to construct objectives.

Flanagan, J. C.; Shanner, W. M.; and Mager, R. F. *Behavioral objectives—A guide to individualizing learning.* Palo Alto, Cal.: Westinghouse Learning Press,

1971. Includes objectives for the primary, intermediate, and secondary levels in mathematics, social studies, language arts, and science.

Popham, W. J. *Instructional objectives.* Los Angeles, Cal.: Instructional Objectives Exchange, 1968. Separate booklets of objectives, together with sample test items, are available in a wide variety of content areas, e.g., language arts, home economics, English literature, mathematics, English grammar, reading.

3
THE NATURE AND SPECIFICATION OF AFFECTIVE LEARNING OUTCOMES

SUMMARY PREVIEW STATEMENTS[1]

1. Specifying affective outcomes (e.g., attitudes, interests, values, and the like) may be as important, or more important, than specifying cognitive or psychomotor outcomes.

2. Cognitive and affective outcomes interact to the degree that they are virtually inseparable.

3. Affective outcomes directly influence learning and also constitute legitimate educational outcomes in themselves.

4. How an individual feels about subject matter, school, and learning may be as important as how much he achieves.

5. The major categories of the Affective Domain of the *Taxonomy of Educational Objectives* are:
   a. Receiving (attending and awareness).
   b. Responding.
   c. Valuing.
   d. Organization.
   e. Characterization by a value or value complex.

6. The organizing principle in the Affective Domain of the *Taxonomy of Educational Objectives* is "internalization."

7. Internalization is the inner growth that occurs as the individual becomes aware of and then adopts attitudes, principles, codes, and

---

[1] This chapter is based in part on material taken from D. R. Krathwohl and D. A. Payne, Defining and Assessing Educational Objectives. In *Educational measurement,* 2nd ed., ed. R. L. Thorndike (Washington: American Council on Education, 1971), pp. 17–45. Excerpts reprinted by permission.

sanctions that are basic to his value judgments and guide his behavior.

8. The hierarchical continua of the Affective Domain have the following characteristics:
   a. Increasing emotionality of responses.
   b. Increasingly automatic responses.
   c. Increasing willingness to attend to particular stimuli.
   d. Increasing integration of diverse values.

9. Popham has developed a method for specifying affective objectives that involves:
   a. Generating a general affective statement.
   b. Imagining a hypothetical student who positively typifies the objective.
   c. Imagining a hypothetical student who negatively typifies the objective.
   d. Describing a situation in which these two individuals would respond differentially.

10. Affective outcomes are hard to specify because it is difficult to identify appropriate overt behavioral evidence of the covert affect, and because they are ever-changing.

11. Lack of attention to affective outcomes tends to result in their erosion in the classroom.

12. A teacher will probably need to specify fewer affective than cognitive outcomes.

While most major efforts at test construction and curriculum building have concentrated exclusively on cognitive achievement, criticism of the schools often focuses on students' "poor" attitudes, "low" motivation to achieve, slovenly work habits, and lack of commitment to societal values. Affective goals and objectives seem to have high saliency for educators and noneducators alike. Furthermore, affective objectives have long-range importance, involving as they do not whether a student can but whether he wants to and does behave in educationally desirable ways. Unfortunately, there is little formal recognition of the long-range importance of affective outcomes in the schools' curricula, and measures for the evaluation of these outcomes are seldom developed. Thus, the structured articulation of affective objectives may be even more critical to educational progress than are cognitive objectives. Definition of terms is especially crucial in the affective area.

If confusion exists about the definition of a term like *really under-stand,* consider the variety of possible meanings of a term like *appreciation.* When teachers say they want a child to *appreciate* art, do they mean that he should be aware of works of art? Should he be willing to give them some attention when they are accessible? Should he seek them out—visit museums on his own, for instance? Do they mean that he should regard works of art as valuable? Should he experience an emotional response when he sees a work of art? Should he be able to evaluate it and explain why and how it is effective? Should he be able to compare its aesthetic impact with that of some other art form (e.g., music)?

This list could be enlarged, but it is extensive enough to suggest that the term *appreciation* has a wide variety of meanings. And, worse, not all of its meanings are distinct from the terms *attitude* and *interest.* Thus, if appreciation involves liking a work of art well enough to seek it out, how would one distinguish such behavior from an interest in art —or are interest and appreciation interchangeable? If the student values art, does he have a favorable attitude toward it? Are appreciation objectives and attitude objectives the same, overlapping, or entirely different?

STRUCTURE AND CATEGORIES OF THE AFFECTIVE DOMAIN

Although the authors of the *Taxonomy of Educational Objectives* (Bloom *et al.* 1956) found it possible to structure the cognitive domain on simple-complex and concrete-abstract axes, the authors of the affective domain taxonomy (Krathwohl *et al.* 1964) found it necessary to add the dimension of *internalization* to provide a meaningful hierarchical structure. Internalization is the process by which behavioral control consistent with positive values is exerted from within the individual. At first, this incorporation of new values, or adoption of new behavior, may have only isolated manifestations, but it gradually comes to dominate one's thinking and motivation until one's actions are consistent with his professed value orientation. Inner growth occurs as the individual becomes aware of and then adopts attitudes, principles, codes, and sanctions that are basic to his value judgments and guide his conduct. Internalization has many elements in common with *socialization,* and is best understood by examining the categories in the affective domain of the *Taxonomy* structure. Stripped of their definitions, the sequence of categories and subcategories is as follows (Krathwohl *et al.* 1964, pp. 34–35):

1.0 Receiving (attending)
   1.1 Awareness
   1.2 Willingness to receive
   1.3 Controlled or selected attention
2.0 Responding
   2.1 Acquiescence in responding
   2.2 Willingness to respond
   2.3 Satisfaction in response
3.0 Valuing
   3.1 Acceptance of a value
   3.2 Preference for a value
   3.3 Commitment (conviction)
4.0 Organization
   4.1 Conceptualization of a value
   4.2 Organization of a value system
5.0 Characterization by a value or a value complex
   5.1 Generalized set
   5.2 Characterization

The lowest level of behavior in the structure is the individual's awareness of the stimuli that initiate the affective behavior and form the context in which the affective behavior occurs. Thus, the lowest category is 1.0 *Receiving*. It is subdivided into three categories. At the 1.1 *Awareness* level, the individual's attention is attracted to the stimulus, e.g., he develops some consciousness of the use of shading to convey depth and lighting in a picture. The second subcategory, 1.2 *Willingness to receive*, describes the state of having differentiated the stimulus from others and being willing to give it attention, e.g., he develops a tolerance for bizarre uses of shading in modern art. At 1.3 *Controlled or selected attention*, the student looks for the stimulus, e.g., he is on the alert for uses of shading to create a sense of three-dimensional depth and to indicate the nature of lighting.

At the next level, 2.0 *Responding*, the individual responds regularly to the affective stimuli. At the lowest level of responding, 2.1 *Acquiescence in responding*, he merely complies with expectations, e.g., at the request of his teacher, he hangs reproductions of famous paintings in his dormitory room. He is obedient to traffic rules. At the next level, 2.2 *Willingness to respond*, he responds increasingly to an inner compulsion, e.g., he voluntarily looks for instances of good art in which shading, perspective, color, and design have been well used. He has an interest in social problems broader than those of the local community. At 2.3 *Satisfaction in response*, he responds emotionally as well, e.g., he works with clay to make pottery for personal pleasure. Up to this point, he has differentiated the affective stimuli; now he has begun to seek them out and to attach emotional significance and value to them.

The next level, 3.0 *Valuing*, describes increasing internalization as the person's behavior becomes sufficiently consistent to desire and hold a value. More specifically, Valuing is subdivided into 3.1 *Acceptance of a value*, e.g., he has a continuing desire to develop the ability to write effectively; 3.2 *Preference for a value*, e.g., he actively seeks out examples of good art for enjoyment of them to the level where he behaves so as to further his impression actively; and 3.3 *Commitment*, e.g., faith in the power of reason and the method of experimentation.

As the learner successively internalizes values, he encounters situations in which more than one value is relevant. This necessitates organizing his values into a system, 4.0 *Organization*. And since interrelating values requires conceptualizing them in a form that permits organization, this level is subdivided into: 4.1 *Conceptualization of a value*, e.g., he desires to evaluate works of art he appreciates or to find out and crystallize the basic assumptions which underlie codes of ethics; and 4.2 *Organization of a value system*, e.g., acceptance of the place of art in one's life as one of dominant value, or weighs alternative social policies and practices against the standards of public welfare.

Finally, the internalization and organization processes reach a point at which the individual responds very consistently to value-laden situations with an interrelated set of values and structured view of the world. The *Taxonomy* category that describes this behavior is 5.0 *Characterization by a value or value complex*, which includes the subcategories 5.1 *Generalized set*, e.g., he views all problems in terms of their aesthetic aspects, or readiness to revise judgments and to change behavior in the light of evidence, and 5.2 *Characterization*, e.g., he develops a consistent philosophy of life.

In summary, the major characteristics of the affective domain continuum are: (1) increasing emotional quality of responses; (2) responses increasingly automatic as one progresses up the continuum; (3) increasing willingness to attend to a specified stimulus; and (4) developing integration of a value pattern at the upper levels of the continuum.

ILLUSTRATIVE AFFECTIVE DOMAIN OBJECTIVES

Following are some sample objectives for the affective domain. Refer to the list of affective domain categories on page 61 for the specific classification of each objective.

1.3 Listens to music with some discrimination of mood and meaning and some recognition of the contribution of various musical instruments to the total effect.

2.2 Contributes to group discussions by asking thought-provoking questions.

3.2 Is willing to work for improvement of health regulations.

4.2 Weighs alternative social policies and practices against the standards of the public welfare rather than the advantage of specialized and narrow interest groups.

5.1 Is ready to revise judgments and change behavior in the light of evidence.

It is obvious that the behaviors suggested by affective objectives are much more difficult to define than those associated with cognitive learning outcomes. Nevertheless, affective objectives are important and should be systematically promoted by instructors. As long as an instructor can logically or empirically defend a behavior as representing a particular value, and can communicate his thinking to his students, he can consider affective objectives legitimate goals. One instructor might define "appreciation of art" in terms of the number of times a student visits an art museum during the semester; another instructor might specify other behavior to fulfill this objective. But visits would represent a desired behavior and be observable. The need for behavioral description of affective objectives is as important, if not more so, than that required by cognitive objectives.

Difficulty may arise if students are aware of the affective objectives held for them by teachers. They may attempt to "please" the teacher by making the desired responses or voluntarily engaging in the expected behavior. Some methods of handling this problem when using questionnaires and inventories will be dealt with in Chapter Eight. Suffice it to say, however, that the advantages of considering affective outcomes, even with their attendant measurement problems, far outweigh the disadvantages.

BEHAVIORAL AFFECTIVE CATEGORIES FOR THE TAXONOMY OF EDUCATIONAL OBJECTIVES

One of the criticisms frequently leveled at the *Taxonomy*, particularly by evaluators, is that it is not couched in behavioral terms. The possibility of some latitude in interpreting the various categories of the *Taxonomy* frequently makes the tasks of curriculum evaluation and test construction difficult. Metfessel, Michael, and Kirsner (1969) have made a very practical contribution by listing infinitives and direct objects that can be used to operationalize the *Taxonomy*. Table 3.1 may suggest many important objectives and assist in "behavioralizing" the *Taxonomy*.

TABLE 3.1 Instrumentation of the Taxonomy of Educational Objectives: Affective Domain

Taxonomy Classification	KEY WORDS	
	Examples of Infinitives	Examples of Direct Objects
1.0 Receiving		
1.1 Awareness	to differentiate, to separate, to set apart, to share	sights, sounds, events, designs, arrangements
1.2 Willingness to Receive	to accumulate, to select, to combine, to accept	models, examples, shapes, sizes, meters, cadences
1.3 Controlled or Selected Attention	to select, to posturally respond to, to listen (for), to control	alternatives, answers, rhythms, nuances
2.0 Responding		
2.1 Acquiescence in Responding	to comply (with), to follow, to commend, to approve	directions, instructions, laws, policies, demonstrations
2.2 Willingness to Respond	to volunteer, to discuss, to practice, to play	instruments, games, dramatic works, charades, burlesques
2.3 Satisfaction in Response	to applaud, to acclaim, to spend leisure time in, to augment	speeches, plays, presentations, writings
3.0 Valuing		
3.1 Acceptance of a Value	to increase measured proficiency in, to increase numbers of, to relinquish, to specify	group membership(s), artistic production(s), musical productions, personal friendships
3.2 Preference for a Value	to assist, to subsidize, to help, to support	artists, projects, viewpoints, arguments
3.3 Commitment	to deny, to protest, to debate, to argue	deceptions, irrelevancies, abdications, irrationalities
4.0 Organization		
4.1 Conceptualization of a Value	to discuss, to theorize (on), to abstract, to compare	parameters, codes, standards, goals

Source: W. S. Metfessel, W. B. Michael, and D. A. Kirsner, Instrumentation of Bloom's and Krathwohl's taxonomies for the writing of educational objectives. *Psychology in the Schools* 6 (1969): 227–231. Reprinted by permission of the publisher.

TABLE 3.1 *(Continued)*

	KEY WORDS	
Taxonomy Classification	*Examples of Infinitives*	*Examples of Direct Objects*
4.2 Organization of a Value System	to balance, to organize, to define, to formulate	systems, approaches, criteria, limits
5.0 Characterization by Value of Value Complex		
5.1 Generalized Set	to revise, to change, to complete, to require	plans, behavior, methods, effort(s)
5.2 Characterization	to be rated high by peers in, to be rated high by superiors in, and to be rated high by subordinates in and to avoid, to manage, to resolve, to resist	humanitarianism, ethics, integrity, maturity extravagance(s), excesses, conflicts, exorbitancy/exorbitancies

POPHAM'S STRATEGY FOR SPECIFYING AFFECTIVE OBJECTIVES

In addition to Metfessel, Michael, and Kirsner's list of behavioral terms, the interested teacher may find Popham's relatively simple strategy useful in identifying and specifying affective learning outcomes. Its basic intent is to describe observable student behaviors that reflect attainment or nonattainment of these affective objectives. There are five general steps in the procedure (Popham, undated filmstrip):

1. Begin with a general statement of the broad affective objectives.

Example: At the end of this course, students will have more favorable attitudes toward science.

2. Next, imagine a hypothetical student who personifies the objective. The intent is to describe the behavior likely to be exhibited by a possessor of this positive attitude.

Example: A student who has a positive attitude toward science is more likely to read scientific articles in popular magazines, attend science-fiction movies, and select science book titles.

3. Third, imagine a student who is a nonpossessor of the attitude or has a negative attitude toward the objectives or stimulus.

Example: A student who has a negative attitude toward science would not choose magazine articles dealing with science, would not enjoy courses in science, and would not enjoy or choose to visit a science museum.

At this point, two ends of a behavioral continuum have been described.

4. Describe a situation in which the attribute possessor and nonpossessor would respond differently. Define difference-producing situations in which the hypothetical individuals would behave differently. The situations might be contrived or occur naturally.

Example: When put in a forced-choice situation, students majoring in science will select more hypothetical book titles dealing with scientific topics than will individuals not majoring in science.

It is of great importance that the situations chosen be free of behavior-inducing cues. There should be no external pressure to respond in a particular way. Do not ask for a show of hands to indicate interest or request that students sign a survey of attitudes toward a course. The teacher may, however, wish to work out a code with students so that he can keep track of individual progress toward selected affective objectives.

The use of what Webb *et al.* (1966) call unobtrusive measures is particularly well suited to many kinds of affective outcomes. Such measures are considerably less influenced by the desire of a student to please the teacher.

5. Select those difference-producing situations that most effectively, efficiently, and practically define the intended outcomes.

Some of the many methods that can be used to measure affective learning outcomes are described in Chapter Eight.

IMPLICATIONS OF THE AFFECTIVE DOMAIN TAXONOMY

The existence of an affective domain taxonomy raises questions about the relation between cognitive and affective objectives. The typical statement of objectives specifies behavior in only one domain. This no doubt results from the typical analytic approach to building curricula. Only occasionally do we find a statement like "the student should learn to analyze a good argument with pleasure," which suggests not only the cognitive behavior but also the affect that accompanies it.

In spite of this lack of explicit formulation, nearly all cognitive objectives have an inherent affective component. For example, most instructors hope their students will develop a continuing interest in, and positive attitudes toward, the content or methods of the course. But they leave these goals unspecified. Thus, many objectives classified as cognitive have an implicit but unspecified affective component. If such an objective refers, as it usually does, to the content of the course as a whole, or a sizable segment of it, it may be most convenient to specify it as a separate objective.

In the cognitive domain, the instructor's concern is that the student shall be able to do a task when requested. In the affective domain, his concern is that the student *does do* it when appropriate after he has learned that he *can do* it. Though the school system rewards the student more on a can-do than on a does-do basis, it is the latter that every instructor seeks; first-level objectives nearly always involve what the individual *does do* as a result of his education. By emphasizing this phenomenon, the affective domain brings to light an extremely important consideration often missing from cognitive objectives.

The heuristic value of the affective *Taxonomy* may be its most important contribution. Its very existence may encourage greater attention to the affective components of cognitive objectives. It may encourage people to attempt more fully to operationalize their objectives in this domain.

It is important to note an important difference between the cognitive and affective domains that often remains obscure. Both are concerned with overt and covert behavior. Because covert behavior is by definition unobservable, and because the teacher must deal with observable phenomena, both teaching and evaluation assume that all covert behaviors—e.g., thinking in certain ways—have certain overt consequences that can be identified. This is particularly easy to demonstrate in the cognitive domain, where certain kinds of thinking result in "right" answers or demonstrable abilities to perform in certain ways. This is often true in the affective domain as well; if students enjoy a course, for example, they engage in certain behaviors spontaneously during the period of instruction (attending concerts, reading books in the field, talking to others about the subject, and the like).

In other instances, the link between covert and overt behavior is much less direct, immediate, and observable in the affective domain. Feelings of pleasure in reading, for instance, may have no immediate overt manifestations, and if they occur at a low level it may be a long time before they result in such overt action as, for example, increased reading. Thus, the attempt to state affective goals in terms of observable behavior or performance may be very difficult or impossible. It may be necessary to phrase immediate objectives in terms of internal states of mind that over time will have overt behavioral consequences. This suggests the importance of stating long-term goals and evaluating complete programs as well as single units and courses.

SUGGESTED READINGS

Beatty, W. H, ed. *Improving educational assessment and an inventory of measures of affective behavior.* Washington: Association for Supervision and Curriculum Development, 1969.

Eiss, A. F., and Harbeck, Mary Blatt. *Behavioral objectives in the affective domain.* Washington: National Science Supervisors Association, 1969. An excellent application of the affective domain of the *Taxonomy of educational objectives* to objectives and measures in science.

EPIC, Diversified Systems Corporation. *Affective measures for educational evaluation.* Tucson, Ariz.: Educational Innovators Press, 1972. This brief booklet describes a variety of methods of gathering data related to various affective behaviors.

Lee, B. N., and Merrill, M. D. *Writing complete affective objectives: A short course.* Belmont, Cal.: Wadsworth, 1972. This brief field-tested self-instructional paperback will assist teachers, particularly those at the elementary and secondary level, in developing affective objectives and analyzing student behavior.

Mager, R. F. *Developing attitude toward learning.* Palo Alto, Cal.: Fearon, 1968. Describes three principles that teachers can apply in nurturing favorable attitudes toward subjects of study. Some consideration is also given to measurement.

Raths, L. E.; Harmon, M.; and Simon, S. B. *Values and teaching.* Columbus, Ohio: Charles Merrill, 1966.

Shaw, M. E., and Wright, J. M. *Scales for the measurement of attitudes.* New York: McGraw-Hill, 1967. An extremely valuable sourcebook for a tremendous variety of unpublished affective measures.

4

PLANNING FOR THE DEVELOPMENT, ADMINISTRATION, AND SCORING OF THE MEASURING INSTRUMENT

SUMMARY PREVIEW STATEMENTS

1. In planning for the development of an assessment device, consideration needs to be given to:
   a. The type of measuring procedure used.
   b. Length of the instrument.
   c. The range of difficulty of items.
   d. Time limits.
   e. Objectives to be sampled.
   f. Arrangement of items.
   g. Scoring procedures.
   h. The method of recording and reporting results.

2. The most important decision to be made is what to measure.

3. The development of a table of specifications (a two-way grid contrasting content and behavioral outcomes) can greatly facilitate both the instructional and the test development process.

4. The types of outcomes measured are not readily apparent from the format of the measurement procedure used.

5. Rating scales are useful in summarizing either cognitive or affective outcomes.

6. Anecdotal records, observations, and sociometric methods are valuable tools for examining personal-social outcomes.

7. Oral exams are particularly useful with elementary students and those likely to have difficulty responding to written tests.

8. A great variety of knowledge and higher-order outcomes can be assessed with essay and structured selection-type test items.

9. The main advantage of classroom tests over standardized tests is their greater relevance to the curriculum.

10. Carefully controlled conditions should prevail when administering a test, particularly a standardized test.

11. The directions for taking a test should be as clear and concise as possible.

12. Great care needs to be taken in specifying test scoring procedures.

13. Teachers may profitably use fan, strip, or cut-out keys in test scoring.

14. If all individuals attempt all items, a correction for guessing on objective tests is probably not needed.

15. The greater the variety of outcomes measured and the more frequent the measurement, the greater the reliability of the assessment.

16. The results of all tests should be discussed with individual students and/or the entire class.

17. The teacher should give students samples of the questions he will ask on tests and should allow practice on them to reduce test anxiety and make possible a fairer sampling of behavior.

18. The chances of achieving a passing score by chance on a reliable classroom test are extremely small.

19. The differential weighting of response alternatives on a multiple-choice exam rarely improves its measuring capacity.

To insure the best possible test, one must plan for it. Appropriate planning involves consideration of a large number of factors, including the (1) type of measurement procedure to be used, (2) length of the test, (3) range and difficulty level of the items, (4) arrangement of items, (5) time limits, (6) scoring system, (7) manner of reporting results, (8) method of recording responses, and, most important of all, (9) the subject matter, mental operation, or behavior to be sampled. Several of the more important decision points in test planning will be discussed in this chapter.

OVERVIEW OF THE STEPS INVOLVED IN CONSTRUCTING ASSESSMENT DEVICES

The test development process is a complex one, consisting of a variety of tasks and activities. A flowchart of the major activities is presented in Figure 4.1, which is based on an analysis of the test development process and a PERT (Program Evaluation and Review Technique) chart described by Cook (1966). The system is virtually self-explanatory and should provide the reader with a good perspective on the entire process. Those activities and decisions related to the development of parallel forms are obviously of less relevance to the classroom teacher. The desirability of having available comparable forms of a classroom test to handle the problems of absentees, or testing under crowded conditions in which cheating might be anticipated, or for research purposes, should not be overlooked. The specific form that each activity in the chart takes will, of course, depend on the assessment requirements. Of particular concern are those decisions related to activities 2, 7, 10, 18, 20, and 21. These require skills and knowledges of measurement, evaluation, testing, and assessment. With regard to Activity 3, the reader is referred to Figure 2.1, which describes the development of instructional objectives. In Activity 4, consideration must be given to such factors as item format, time available, directions for administration, behavior measured, and language.

DEVELOPING A TABLE OF SPECIFICATIONS

Ordinarily the first step a teacher would take in developing a measuring instrument would be to review the objectives of his instructional program, both those originally proposed and those actually attended to. A convenient way to conduct this review is through the use of a "table of specifications." This table is simply a two-way grid relating the two major components of an educational objective: the "content" element and the "behavioral" element. In addition, the table should contain percentages that reflect the relative emphases given each objective in the instructional situation. A sample table of specifications is presented in Table 4.1.

It should be noted that the Behavior Dimension uses the first four categories of the *Taxonomy of Educational Objectives*. There are, obviously, alternative ways of viewing this dimension. Some of these schemes have been summarized in Table 4.2. These alternative methods range from the very general (Smith and Tyler) to the specific (Walbesser). All deserve the readers' consideration. The behavior categories selected for use in a table of specifications will be heavily

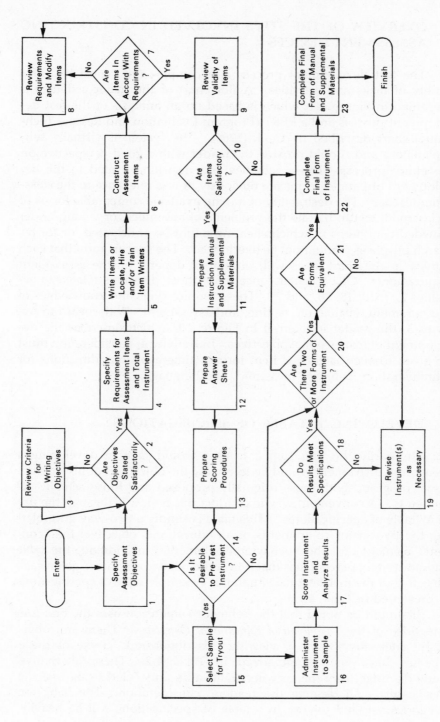

FIGURE 4.1. Flowchart Describing Process of Constructing Assessment Devices

TABLE 4.1 Sample Abbreviated Table of Specifications for a Course in Educational Tests and Measurement Used in Developing Mid-Semester Exam

	Behavior Dimension								
Content Dimension	Recall		Compre-hension		Applica-tion		Analysis		Total Content Dimension
	Cell #	%	Cell #	%	Cell #	%	Cell #	%	
History of Testing	(1)	5	(8)		(15)		(22)		5
Uses of Tests	(2)	3	(9)	4	(16)		(23)		7
Measurement Terminology	(3)	3	(10)	2	(17)		(24)		5
Planning the Test	(4)	1	(11)	6	(18)	3	(25)		10
Constructing Supply-Type Questions	(5)	2	(12)	11	(19)	8	(26)	3	24
Constructing Selection-Type Items	(6)	4	(13)	6	(20)	12	(27)	7	29
Constructing and Scoring Essay Tests	(7)	4	(14)	8	(21)	5	(28)	3	20
Total Behavior Dimension		22		37		28		13	100%

influenced by the level of the student and the nature of the subject matter.

In practice the content categories would probably be more detailed than those in Table 4.1. Let us repeat that the greater the detail in the test blueprint, as summarized in a table of specifications, the easier will be the item construction task. Some compromise between the extremes of objectives—highly specific and highly general—will result in a reasonably balanced test.

Having developed a table of specifications the teacher-evaluator will now write items corresponding to each cell in the table. He will write a number of independent items in proportion to the representation of each objective in the table. Again, with reference to Table 4.1 he would construct 5 percent of the items (assuming the use of short-answer varieties) on the midsemester exam to measure the objectives of

TABLE 4.2 Alternative Ways of Conceptualizing the Behavior Dimensions of Tables of Specification

Smith and Tyler (1942)	Ebel (1965a)
1. Development of effective thinking methods	1. Understanding of terminology, vocabulary
2. Cultivation of useful work habits and study skills	2. Understanding of fact, principle, or generalization
3. Acquisition of wide range of significant interests	3. Ability to explain or illustrate
4. Appreciation of aesthetic experiences	4. Ability to calculate
5. Development of social sensitivity	5. Ability to predict under specified conditions
6. Personal social adjustment	6. Ability to recommend appropriate action
7. Acquisition of important information	7. Ability to make an evaluative judgment
8. Development of physical health	
9. Development of consistent life philosophy	

Raths (1938)	Walbesser (1965)
1. Functional information	1. Identifying
2. Various aspects of thinking	2. Distinguishing
3. Attitudes	3. Naming
4. Interest, aims, purposes, appreciations	4. Ordering
5. Study skills and work habits	5. Describing
6. Social adjustments and sensitivity	6. Applying rules
7. Creativeness	7. Stating rules
8. Functional social philosophy	8. Demonstrating
	9. Interpreting

Cell 1, 3 percent of Cell 2, and so on. If an instructor is using essay items, the percentages might reflect the amount of time and scoring weight given to certain items. In this way the evaluator insures proportionality, or what was referred to in Chapter One as "balance" in the test. Balance is interpreted relative to the amount of time spent on certain topics and skills in class, which in turn reflects the importance of selected objectives.

In summary, the use of a table of specifications in test development will help insure (1) that only those objectives actually pursued in instruction will be measured, (2) that each objective will receive the appropriate relative emphasis in the test, and (3) that by using subdivisions based on content and behavior, no important objectives will be overlooked or misrepresented.

SELECTING APPROPRIATE MEASUREMENT PROCEDURES

The table of specifications indicates the relative importance of each instructional objective. But a question now arises about how best to measure each objective. Many different techniques are available. Some measurement methods lend themselves more readily than others to assessing certain outcomes. The decision is frequently a difficult one. Properly matching objective and assessment procedure requires, in addition to sophistication in the theory and practice of measurement, competence in the subject matter and knowledge about the psychology of learning.

In order to make an intelligent selection of a measurement procedure, one needs to be aware of the relative advantages and disadvantages of the many techniques available. Data-gathering procedures may conveniently be classified in "test" and "nontest" categories. The relative strengths and limitations of these two types of techniques will be discussed in this section. "Nontest" methods are treated more extensively in Chapter Sixteen.

Nontest Procedures

In one sense the label "nontest" is a misnomer, inasmuch as any systematic sampling of behavior may be considered testing. Nontest procedures differ from test procedures in that (1) the student is unaware that data are being gathered, and (2) the student is not involved in recording responses.

It is not our intent to consider nontest procedures in detail. It might be helpful, however, to mention some of the techniques that are available, discuss selected situations in which they might be applied, and briefly illustrate such applications.

Rating and Checklist Procedures. Rating scales and checklists may be developed to assess cognitive or affective outcomes of instruction. For example, a checklist might be developed to describe how well a student can use a microscope or complete a dissection in zoology class. The instructor might use such a checklist while observing a particular student or group of students.

Guilford (1954, pp. 263–301) has identified five broad categories of rating scales: numerical, graphic, standard, cumulated points, and forced-choice. The most frequently used technique by far is the numerical scale. For example, an instructor in art might check on a nine-point scale the degree to which a student's painting represents a symmetrical relationship of central to peripheral elements. A series of scales like the following might be used to assess a variety of outcomes.

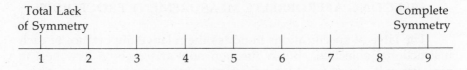

The rating scale has the advantage of being easily constructed and applied. It is a very flexible and adaptable technique in that responses may be recorded by an observer or a teacher. Rating procedures generally involve recording the relative degree to which a particular objective has been met or the extent to which a student's behavior indicates achievement. Because of problems of reliability it is suggested that ratings be obtained from a number of different observers.

Anecdotal Records and Observations. Anecdotal material is an excellent source of information primarily useful in evaluating the noncognitive outcomes of education. Variables such as interest, adjustment, and attitude may be described by recording factual accounts of behaviors relating to these variables. The primary advantage of this method of data gathering is that it is recorded by someone other than the student and is, therefore, more likely to be objective. A rich source of data is available in the wide variety of situations in which the teacher may observe his students. The chief drawback of observational techniques is their susceptibility to distortion arising from the idiosyncrasies of the recorder. In order to insure objectivity and attempt to control distortion, it is suggested that one first describe the situation, and then evaluate it in a separate paragraph.

Sociometric Methods. Occasionally a teacher, particularly in the elementary grades, is interested in describing the personal-social adjustment of his students. The teacher might ask each student to identify three peers he likes to sit by or work with on projects. By summarizing the choices in the form of a sociogram (a chart relating names by connected lines), the teacher can identify clique(s) and isolate(s). Such information is useful in describing interpersonal relationships and may identify individuals whose behavior in or outside the classroom might profitably be observed further.

Test Procedures

The four most frequently used test procedures for measuring educational achievement are oral exams, essay tests, teacher-made objective tests, and standardized tests.

Oral Exams. The oral exam is commonly used with (1) elementary-school children, (2) graduate students, and (3) students physically unable to take written tests. Although not used systematically in American education, the oral exam is a potentially useful technique. Certain measurement purposes can be better achieved with this technique than any other.

The value of oral exams is readily apparent. While written exams assume that the examinee understands the questions, the oral examiner can see if his question is understood. Further, the examiner can probe the depth of a student's understanding of a topic. Such probing also gives some indication of the thought processes used by the student. Not to be overlooked is the advantage of flexibility, i.e., the variety of behaviors that can be sampled. The technique of oral examination allows for the testing of both generalization and specific fact. In addition, the examiner(s) can observe a wide range of reactions to different stimulus questions. If a student hesitates in responding, fumbles for appropriate words, and manifests signs of stress, these reactions may be taken into account in appraising his degree of competence. It is with these types of behavior that examiners of doctoral candidates are frequently concerned. They are interested not only in how much the candidate knows, but also in how he expresses and handles himself in front of a group. In this respect the oral examination is realistically related to contemporary life. Prospective teachers, for example, must be able to use their knowledge in speaking. In many other vocational activities the spoken use of knowledge far exceeds its application in other ways.

Despite their potential advantages, several serious weaknesses of oral exams inhibit their use. Probably the most thoroughly documented weakness of the oral examination is its unreliability. The difficulty of maintaining comparable standards of judgment, selective perceptions, and interpretation on the part of different examiners, and the limited sampling of the breadth of the student's knowledge, potentially contribute to both unreliability and invalidity. Such factors as (1) lack of precision in the conduct of an oral exam, (2) failure to preplan the questions, and (3) the relative inefficiency of the oral exam in terms of faculty time serve to detract from its usefulness. The oral exam, nevertheless, has a great deal to offer as an assessment procedure. The use of the technique requires careful planning. Some of the factors that should be considered in the planning and use of oral exams are summarized in Table 4.3.

Essay Tests. The essay item and test are particularly valuable in the appraisal of certain kinds of behavioral changes. Essay items provide latitude for a student to express himself in characteristic ways. They allow him to impose his own organization on the material and to present it in his own words. They allow an instructor to assess objectives related to expression (spelling, grammar, and punctuation) as well as to

TABLE 4.3 Principles of Oral Examinations

1. Use oral examinations only for the purposes for which they are best suited, i.e., to obtain information as to the depth of students' knowledge, where oral presentation is clearly a purpose of the course or program, or where other means are simply inappropriate.
2. Prepare in advance a detailed outline of materials to be sampled in the examination even to the extent of writing questions which will be asked.
3. Determine in advance how records of student performance will be kept and what weights will be assigned various factors.
4. Keep the questioning relevant to the purposes of the course or program.
5. Word questions in such a way that the students can see the point of the question with minimum difficulty.
6. Where several examiners are involved, make each one responsible for questions on a specified part of the full examination.
7. Judge students on the basis of their performance precisely defined—not in terms of a generalized impression of their total appearance.
8. Pose questions which students with the training which has preceded a particular examination can reasonably be expected to know. An examination is not the place for an instructor to demonstrate his own erudition.
9. Use both general and specific questions but do so in some logical order.
10. Do not spend a disproportionate time probing for the answer to one question. If the first several questions do not elicit the desired response, move on to some other matter.
11. Develop some facility with several basic techniques for successful oral examining, such as (a) creating a friendly atmosphere, (b) asking questions, and (c) recording responses.
12. Make a written record of the student's performance at the time it is given. However, do so without disturbing the student or disrupting the flow of the examination.
13. In most situations allow students ample time to think through and make responses to questions.
14. Avoid arguing with the student. It is his show—let him make the most of it.

Source: Reprinted and abridged with permission from *Testing Bulletin No. 7*, published by the Office of Evaluation Services, Michigan State University, 1967.

mastery of subject matter. The essay item lends itself well to the assessment of higher-order mental abilities, particularly levels 5 (Synthesis) and 6 (Evaluation) of the *Taxonomy of Educational Objectives*.

Gronlund (1965) has identified twelve complex learning outcomes that can be measured effectively with essay items. These are the abilities to:

Explain cause-effect relationships.

Describe applications of principles.

Present relevant arguments.

Formulate tenable hypotheses.

Formulate valid conclusions.

State necessary assumptions.

Describe the limitations of data.

Explain methods and procedures.

Produce, organize, and express ideas.

Integrate learnings in different areas.

Create original forms (e.g., designing an experiment).

Evaluate the worth of ideas.

This list is not exhaustive but should highlight some of the potential learning outcomes that may be assessed by essay items and tests. In addition, some advocates of the essay item claim that it can be used to elicit creative behavior. Attempts to assess creativity through such methods, however, are still in the early stages of development.

A primary weakness of essay items is their susceptibility to scoring unreliability. A reader may very well judge a paper as failing on one day and passing the next. He may judge the first paper in a set more or less rigorously than the last. He may also be influenced by such irrelevant factors as handwriting, prior work by the student, or volume of material presented. This is not to say that essay items cannot be scored quite objectively. They can, but the task is time-consuming and requires considerable planning and effort.

Essay tests frequently require extended responses to a few questions. This procedure, by limiting the samples of behavior, may result in low instrument reliability and reduced relevance.

Teacher-Made Objective Tests. Objective teacher-made tests were first used in an attempt to overcome the weaknesses of other forms of testing, particularly oral and essay exams. Oral and extended-response essay tests tend to yield unreliable measurements because of the influence of such factors as the mental set of the examiner or scorer, past student performance, and limited sampling of course material. A series of questions and alternative answers provides more consistent and comparable responses, which in turn leads to greater reliability of measurement.

An objective test is a flexible instrument capable of appraising recall of knowledge and more complex cognitive abilities. It is an efficient procedure, allowing broad coverage of objectives in a reasonable period of time. Because student responses can be scored objectively, and a large number of responses gathered, the technique generally yields reliable results.

There are two general classes of objective items, *supply* and *choice* (or selection). In the supply type, the student responds to a simple direct question, e.g., What are the two main gases found in air? or to an incomplete statement, e.g., The two main gases found in air are _____. He is required to construct or supply his own answer. This item type is a good measure of recall of knowledge, although it is sometimes scored less objectively than are selection- or choice-type items.

Three major kinds of choice-type items have been found useful in achievement testing: true-false, multiple-response, and matching. Of the three, the multiple-response or multiple-choice item is the most commonly used. It is probably the most adaptable of the objective item types, allowing testing for command of factual information or of more complicated thought processes. Students are presented with a question or statement followed by four or five options or alternatives, one of which is correct; the others are distractors or foils. If a relatively large number of possible responses is given with each item, the effect of chance selection of correct answers is reduced. Research by Tversky (1964), however, seems to indicate that, at least from the standpoint of information theory, only three alternatives or options may be necessary.

Another form of objective item that has been found useful in accomplishing a quick survey of knowledge is the key-list or matching item. Students are given two lists of objects and are asked to match them on the basis of some indicated relationship. Such an exercise might involve matching inventions with their inventors or battles with dates. The reader is referred to Chapter Five for specific suggestions useful in constructing teacher-made objective tests.

Standardized Tests. A standardized test is an instrument that (1) contains a specified set of items, (2) includes explicit and standardized directions for administration and scoring, and (3) has usually been administered to a representative population of individuals for the purpose of securing normative data. The availability of normative data useful in interpreting individual scores is considered by some to distinguish standardized tests from other types of instruments. Other important characteristics of standardized tests are the high quality of items and high reliability. The key factor, however, is the uniformity of administration and scoring.

Standardized achievement tests are generally published as a battery, which contains a series of individual tests standardized on the same population, or as individual subject-matter tests.

Standardized achievement tests are useful for the purposes of testing outlined in Chapter One (e.g., planning, assessing, and reporting the results of educational experiences) to the extent that the items measure the specific objectives of instruction. In general, they measure outcomes and content common to educational programs in the United States. They are less well suited to measuring learning outcomes unique to a particular class or school. The concept of relevance, then, is a crucial one when selecting a standardized achievement test to evaluate learning outcomes. The items should measure the same behavior and content dimensions as would a teacher-made test. An item-by-item examination of the test should be undertaken, using a table of specifications to guide the analysis.

The relative strengths and weaknesses of nonstandardized (e.g., essay and teacher-made objective) and standardized tests are summarized in Table 4.4. In matching measurement procedure to instruc-

TABLE 4.4 Advantages and Limitations of Standardized and Nonstandardized Tests With Respect to the Criteria of Validity, Reliability, and Usability

	Standardized	
Criterion	Advantages	Limitations
1. Validity		
a. Curricular	Careful selection by competent persons. Fits typical situations.	Inflexible. Too general in scope to meet local requirements fully, especially in unusual situations.
b. Statistical	With best tests, high.	Criteria often inappropriate or unreliable. Size of coefficients dependent upon range of ability in group tested.
2. Reliability ·	For best tests, fairly high —often .85 or more for comparable forms.	High reliability is no guarantee of validity. Also, reliability depends upon range of ability in group tested.
3. Usability		
a. Ease of Administration	Definite procedure, time limits, etc. Economy of time.	Manuals require careful study and are sometimes inadequate.
b. Ease of Scoring	Definite rules, keys, etc. Largely routine.	Scoring by hand may take considerable time and be monotonous. Machine scoring preferable.
c. Ease of Interpretation	Better tests have adequate norms. Useful basis of comparison. Equivalent forms.	Norms often confused with standards. Some norms defective. Norms for various types of schools and levels of ability are often lacking.

Julian C. Stanley, *Measurement in today's schools,* Fourth Edition © 1964. Reprinted by permission of Prentice-Hall, Inc., Englewood Cliffs, New Jersey.

TABLE 4.4 *(Continued)*

	Standardized	
Criterion	*Advantages*	*Limitations*
Summary	Convenience, comparability, objectivity. Equivalent forms may be available.	Inflexibility. May be only slightly applicable to a particular situation.

	Nonstandardized	
	Essay	
Criterion	*Advantages*	*Limitations*
1. Validity a. Curricular	Useful for English, advanced classes; affords language training. May encourage sound study habits.	Limited sampling. Bluffing is possible. Mixes language factor in all scores.
b. Statistical		Usually not known.
2. Reliability		Reliability usually quite low.
3. Usability a. Ease of Administration	Easy to prepare. Easy to give.	Lack of uniformity.
b. Ease of Scoring		Slow, uncertain, and subjective.
c. Ease of Interpretation		No norms. Meaning doubtful.
Summary	Useful for part of many tests and in a few special fields.	Limited sampling. Subjective scoring. Time-consuming.

	Nonstandardized	
	Objective	
Criterion	*Advantages*	*Limitations*
1. Validity a. Curricular	Extensive sampling of subject matter. Flexible in use. Discourages bluffing. Compares favorably with standard tests.	Narrow sampling of functions tested. Negative learning possible. May encourage piecemeal study.

TABLE 4.4 *(Continued)*

| | | Nonstandardized | |
| | | Objective | |
Criterion	Advantages		Limitations
b. Statistical			Adequate criteria usually lacking.
2. Reliability	Sometimes approaches that of standard tests.		No guarantee of validity.
3. Usability			
a. Ease of Administration	Directions rather uniform. Economy of time.		Time, effort, and skill required to prepare well.
b. Ease of Scoring	Definite rules, keys, etc. Largely routine. Can be done by clerks or machine.		Monotonous.
c. Ease of Interpretation	Local norms can be derived.		No norms available at beginning.
Summary	Extensive sampling. Objective scoring. Flexibility.		Preparation requires skill and time.

tional objective, such factors as flexibility of technique, nature of the objective (with respect to both content and behavior), level of student, and time available for test administration and scoring will need to be considered. It is unlikely that any single procedure will be used exclusively. A combination of methods will generally provide the most valid measurement.

TEST ADMINISTRATION

After deciding on the measurement procedures to be used, several important additional decisions must be made. The teacher-evaluator must decide on the administration procedures to be followed. If he has selected a standardized test, many of the decisions have already been made for him. The test manual will contain very detailed directions which must be followed precisely. If the scores derived from testing his group are to be legitimately compared with those of the standardization group, an attempt to duplicate the standardization testing conditions must be made.

Rigidly controlled administration is just as important to a teacher-made test as to a standardized test. This is particularly true if a teacher anticipates combining the score distributions from a number of different tests or sections of the same course in order to arrive at evaluations.

Many factors are involved in test administration. The form in which the test is presented, the preparation of the students for the test, and the actual conditions of testing need to be considered. Obviously, each student should have a copy of the test. Films, oral presentation, and slides have been used to administer tests with some degree of success. The most noteworthy characteristic of these methods, which is at once an advantage and a drawback, is the control of presentation. The fixed rate, even if generous, does not allow all students to manifest their natural test-taking behavior or to review questions. The feeling of excessive pressure would not seem desirable, but concern and involvement in and focused attention on the test-taking task would be necessary.

Guidelines for Test Administration

If test scores are to have any meaning, they must be gathered under uniform and optimal conditions. This is particularly true if the intent is to make comparisons between individuals or against an absolute scoring standard. Anyone who ever has been involved in large-scale testing programs knows the importance of preparation. The administration of any group test, particularly a standardized test, is a complex task. To facilitate the process of test administration, Prescott (undated) has prepared a set of guidelines for administrative activity before, during, and after the test. These guidelines, although most relevant to standardized tests, can be applied to classroom tests as well. Prescott's suggestion that the examiner take the test is a very good one. The guidelines are as follows:[1]

Before the Testing Date

1. Understand nature and purposes of the testing:
   a. Tests to be given.
   b. Reasons for giving tests.
2. Decide on number to be tested at one time.
3. Decide on seating arrangements.
4. Decide on exact time of testing.
   a. Avoid day before holiday.
   b. Avoid conflicts with recess of other groups.
   c. Make sure there is ample time.
5. Procure and check test materials:
   a. Directions for administering.

---

[1] From George A. Prescott, *Test Service Bulletin 102, Test Administration Guide.* Formerly issued by the Test Department of Harcourt Brace Jovanovich, undated.

    b. Directions for scoring.
    c. Test booklets:
       (1) One for each pupil and examiner.
    d. Answer sheets:
       (1) One for each pupil and examiner.
    e. Pencils (regular or special).
    f. Stopwatch or other suitable timer.
    g. Scoring keys.
    h. "Testing—Do Not Disturb" sign.
    i. Other supplies (scratch paper, etc.).

6. Study test and directions carefully.
    a. Familiarize yourself with:
       (1) General make-up of test.
       (2) Time limits.
       (3) Directions.
       (4) Method of indicating answers.
    b. Take the test yourself.

7. Arrange materials for distribution.
    a. Count number needed.

8. Decide on order in which materials are to be distributed and collected.

9. Decide what pupils who finish early are to do.

Just Before Testing

1. Make sure central loudspeaker is disconnected.
2. Put up "Testing—Do Not Disturb" sign.
3. See that desks are cleared.
4. See that pupils have sharpened pencils.
5. Attend to toilet needs of pupils.
6. Check lighting.
7. Check ventilation.
8. Make seating arrangements.

During Testing

1. Distribute materials according to predetermined order.
2. Caution pupils not to begin until you tell them to do so.
3. Make sure that all identifying information is written on booklet or answer sheet.
4. Read directions exactly as given.
5. Give signal to start.
6. Write starting and finishing times on the chalkboard.

7. Move quietly about the room to:
    a. Make sure pupils are marking answers in the correct place.
    b. Make sure pupils are continuing to the next page after finishing the previous page.
    c. Make sure pupils stop at the end of the test.
    d. Replace broken pencils.
    e. Encourage pupils to keep working until time is called.
    f. Make sure there is no copying.
    g. Attend to pupils finishing early.
8. Permit no outside interruptions.
9. Stop at the proper time.

Just After Testing

1. Collect materials according to predetermined order.
2. Count booklets and answer sheets.
3. Make a record of any incidents observed that may tend to invalidate scores made by pupils.

The directions for taking the test should be as complete, clear, and concise as possible. The student must be made aware of what is expected of him. The method of responding should be kept as simple as possible. Reducing the possible mechanical complexities involved in responding is very important for younger students. Instead of using one of the many convenient IBM or other preprinted answer sheets, the student (up to Grade Four) might be allowed to respond on the test booklet. The directions should also contain instructions on guessing. This problem will be discussed in greater detail in the next section.

Criteria for Preparing Test Directions

Traxler (1951) has offered seven excellent commonsense criteria that should be kept in mind when writing the directions for a test. These are:

1. Assume that the examinees and examiner know nothing at all about objective tests.

2. In writing the directions, use a clear, succinct style. Be as explicit as possible, but avoid long drawn-out explanations.

3. Emphasize the more important directions and key activities through the use of underlining, italics, or different type size or style.

4. Give the examiner and each proctor full instructions on what is to be done before, during, and after the administration.

5. Field or pretest the directions with a sample of both examinees and examiners to identify possible misunderstandings and inconsistencies and gather suggestions for improvement.

6.   Keep the directions for different forms, subsections, or booklets as uniform as possible.

7.   Where necessary or helpful, give practice items (or, if possible, tests) before each regular section. This is particularly important when testing the young or those unfamiliar with objective tests or separate answer sheets, e.g., the educationally or culturally disadvantaged, foreign students, or special education students.

Any important test should be announced well in advance, rather than dangling the threat of a surprise test over the students' heads. Such an "announced test" procedure is more likely to result in effective study.

If possible, practice should be given in taking tests. This is very important if unusual items or ways of asking questions (e.g., analogy items) are to be used. Again, the younger student would probably benefit most from this practice.

Obviously, the testing room should be as conducive as possible to concentration on the task at hand. Very little research has been done on the effect of distractions on test results. The results of the few investigations that have been undertaken seem to indicate that absolute quiet may not be as important as one might expect. The same general conclusion has been reached concerning the general physical health of a student at the time of testing. Nevertheless, freedom from distractions would seem desirable.

Unless an instructor considers time a major factor in learning, achievement tests should be administered in a way that allows all, or nearly all, students enough time to finish. In general, speed of response is not a relevant variable; allowing sufficient time for the test tends to reduce wild guessing and results in a more reliable measure, particularly if one's concern is with relative achievement performance. There are, of course, situations in which speed alone or a combination of speed of response and level of performance are significant.

It is probably a sound idea to arrange items on the basis of increasing difficulty (actual or estimated). Locating easy items at the beginning of the test, thereby providing success experiences, makes good psychological sense. It is also desirable to group together items requiring similar types of responses. Such a grouping tends to allow the development of a mental or mechanical set conducive to answering a particular type of item.

TEST SCORING

Common sense probably yields more helpful suggestions for test scoring than does prolonged discussion. Obviously, responses need to be recorded in a convenient form so that scoring can proceed efficiently. If scoring is to be done by hand, it should be checked. A number of devices and machines utilizing mark-sensing methods of a mechanical, electrical, or optical nature are available to assist in test scoring. Their cost, however, is still beyond the budgets of most schools. Answer keys and scoring rules should of course be prepared before actual scoring. This is very important if supply questions, particularly extended-response essay questions, are used. (See Chapter Six for suggestions for scoring essay items.) In addition, it is an excellent idea to have a colleague check the content, phrasing, and keying of the items.

Developing Hand-Scoring Answer Keys

If standard commercial or separate preprinted answer sheets are to be used, the punch-out overlay scoring template can be applied. These templates are available from most commercial test and answer sheet producers and service organizations. Many teachers, because of the peculiarities of the subject matter, behavior, or examinee involved, must develop their own answer sheets. Traxler (1951) has described three major types of hand-scoring answer keys: the fan (or accordion), strip, and cut-out key.

Fan Key. This key consists of a series of columns, extending from the top to the bottom of the page, on which are recorded acceptable answers or directions scored for the individual items. The key and answer sheet are the same size and identically spaced. Usually each column corresponds to a page of the test. The key is folded along vertical lines separating its columns and is superimposed on the appropriate page of the test or next to the appropriate column of the answer sheet and matched to the corresponding responses.

Strip Key. Similar to the fan key, this method employs the use of separate columns, usually on cardboard.

Cut-Out Key. Windows are cut out to reveal letters, numbers, words or phrases on the answer sheet. The key is superimposed on a page of the test or answer sheet.

Two of the most common problems encountered in making decisions about test scoring involve the weighting of responses and corrections for guessing.

Weighting Test Items and Alternatives

Teachers often believe that differential weighting of items or alternative answers provide more discriminating measures. To some extent this is true. If differential weights can be identified and applied on the basis of quality of response, difficulty level, or some other basis that is at least logically if not empirically justified, there is a tendency for the weighted items and tests to be more reliable. The difference in the reliabilities of weighted and unweighted items is generally quite small, especially if the test is reliable to begin with. If a test is of moderate reliability, differential weighting may slightly increase the consistency of measurement. The scoring task is, of course, thereby made more complex. Differential weighting may have some value for test items susceptible to the effects of guessing, e.g., true-false items. Ebel (1965b), for example, has prepared a *confidence weighting* scheme for true-false items. This system, outlined in Table 4.5, in a sense turns the two-choice item into a multiple-choice item. One would expect an increase in the reliability of a test using this system over that obtained by conventional scoring procedures. Such has been the result of comparative studies that have been completed, although most of the increases are slight.

TABLE 4.5 A System for the Confidence-Weighting of True-False Items

Response Number	Significance of the Response	Score Value		
		Right	Wrong	Omit
1	The statement is probably true	2	−2	
2	The statement is possibly true	1	0	
3	I have no basis for response			0.5
4	The statement is possibly false	1	0	
5	The statement is probably false	2	−2	

Source: From Ebel (1965b, p. 49).

Most of the recommendations concerning differential weighting have been well summarized by Guilford (1954), and Wang and Stanley (1970). In light of his own research and the results of other investigations, Guilford concluded that "Differential weighting of items is most effective in short tests and usually pays little dividends when there are more than 10 to 20 items" (p. 447). Weights of 1 or 0 (i.e., right or wrong) are appropriate for most achievement, aptitude, and general mental ability tests, and in general differential weighting is not worth the trouble it entails.

Correction for Guessing

Researchers have for the past thirty years been investigating the problem of whether or not to correct for guessing. There is still no definite answer or agreement among the experts. The main purpose of applying corrections is to discourage dishonest or "wild" guessing by extracting a penalty for it. Guessing's most important effect is not on individual scores but on the reliability of the test. If the test is reliable to begin with, chance success is relatively unimportant and its effects are negligible.

If guessing is thought to be a problem on a particular test, two methods are available to control it. Some technicians favor the use of "instructions" against guessing, the rationale being that a request not to guess will in fact inhibit guessing, thereby decreasing the element of chance success. The problem with such instructions is that students do not know when they have complete knowledge, no knowledge, or partial knowledge. Therefore, they may make guesses that are not pure, while a pure guess is based on no knowledge. Instructions usually introduce personality variables and tempt students' gambling instincts. The bold take more chances than the timid and are, therefore, more likely to gain an advantage.

Some experts prefer to use correction formulas, usually in conjunction with but sometimes without "do not guess" directions. The most frequently used formula is:

$$\hat{S} = R - \frac{W}{n-1},$$ (Equation 4.1)

where $\hat{S}$ = the corrected score;

R = the number of correct responses;

W = the number of wrong responses, not counting omitted items, and

n = the number of options for each item.

It is obvious that as the number of choices per item increases the likelihood of guessing correctly decreases. Such a formula is really a correction for the number of omitted responses. If no items are omitted, scores corrected for guessing, by subtracting a fraction of the wrong responses, correlate perfectly with uncorrected scores. In general, corrected and uncorrected scores rank students in about the same relative positions. This is particularly true if all students attempt all items and the test is reliable to begin with.

Traub, Hambleton, and Singh (1968) have demonstrated the effectiveness of what might be considered a "psychological" correction for guessing. The formula for the correction is as follows:

$$\hat{S} = R + \frac{0}{n}$$ (Equation 4.2)

The terms are defined as before, with the addition of the term

0 = the number of omitted items.

The corrected score is considered to be a correction due to the fact that the student is given proportional credit for not guessing on items.

Although Equation 4.2 correlates perfectly with Equation 4.1, it may have a different psychological impact on the examinee. It is, of course, necessary to alert students to the fact that this correction is to be applied and to explain the terms.

Generally, directions concerning guessing like the following are sufficient: "Answer every item without omissions. Select the alternative you feel is best even though you are not absolutely sure."

SUGGESTED READINGS

Cronbach, L. J. *Essentials of psychological testing,* 3rd ed. New York: Harper & Row, 1970. Chapters 3 (Administering Tests) and 4 (Scoring) are excellent summaries based on experience and research.

Furst, E. J. *Constructing evaluation instruments.* New York: Longmans, Green, 1958. See Chapter 7, "Planning the Test," and Chapter 8, "Constructing Items to Fit Specifications."

Gronlund, N. E. *Measurement and evaluation in teaching.* New York: Macmillan, 1971. See Chapter 2, "Defining Objectives for Evaluation Purposes"; Chapter 3, "Relating Evaluation Procedures to Objectives"; and Chapter 6, "Principles and Procedures of Classroom Testing."

Henry, N. B., ed. *The measurement of understanding.* Forty-Fifth Yearbook of the National Society for the Study of Education, Part I. Chicago: University of Chicago Press, 1946.

Lindquist, E. F., ed. *Educational measurement.* Washington: American Council on Education. The following chapters probably contain the most comprehensive treatment of the topics discussed in this chapter: Chapter 5, "Preliminary Considerations in Objective Test Construction," by E. F. Lindquist; Chapter 6, "Planning the Objective Test," by K. W. Vaughn; and Chapter 10, "Administering and Scoring the Objective Test," by Arthur E. Traxler.

Thorndike, R. L., ed. *Educational measurement,* 2nd ed. Washington: American Council on Education, 1971. The following chapters are representative of current thought on the topics of this chapter: Chapter 3, "Planning the Objective Test," by Sherman N. Tinkelman; Chapter 6, "Reproducing the Test," by Robert L. Thorndike; Chapter 7, "Test Administration," by William V. Clemans; and Chapter 8, "Automation of Test Scoring, Reporting and Analysis," by Frank B. Baker.

Wright, H. F. *Recording and analyzing child behavior.* New York: Harper & Row, 1967. This interesting paperback volume concerns methods of describing and evaluating the behavior of individuals in naturally occurring situations.

III
INSTRUMENT DEVELOPMENT

5
CONSTRUCTING SHORT–ANSWER ACHIEVEMENT TEST ITEMS

SUMMARY PREVIEW STATEMENTS

1. The writing of test items, questions, or exercises basically involves finding the most suitable manner in which to pose problems to students.

2. A supply-type item requires the examinee to construct his own response to a direct question or incomplete statement.

3. A selection-type item requires the student to decide between two or more possible answers.

4. Common shortcomings of teacher-made tests include:
   a. Too great a reliance on subjective but presumably absolute standards.
   b. Hasty development and insufficient length.
   c. Focusing on trivia and easily measured outcomes to the exclusion of important achievements.
   d. Poor format, structure, and grammar.

5. Prerequisites for writing good achievement test items include:
   a. A rational philosophy of education.
   b. Command of verbal communication skills.
   c. Command of subject matter.
   d. Command of item-writing techniques.
   e. Knowledge about how students learn and develop.

6. General guidelines for writing "objective" items include:
   a. Avoiding obvious, trivial, meaningless, obscure, or ambiguous content.
   b. Following accepted rules of grammar.
   c. Avoiding irrelevant clues.
   d. Avoiding interrelated items.

    e. Using items whose scoring would be agreed upon by experts.

    f. Stating questions in clear explicit terms.

    g. Providing equal credit for equally correct answers.

    h. Specifying the terms in which the answer is to be stated.

    i. Minimizing textbook expressions and stereotyped language.

    j. Stating items in the form of direct questions.

    k. Avoiding the use of "specific determiners" such as "only," "all," "none," "always," and "could," "might," "may," or "generally."

7. Supply items have the advantages of:
   a. Minimizing the effect of guessing.
   b. Being adaptable to actual classroom instructional practice, e.g., the Socratic method.
   c. Providing good measures of knowledge.

8. The scoring of supply items is not always completely objective.

9. The use of true-false items is an objective and efficient method for surveying student knowledge.

10. False items tend to be more discriminating than true items and should probably constitute about 60 percent of the true-false items used.

11. There is no evidence that mislearning or rote learning is stimulated by the use of true-false items, particularly if the test results are reviewed with students.

12. Although it influences scores to some extent, the effect of guessing on constant-alternative items is minor.

13. Multiple-choice or changing-alternative items provide a flexible method of measuring a great variety of outcomes, particularly at the higher levels of mental ability.

14. Multiple-choice items should include logically related and arranged alternatives, provide a correct or preferable answer, and list plausible, grammatically parallel, but incorrect answers.

15. The use of a "None of the Above" or an "All of the Above" alternative should be cautious, particularly when it is keyed as the correct answer.

16. The more similar the alternatives in a multiple-choice item, the higher the likelihood of good discrimination between high- and low-achieving students.

17. Many useful ideas for achievement test items can be found in the *Taxonomy of Educational Objectives,* Handbook I—Cognitive Domain.

18. Graphic materials can provide a basis for measuring outcomes in a variety of subject-matter fields.

19. The matching item is a variation on the multiple-choice item and is useful in surveying knowledge of the who, what, when, and where variety.

20. Matching items should:
    a. Include very detailed directions for responding.
    b. Be limited to a single page.
    c. Be limited to about 10–15 pairs.
    d. Use mutually exclusive categories.
    e. Present stimuli and responses in some logical order.

21. Great care must be taken in developing test materials for young children.

Effective educational assessment will result from careful planning, imaginative and skillful question writing, careful formulation of questions into a total test, and fair and proper administration and scoring. Effectiveness also depends on the quality of instruction preceding testing and on the intelligent subsequent interpretation and use of test scores. The author noted in the previous three chapters that test planning, whose importance is often underestimated, involves decisions about learning outcomes, the contexts in which they are most likely to be demonstrated, and the kinds of stimuli necessary or likely to elicit them. Item writing would follow logically from the test development sequence outlined above.

The writing of test questions, items, or exercises basically involves finding the most suitable manner in which to pose problems to students. Such problems may involve the recall of learned information or the use of some higher-order mental abilities. This chapter will present guidelines and suggestions that have been found useful in constructing two of the major classes of "objective" short-answer items—supply and selection (Ebel 1956, p. 193). The supply items examined will be simple direct questions and completion items. The selection items discussed will be of the true-false, multiple-choice, and matching varieties. The essay question is considered by some experts to fall in the "supply" category, and a distinction is sometimes made between extended-response and restricted-response supply questions. We are here considering only the short-answer (e.g., a single word, phrase, or sentence) supply item. Essay or extended free-response items will be considered in Chapter Six.

Historically, supply items have been referred to as "recall" items, and selection items as "recognition" items. The distinction is unwarranted, implying as it does that we are only measuring qualitative differences in memory. Nothing could be further from the truth. All of these items refer only to the form in which the response to a test item is to be made. The student either constructs his own response or identifies the correct answer in a list of alternatives. The instructional objective being measured depends upon the content and structure of the item itself, rather than on the form of the response. There is some data in the literature of experimental psychology to suggest that tests of recognition yield higher scores than do tests of recall (Postman and Rau 1957). If we can accept length of retention as a criterion of success, however, we also have evidence that recall and recognition activities are very highly correlated (Bahrick 1964). Thus supply and selection items can measure the same behavior, and the decision about the type to use will probably be arbitrary or dictated by such practical considerations as ease of scoring.

Item construction, if approached seriously, requires considerable expenditure of time and effort. But there are other requisites for sound item construction, some of which will be discussed in the following section.

PRELIMINARY CONSIDERATIONS

By way of preview, let us point out five principles that need to be considered as one prepares to construct items:

1. Adequate provision should be made for measuring all of the important outcomes of instruction.

2. The test and its items should reflect the approximate emphases given various objectives in the course.

3. The nature of the test and its items must take into account the nature of the group to be examined.

4. The nature of the test and its items must take into consideration the conditions under which the test is to be administered.

5. The nature of the test and its items must take into consideration the purpose it is to serve.

Implicit in these principles are several prerequisites for sound item construction. The first and probably most obvious prerequisite is competence in the subject matter to be examined. The test constructor should be a scholar in the broadest and finest sense of the word. The basic principles and knowledges, as well as the common fallacies, should be at his command.

But command of the subject matter is a necessary but not sufficient condition for writing effective items. The test constructor must also possess skill in item writing. He must be aware of the various ways in which questions can be asked and the kinds of objectives for which each is best suited. Some of these knowledges may be acquired in courses in test construction or from the references listed at the end of this chapter. The best approach is, of course, a combination of formal study and experience. One must actually write many items of various types, and try them out with students, before he can develop skill and perspective on the relative advantages and disadvantages of the various question forms.

An integral aspect of item-writing skill is, of course, mastery of verbal communication. The item writer must be able to apply the rules of grammar and rhetoric. Test items are probably read more closely than any other type of nonlegal written communication. Skill in conducting item analyses and estimating reliability and validity are also desirable.

If item construction and test development do not proceed from a rational and well-developed philosophy of education, the resulting items are likely to treat only superficial aspects of instruction. The resulting test would be of variable quality. The specification of defensible instructional objectives is of paramount importance in test construction.

And finally, the item writer must be an educational and developmental psychologist. He must possess knowledge of how students learn and develop. Such knowledge of individual differences will allow him to accomplish an optimal matching of test questions and students. One would not, for example, use analogy items with third-grade students, because the mechanically contrived way of asking questions does not correspond to the usual instructional program at this level and students are unfamiliar with the form. We do not want the mechanics of a test question to interfere with measurement.

Let us now turn our attention to some guidelines for writing items. Many of the suggestions in the remainder of this chapter will be considered common sense. But, unfortunately, the application of common-sense principles in test development is often found wanting. If, in the following five sections, we can underscore the importance of common sense in item writing, we will have made a worthwhile contribution.

GENERAL GUIDELINES FOR ITEM WRITING

Before considering specific item types, it would be profitable to consider some general principles for item writing. Remmers, Gage, and

Rummel (1965) have summarized six principles applicable to all short-answer items:

1. *Avoid using items which, in terms of either content or structure, could be considered obvious, trivial, meaningless, or ambiguous.* If a test developer does not rely heavily upon a table of specifications to guide item and test development, these types of unsatisfactory items may result.

2. *Follow the rules of punctuation, grammar, and rhetoric.* Again the importance of command of language and expressive skills in item development is emphasized.

3. *Use items that have a "right" or "definitely correct" answer, or at least an answer upon which experts agree.* These item characteristics were described in Chapter One as "objectivity."

4. *Avoid items that rely on obscure or esoteric language.* Unless one's intent is to test vocabulary, it is not desirable to elicit responses whose correctness depends upon size of vocabulary or reading ability. If key words are obscure, even the better students will fail to give them sufficient attention, and the items may become "trick" or "catch" questions.

5. *Avoid interrelated items.* This situation arises when the content of one item (e.g., the stem or alternatives in a multiple-choice item) furnishes the answer to other items. Inasmuch as we frequently test the same content area a number of times, it is difficult to avoid interrelated items, and only very careful inspection of the test will reveal them.

6. *Avoid items containing "irrelevant cues."* Irrelevant cues probably constitute the chief fault of most classroom tests. Irrelevant cues are a class of defect that leads a student to the correct answer independent of his knowledge or skill. Such defects may take the forms of grammatical clues, word associations or definitions, a systematic difference in the correct answer, or stereotyped language, to name only a few. The type of cue will vary with the type of item. A test that contains a large number of items with irrelevant cues is probably measuring nothing more than test wiseness or intelligent test-taking behavior.

The effect of the violation of some of these guidelines has been investigated by McMorris *et al.* (1972).

Some general questions relating to the quality of item content and structure are summarized in Table 5.1.

Let us now turn our attention to specific item types and guidelines for their construction. Many of the suggestions for certain item types are applicable to the other types as well, and the suggestions given here were selected on the basis of practical applicability.

TABLE 5.1   Critical Questions Useful in Reviewing Educational
Achievement Test Items

Item Content

1. Content is trivial. Does the item deal with facts, principles, understandings, skills, etc., of sufficient importance to merit inclusion in an achievement test?
2. Content is too factual. Does the item measure sheer recall of relatively unimportant material or does it call for knowledge and understanding of important facts, concepts, etc.?
3. Content is too specific. Is the content related specifically to a particular grade level, course of study, textbook, or region of the country?
4. Content is outmoded and no longer has significance.
5. Intent of the item is not clear. Does the item call for judgments which the student is not in the position to make?
6. Item is incorrectly classified. Does the item belong in another section of the test?
7. Item is too easy or too difficult for designated grade level.
8. Vocabulary level is not appropriate for designated grade levels. Is vocabulary too technical, too literary, too textbookish, etc.?

Item Structure

1. Items are not entities. Is the student required to use the response obtained in one item in answering another item?
2. Item could be better cast as another type (e.g., as true-false rather than multiple-choice).
3. The statement of the problem is badly worded. Does the item contain superfluous information? Might a student who understands the issue involved be likely to miss the item because of its wording? Is the wording ambiguous?
4. The item has more than one correct response. Are optional responses mutually exclusive?
5. Clues to the correct response are given. Does the correct response to one item give clues to the correct response for a different item? Are there words or phrases from the item stem repeated only in the correct response?
6. Optional responses are not plausible. Can the student quickly eliminate one or more responses because they are unrelated to the problem?
7. Optional responses are not grammatically consistent.
8. Optional responses vary noticeably in length. Do the longest (or shortest) responses tend to be the correct response?

Source: Developed by Dr. Harold F. Bligh, Managing Editor of the Test Division, Harcourt, Brace and World, Inc., New York, 1962. Reprinted by permission of the author.

WRITING SUPPLY ITEMS

Supply items are generally of two types: simple direct questions (e.g., Who was the first American astronaut to fly in space?) and completion items (e.g., The name of the first American astronaut to fly in space is _____.) The chief advantage of the supply item is that it minimizes the effect of guessing. Because the student is required to construct his own response, supply items constitute one of the best ways of measuring objectives associated with the first level (Knowledge) of the *Taxonomy of Educational Objectives*. Such an emphasis on memory, in moderation, is probably not unreasonable. Students must possess a certain amount of knowledge or factual information before they can do anything else. Thus an instructor's decision to check on specific facts, which are requisite to further work with supply items, is entirely justified in many instances.

Another outstanding advantage of supply items, particularly for those teaching and testing in the early grades, is that they are "natural." Teaching in the elementary grades frequently employs the so-called Socratic question-and-answer format. In testing, then, the use of simple direct questions follows logically from the method of instruction. Supply items are also efficient from the instructor's standpoint, i.e., they allow the student to summarize long and often complex problem-solving processes in a single brief statement, thereby facilitating scoring.

The chief disadvantage of supply items is that scoring is not always completely objective. It is surprising how often students will come up with correct but unanticipated answers. Unless the scoring key is revised in light of alternative correct answers, serious injustices may be perpetrated on students. Lack of objectivity can frequently be traced to the use of ambiguous words in the item. Because they are easily prepared, supply items too frequently become *only* a matter of identification and/or naming. It is unlikely that a test composed primarily of these kinds of items would reflect all relevant instructional objectives.

It should be noted that the following specific guidelines are not "rules" in the strict sense of the word, but ways of asking questions that have been found useful. In many instances the choice of style will depend on the personal preferences of the item writer.

1. *Require short, definite, clearcut, and explicit answers.* An indefinite statement is likely to lead to scoring problems for instructors and response problems for students.

FAULTY: Ernest Hemingway wrote _____.
IMPROVED: *The Old Man and the Sea* was written by _____.

2. *Avoid multi-mutilated statements.* Merely introducing blanks liberally into a statement, from a text for example, can only lead to ambiguity. In addition, the instructor is not sure which portion of the statement the student is responding to and therefore which objective is being measured. One can end up with a nonsensical sequence of blanks.

FAULTY: _____ pointed out in _____ that freedom of thought in America was seriously hampered by _____ _____ _____ _____.

IMPROVED: That freedom of thought in America was seriously hampered by social pressures toward conformity was pointed out in 1830 by (De Tocqueville).

3. *If several correct answers* (e.g., synonyms) *are possible, equal credit should be given to each one.*

4. *Specify and announce in advance whether scoring will take spelling into account.*

5. *In testing for comprehension of terms and knowledge of definitions, it is often better to supply the term and require a definition than to provide a definition and require the term.* The student is less likely to benefit from verbal association cues if this procedure is followed. In addition, asking the student to supply the definition is a better measure of his knowledge.

FAULTY: What is the general measurement term describing the consistency with which items in a test measure the same thing?
IMPROVED: Define "internal consistency reliability."

6. *It is generally recommended that in completion items the blanks come at the end of the statement.* Beginning an item with a blank is awkward for the student and may interfere with his comprehension of the question. In general, the best approach is a simple and direct one.

FAULTY: A (an) _____ is the index obtained by dividing a mental age score by chronological age and multiplying by 100.
IMPROVED: The index obtained by dividing a mental age score by chronological age and multiplying by 100 is called a (an) _____.

7. *Minimize the use of textbook expressions and stereotyped language.* When statements are taken out of context, they tend to become ambiguous. The use of paraphrased statements, however, will reduce the incidence of correct responses that represent meaningless verbal associations. In addition, it should reduce the temptation to memorize the exact wording of the text or lecture material.

8. *Specify the terms in which the response is to be given.*

FAULTY: Where does the Security Council of the United Nations hold its meetings?

IMPROVED: In what city of the United States does the Security Council of the United Nations hold its meetings?

A high degree of precision is particularly important in mathematics questions stated in free-response form. Otherwise, the student may be faced with the problem of trying to guess the degree of error to be tolerated. Is one decimal place accuracy sufficient? Two decimal place accuracy? Different students may come to different conclusions.

FAULTY: If a circle has a 4-inch diameter, its area is _____.
IMPROVED: A circle has a 4-inch diameter. Its area, correct to two decimal places, is (<u>12.56</u>) square inches.

9. *In general, direct questions are preferable to incomplete declarative sentences.*

FAULTY: Gold was discovered in California in the year _____.
IMPROVED: In what year was gold discovered in California? _____.

10. *Avoid extraneous clues to the correct answer.* The grammatical structure of an item may lead a student to the correct answer, independent of his knowledge, particularly if the number of alternative answers is small.

FAULTY: A fraction whose denominator is greater than its numerator is a _____.

IMPROVED: Fractions whose denominators are greater than their numerators are called _____ fractions.

In the faulty item above, the article "a" functions as an irrelevant clue. Similarly, blanks should be of uniform length so as not to suggest the extensiveness of the expected response.

WRITING CONSTANT–ALTERNATIVE SELECTION ITEMS

In responding to a constant-alternative selection item, the examinee chooses one of two or more alternatives that remain the same throughout a series of items. The alternative answers are usually True and False. Other forms, however, may be used: yes-no, right-wrong, true-false-depends, correct-incorrect, same-opposite, true-false and converse true or converse false, true-false with correction variety, and true-false-qualification. Because it is the most common representative constant-alternative type, the true-false item will be used as an example in this section.

Of all the types of items used in educational measurement, the true-false variety is probably the most controversial. At one extreme we have such statements as:

> True-false items undoubtedly have more popularity than merit. A true-false test tends to give inconsistent results. . . . The use of true-false items in classroom tests is not recommended. (Gorow 1966)

At the other end of the opinion continuum, we have:

> Acquiring command of knowledge is . . . the central purpose of education. All knowledge is knowledge of propositions. . . . The essential purpose of logical reasoning is to test the truth or falsity of deductive propositions. Propositions are expressed in sentences which may be true or false. This is the stuff of which human knowledge (and true-false tests) are made. (Ebel 1965a)

It is the author's feeling that, despite some difficulties in constructing such items, the true-false question is a potentially valuable data-gathering procedure. There are a number of advantages to the use of true-false items. Most prominent among these is efficiency. An instructor can present a large number of such items per unit of testing time. This allows him to survey large content areas to obtain an estimate of students' knowledge. Scoring of true-false items and tests is, of course, rapid and easy. If great care is exercised in their construction, such items can be used to test understanding of principles and generalizations. In addition, they can profitably be used to assess persistence of popular misconceptions, fallacies, and superstitions (e.g., Swallowing watermelon seeds will result in appendicitis). As a footnote, it should be pointed out that the learning of significant amounts of misinformation from true-false items has *not* been demonstrated. What little mislearning does take place can be "washed out" if the test is reviewed by students and instructor. This is, of course, a recommended class activity no matter what type of item is used. Finally, true-false items are well adapted to testing situations in which only two responses are possible (e.g., School emergency exits should open inwardly).

The disadvantages and limitations of true-false items may outweigh their merits unless thoughtful judgment and intelligence are exercised. Some experts say that, although seemingly easy to construct, meaningful and error-free constant-alternative items are the most difficult of all "objective" questions to write. Quality and precision of language are crucial to these items. Ambiguous terminology and reading ability probably have the greatest effect on true-false items, since a student must respond, in most instances, to a single unqualified statement. Obviously, the smaller the stimulus the greater the chance for misinterpretation. Guessing can also have a significant effect. On a 50-item true-false test "blind guessing" is likely to result in a score of 25. The result, of course, is to reduce the usable range of scores from 50 (zero to 50) to 25 (25 to 50). It would, however, be a rare event for a student to respond blindly. Almost all students will have some information about an item. In addition, although the odds of a chance score of 25 on a 50-item test are 1 in 2, those of a chance score of 35 are 1 in 350. Once the indifference point (50–50) is passed, chance responses through guessing will work *against* the student. The solution is to increase test reliability by using a fairly large number of items, thereby reducing the overall effect of guessing. Another procedure to reduce the effect of guessing would be to use Ebel's confidence weighting technique (Ebel 1965b), described in Chapter Four.

One final limitation of the true-false variety of constant-alternative items involves their susceptibility to "response sets." Response sets are tendencies to respond to test items on the basis of form rather than content. A response set labeled "acquiescence"—the reliable tendency to respond "true" when in doubt about a particular item—has been identified. This behavior, although constant and reliable, is unrelated to the purpose of the item and test, and therefore confounds the meaning of the scores. The best way to overcome this problem is to construct a reliable test to begin with. In addition, balancing the number of true and false items might help. There is some evidence, however, that false items discriminate better; perhaps a 60–40 split in favor of the false statements is the best recommendation.

Despite the seemingly overwhelming evidence of the limitations of true-false items, they can prove useful in classroom tests if used in moderation with upper-level students. One would not recommend a test entirely composed of constant-alternative items. Specific suggestions for improving true-false items follow.

1. *Avoid the use of "specific determiners."* Specific determiners are a class of words that function as irrelevant cues. For example, it has been found that, on most classroom tests, items that include the words "only," "all," "no," "none," "always," "never," etc., are generally false. On the other hand, items containing words like "could," "might," "can," "may," and "generally" will usually be true.

FAULTY: No picture and no sound in a television set may indicate a bad 5U4G tube.
IMPROVED: A bad 5U4G tube in a television set will result in no picture and no sound.

A test-wise but unknowledgeable student would be likely to decipher the correct answer in the imprecise wording of the item. If the number of true and false specific determiners is evenly balanced, their influence is reduced. There are, of course, situations in which an instructor may successfully use specific determiners in true-false items whose answers are the opposite of those suggested by the words in question (e.g., The area of a rhombus is always equal to one half the product of its diagonals).

2. *Base true-false items upon statements that are absolutely true or false, without qualifications or exceptions.* This is a difficult requirement in some subject-matter areas (e.g., history, literature) where trends, generalizations, and principles are hard to demonstrate empirically. Statements that are not absolutely true or false are likely to perplex examinees, particularly the more knowledgeable. Examinees may read different assumptions into the statement, and one can no longer be sure what the item is measuring.

FAULTY: If a test is valid it is reliable.

This appears to be an excellent item, but appearances can be deceiving. Responses to the item will depend upon one's definition of validity. A test may have been judged to possess a high degree of content validity, but when administered be found to lack reliability. If, however, one defines validity correlationally, a high validity coefficient will also mean that the test is reliable.

IMPROVED: If an investigator obtains a correlation of .90 between a test and a criterion, he knows the test is highly reliable.

3. *Avoid negatively stated items when possible and eliminate all double negatives.* Such phrasing may cause a student to miss an item because he does not comprehend the question. Double negatives are frequently interpreted as emphatically negative. Such items might be used to measure translating ability in an English course, but their general usefulness is negligible; they should be avoided.

FAULTY: It is not infrequently observed that copper turns green as a result of oxidation.
IMPROVED: Copper will turn green upon oxidizing.

4. *Use quantitative and precise rather than qualitative language where possible.* Again, the specificity of word meanings comes into play in judging the effectiveness of an item. Such words as "few," "many," "young," "long," "short," "large," "small," and "important," unless accompanied by a standard of comparison, are open to interpretation and thus ambiguous.

FAULTY: Many people voted for Richard Nixon in the recent Presidential election.
IMPROVED: Richard Nixon received more than 60% of the votes cast in the Presidential election of 1972.

5. *Avoid stereotypic and textbook statements.* Such statements, when taken out of context, are ambiguous and frequently meaningless and trivial (e.g., From time to time efforts have been made to explode the notion that there may be a cause-and-effect relationship between arboreal life and primate anatomy). A related problem arises when text material is quoted verbatim and turned into a true-false statement by inserting *no* or *not.* Such statements may appear ambiguous and place too great a premium on rote memorization.

6. *Avoid making the true items consistently longer than the false items.* There is a tendency, particularly on the part of the beginning teacher and item writer, to write systematically longer true items. This phenomenon results from concern that all necessary qualifications be made, so that there can be no doubt that the item is in fact true.

7. *Avoid the use of unfamiliar or esoteric language.* Comprehension of an item is determined by its difficulty. It is always best to keep its language simple and straightforward and not to confound the student with five-dollar words when fifty-cent ones will do.

FAULTY: According to some peripatetic politicos, the *raison d'être* for capital punishment is retribution.
IMPROVED: According to some politicians, justification for the existence of capital punishment can be traced to the Biblical statement, "An eye for an eye."

8. *Avoid complex sentences with many dependent clauses.* Highly involved sentences and compound statements tend to distract the examinee from the central idea of the item. It is a poor practice to make one of the dependent clauses in a true-false item, false. It is likely that students will not focus on such seemingly unimportant parts of the statement, and the item becomes a "trick" or "catch" question. With compound statements, the student does not know which element is to be judged true or false.

FAULTY: Jane Austen, an American novelist born in 1790, was a prolific writer and is best known for her novel *Pride and Prejudice,* which was published in 1820.

There are so many details in this item that the student does not know on which one to focus. The item is false for many reasons (Austen was a British novelist, 1775–1817, and the book was published in 1813), and different students will get credit for different amounts of knowledge.

IMPROVED: Jane Austen is best known for her novel *Pride and Prejudice.*

9. *It is suggested that the crucial elements of an item be placed at the end of the statement.* The function of the first part of a two-part statement is to "set

the problem." To focus on the effect in a cause-and-effect relationship, for example, one should state the true cause in the first portion of the statement, and a false effect at the end. Conversely, to focus on the cause, one should state the true effect first, and a false cause at the end of the statement. This procedure is suggested because the student is likely to focus on the last portion of a statement he reads. Thus the instructor's objective and the student's attention will be synchronized. The following item is intended to focus on the effect.

FAULTY: Oxygen reduction occurs more readily because carbon monoxide combines with hemoglobin faster than oxygen does.

IMPROVED: Carbon monoxide poisoning occurs because carbon monoxide dissolves delicate lung tissue.

Obviously, "true" cause-and-effect items are also useful.

WRITING CHANGING–ALTERNATIVE SELECTION ITEMS

Changing-alternative items require the examinee to select an answer from among several alternatives, which change with each item. Such items are usually referred to as multiple-choice. The selection may be made on any number of bases, e.g., correct or best, most inclusive, cause or effect, most similar or dissimilar, and so on.

Each item is composed of a stem or lead, which sets the problem, and alternative responses. The stem may be an incomplete statement (to be completed by the alternatives) or a direct question. Only one response is correct, and the others should be plausible but incorrect. For this reason the incorrect alternatives are sometimes referred to as "foils" or "distractors." They serve to distract the less knowledgeable and skillful student away from the correct answer.

The most common form of changing-alternative item, and the one we will concentrate on in this section, is the multiple-choice item. Probably the most flexible of all item types, it can be used to assess knowledge as well as such higher mental processes as application and analysis. Since alternative answers serve as a standard of comparison, these items are relatively free from ambiguity. This characteristic is one of their advantages over true-false items. Furthermore, the effect of guessing is markedly reduced, though not eliminated. In a ten-item four-alternative multiple-choice test, the probability of obtaining a score of seven by chance alone is 1 in 1000. To achieve freedom from guessing comparable to that of a four-alternative 25-item multiple-choice test would require a true-false test of 200 items. The effectiveness of the multiple-choice item is, therefore, obvious. Multiple-choice items are generally preferable when the correct answer is long or can be expressed in a variety of ways. The use of plausible incorrect alternatives therefore can test fine discriminations and allow the test constructor easily to control the difficulty level of the items by varying the homogeneity of responses. The multiple-choice item is relatively free of "response sets" of the type described in connection with true-false items (Cronbach 1950). As contrasted with true-false items, multiple-choice items can provide valuable diagnostic information if the alternatives are carefully constructed and represent different degrees of "correctness."

The primary limitation of multiple-choice items is that they are difficult to construct well. Plausible distractors are often difficult to find or construct (particularly that fourth or fifth incorrect option). One excellent source of alternatives is the pool of incorrect answers supplied when the stem of the multiple-choice item is administered as a free-response item. Multiple-choice items are subject to almost as many irrelevant cues as is any other type of short-answer question. The relatively greater amount of written stimulus material contributes to this situation, and also increases reading time and reduces the number of items (as compared with supply and selection items) than can be presented per unit of time. Their greater flexibility and reliability, however, more than compensate for this lessened efficiency. Some suggestions for writing multiple-choice items follow.

1. *It is recommended that the stem be a direct question.* Although there is no research evidence to support the preferability of the direct question lead over the incomplete statement, it has been found in practice that the novice item writer will produce fewer weak and ambiguous items if the direct question lead is used.

2. *The stem should pose a clear, definite, explicit, and singular problem.* This suggestion follows from the preceding one. The major potential weakness of incomplete statements leads is that they are frequently too incomplete; in many instances the examinee must read the alternatives in order to determine what the question is. The direct question stem is more likely to make explicit the basis on which the correct response is to be chosen. It is generally easier for an item writer to express complex ideas with the direct question format. If the incomplete statement lead is used, it should be meaningful in itself and imply a direct question rather than leading into a collection of unrelated true-false statements.

FAULTY: Salvador Dali is
    a. a famous Indian statesman.
    b. important in international law.
    c. known for his surrealistic art.
    d. the author of many avant-garde plays.
IMPROVED: With which one of the fine arts is Salvador Dali associated?
    a. Surrealistic painting
    b. Avant-garde theatre

    c. Polytonal symphonic music
    d. Impressionistic poetry

3. *Include in the stem any words that might otherwise be repeated in each response.* Streamlining an item in this way reduces reading time and makes for a more efficient question.

FAULTY: Milk can be pasteurized at home by
    a. heating it to a temperature of 130°.
    b. heating it to a temperature of 145°.
    c. heating it to a temperature of 160°.
    d. heating it to a temperature of 175°.
IMPROVED: The minimum temperature that can be used to pasteurize milk at home is:
    a. 130°.
    b. 145°.
    c. 160°.
    d. 175°.

4. *Items should be stated simply and understandably, excluding all nonfunctional words from the stem and alternatives.* The inclusion of extraneous words increases reading time and thereby reduces item efficiency. In addition, the central problem may become obscured, which leads to ambiguity.

FAULTY: Although the experimental research, particularly that by Hansmocker, must be considered equivocal and the assumptions viewed as too restrictive, most testing experts would recommend as the easiest method of significantly improving paper-and-pencil achievement test reliability to
    a. increase the size of the group being tested.
    b. increase the differential weighting of items.
    c. increase the objectivity of scoring.
    d. increase the number of items.
    e. increase the amount of testing time.
IMPROVED: Assume a ten-item, ten-minute paper-and-pencil multiple-choice achievement test has a reliability of .40. The easiest way of increasing the reliability to .80 would be to increase
    a. group size.
    b. scoring objectivity.
    c. differential item scoring weights.
    d. the number of items.
    e. testing time.

5. *Avoid interrelated items.* Instructors occasionally and unintentionally write items that overlap. That is, the stem or alternatives to one item give away the answer to other items. This is more likely to happen

when the test is long. It may be necessary in some cases to index key words or concepts to check on overlap. Casual perusal is rarely sufficient.

6. *Avoid negatively stated items.* Every attempt should be made to keep the use of such items to a minimum, as they are frequently awkward and difficult to comprehend. If "not," "no," "never," "none," "except," or a similar term is to be used, it should be highlighted for the student by underlining or capitalizing it. One is often better off rewriting the item positively.

FAULTY: None of the following cities is a state capital except
    a. Bangor
    b. Los Angeles
    c. Denver
    d. New Haven
IMPROVED: Which of the following cities is a state capital?
    a. Bangor
    b. Los Angeles
    c. Denver
    d. New Haven

7. *Avoid making the correct alternative systematically different from other options.* The usual example of a "systematically different correct alternative" is a correct answer that is obviously longer and more precisely stated than the distractors. There is an unconscious tendency to include *all* relevant information so that the correct alternative will be unequivocally correct. A related error is the attempt to make the correct alternatives more technical than the foils.

8. *If possible, the alternatives should be presented in some logical, numerical, or systematic order.* Again, our purpose is to so structure the question that responding to it will be facilitated. Alphabetizing single-word, concept, or phrase alternatives has *not* been shown to bias responses.

9. *Response alternatives should be mutually exclusive.* Overlapping or synonymous responses should be eliminated because they reduce the discrimination value of an item and allow examinees to eliminate two or more alternatives for the price of one.

FAULTY: Who wrote *Penrod*?
    a. Booth Tarkington
    b. Samuel Clemens
    c. Lewis Carroll
    d. Mark Twain
IMPROVED: Who wrote *Penrod*?
    a. Mark Twain

    b. Booth Tarkington
    c. Lewis Carroll
    d. Bret Harte

FAULTY: If a test has a reliability of .78, what percentage of an observed score is attributable to errors of measurement?
    a. Over 5%
    b. Over 10%
    c. Over 20%
    d. Over 30%

The precise answer is 22%, but because of the way the alternatives are phrased, an examinee is likely to be unsure how to respond. The closest answer is "c," but alternatives "a" and "b" overlap "c" and must also be considered correct.

IMPROVED: If a test has a reliability of .50, what percentage of an observed score can be attributed to errors of measurement?
    a.   2.5%
    b.   5%
    c. 25%
    d. 50%

10. *Make all responses plausible and attractive to the less knowledgeable or skillful student.* The options to a multiple-choice item should include distractors that will attract the unprepared student. Foils should include the common misconceptions and/or errors. They should be familiar, natural, and reasonable.

FAULTY: Which of the following statements makes clear the meaning of the word "electron"?
    a. An electronic tool
    b. Neutral particles
    c. Negative particles
    d. A voting machine
    e. The nuclei of atoms

IMPROVED: Which of the following phrases is a description of an "electron"?
    a. Neutral particle
    b. Negative particle
    c. Neutralized proton
    d. Radiated particle
    e. Atom nucleus

11. *The response alternative "None of the above" should be used with caution, if at all.* Although some testing experts recommend the use of this alternative, particularly with mathematics items, the author does not recommend its use. When "None of the above" is the correct answer

there is no assurance that the examinee does, in fact, know the answer. Consider the following elementary example:

FAULTY: What is the area of a right triangle whose sides adjacent to the right angle are 4 inches and 3 inches long respectively?
    a. 7
    b. 12
    c. 25
    d. None of the above

The answer is 6 square inches, and the knowledgeable student would select alternative "d." But a student who solved the problem incorrectly (e.g., solving for the hypotenuse, which is 5), and came up with an answer not found among the alternatives, would also select the correct answer, "d," thereby getting the item right for the wrong reason. The response "None of the above" may function very well as an alternative if the correct answer is included among the preceding alternatives. In such a situation, it would function as an all-inclusive incorrect alternative covering a multitude of sins.

IMPROVED: What is the area of a right triangle whose sides adjacent to the right angle are 4 inches and 3 inches respectively?
    a. 6 sq. inches
    b. 7 sq. inches
    c. 12 sq. inches
    d. 25 sq. inches
    e. None of the above

12. *Make options grammatically parallel to each other and consistent with the stem.* Lack of parallelism makes for an awkward item and may cause the examinee difficulty in grasping the meaning of the question and of the relationships among the alternative answers.

FAULTY: As compared with the American factory worker in the early part of the nineteenth century, the American factory worker at the close of the century
    a. was working long hours.
    b. received greater social security benefits.
    c. was to receive lower money wages.
    d. was less likely to belong to a labor union.
    e. became less likely to have personal contact with employers.

IMPROVED: As compared with the American factory worker in the early part of the nineteenth century, the American factory worker at the close of the century
    a. worked longer hours.
    b. had more social security.
    c. received lower money wages.
    d. was less likely to belong to a labor union.
    e. had less personal contact with his employer.

Lack of parallelism between stem and alternatives may also lead to a "grammatical clue" to the correct answer.

FAULTY: A two-way grid summarizing the relationship between test scores and criterion scores is sometimes referred to as an
    a. correlation coefficients.
    b. expectancy table.
    c. probability histogram.
    d. bivariate frequency distribution.
The article *an* leads the student to the correct answer.
IMPROVED: Two-way grids summarizing test-criterion relationships are sometimes called
    a. correlation coefficients.
    b. expectancy tables.
    c. bivariate frequency distributions.
    d. probability histograms.

13. *Avoid such irrelevant cues as "common elements" and "pat verbal associations."* Because multiple-choice items require association between several options and a lead statement, any similarity between key words in the stem and alternatives may function as irrelevant cues. The term "irrelevant cue" describes an item fault that leads the examinee to the correct answer regardless of his knowledge of the topic under examination. Common elements in the stem and correct alternative are the most obvious type of irrelevant cue.

FAULTY: The "standard error of estimate" refers to
    a. the objectivity of scoring.
    b. the percentage of reduced error variance.
    c. an absolute amount of possible error.
    d. the amount of error in estimating criterion scores.
The test-wise but unknowledgeable student, seeing the terms "estimate" in the stem and "estimating" in the fourth option, would be led to the correct answer.
FAULTY: The "standard error of estimate" refers to
    a. scoring errors.
    b. sampling errors.
    c. standardization errors.
    d. administration errors.
    e. prediction errors.
Although we have made the alternatives more homogeneous and eliminated the common elements, we are still left with a faulty item. The problem now is the verbal association between "estimate" and "prediction," which would again lead the student to the correct answer.
IMPROVED: The "standard error of estimate" is most directly related to which of the following test characteristics?

    a. Objectivity
    b. Reliability
    c. Validity
    d. Usability
    e. Specificity

14. *In testing for understanding of a term or concept, it is generally preferable to present the term in the stem and alternative definitions in the options.* The examinee is less likely to benefit from pat verbal associations, particularly if the correct answer is a paraphrase, rather than a verbatim extract from the text.

15. *Use "objective" items.* In other words, use items on whose correct answers virtually all experts would agree. It is an interesting, humbling, and informative experience to have a colleague key one's tests. But it is perhaps of greater importance to go over each test with one's students, who are probably the best "test critics."

ILLUSTRATIVE SELECTION ITEMS FOR THE COGNITIVE DOMAIN OF THE TAXONOMY OF EDUCATIONAL OBJECTIVES

The *Taxonomy of Educational Objectives,* as was noted in Chapter Two, is a highly valuable source of ideas for achievement test items. The following items are presented to illustrate the variety of outcomes that can be measured using the *Taxonomy* as a guide. Each item is keyed to a specific *Taxonomy* classification:[1]

1.12 Knowledge of Specific Facts

    1. The Monroe Doctrine was announced about ten years after the
        a. Revolutionary War.
        b. War of 1812.
        c. Civil War.
        d. Spanish-American War.

1.31 Knowledge of Principles and Generalizations

    2. Which of the following statements of the relationship between market price and normal price is true?
        a. Over a short period of time, market price varies directly with changes in normal price.
        b. Over a long period of time, market price tends to equal normal price.

---

[1] From the book *Taxonomy of educational objectives, Handbook II: The cognitive domain,* edited by B. Bloom, D. Krathwohl, and B. Masia. (New York: David McKay Company, Inc., 1956.) Reprinted by permission of the publisher.

   c. Market price is usually lower than normal price.
   d. Over a long period of time, market price determines normal prices.

2.10 Translation from Symbolic Form to Another Form, or Vice Versa

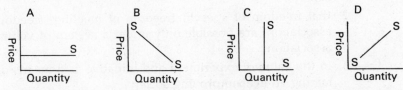

3. Which of the above graphs best represents the supply situation where a monopolist maintains a uniform price regardless of the amounts which people buy?
   a.
   b.
   c.
   d.

3.00 Application

In the following items you are to judge the effects of a particular policy on the distribution of income. In each case assume that there are no other changes in policy which would counteract the effect of the policy described in the item. Mark the item:

   A. if the policy described would tend to *reduce* the existing degree of inequality in the distribution of income,
   B. if the policy described would tend to *increase* the existing degree of inequality in the distribution of income, or
   C. if the policy described would have no effect, or an indeterminate effect, on the distribution of income.

___ 4. Increasingly progressive income taxes.

___ 5. Confiscation of rent on unimproved urban land.

___ 6. Introduction of a national sales tax.

___ 7. Increasing the personal exemptions from income taxes.

___ 8. Distributing a subsidy to sharecroppers on Southern farms.

___ 9. Provision of educational and medical services, and low-cost public housing.

___ 10. Reduction in the degree of business monopoly.

___ 11. Increasing taxes in periods of prosperity and decreasing them in periods when depressions threaten.

4.00 Analysis

12. An assumption basic to Lindsay's preference for voluntary associations rather than government orders . . . is a belief
   1. that government is not organized to make the best use of experts.
   2. that freedom of speech, freedom of meeting, freedom of association, are possible only under a system of voluntary associations.
   3. in the value of experiment and initiative as a means of attaining an ever-improving society.
   4. in the benefits of competition.

13. The relation between the definition of sovereignty given in Paragraph 2 and that given in Paragraph 9 is best expressed as follows:
   a. There is no fundamental difference between them, only a difference in formulation.
   b. The definition given in Paragraph 2 includes that given in Paragraph 9 but in addition includes situations which are excluded by that given in Paragraph 9.
   c. The two definitions are incompatible with each other; the conditions of sovereignty implied in each exclude the other.

5.20 Production of a Plan, or Proposed Set of Operations

Several authorities were asked to participate in a round-table discussion of juvenile delinquency. They were given the following data about City X and communities A, B, and C within City X.

	For City X as a Whole	For Community A	For Community B	For Community C
Juvenile Delinquency Rate (annual arrests per 100 persons ages 5–19)	4.24	18.1	1.3	4.1
Average Monthly Rental	$60.00	$42.00	$100.00	$72.00
Infant Death Rate (per 1000 births)	52.3	76.0	32.1	56.7
Birth Rate (per 1000 inhabitants)	15.5	16.7	10.1	15.4

In addition, they were told that in Community A the crimes against property (burglary, etc.) constituted a relatively higher proportion of the total juvenile offenses than in Communities B and C, where crimes against persons (assault, etc.) were relatively greater.

14. How would *you* explain the differences in these juvenile delinquency rates in light of the above data? (You may make use of any theory or material presented in the course.)

15. In light of your explanation of the data, what proposals would you make for reducing the juvenile delinquency rate in each of the three communities?

6.20 Judgments in Terms of External Criteria: Given Possible Bases for Judgments about Accuracy, Recognize Criteria Which Are Appropriate

For items 16–21, assume that in doing research for a paper about the English language you find a statement by Otto Jespersen which contradicts one point of view on language which you have always accepted. Indicate which of the statements would be significant in determining the value of Jespersen's statement. For the purpose of these items, you may assume that these statements are accurate.

Key: A. Significant positively—i.e., might lead you to trust his statement and to revise your own opinion.

B. Significant negatively—i.e., might lead you to distrust his statement.

C. Has no significance.

__ 16. Mr. Jespersen was Professor of English at Copenhagen University.

__ 17. The statement in question was taken from the very first article that Mr. Jespersen published.

__ 18. Mr. Jespersen's books are frequently referred to in other works that you consult.

__ 19. Mr. Jespersen's name is not included in the *Dictionary of American Scholars*.

__ 20. So far as you can find, Jespersen never lived in England or the United States for any considerable length of time.

__ 21. In your reading of other authors on the English language, you find that several of them went to Denmark to study under Jespersen.

ILLUSTRATIVE SELECTION ITEMS USING GRAPHIC MATERIALS

Instructors in all subject areas encounter situations in which only pictorial, diagrammatic, or visual material is suitable for purposes of measurement. The use of such materials allows for great flexibility in the assessment of a variety of content areas and learning outcomes. Such stimuli can be used equally well to measure knowledge, comprehension, and application. Complex learning outcomes can be measured with items based on graphic materials. To illustrate this contention, the following items and explanations have been reproduced from *Multiple-choice Questions: A Close Look,* a pamphlet published by Educational Testing Service.[2] The items are intended for high-school and college students.

QUESTION 1

The shading on map [in Figure 5.1] is used to indicate

*A. population density.
 B. percentage of total labor force in agriculture.
 C. per capita income.
 D. death rate per thousand of population.

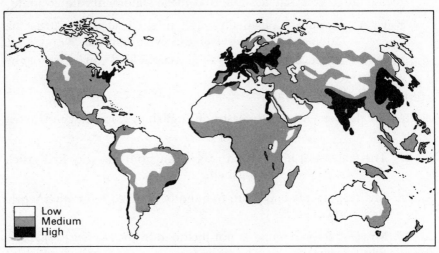

FIGURE 5.1

Many of the multiple-choice questions included in tests in the social sciences require the student to make use of his general knowledge in the

---

interpretation of materials. Thus, this question does not simply ask: What areas of the world have the highest population densities? Rather, it presents a novel situation in which the student must infer that only one of the choices offered provides a plausible explanation of the shadings on the map.

An examination of the map clearly shows that choice A, population density, is the proper response. The darkest shading, which according to the map's legend indicates the highest degree of whatever the shading represents, covers such high-density areas as the northeastern part of the United States, a large part of Europe, the Nile valley, India, Japan, and Eastern China. If this is not a sufficient clue, the areas with the lightest shading include such underpopulated areas as the Arctic regions, tropical South America, the Sahara and Arabian deserts, and most of Australia.

Choice B, the percentage of the total labor force in agriculture, though attractive if only India and China are examined, is clearly incorrect when applied to the northeastern United States.

Choice C, per capita income, is plausible only if the student's analysis of the map is limited to the dark shading in the United States and Western Europe (and even there it is not entirely correct); the dark shadings in China and India certainly do not indicate high per capita income. The reverse is true of choice D, death rate per thousand of population, since the latter might be expected to be high for India and China, but low for the United States and Europe.

QUESTION 2

The graph [in Figure 5.2] represents the political composition from 1922 to 1955 of which of the following?

 A. German Bundestag
 B. French National Assembly
 C. Italian Chamber of Deputies
*D. British House of Commons

To answer this question correctly, the student must be able to do several things. First, he must be able to read the graph. Then, using the information he can infer from it, he must interpret it in the light of his knowledge of European history and government from 1922 to 1955 and conclude which legislative body may properly be so depicted. In such a process, it is possible for different students to make use of different information to arrive at the correct answer.

In examining the graph, the student should note that the party system shown is essentially a two-party one, although there is a third party that, for most of the period shown, decreased in representation. He may also note the years in which elections were held, the years that Party A received majorities, the fact that Party B did not receive a major-

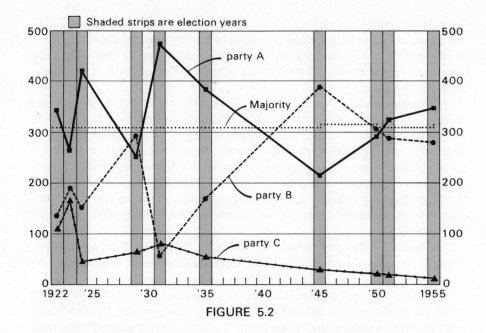

FIGURE 5.2

ity until 1945, and the fact that in the elections of 1923 and 1929 neither party received a majority.

In considering the first of the four possible answers, the German Bundestag, the student should recognize that during the period through 1932, that of the Weimar Republic, no single party in Germany was able to attain a majority, partly because of the multiplicity of parties. After Hitler came to power in 1933, parties other than the Nazi Party were outlawed. These facts do not fit the graph.

The French National Assembly, the second possible answer, contained far more than three parties both before and after World War II. The Italian Chamber of Deputies should also be rejected as a possible answer because, after Mussolini came to power in 1924, it became less and less important until, in 1938, it was superseded by a Chamber of Fasci and Corporations and political parties were suppressed.

QUESTION 3

In the following question you are asked to make inferences from the data given you in Figure 5.3, a map of the imaginary country Serendip. The answer must be a probability rather than a certainty. The relative sizes of towns and cities are not shown. To assist you in the location of the places mentioned in the questions, the map is divided into squares lettered vertically from A to E and numbered horizontally from 1 to 5.

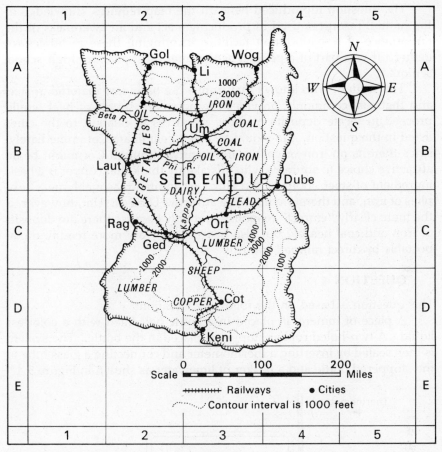

FIGURE 5.3

Which of the following cities would be the best location for a steel mill?

A. Li   (3A)
*B. Um   (3B)
C. Cot   (3D)
D. Dube   (4B)

A map of an imaginary country such as this offers numerous possibilities for questions measuring important understandings. One could ask several questions requiring an understanding of the symbols used on the map. To measure student comprehension of the meaning of contour lines, for example, one might ask which railroad has the steepest grades to climb. Similar questions can be developed requiring knowledge of the factors influencing population distribution, economic activities, and the like.

The question reproduced beneath the map requires knowledge of the natural resources used in producing steel and an awareness of the importance of transportation facilities in bringing these resources together. It was part of a general achievement test given to high-school seniors.

The student who knows that iron is the basic raw material in steel and that coal commonly provides the necessary source of heat would proceed to locate deposits of these resources in relation to the cities listed in the question. He would be able to eliminate Cot immediately, since there is no iron or coal in its vicinity, although Cot might be an attractive choice to students who mistakenly think that copper is a basic ingredient of steel. Both Li and Dube are located reasonably near supplies of iron, and therefore might be attractive choices. Um, however, is the more clearly "correct" response, not only because there are deposits of iron and coal nearby, but also because they are more readily transportable by direct railroad routes.

QUESTION 4

This question is based on the following situation:

A piece of mineral is placed in a bottle half-filled with a colorless liquid. A two-holed rubber stopper is placed in the bottle. The system is then sealed by inserting a thermometer and connecting a glass tube to the stoppered bottle and a beaker of limewater as shown in Figure 5.4.

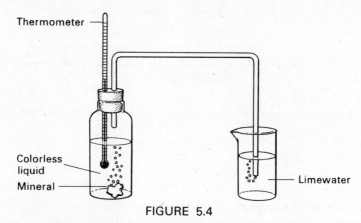

FIGURE 5.4

The following series of observations is recorded:

I. Observations during the first few minutes:

1. Bubbles of a colorless gas rise to the top of the stoppered bottle from the mineral.
2. Bubbles of colorless gas begin to come out of the glass tube and rise to the surface of the limewater.

3. The limewater remains colorless throughout this period of time.
4. The thermometer reads 20°C.

II. Observations at the end of thirty minutes:

1. Bubbles of colorless gas continue to rise in the stoppered bottle.
2. The piece of mineral has become noticeably smaller.
3. There is no apparent change in the level of the colorless liquid in the bottle.
4. The liquid in the bottle remains colorless.
5. The thermometer reads 24°C.
6. The limewater is cloudy.

Which of the following is the best explanation for the appearance of gas bubbles at the end of the tube in the beaker of limewater?

  A. The pressure exerted by the colorless liquid is greater than that exerted by the limewater.
*B. The bubbles coming from the mineral cause an increased gas pressure in the stoppered bottle.
  C. The temperature increase at the end of thirty minutes causes an expansion of gas in the stoppered bottle.
  D. The decrease in the size of the piece of mineral causes reduced pressure in the stoppered bottle.
  E. The glass tube serves as a siphon for the flow of gas from the bottle to the beaker.

This question is taken from a test designed to be used with a new curriculum in high-school chemistry. The question is only one of a series based on the experimental situation described. Questions in the series are grouped in sequence in order to permit the student to think intensively about one situation for an extended period of time. The student is asked to deal with a realistic laboratory situation—one he has not yet encountered in the course—and to employ scientific problem-solving ability in using the data given to answer the questions.

Choice A is both vague and irrelevant. It is unspecific about where the pressure is exerted and has nothing to do with the cause of the bubbles.

Choice C sounds plausible. In itself, the statement is not incorrect, since the temperature increase will cause an increase in gas pressure in the stoppered bottle. However, students who are in command of the subject will realize that the increase in gas pressure due to the rise in temperature is insignificant compared with that caused by the bubbles coming from the mineral.

Choice D is incorrect. Some students may not realize this, but even if the statement were correct, it would offer an incorrect explanation for the appearance of the bubbles in the beaker.

Many good students reject choice E, but many less able students choose it, probably because the arrangement looks somewhat like a siphon and they have heard of the use of siphons in transferring fluids.

Students who understand the forces at work in the situation described will know that bubbles would appear at the end of the tube in the beaker when the pressure exerted by the gas from the stoppered bottle exceeded the pressure exerted by the limewater at the end of the tube. They will also realize that the limewater pressure would remain essentially constant. Choice B, therefore, accounts best for the appearance of gas bubbles at the end of the tube in the beaker.

In addition to the kinds of items presented here, many other possibilities exist. Drawings, blueprints, paintings, photographs, and the like may also profitably be used as stimulus material. In addition to being efficient, the use of such materials can stimulate student interest. Test materials that use pictorial representation are intrinsically interesting, succinct, understandable, and realistic. Two difficulties exist: it is sometimes difficult to locate appropriate material, and reproduction can be complicated. The availability of copying machines (e.g., Xerox) can make duplication of graphic test material practical.

GUIDELINES FOR SELECTION OF READING COMPREHENSION PASSAGES AND WRITING OF QUESTIONS BASED ON THEM

At virtually all levels of education, instructors are concerned with assessing a student's ability to comprehend written material. One must absorb and understand information before he can be expected to do anything with it. Following is a set of guidelines useful in selecting reading passages and writing reading comprehension items. These suggestions should prove helpful to those involved in language arts and, to some extent, foreign language instruction.

A reading comprehension passage should:

1. Represent a reading load that is reasonable in proportion to the number of items based on it so that examinees do not have to spend precious minutes reading a long selection that adds only three or four points to their raw scores.

2. Contain several distinct ideas that lend themselves to questions clearly differing in content.

3. Be interesting and appropriate to the intellectual level and social maturity of the examinees.

4. Be culturally genuine and a representative sample of the literature tested.

5. Be selected from materials that examinees are not likely to know (textbooks and other materials frequently read in schools or colleges should be avoided).

6.   Be clear and free from ambiguities of content or style, unless such ambiguity is made the object of a test item.

7.   Be written in a good literary style.

8.   Contain no excess verbiage or content irrelevant to the items based on it. All superfluous material should be cut, keeping in mind that material on which distractors are based is just as essential as that suggesting the right answer.

An item based on a reading comprehension passage should be:

1.   Checked from all points of view to ascertain that it *cannot* be answered without reading the passage.

2.   Addressed to significant aspects of content and style rather than minor details.

3.   Checked against the entire passage, even if it refers only to a part, so as to avoid contradictions or ambiguities.

4.   Of a level of difficulty comparable to that of the reading selection, neither considerably easier nor more difficult or esoteric in content or wording.

5.   Answerable solely on the basis of the content or implications of the passage, if its purpose is to test reading comprehension rather than concepts related to style, literary history, and the like.

6.   Independent of all other items, so that the examinee need not know the answer to one question in order to answer the next correctly.

7.   Significantly different from every other item without overlap in either content or wording.

8.   Free of clues to any other items.

9.   Paraphrased rather than repeating the wording of the selection.

WRITING MATCHING EXERCISES

The matching exercise is a variation of the multiple-choice question. While the multiple-choice question usually presents a single problem and several solutions, the matching exercise presents several problems and several solutions. The list of alternative solutions is constant for each new problem or stimulus. It is because of this constancy of alternatives that the quality and homogeneity of options so significantly influence the effectiveness of the entire exercise. Matching exercises may concentrate on form or content. Pictorial material can be used with success in these types of exercises. Content might be related to events, inventions, results, definitions, quotations, dates, or locations. At a more sophisticated level, matching (classification or key-list) items may concern (1) cause-and-effect relationships, (2) theoretical statements and experimental bases, and (3) a phenomenon and its explanation in terms of principles, generalizations, or theories.

Most such exercises contain two columns, that on the left-hand side of the page containing the stimuli or premises, and the right-hand list containing responses. Compound matching exercises (e.g., state–major industry–city or authors-novels-nationalities) are, of course, possible, but are used infrequently.

The matching exercise's chief advantage is efficiency in time and space. It uses the same set of response alternatives for a whole group of items. The matching exercise is, therefore, a compact and efficient method of rapidly surveying knowledges of the who, what, when, and where variety.

The matching exercise is not well adapted to the measurement of higher-order abilities. It is particularly susceptible to irrelevant cues, implausible alternatives, and the awkward arrangement of stimuli or responses; thus, great care is needed in development. Several suggestions for constructing or revising matching exercises follow:

1. *Matching exercises should be complete on a single page.* Splitting the exercise is confusing, distracting, and time-consuming for the student.

2. *Use response categories that are related but mutually exclusive.* If this suggestion is not followed, ambiguous items or items requiring multikeying will result. Responses should be drawn from the same domain (e.g., do not mix dates and names of inventors in the same response list) but should not overlap. The degree of relatedness among stimuli and/or responses will, of course, dictate the degree of difficulty of the exercise.

3. *Keep the number of stimuli relatively small (e.g., 10–15), and let the number of possible responses exceed the number of stimuli by two or three.* This is, admittedly, an arbitrary suggestion but is related to a point well worth considering. If a matching exercise is too long, the task becomes tedious and the discrimination too fine. A related problem is the possibility that the use of matching items might "overweight" the test. Because of their compactness, their weight in the test relative to the objectives and other item types may become disproportionate. One should also avoid matching the numbers of stimuli and responses, as this increases the likelihood that a student will benefit from guessing or the process of elimination. In this regard the cautious use of the response "None of the above" may be recommended. One might include a statement in the test directions to the effect that the responses may be used more than once.

4. *The directions should clearly specify the basis for matching stimuli and responses.* Although the basis for matching is usually obvious, sound testing practice dictates that the directions spell out the nature of the task. It is unreasonable that he should have to read through the stimulus and response lists in order to discern the intended basis for matching.

5. *Keep the statements in the response column short and list them in some*

logical order. **This** suggestion is intended to facilitate response to the exercise. The responses should be so stated and arranged (e.g., alphabetically, chronologically, etc.) that the student can scan them quickly.

The following matching exercise does not embody the suggestions made above.

FAULTY: Directions—Match List A with List B. You will be given one point for each correct match.

	List A		*List B*
a.	cotton gin	a.	Eli Whitney
b.	reaper	b.	Alexander Graham Bell
c.	wheel	c.	David Brinkley
d.	TU54G tube	d.	Louisa May Alcott
e.	steamboat	e.	None of these

The primary shortcomings of this matching exercise may be summarized as follows:

1. The directions fail to specify the basis for matching or mechanics for responding.
2. The two lists are enumerated identically.
3. The responses are not listed logically—in this case, alphabetically.
4. Both lists lack homogeneity.
5. There are equal numbers of elements in both lists.
6. The use of "None of these" is questionable in this exercise, serving as a giveaway to List A elements "c" and "d." Furthermore, if a student uses it for element "e" of List A, it is not clear that he knows who did in fact invent the steamboat.

An improved version of the exercise follows:

IMPROVED: Directions—Famous inventions are listed in the left-hand column, and inventors in the right-hand column below. Place the letter corresponding to the inventor in the space next to the invention for which he is famous. Each match is worth 1 point, and *"None of these"* may be the correct answer. Inventors may be used more than once.

	Inventions		*Inventors*
____	1. steamboat	a.	Alexander Graham Bell
____	2. cotton gin	b.	Robert Fulton
____	3. sewing machine	c.	Elias Howe
____	4. reaper	d.	Cyrus McCormick
		e.	Eli Whitney
		f.	None of these

Many other types of short-answer items could be discussed. Such question forms as the rearrangement exercise (Cureton 1960), interpretive exercise (Gronlund 1965), analogies (Remmers, Gage, and Rummel

1965, pp. 258–259), and problem-solving items (Adams 1964, pp. 345–347) have been found useful in educational measurement. Space limitations will not allow us to consider these forms here, but the reader is referred to the above references and the suggested readings at the end of the chapter for additional treatments of item writing.

WRITING TEST ITEMS FOR ELEMENTARY AND JUNIOR HIGH-SCHOOL STUDENTS

The development of test items for young students is a difficult task.[3] This is particularly true if the teacher has decided to use so-called "objective" or short-answer questions. Two of the main difficulties in writing items for the young involve (1) the development of comprehensible and appropriate stimulus materials, and (2) the development of a scheme for recording student responses efficiently.

At the kindergarten level, the best way to record answers is perhaps to have the youngsters draw an X on a picture. A series of pictures can be accompanied by a series of questions, as shown in Figure 5.5:

FIGURE 5.5

<hr>

[3] The material in this section is based on Dr. Clarence Nelson's monograph *Improving objective tests in science* (1967), pp. 18–21. Sample items reproduced by permission of the National Science Teachers Association.

1. Put an X on the pictures of things that are alive.

2. Put a Y on the picture of each thing that is an animal.

3. Put a Z on the picture of each thing that is a mammal.

4. One of these three pictures is a kitty. Put an X on that picture.

5. One of these three pictures shows what happens when something is heated or becomes warm. Put an X on that picture.

To test for understanding of concepts, it is desirable to use a picture card illustrating objects similar but not identical to those discussed in class. If identical objects are used, one may be measuring recall rather than understanding.

A similar method of recording responses can be used at the first-grade level. Using pictorial material, the teacher may read the questions to the students. Following are two examples.

6. (The teacher demonstrates boiling, filtering, and straining of water, and then reads the text question.) Pure water can be taken out of salt water by:

7. Salt has been mixed with chopped ice. If some of this chopped ice is packed around a container full of water, what will probably happen to the water in the container?

Second- and third-graders can probably use a special answer sheet. The teacher may wish to make an answer sheet containing lettered or numbered squares like the following:

8.	a	b	c		10.	a	b	c
	□	□	□			□	□	□

9.	a	b	c		11.	a	b	c
	□	□	□			□	□	□

An alternative is to have the students circle the letters on an answer sheet. The questions could be handed out in duplicated form, and after the method for recording the answers is explained, the questions and answers could be read slowly to the students.

8. When a watch is laid flat on a table, if 12 on the dial represents north, then 9 on the dial represents
   a. south.
   b. east.
  *c. west.

9. If 12 on your watch dial represents north, what represents southeast?
  *a. 4:30
  b. 7:30
  c. 10:30

10. A person standing at the seashore looking at a ship several miles from the shore can see the
   a. entire ship.
  *b. upper part of the ship only.
   c. lower part of the ship only.

11. The horizon would be farthest away
   a. if you were standing on the seashore and looking out over the ocean.

b. if you were on top of the Empire State Building or the Washington Monument and looking straight ahead.

*c. if you were looking out of an airplane window while flying four miles above the earth.

Junior high-school students can use commercially available (e.g., IBM) answer sheets. A commercial scoring template may be used for hand scoring. If the answer sheet is teacher-made, a fan, strip, or cut-out key (see Chapter Four) may be used. Following is a series of test items aimed at measuring the junior high-school student's understanding of land-feature diagrams. The test item should not be one previously studied in class.

Items 12–16 refer to the cross-sectioned land-feature diagram in Figure 5.6. Formations are indicated by Roman numerals.

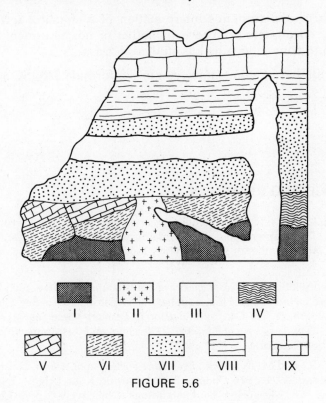

FIGURE 5.6

12. Fossils would be least likely to occur in

*a. III.

b. V.

c. VII.

d. VIII.

e. IX.

13. An unconformity exists between
    a. I and III.
    b. III and VI.
    *c. V and VII.
    d. VII and VIII.
    e. VIII and IX.

14. The youngest formation is
    a. I.
    b. II.
    c. III.
    d. V.
    *e. IX.

15. The oldest formation is
    *a. I.
    b. II.
    c. III.
    d. V.
    e. IX.

16. Which formation is made up of igneous rock?
    *a. III.
    b. V.
    c. VII.
    d. VIII.
    e. IX.

Similarly, the student's interpretation of a chemical formula not previously encountered can reveal whether or not he understands the symbols and conventions he has studied in class.

17. The number of atoms of oxygen in the formula $2Al_2(SO_4)_3$ is
    a. 4.
    b. 7.
    c. 8.
    d. 12.
    *e. 24.

SUGGESTED READINGS

The following references contain general discussions of item construction principles. The chapters cited deal primarily with supply and selection items, useful in a large number of subject-matter fields and with a variety of levels of students.

Adams, Georgia Sachs. *Measurement and evaluation in education, psychology, and guidance.* New York: Holt, Rinehart & Winston, 1964. See Chapter 10, "Development, Try-Out, and Revision of Teacher-Made Tests," and Chapter 11, "The *Taxonomy of Educational Objectives* and Test Items Illustrative of Its Major Categories."

Ahmann, J. S., and M. D. Glock. *Evaluating pupil growth, 4th ed.* Boston: Allyn and Bacon, 1971. See Chapter 3, "Measuring Knowledges Objectively," Chapter 4, "Measuring Understandings Objectively," and Chapter 6, "Evaluating Procedures and Products."

Ebel, R. L. Writing the test item. In *Educational measurement,* ed. E. F. Lindquist. Washington: American Council on Education, 1951.

Ebel, R. L. *Essentials of educational measurement.* Englewood Cliffs, N.J.: Prentice-Hall, 1972. See Chapter 7, "True-False Test Items," and Chapter 8, "How to Write Multiple-Choice Test Items."

Furst, E. J. *Constructing evaluation instruments.* New York: Longmans, Green, 1958. See Chapter 8, "Constructing Items to Fit Specifications," Chapter 9, "Constructing Supply-Type Questions," and Chapter 10, "Constructing Choice-Type Items."

Gerberich, J. R. *Specimen objective test items: A guide to achievement test construction.* New York: Longmans, Green, 1956.

Gronlund, N. E. *Measurement and evaluation in teaching.* New York: Macmillan, 1971. See Chapter 7, "Constructing Objective Test Items: Simple Forms," Chapter 8, "Constructing Objective Test Items: Multiple-Choice Form," and Chapter 9, "Measuring Complex Achievement: The Interpretive Exercise."

Henry, Nelson B., ed. *The measurement of understanding.* Forty-Fifth Yearbook of the National Society for the Study of Education, Part I. Chicago: University of Chicago Press, 1946.

Mehrens, W. A., and Lehmann, S. J. *Measurement and evaluation in education and psychology.* New York: Holt, Rinehart and Winston, 1973. An excellent introductory but comprehensive and readable text.

Remmers, H. H.; Gage, N. L; and Rummel, J. F. *A practical introduction to measurement and evaluation,* 2nd ed. New York: Harper & Row, 1965. See Chapter 8, "Constructing Teacher-Made Tests."

Stanley, J. C. *Measurement in today's schools,* 4th ed. Englewood Cliffs, N.J.: Prentice-Hall, 1964. See Chapter 7, "Constructing Specific Types of Objective Tests."

Test Development Division. *Multiple-choice questions: A close look.* Princeton, N.J.: Educational Testing Service, 1963.

Wesman, A. G. Writing the Test Item. In *Educational measurement,* ed. R. L. Thorndike. Washington: American Council on Education, 1971. See Chapter 4.

The following references deal with test and item construction principles unique to selected subject-matter areas or useful with particular types of students.

Ahmann, J. S.; Glock, M. D.; and Wardenberg, Helen L. *Evaluating elementary school pupils.* Boston: Allyn & Bacon, 1960.

Arny, Clara B. *Evaluation in home economics.* New York: Appleton-Century-Crofts, 1953.

Austin, Mary. *Reading evaluation: Appraisal techniques for schools and classrooms.* New York: Ronald Press, 1971.

Berg, H. D., ed. *Evaluation in social studies.* Thirty-Fifth Yearbook of the National Council for the Social Studies. Washington: National Education Association, 1965.

Clark, J. L. D. *Foreign language testing: Theory and practice.* Philadelphia: The Center for Curriculum Development, 1972.

Clarke, H. H. *Application of measurement to health and physical education,* 3rd ed. Englewood Cliffs, N.J.: Prentice-Hall, 1959.

Dressel, P. L., *et al. Evaluation in higher education.* Boston: Houghton Mifflin, 1961.

Evaluation in mathematics. Twenty-Sixth Yearbook of the National Council of Teachers of Mathematics. Washington: NCTM, 1961.

Farnsworth, P. R. *Musical taste: Its measurement and cultural nature.* Stanford University Press, 1950.

Gerberich, J. R.; Greene, H. A.; and Jorgensen, A. N. *Measurement and evaluation in the modern school.* New York: David McKay, 1962. Part 5 of this comprehensive reference text contains 11 chapters, each of which deals with the measurement problems encountered in selected subject fields.

Hardaway, Mathilde, and Maier, T. G. *Tests and measurements in business education,* 2nd ed. Cincinnati: South-Western, 1952.

Horrocks, J. E., and Schoonover, Thelma I. *Measurement for teachers.* Columbus, Ohio: Charles Merrill, 1968. Several chapters of this book describe procedures useful in assessing outcomes in reading, mathematics, language arts, sciences, and the fine and applied arts.

Lado, R. *Language testing* (The construction and use of foreign language tests). New York: McGraw-Hill, 1961.

Nedelsky, L. *Science teaching and testing.* New York: Harcourt, Brace & World, 1965.

Thomas, R. M. A rationale for measurement in the visual arts. *Educational and Psychological Measurement* 25 (1965): 163–189.

Valette, Rebecca M. *Modern language testing: A handbook.* New York: Harcourt Brace Jovanovich, 1967.

6

CONSTRUCTING AND SCORING ESSAY ITEMS AND TESTS

SUMMARY PREVIEW STATEMENTS

1. Essay items and tests can be used to assess a variety of learning outcomes, particularly those related to an individual's ability to organize, analyze, synthesize, and express evaluations of material, ideas, facts, and concepts.

2. The use of extended-response essay items allows the examinee to express himself freely and the instructor to explore in depth a sampling of student knowledge and skills.

3. The use of restricted-response essay items provides for an efficient survey of a moderately large content area.

4. The answer to an essay item may be strictly evaluated in terms either of accuracy of content or clarity of expression (including organization).

5. Reliability of grading is one of the major obstacles to the effective use of essay items and tests.

6. Reliability of the sampling of student knowledges and skills is another potential problem area in essay testing.

7. The validity of essay items and tests in terms of objectives must be a matter of great concern to the examiner.

8. An instructor should almost never rely exclusively on essay items to assess the total learning outcomes of a unit or course of study.

9. The global rating of the components of an essay item—such as organization, style, and mechanics of expression—is one approach to scoring.

10. It is recommended that an analytic method be applied in scoring essay items.

11. An instructor should write an "ideal" answer to a given essay question for use as a guide in evaluating individual student answers.

12. Use of the Checklist Point Score method allows each element of an essay answer to be objectively assessed.

13. Essay items may be used to explore various affective learning outcomes.

14. The use of computers to score essay items has not yet realized its full potential.

15. Essay items should:
    a. Be relevant and limited in scope.
    b. Contain clearly defined tasks.
    c. Be scored anonymously.
    d. Be scored using the Checklist Point Score method.
    e. Be the same for all students.

Many instructors, particularly neophytes, believe that essay tests are the easiest type of measuring instrument to construct and score. Nothing could be further from the truth. The expenditure of considerable time and effort is necessary if essay items and tests are to yield meaningful information. Essay tests allow for direct assessment of the attainment of a variety of objectives and goals. By contrast with traditional "objective" item types, they demand less construction time per fixed unit of student time, and according to some investigators encourage more appropriate study habits. See Balch (1964) for a review of the relevant literature.

This chapter will discuss some of the problems and procedures involved in constructing and administering essay items and tests, as well as scoring procedures.

GENERAL TYPES OF ESSAY ITEMS

Essay items may be classified according to a number of different but relevant criteria. Two categories that have been found particularly useful will be discussed in the following section.

Extended vs. Restricted Response

One can differentiate the many types of essay items on the basis of the extensiveness of the student's response. The relative freedom of response has obvious practical implications for both instructor and student. From the instructor's standpoint, an extensive response to a few broadly based questions allows for an in-depth sampling of a student's knowledge, thinking processes, and problem-solving behavior relative to a particular topic. The open-ended nature of the task posed by an instruction such as "Discuss essay and objective type tests" is challenging to a student. In order to respond correctly, the student must recall specific information and organize, evaluate, and write an intelligible composition. On the other hand, such free-response essay items tend to yield a variety of responses from examinees, both with respect to content and organization, and thus to inhibit reliable grading. The potential ambiguity of an essay task is probably the single most important contributor to unreliability. In addition, the more extensive the responses elicited, the fewer questions an instructor may ask—which, in turn, may lower the content validity of the test.

It follows, therefore, that a restricted-response essay item and/or test is in general preferable. An instruction such as "Discuss the relative advantages and disadvantages of essay and short-answer tests with respect to (1) reliability, (2) objectivity, (3) content validity, and (4) usability" presents a well-defined task that lends itself to reliable scoring and yet allows the student sufficient latitude to organize and express his thoughts creatively.

Content vs. Expression

It is frequently claimed that the essay item or test allows the student to present his knowledge and understanding and organize the material in a unique form and style. More often than not, such factors as expression, grammar, spelling, and the like are evaluated in conjunction with content. If the instructor has attempted to develop students' expressive skills, and if this learning outcome is included in his table of specifications, the evaluation of such skills is legitimate. If expressive skills are not part of the instructional program, it is not ethical to evaluate them. If the score of each essay item includes an evaluation of the mechanics of English, this should, obviously, be brought to the attention of the student. If possible, separate scores should be computed for content and expression.

The decision to include either or both of these elements in a score, and the relative weighting of each, should be dictated by the table of specifications.

SPECIFIC TYPES OF ESSAY QUESTIONS

The following set of essay questions[1] is presented to illustrate how the phrasing of an essay item can be framed to elicit particular behaviors and levels of response.

I.   **Recall**

    A. Simple recall
       1. What is the chemical formula for hydrogen peroxide?
       2. Who wrote "The Emergence of Lincoln"?

    B. Selective recall in which a basis for evaluation or judgment is suggested
       1. Which three individuals in the nineteenth century had the most profound effect on contemporary life?

II. **Understanding**

    A. Comparison of two phenomena on a single designated basis
       1. Compare the writers of the English Renaissance to those of the nineteenth century with respect to their ability to describe nature.

    B. Comparison of two phenomena in general
       1. Compare the French and Russian Revolutions.

    C. Explanation of the use or exact meaning of a phrase or statement
       1. The Book of John begins "In the beginning was the word . . ." From what philosophical system does this statement derive?

    D. Summary of a text or some portion of it
       1. State the central thesis of the Communist Manifesto.

    E. Statement of an artist's purpose in the selection or organization of material
       1. Why did Hemingway describe in detail the episode in which Gordon, lying wounded, engages the oncoming enemy?
       2. What was Beethoven's purpose in deviating from the orthodox form of a symphony in Symphony No. 6?

III. **Application.** It should be clearly understood that whether or not a question elicits application depends on the preliminary educational

---

[1] Reprinted and modified with permission from *Testing Bulletin No. 2,* "The Writing of Essay Questions," published by the Office of Evaluation Services, Michigan State University, September 1967.

experience. If an analysis has been taught explicitly, a question involving that analysis is a matter of simple recall.

A. Causes or effects
   1. Why may too frequent reliance on penicillin for the treatment of minor ailments eventually result in its diminished effectiveness against major invasion of body tissues by infectious bacteria?
   2. Why did fascism flourish in Italy and Germany but not in England and the United States?

B. Analysis (It is advisable not to use the word *analysis* in the question itself)
   1. Why was Hamlet torn by conflicting desires?
   2. Why is the simple existence of slavery an insufficient explanation for the outbreak of the American Civil War?

C. Statement of relationship
   1. It is said that intelligence correlates with school achievement at about .65. Explain this relationship.

D. Illustrations or examples of principles
   1. Name three examples of uses of the lever in typical American homes.

E. Application of rules or principles in specified situations
   1. Would you weigh more or less on the moon? on the sun? Explain.

F. Reorganization of facts
   1. Some writers have said that the American Revolution was not merely a political revolution against England but also a social revolution, within the colonies, of the poor against the wealthy. Using the same evidence, what other conclusion is possible?

IV. Judgment

A. Decision for or against
   1. Should members of the Communist Party be allowed to teach in American colleges? Why or why not?
   2. Is nature or nurture more influential in determining human behavior? Why?

B. Discussion
   1. Discuss the likelihood that four-year private liberal arts colleges will gradually be replaced by junior colleges and state universities.

C. Criticism of the adequacy, correctness, or relevance of a statement
   1. The discovery of penicillin has often been called an accident. Comment on the adequacy of this explanation.

D. Formulation of new questions
   1. What should one find out in order to explain why some students of high intelligence fail in school?
   2. What questions should a scientist ask in order to determine why more smokers than nonsmokers develop lung cancer?

SPECIAL PROBLEM AREAS

The relative strengths and weaknesses of the essay approach to measuring learning outcomes were discussed in Chapter Four. Three specific sources of difficulty likely to be encountered in the use of essay tests, and ways of minimizing them, are still in need of elaboration.

Reader Reliability

The classic studies of the reliability of grading free-response test items were undertaken in 1912 and 1913 by Starch and Elliott (1912, 1913a and b). In three studies focusing on high-school English, history, and mathematics, Starch and Elliott found tremendous variation in the independent gradings of a standard set of papers. They found discrepancies of up to 48 points in English, 49 points in geometry, and 70 points in history. Even recent research, employing highly sophisticated designs and analysis procedures, has failed to demonstrate consistently satisfactory agreement among essay graders. A study by Myers, McConville, and Coffman (1966) involving 145 readers, 80,000 essays, and a five-day reading period found average single-reader reliabilities of .41. When the number of readers was increased to four, the average reliability rose to .73. This significant increase in reliability was obtained under controlled conditions, with trained graders who read "holistically" and used a four-point scale. The implication of this research is clear: several readers should participate in the grading of essay exams. The fallibility of human judgment cannot be underestimated as a source of unreliability in the scoring of essay examinations.

Recent research has shed light on some of the specific contributory factors in lack of reader reliability. Marshall and Powers (1969), for example, have experimentally demonstrated that preservice teachers are influenced by such factors as quality of composition and penmanship, even when they are explicitly instructed to grade on content alone.

Instrument Reliability

Even if an acceptable level of scoring reliability is attained, there is no guarantee that we are measuring consistently (see Chapter Eleven). There remains the issue of the sampling of objectives or behaviors represented by the test. Traxler and Anderson (1935), for example, found that although experienced readers could agree on the scoring of two different forms of an essay test, the correlation between the forms was only .60. Thus it is possible for the reliability of scoring to exceed the reliability of the instrument itself.

It has been suggested by some experts that the essay test is less susceptible than the objective test to the effect of guessing. This may not be the case. If the examinee is torn between two or more responses to an open-ended question, he still must guess between them. Such guessing, if widespread, can contribute to increased error and decreased reliability. The only difference between guessing on essay and objective tests is that the essay writer devises his own alternatives, while the alternatives are provided on an objective test.

One way to increase the reliability of an essay test is to increase the number of questions and restrict the length of the answers. The more specific and narrowly defined the questions, the less likely they are to be ambiguous to the examinee. This procedure should result in more uniform comprehension and performance of the assigned task, and hence in the increased reliability of the instrument and scoring. It also helps insure better coverage of the domain of objectives.

Instrument Validity

The number of questions on the test influences validity, as well as reliability (see Chapter Eleven). It has been suggested that the first step in developing an achievement test is to summarize the instructional objectives in the form of a table of specifications. As commonly constructed, an essay test contains a small number of items; thus, the sampling of desired behaviors represented in the table of specifications will be limited, and the test will suffer from lowered validity—specifically, decreased content validity. The limited sampling affects not only the behavior measured, but also coverage of subject matter. Stanley (1964) has summarized studies showing that an essay exam elicits about half the knowledge an individual possesses about a particular topic, but requires twice as much time as a short-answer test.

There is another sense in which the validity of an essay test may be questioned. Theoretically, the essay test allows the examinee to construct a creative, organized, unique, and integrated communication. Very frequently, however, he spends most of his time simply recalling and assembling information, rather than integrating it. The behavior elicited by the test, then, is not that hoped for by the instructor or dictated by the table of specifications. Obviously, validity suffers in a situation such as this. Again, one way to handle the problem is to increase the number of items on the test.

SCORING ESSAY TESTS

Most instructors would agree that the scoring of essay items and tests is among the most time-consuming and frustrating tasks associated with conscientious classroom measurement. Instructors are frequently unwilling to set aside the large chunks of time necessary to score a stack of "blue books" carefully. It almost goes without saying that if reliable scoring is to be accomplished an instructor must expend considerable time and effort.

Before turning to specific methods of scoring, several general comments are in order. First, it is critical that the instructor prepare in advance a detailed "ideal" answer. This answer will serve as the criterion by which each student's answer will be judged. If this is not done, the results could be disastrous. The subjectivity of the instructor could seriously inhibit consistent scoring, and it is also possible that student responses might dictate correct answers. Second, it is generally recommended that student papers be scored anonymously, and that all the answers to a given item be scored at one time, rather than grading each student's total test separately.

The mechanics of scoring generally take one of two forms.

Rating Methods

The rating method involves evaluating a number of categories, generally less than ten. Qualitative judgments are then made within categories. In general, this method emphasizes the totality of the response and is used when the instructor is focusing on expression rather than content. Rating methods are generally efficient, but their reliabilities are very much tied to the number of categories and subdivisions within categories. The categories chosen will usually be determined by the "ideal" answer constructed by the instructor. Another useful approach is to use a standard set of categories, particularly if one's primary interest is in evaluating English composition. A rating method found useful by Paul Diederich in his research on writing ability, and by many classroom teachers, is presented in Table 6.1. This scale weighs organization 50 percent, style 30 percent, and mechanics 20 percent. By using appropriate, if arbitrary, multiplications, the 40-point

TABLE 6.1 Diederich's Scale for Grading English Composition

1 = Poor	2 = Weak	3 = Average	4 = Good	5 = Excellent

Quality and development of ideas	1 2 3 4 5		
Organization, relevance, movement	1 2 3 4 5	_____× 5 =_____	
		Subtotal	
Style, flavor, individuality	1 2 3 4 5		
Wording and phrasing	1 2 3 4 5	_____× 3 =_____	
		Subtotal	
Grammar, sentence structure	1 2 3 4 5		
Punctuation	1 2 3 4 5		
Spelling	1 2 3 4 5		
Manuscript form, legibility	1 2 3 4 5	_____× 1 =_____	
		Subtotal	
		Total grade _____%	

Source: Adapted from A. Jewett and C. E. Bish, eds., *Improving English composition.* Washington: National Education Association, 1965. Reprinted by permission of the National Education Association.

scale translates into a 100-point scale. Such a translation is useful if an instructor is disposed or required to report percentage grades.

Analytic Method

The analytic—or, as Remmers, Gage, and Rummel (1965, p. 229) call it, the Checklist Point Score—method involves partitioning the "ideal" response into a series of points or features, each of which is specifically defined. It is a scoring technique particularly useful if the content is to be emphasized over expression. Each element in the answer is identified and a credit value attached to it. If possible, the instructor's table of specifications should be used as a guide for determining credits.

As an illustration of this method, consider the following restricted-response question: "What are the principal reasons why research in the social sciences has not progressed as far as has that in the biological and physical sciences?" The instructor's ideal answer might be: "Since the social scientist is himself part of what he is attempting to study, he cannot achieve the objectivity possible in the more precise sciences. Further, the conclusions he reaches frequently run counter to deeply held prejudices and are therefore unacceptable. Feeling that many of the social affairs of men are not susceptible to scientific study, people have been less willing to subsidize social research than medicine, for example. Finally, the scientific study of nature has a much longer history than the scientific study of man. This history has provided a much larger body of data and theory from which to progress."

The essential elements in this ideal answer are identified and quantitative weights are assigned to each. The checklist/point-score sheet might look something like this:

Element of Answer	Possible Points
1. Scientist part of his subject	2
2. Prejudice	3
3. Lack of financial support	2
4. Short history	1
5. Small body of facts and theory	1
6. Organization	1
7. Language usage	1

This approach to scoring has several advantages, as noted by Ahmann and Glock (1963). An analysis of the instructor's ideal response quite frequently reveals that the original question needs to be recast in order to elicit the desired response, which may result in a readjustment of time limits. A final advantage of the checklist point score method is its reliability. If used conscientiously, the analytic method can yield consistent scores on restricted-response essay items for different graders.

Many of the suggestions for using essay items discussed in this chapter, as well as other recommendations by measurement authorities, are summarized in Table 6.2. All are self-explanatory with the exception of number 8. Testing experts generally recommend against the use of optional questions. Their use results in essay tests that measure what the student knows, rather than what he doesn't know. If a test is to provide useful information about learning outcomes, negative as well as positive evidence should be gathered. We are emphasizing here the diagnostic use of essay tests. There may be situations in which it is legitimate to allow a student to select the questions he will answer. Such a situation might be a statewide testing program with little control of the curriculum, in which an optional choice would probably constitute a fairer testing practice. But in a classroom testing situation, allowing a choice of questions is generally not recommended.

Scoring Essay Items for Affective Outcomes

The extended-response essay item may be used to examine a variety of affective outcomes. The wealth of material provided by responses to problematic situations may be subjected to a content analysis. Recurring themes in the essays of individuals or whole classes may be related to attitudes toward subject matter or the learning environment. Whether or not a given teacher wishes to investigate changes in attitudes will, of course, depend on his particular instructional objectives.

TABLE 6.2 Suggestions for Constructing, Evaluating, and Using Essay Exams

1. Limit the problem which the question poses so that it will have an unequivocal meaning to most students.
2. Use words which will convey clear meaning to the student.
3. Prepare enough questions to sample the material of the course broadly, within a reasonable time limit.
4. Use an essay question for the purposes it best serves, i.e., organization, handling complicated ideas, and writing.
5. Prepare questions which require considerable thought, but which can be answered in relatively few words.
6. Determine in advance how much weight will be accorded each of the various elements expected in a complete answer.
7. Without knowledge of students' names, score each question for all students. Use several scores and scorers if possible.
8. Require all students to answer all questions on the test.
9. Write questions about materials immediately germane to the course.
10. Study past questions to determine how students performed.
11. Make gross judgments of the relative excellence of answers as a first step in grading.
12. Word a question as simply as possible in order to make the task clear.
13. Do *not* judge papers on the basis of external factors unless they have been clearly stipulated.
14. Do *not* make a generalized estimate of an entire paper's worth.
15. Do *not* construct a test consisting of only one question.

Source: Adapted with permission from *Testing Bulletin No. 1*, Essay tests: General considerations. Published by the Office of Evaluation Services, Michigan State University, 1971.

Sims (1948) has suggested that a student's interests and values may more strongly influence his response to an essay question than does the question itself. Clinical psychologists have, of course, long used the "free-response mode" to gain insights into personality dynamics. The main difficulty in using the essay in this fashion involves the enormous amount of effort required to standardize procedures. As an exploratory technique, it has a great deal to recommend it.

Scoring Essays by Computer

Although it may sound like a flirtation with science fiction, claims are being made for the computer as an instrument capable of effective essay scoring. Ellis Page (1966) has spearheaded the movement for computer applications. He has demonstrated that such central traits of writing as ideas, organization, style, mechanics, and even creativity may be as accurately assessed by computer as by the expert English teacher. Although moderate agreement has been shown between computer- and human-scored essays, the relationship is not strong enough to justify complete acceptance of this application of technology.

SUGGESTED READINGS

Ahmann, J. S., and Glock, M. D. *Evaluating pupil growth*, 4th ed. Boston: Allyn and Bacon, 1971. Chapter 5, "Preparing Essay Achievement Tests," is a very practical, teacher-oriented presentation of material related to the development and use of essay tests.

Coffman, W. E. Essay examinations. In *Educational measurement*, 2nd ed., ed. R. L. Thorndike. Washington: American Council on Education. This 32-page chapter contains the most recent, comprehensive, and integrated survey of the research and practice of essay testing.

Ebel, R. L. *Essentials of educational measurement.* Englewood Cliffs, N.J.: Prentice-Hall, 1972. In Chapter 6 Professor Ebel, one of the foremost authorities in the field of educational measurement, describes the salient characteristics and uses of essay tests. He discusses both the similarities and differences between essay and objective testing.

Godshalk, F. I.; Swineford, Frances; and Coffman, W. E. *The measurement of writing ability.* New York: College Entrance Examination Board, 1966.

Green, J. A. *Teacher-made tests.* New York: Harper & Row, 1963. Chapter 5 is a brief overview of essay-test construction and scoring.

Stalnaker, J. M. The Essay Type of Examination. In *Educational measurement*, ed. E. F. Lindquist. Washington: American Council on Education, 1951. Chapter 13 is one of the most comprehensive discussions available on essay testing.

Stanley, J. C. *Measurement in today's schools,* 4th ed. Englewood Cliffs, N.J.: Prentice-Hall, 1964. Chapter 8, in addition to offering very useful suggestions for constructing essay tests, summarizes many significant studies.

7

GENERAL CONSIDERATIONS IN DEVELOPING MEASURES OF AFFECTIVE LEARNING OUTCOMES

SUMMARY PREVIEW STATEMENTS

1. Attitudes, values, interests, and other affective characteristics are learned in the classroom.

2. It is important for teachers to be concerned with affective learning outcomes, which influence the student's:
   a. Eventual ability to participate effectively in society.
   b. Development of a healthy personality.
   c. Occupational and vocational satisfaction.
   d. Learning.

3. Among the most pervasive affective variables are attitudes. These predispositions to act or respond in particular ways have the following characteristics:
   a. A range of degrees of "favorableness."
   b. A range of intensity.
   c. Ability to be learned.
   d. Emphases on a variety of social objects.
   e. A relatively high degree of stability.
   f. Varying degrees of interrelatedness.
   g. Variability in the ease with which they can be aroused.

4. There is a wide range of verbal and nonverbal measures of affective variables, among them:
   a. Amount of time, money, and energy spent on a particular activity.
   b. Formal verbal responses to such scales as the semantic differential, Likert, and Thurstone scales.
   c. Reaction time.
   d. Amount of knowledge about a particular referent.
   e. Examination of personal documents.
   f. Sociometric measures.

    g. Projective techniques.

    h. Observational and performance measures.

    i. Physiological measures.

    j. Memory measures.

5. Among the many problems associated with assessing affective learning outcomes are:

    a. Teachers' and administrators' reluctance to consider affective variables.

    b. Lack of teacher time to develop measures.

    c. Lack of faith that we can measure affective outcomes.

    d. The artificiality of the measures of affective variables.

    e. Students' reluctance to reveal their true feelings.

    f. The instability of some affective outcomes.

    g. The influence of "social desirability" on responses to inventories.

    h. The fakability of many instruments.

    i. Semantic difficulties in communicating about affective variables.

    j. Lack of knowledge about available measures and techniques.

    k. Distortion of responses to certain kinds of instruments due to the influence of response sets and styles.

    l. Difficulties in establishing the validity of affective measures.

6. In building verbal measures of affective variables, the developer should use statements that are:

    a. Couched in the present tense.

    b. Nonfactual.

    c. Singularly relevant to the object.

    d. Representative of a wide range of feelings.

    e. Simple, clear, direct, and short.

A definite, strong, and pervasive evolutionary change is taking place in education. This upheaval involves what were described in Chapter Three as affective learning outcomes. Its impact is evident in the type and extent of research on affective outcomes published in the professional journals the papers presented and discussed at professional educational and research meetings, the sensitizing experiences being introduced into teacher training programs, and books on humanizing the school curriculum being published. Nearly every teacher is aware that, no matter what he does, affective learning takes place. Gagné (1965, p. 23), for example, has noted that

. . . there are many aspects of the personal interaction between a teacher and his students that do not pertain, in a strict sense, to the acquisition of skills and knowledges that typically form the content of a curriculum. These varieties of interaction include those of motivating, persuading, and the establishment of attitudes and values. The development of such human dispositions as these is of tremendous importance to education as a system of modern society. In the most comprehensive sense of the word "learning", motivations and attitudes must surely be considered to be learned.

Affective and cognitive phenomena are not separable. They develop together and influence one another (Gordon 1970). Concern with both kinds of outcomes, then, is evidence of concern for the "whole child."

THE NEED TO ASSESS AFFECTIVE OUTCOMES

There are four primary reasons why affective outcomes need to be assessed:

Affective variables influence an individual's ability to participate effectively in a democratic society. Attitudes toward institutions, practices, social groups, and the like, affect and are affected by the efforts of society to maintain itself and meet the needs of its members. If for no other reason than this, affective objectives must be considered legitimate outcomes of concern to educators (Scriven 1966; Smith 1966).

The development of skills and abilities related to the acquisition and growth of attitudes and values is necessary for a healthy and effective life. The development of rational attitudes and values is the result of intelligent examination of society's needs and those of the individual. Affective skills are necessary to the overall effective functioning of the individual in society. This observation has many implications for mental health (Jackson and Getzels 1959). The development of attitudes and values can be a rational process and is therefore amenable to modification. That affective variables can be manipulated and changed has been repeatedly demonstrated. Breer and Locke (1965) have shown that the kinds of experiences an individual has with a variety of tasks will influence the kinds of attitudes he develops. They were able to show experimentally, for example, that the experience of failure or success at a task is causally related to a variety of beliefs and values associated with the concept of achievement. Similarly, Atkinson (1958) has shown that tasks that are either too easy or too hard are less motivating than those of moderate difficulty.

Affective outcomes interact with occupational and vocational satisfaction. In maintaining himself economically, an individual must (1) relate effectively with his associates, (2) enjoy his work, (3) believe it possible to make maximal use of his abilities, and (4) feel that he is making a contribution to society. Kahl (1965) reasons that the values of mastery, activism, trust of others, and independence of family should be considered legitimate educational objectives, since they have been empirically related to socioeconomic achievement and upward mobility in our heavily industrialized society.

Affective variables influence learning. This postulate has been well documented (Lehmann 1958; Ripple 1965). The interaction of teachers' and students' affective characteristics influences progress toward the attainment of classroom goals. Ripple (1965), in summarizing research on the affective characteristics of the learning situation, concluded that the attainment of classroom objectives is facilitated by (1) a generalized feeling of warmth in the learning environment, (2) tolerance of emotional and feeling expressions on the part of students, (3) democratic group decisionmaking leading to stimulating activities, (4) the use of nonpunitive control techniques of considerable clarity and firmness, (5) reduced frustration and anxiety in learning tasks, and (6) shifting states of order based on the organization of emotions toward the achievement of goals. More specifically, Domino (1971) has experimentally demonstrated interaction between a student's achievement values, the instructor's teaching style, and the amount of, and satisfaction with, learning. If students are learning material that interests them, they are likely to develop positive attitudes toward it. Attitudes have also been shown to be related to achievement. Bassham, Murphy, and Murphy (1964) have demonstrated with a sample of sixth-grade students a relationship between positive attitudes and achievement in arithmetic.

A cautionary note needs to be added. The desire to improve, modify, adjust, expand, or in some way influence and alter attitudes and values should not obscure our primary concern with learning, not just making students feel better. Heath suggests that ". . . we need to educate youth, not just his head nor his heart. The promise of affective education is that it will stimulate us to recover the person lost among our abstractions; its danger is that it may devalue man's most promising adaptive and educable skill: a disciplined intellect" (1972, p. 371).

CHARACTERISTICS OF AFFECTIVE VARIABLES

There are, as we noted in Chapter Three, a number of levels of affective variables. Many terms have been used to describe these variables, including attitude, value, interest, opinion, belief, appreciation, and motive. Because the concept of "attitude" holds a central position in research and literature on curriculum, it will be the focus for discussion of affective variables. The observations in this chapter will draw primarily upon material on attitudes, but their implications are germane to the entire affective area.

Relationships between some of the terms used to describe affective outcomes and the various levels of the *Taxonomy of Educational Objectives* (see Chapter Three) are illustrated in Figure 7.1. It will be recalled that the degree to which a feeling concept has been internalized is the factor that unifies the Affective Domain of the *Taxonomy*. Interests are considered more transitory and therefore less fully internalized. The development of a value system that strongly controls one's behavior is a relatively lasting general characteristic of the individual and is highly internalized. In the middle range of internalization we find attitudes. They are somewhat internalized, and therefore influence behavior, but are not so rigidly inculcated that they cannot be changed.

Rokeach has defined an attitude as a . . . "relatively enduring organization of beliefs around an object or situation predisposing one to

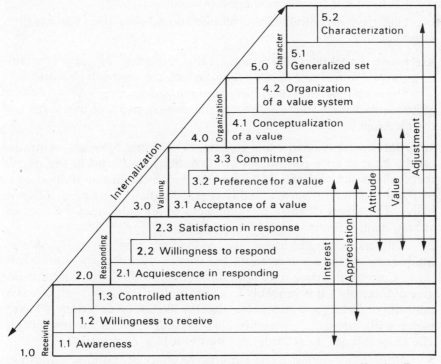

FIGURE 7.1. Range of Meanings Associated with Common Affective Terms as Defined by the *Taxonomy of Educational Objectives*

respond in some preferential manner" (1968, p. 112). The key phrases in this definition are *relatively enduring* and *organization of beliefs*. The fact that attitudes are relatively lasting suggests their potency in influencing behavior over fairly long periods of time. For example, an unfavorable attitude toward school, whether held by student or parent, has many potentially significant implications. Considering the total amount of time spent in formal educational settings, an unfavorable attitude could have serious inhibitory effects on learning. Most authorities agree that an attitude is not an irreducible element within personality, but represents a cluster of two or more interrelated elements. *A belief is a single proposition, conscious or unconscious, inferred from what a person says or does.* The content of a belief may characterize the object of belief as true or false, correct or incorrect, good or bad, or may advocate a course of action. Following are three kinds of beliefs (Rokeach 1968):

I believe that the sun rises in the east (Descriptive).

I believe this ice cream is good (Evaluative).

I believe it is desirable that children should obey their parents (Prescriptive).

Krech and Crutchfield (1948) suggest that attitudes designate favorable or unfavorable feelings about beliefs, which are themselves neutral.

Shaw and Wright (1967) have summarized six major dimensions of attitudes that have implications for the development of measures and their application:

1. *Attitudes are evaluative and give rise to motivated behavior.* Attitudes can be located on a continuum of "favorableness," and to the degree that feelings can motivate behavior they will influence an individual to respond in different ways, and different individuals to respond differentially. The object of this "favorableness of attitude" may be an individual, institution, concept, idea, or thing.

2. *Attitudes vary in intensity.* Two individuals may have favorable attitudes toward the same referent, but vary in the intensity of their feelings. Conversely, they may hold different attitudes with the same degree of intensity. It is probably true that motivational strength is tied to intensity of feeling and, therefore, that the likelihood of certain behavior varies with intensity. Intensity also has implications for instruction. The more intense an attitude, the harder it is to change it.

3. *Attitudes are learned.* The cumulative effect of training, education, childrearing, and formal and informal social interactions influences the development of attitudes.

4. *Attitudes have specific social referents.* These referents need not always be concrete objects, but may include abstract referents related, for example, to world or political issues or to theology.

5. *Attitudes represent varying degrees of interrelatedness.* Attitudes toward similar objects are more likely to be interrelated than attitudes toward dissimilar objects. Complex clusters of interrelated beliefs, e.g., toward the women's liberation movement, and its subissues of abortion, equal pay for equal work, and the like, are more difficult to change than single narrowly referenced attitudes. This dimension is sometimes referred to as *generality*.

6. *Attitudes are relatively stable and enduring.* The history of reinforcement of an attitude in a particular individual is the primary determinant of the stability of the attitude. Affective predispositions are difficult to change. The role of family and school—the primary social institutions —in developing and modifying attitudes cannot be underestimated.

One additional dimension should be added to Shaw and Wright's list:

7. *Attitudes vary in salience.* Remmers, Gage, and Rummel (1965) note that attitudes vary in the ease with which they can be aroused. *Salience* is an attitude's "proximity to the surface" of a person's mind.

APPROACHES TO THE ASSESSMENT OF AFFECTIVE OUTCOMES

Approaches to the assessment of affective variables are limited only by the creativity and motivation of the teacher. Many methods have been developed by psychologists and sociologists in their studies of human behavior, but few have been communicated to, or translated for use by, educators. One of the attendant problems, in addition to those described in the following section, involves the difference between scaling an attitude dimension and using an instrument developed in the process of scaling research to measure individual differences in attitudes. The methods of equal-appearing intervals, paired comparison, and summated ratings, for example, were developed by researchers to investigate various attributes of an attitude itself. As a kind of by-product of the scaling process, instruments useful in the assessment of many important activities and outcomes became available. Some of the methods described in this section were developed to investigate an attitude domain; others are designed as direct measures of attitudes for application to human subjects.

Cattell, Heist, and Stewart (1950), after extensive review of the literature and personal research, have identified numerous methods that can be applied in the assessment of attitudes and sentiments, or, as they refer to them, "dynamic traits." Selections from their list and some additional methods follow:

1. *Money.* The amount of money an individual spends on certain activities and courses of action is a direct reflection of his attitude and interest.

2. *Time.* The amount of time an individual devotes to certain activities is, to some extent, a reflection of his attitude toward them.

3. *Verbal expressions.* A host of assessment methods use verbal expressions of attitudes. The Thurstone, Likert, Semantic Differential, and opinionnaire methods described in the next chapter, are illustrative. Deri *et al.* (1948) have identified six types of questionnaires commonly used in attitude measurement: preference, stereotype, situational, social distance, opinions, and self-rating. The interview, either free-response or structured, might also be placed in this category.

4. *Measures of attention/distraction.* Records of the length of time an individual attends to a stimulus, or a ranking of stimuli (e.g., pictorial) according to responsiveness to them, could profitably be used as measures of attitudes. Failure to respond to certain stimuli is also meaningful behavior.

5. *Fund of information.* The amount or type of information an individual possesses about a certain object, individual, or issue is to some extent a reflection of his attitude.

6. *Speed of decision (reaction time).* It may be that decisions are made more quickly about questions on which the subject has the strongest convictions.

7. *Written expressions (personal documents).* Analysis of such documents as biographies, diaries, records, letters, autobiographies, journals, and compositions can be very revealing of an individual's attitudes. A *personal document* has been defined by Allport (1942) as any self-revealing record that intentionally or unintentionally yields information about the structure, dynamics, and functioning of the author's mental life.

8. *Sociometric measures.* Analysis of friendship choices, social distances, preferences, and the general social structure of a classroom can be very informative about attitudes. Some consideration will be given to these methods in Chapter Sixteen.

9. *Misperception/apperception methods.* Provided with ambiguous stimuli, an individual may be tempted to perceive them in accordance with his own interests, attitudes, and wishes. A great many *projective techniques* have been based on this assumption.

10. *Activity level methods.* There are a number of measures of the individual's general excitement level in response to a stimulus, among them (a) fluency (amount written), (b) speed of reading, and (c) work-endurance.

11. *Observations.* The use of standardized reports systemically gathered by trained recorders operating within the limits of an explicitly stated

frame of reference has provided extremely valuable data on attitudes *per se* and on the operation of these attitudes within the individual. The use of categorical observational systems will be considered in Chapter Sixteen. (See also Amidon and Hough 1967.)

12. *Specific performances and behaviors.* An individual's behavior can illustrate his attitudes and their influences. It is argued by some that behavioral measures are by far the most valid. The indirect methods we commonly use, however, can provide valid data if reasonable precautions are taken and stringent criteria employed during the developmental stages. Webb *et al.* (1966) have written an extremely valuable reference work with examples of behavioral measures and observational methods.

13. *Physiological measures.* The use of autonomic and metabolic measures can provide useful data in controlled situations. Psychogalvanic response, pulse rate, muscle tension and pressure, and metabolic rate are some of the procedures employed.

14. *Memory measures.* Instructing an individual to learn given material, varying the controversial nature of the content, introducing an unrelated activity to distract the subject, and then asking him to recall all or part of the original material is one approach to the use of memory as an instrument of attitude assessment. The selective operation of memory in reminiscence, dream, or fantasy may also be analyzed.

PROBLEM AREAS IN SCALE DEVELOPMENT AND APPLICATION

A number of factors—both characteristic teacher and technical problems—have inhibited the development and use of affective measures in the classroom.

Reluctance to Consider Affective Variables

Many teachers are reluctant to become involved in teaching and evaluating affective objectives. Some feel that these learning outcomes are of minor importance or that this is an area in which education has no business. Admittedly, affective objectives can prove to be a source of controversy, particularly in this age of parental involvement and concern with school programs. But the conscious refusal to address affective objectives directly represents an affective stance in itself. It is becoming increasingly difficult to maintain a value-free posture in contemporary society. By now the reader must agree that affective and cognitive outcomes are equally important and deserve equal treatment and time.

Lack of Time

The harried classroom teacher frequently complains that he has insufficient time to develop and apply adequate assessment procedures. Affective assessment is invariably the first type to be shortchanged. It is a matter of priorities. Time must be found to consider these important variables. Some time may justifiably be stolen from instructional activities because of the particularly intimate association between teaching for values and testing for them.

Lack of Faith

Disbelief that paper-and-pencil inventories and scales can measure variables related to meaningful behaviors is difficult to overcome. Evidence in support of the contention that measured attitudes do relate to important school outcomes was cited at the beginning of this chapter.

Artificiality of the Situation

The problem of artificiality relates to the larger problem of validity. To ask an individual what he would do in a given situation and then assume that he would in fact do so if the opportunity presented itself is somewhat artificial. The fact that considerable reliance is often placed on *inference* in assessing affective outcomes must be accepted, but there remains the question of the relation of verbalized and actual behavior. All possible efforts must be made to insure that the relationship is as strong as possible.

It might be worthwhile to note two of the classic studies cited in support of the conclusion that the artificiality of attitude measures precludes valid assessment. Corey (1937) found a near-zero correlation between professed attitudes toward cheating and actual cheating on a series of classroom examinations. By allowing students to correct their own papers after the teacher had secretly copied and scored them, a cheating behavior measure was obtained. It was noted, however, that positive attitudes toward cheating were more prevalent on unsigned than signed questionnaires. La Piere (1934) traveled around the United States with two well-dressed Oriental companions and visited several hundred hotels and restaurants. Only once were they refused service. When a mail survey was conducted several months later, over 90 percent of the respondents stated categorically that they would not serve Chinese. The authors concluded that general appearance, neatness, cleanliness, and quality clothing and luggage were more influential than physical characteristics. Does the foregoing suggest that we should discount attitudes and values? No indeed! It does mean that great care needs to be exercised in assessing such variables. That an individual is willing to respond to an inventory has some meaning. The less person-ally controversial or threatening the attitude assessed, the greater the likelihood of a valid response.

Public vs. Private Attitudes

The soundest approach to the interpretation of self-report state-ments on affective measures is to accept them as public declarations, rather than reflections of typical or private characteristics. Context plays an important part in determining the validity of self-reports. The women's movement, auto styles, men's clothing, and political affairs are relatively nonthreatening general topics. But when an individual is pressed to make specific revelations about his attitudes to his wife's independence, relations with minority-group members, or candidates in the last election, he is more likely to attempt to conceal his true feelings. Many of the affective variables dealt with in the classroom setting, however, are of the less personally threatening variety, and therefore lend themselves more readily to assessment.

Stability of Affective Outcomes

Affective characteristics generally maintain themselves over a long period of time. Kelly (1955) has shown that test-retest reliabilities of economic and political values are as high at .50 over a twenty-year period. Stability decreases as the referent becomes more and more specific. In Kelly's study, for example, it was found that attitudes to-ward marriage were quite unstable.

Lack of Knowledge of Techniques

Lack of familiarity with methods that can be employed to measure affective outcomes obviously inhibits any assessment program. Most teacher-training programs fail to devote any systematic attention to the specification or measurement of affective outcomes. Even test and measurement classes devote only minimal time to the topic. Little wonder, then, that teachers in the field pay slight attention to formal measurement of affective variables. Perhaps they are adequately aware of the affective information they are collecting informally.

Problems of Semantics

The specification of objectives and the development of items for instruments require careful consideration of the meanings of words. Reading level, for example, needs to be considered.

Fakability

Depending upon the way in which the data are to be used, a given respondent may desire to distort inventory results and present an image of himself he believes will be to his advantage. Unconscious distortion also may take place, of course. Faking is most likely to occur on personality and interest inventories that are being used for employee selection. That an inventory *can* be faked does not, however, imply that it will be faked. And faked information is in itself revealing in that it communicates how a person thinks it most desirable to appear.

Social Desirability

One type of faking involves the attempt of an examinee to present a socially acceptable image of himself. This type of distortion might be fairly prevalent in a classroom situation, due to a student's desire to please the teacher or tell him what the student thinks he wants to hear. Edwards (1957b) and Crowne and Marlowe (1960, 1964) have conducted considerable research on the influence of social desirability on self-report inventory scores. They have developed scales that can be used to assess the general tendency of an individual to present a socially desirable picture of himself. These scales may be used during the development of an affective inventory to control for social desirability. By eliminating those items that correlate with the social desirability measure, some degree of control can be exercised. It might also be possible to obtain from a group of judges indications of the social desirability of the items or choices being presented, and to select all the items that fall within a relatively narrow range of social desirability or to match alternatives for equal social desirability.

Response Sets and Styles

The use of certain fixed categories of responses, e.g., "yes," "agree," and "like" may introduce the possibility of response biases. Certain individuals, when in doubt, tend to choose the *agree* category irrespective of the content of the items. This phenomenon obviously distorts the meaning of the scores. Reviews of the relevant research by Cronbach (1946, 1950) and Block (1965) suggest that the forced-choice format can be employed to reduce response sets when fixed-response items or instruments are used.

Scale Validation Procedures

The following five methods may be employed in validating effective measures. Validating procedures will be described in more detail in

Chapter Eleven. In addition Ryans (1957) has published an excellent summary of designs that may be employed in validating inventories.

1. *Content validation.* The usual procedure for validating affective measures is to "build in validity." It is assumed that the domain or area to be assessed has been well described, ideally in behavioral terms. If scale items are tied very closely to behavioral objectives, some measure of validity can be assured.

2. *Contrasted groups.* Groups known or assumed to differ with regard to the affective variable are used to examine item responses or total scores on the instrument. Thurstone and Chave (1929), for example, contrasted churchgoers and nonchurchgoers in validating their scale measuring attitudes toward the church. A more contemporary example can be found in the work of Moore and Sutman (1970), who have reported the development and validation of an instrument to assess high-school students' attitudes toward science. The instrument was composed of 60 items and used a four-point rating scale (1 = agree strongly—4 = disagree strongly). Following are four sample items:

Anything we need to know can be found out through science.

Science is so difficult that only highly trained scientists can understand it.

Scientists discover laws which tell us exactly what is going on in nature.

The products of scientific work are mainly useful to scientists, they are not useful to the average person.

To validate the scale, the researchers developed instructional lessons aimed at *changing the attitudes of the students.* Experimental and control (regular science instruction) groups were shown to differ in the expected direction after treatment.

3. *Correlations with self-reported behaviors.* The investigator gathers attitude scores and then surveys the respondents' past behavior verifying these attitudes. Differing descriptions of behavior should correspond to differing scores if the instrument has validity.

4. *Expert judgments.* A group of experts could be polled regarding which responses indicate which attitudes. A high index of agreement would be required.

5. *Correlations with actual behavior.* It is possible, particularly through observation, to discern how different students react in different situations. One then needs to determine whether this behavior is in line with the students' expressed attitudes or preferences. One educational researcher, for example, has demonstrated the feasibility of using empirical keying and validation procedures traditionally associated with aptitude tests to develop a predictive academic interest inventory for use with college freshmen. The procedure involves administering a pool of

items theoretically related to a variable of concern, in this case academic field of interest upon entering school. After the passage of considerable time (e.g., two years), a student's major field of study is correlated with his responses to the inventory items previously administered. This approach to interest inventory development has the distinct advantage of increasing, and to some extent assuring, validity. The inventory items are correlated with actual behavior. This approach is much more likely to yield a valid instrument than is merely asking a student to respond to such a statement as "I think teaching would appeal to me" and assuming validity.

WRITING ITEMS FOR SELF–REPORT AFFECTIVE MEASURES

General guidelines and criteria are crucial to the development of statements for affective measures. Obviously, the statements themselves are of critical importance. All the sophisticated analytic techniques in the world will not overcome an inferior item that does not communicate. Edwards (1957a, b) has provided a list of informal criteria for development and editing activities:[1]

1. Avoid statements that refer to the past rather than to the present.

2. Avoid statements that are factual or capable of being interpreted as factual.

3. Avoid statements that may be interpreted in more than one way.

4. Avoid statements that are irrelevant to the psychological object under consideration.

5. Avoid statements that are likely to be endorsed by almost everyone or by almost no one.

6. Select statements that are believed to cover the entire range of the affective scale of interest.

7. Keep the language of the statements simple, clear, and direct.

8. Statements should be short, rarely exceeding 20 words.

9. Each statement should contain only one complete thought.

10. Statements containing universals such as *all, always, none,* and *never* often introduce ambiguity and should be avoided.

11. Words such as *only, just, merely,* and others of a similar nature should be used with care and moderation in writing statements.

12. Whenever possible, statements should be in the form of simple sentences rather than in the form of compound or complex sentences.

---

13. Avoid the use of words that may not be understood by those who are to be given the completed scale.

14. Avoid the use of double negatives.

Other guidelines, with examples, can be found in an article by Wang (1932) and a book by Payne (1951).

SUGGESTED READINGS

Cohen, A. R. *Attitude change and social influence.* New York: Basic Books, 1964.

Fishbein, M. *Readings in attitude theory and measurement.* New York: John Wiley, 1967.

Greenwald, A. G.; Brock, T. C.; and Ostrom, T. M., eds. *Psychological foundations of attitudes.* New York: Academic Press, 1968.

Insko, C. A. *Theories of attitude change.* New York: Appleton-Century-Crofts, 1967.

Jahoda, Marie, and Warren, N., eds. *Attitudes.* Baltimore: Penguin Books, 1966.

Kiesler, C. A.; Collins, B. E.; and Miller, N. *Attitude change: A critical analysis of theoretical approaches.* New York: John Wiley, 1969.

Malec, M. A., ed. *Attitude change.* Chicago: Markham, 1971.

Rosenberg, M. J.; Hovland, C. I.; McGuire, W. J.; Abelson, R. P.; and Brehm, J. W. *Attitude organization and change: An analysis of consistency among attitude components.* New Haven: Yale University Press, 1960.

Suedfeld, P., ed. *Attitude change: The competing views.* Chicago: Aldine-Atherton, 1971.

Summers, G. F., ed. *Attitude measurement.* Chicago: Rand McNally, 1970.

Triandis, H. C. *Attitude and attitude change.* New York: John Wiley, 1971.

Wagner, R. W., and Sherwood, J. J. *The study of attitude change.* Belmont, Cal.: Brooks/Cole, 1969.

8

THE DEVELOPMENT OF SELF–REPORT AFFECTIVE ITEMS AND INVENTORIES

SUMMARY PREVIEW STATEMENTS

1. Attitude statements and inventories can be developed from free-response questions submitted to students.

2. Most methods of developing affective measures initially involve the identification of a series of statements reflecting gradations of favorableness or affect, from which a representative set is selected.

3. Forced-choice methods require selection between two or more alternatives that reflect either (a) gradations of favorableness or (b) different content, actions, or decisions that can be correlated with variations in feelings.

4. Forced-choice methods tend to produce instruments that yield more uniform distributions of scores and are efficient, easily scored, objective, reliable, and less fakable than other instruments.

5. The Affective Domain Handbook of the *Taxonomy of Educational Objectives* contains excellent suggestions on the content and format of affective measures.

6. Generalized standard scales use a uniform set of statements and scale values to assess differing objects.

7. The paired-comparison method requires a group of judges to select between pairs of statements the one that indicates the greater degree of favorableness.

8. For the paired-comparison method, scale values and distances between statements are derived from percentage data indicating the frequency with which one statement is judged more favorable than other alternatives.

9. After their final selection by the paired-comparison method is made, statements are presented to the target group. Subjects are

asked to indicate those statements with which they agree, and an average of the scale values for those statements calculated. Each subject's average represents his affective inventory score.

10. The method of equal-appearing intervals requires judges to evaluate the degree of favorableness of a series of statements on an 11-point continuum.

11. By the method of equal-appearing intervals, scale values are calculated as the median ratings (P_{50}) of each statement, and the measure of statement ambiguity is the interquartile range (I).

12. Selection of statements by the method of equal-appearing intervals is based on the desire for a range of scale values, but relatively low I values.

13. A subject's affective inventory score is an average of the scale values derived by the method of equal-appearing intervals for the statements with which he agrees.

14. The method of summated ratings employs a five-point scale (strongly agree, agree, undecided, disagree, and strongly disagree) with statements reflecting positive (favorable) or negative (unfavorable) affect.

15. By the method of summated ratings, statements are selected for the final form of the instrument that discriminate between individuals with high positive scores and those with high negative scores.

16. In developing affective measures, it is best to begin with at least three times as many items as the final form is expected to contain.

17. Judges should agree at least 80 percent of the time on whether a given statement is favorable or unfavorable.

18. In administering an affective inventory, one should urge subjects to express their initial reaction.

19. The semantic differential technique is a generalized method that uses pairs of bipolar adjectives to evaluate the connotative meanings of concepts.

20. The opinionnaire and other free-response methods may profitably be used to gather affective data.

21. Opinionnaires should be brief, relevant, comprehensive, non-threatening, and concise.

22. Content analysis is a valuable tool for examining the data gathered with an opinionnaire or the free-response method.

This chapter introduces briefly eight methods useful in constructing affective measures: (1) Corey's simplified scale development technique, (2) forced-choice selection methods, (3) Remmer's standard scales, (4) paired comparisons, (5) equal-appearing intervals, (6) summated (Likert) ratings, (7) the semantic differential technique, and (8) free-response or opinionnaire procedures. These methods have primarily been derived from the literature of psychology, particularly social psychology, with many adaptations to educational settings. This chapter focuses on methods employed in scaling and measuring attitudes. The techniques to be described are, however, flexible enough to assess a variety of affective outcomes.

COREY'S SIMPLIFIED SCALE CONSTRUCTION TECHNIQUE

Three of the scale construction techniques to be described later in this chapter (paired comparisons, equal-appearing intervals, and summated ratings) require the expenditure of considerable time and energy, both at a premium for the classroom teacher. Corey (1943) has described a relatively efficient method for constructing an attitude scale. The test development process itself can serve as a learning experience for the students and teacher. Its steps are as follows:

1. *Collect a pool of statements.* Each student, for example, might be asked to write three or four statements representing various attitudes toward cheating. Illustrative statements might be:

> Cheating is as bad as stealing.
> If a test isn't fair, cheating is all right.
> I won't copy, but I often let someone else look at my paper.
> A little cheating on daily tests doesn't hurt.

2. *Select the best statements.* Using the criteria for constructing attitude statements described in Chapter Seven, about 50 items might be culled from the initial pool of 100 or 150 statements. Duplicates are eliminated, as are statements that are obviously ambiguous to the teacher or students. The students, for example, might be asked to indicate all those statements on the master list that represent opinions favoring cheating (with a plus sign) and those representing negative opinions about cheating (with a minus sign). An agreement criterion of 80 percent is suggested; a show of hands is an efficient way to gather these data.

3. *Administer the inventory.* The following directions might be used:

> Directions: This is not a test in the sense that any particular statement is right or wrong. All these sentences represent opinions that some people hold about cheating on tests. Indicate whether you agree or disagree with the statements by putting a plus sign before all those with which you agree and a minus sign before those with

which you disagree. If you are uncertain, use a question mark. After you have gone through the entire list, go back and draw a circle around the plus signs next to the statements with which you agree very strongly, and a circle around the minus signs if you disagree very strongly.

The inventory may be duplicated and distributed or administered orally. Discussion should be discouraged. Anonymous administration is preferable.

4. *Score the inventory.* Scoring may be accomplished by either teacher or student. The first step involves identifying those statements that were judged by the entire group (in Step 2) as *favoring classroom cheating.* Next, the following score values are applied: a plus sign with a circle receives five points, a plus sign alone four points, a question mark three points, a minus sign two points, and a minus sign with a circle one point. Thus, when a person disagrees very strongly with a statement that favors classroom cheating, he earns one point; if he agrees very strongly with the same statement, he gets five points.

Those statements that express *opposition to cheating* are scored in the opposite fashion: a plus sign with a circle receives one point, a plus sign alone two points, a question mark three points, a minus sign four points, and minus sign with a circle five points. In other words, a student who disagrees very strongly with a statement that opposes cheating actually has a very favorable attitude toward such a practice.

If the inventory contains 50 items, the maximum score possible is 250, which indicates a favorable attitude. The minimum score possible is 50, and an indifference score is in the neighborhood of 150.

FORCED–CHOICE SELECTION METHODS

A forced-choice item (Travers 1951) requires the respondent to select among choices that differ in content, rather than degree of favorableness or intensity. The examinee is directed to indicate which of several actions, contents, or objects is most characteristic of him. The number of choices usually ranges from two to four. The format may resemble that of a multiple-choice item—a stem and several alternatives—or may be a description of a situation with associated questions, or a pair of choice-statements. When used in a two-choice situation with systematically varying content, the forced-choice technique is similar to the paired-comparison method to be described later in the chapter, with the difference that an analysis of scale values is not undertaken. The score is simply the number of times a particular choice is made from a large number of possible choices. One or more of the choices may be scored on a particular scale. Guilford (1954) and others claim as the primary advantages of the forced-choice pattern that it:

1.   Minimizes the subjective element in judgment.

2.   Reduces the respondent's ability to produce a desired outcome and is therefore less fakable.

3.   Produces a better distribution and spread of scores with less piling up and skewness.

4.   Is quick, efficient, objective, and lends itself to machine-scoring.

5.   Produces scores easily analyzed with respect to reliability and validity.

The forced-choice format has been widely adopted in the construction of personality inventories. The *Kuder Preference Record-Personal, Strong Vocational Interest Blank,* and *Edwards Personal Preference Schedule* are representative applications of the method. (See Zavala 1965 for an informative review of the research on forced-choice methodology.)

This method has many possibilities for use in classroom measurement. Two examples will illustrate possible applications. The first is from a scale, the *Personal VEMS* test (*VEMS* stands for Values: Ethical, Moral, and Social), developed by Gardner and Thompson (1963) in their investigation of social values governing interpersonal relations among adolescent youth and their teachers. The VEMS requires a verbal response indicating the action that ought to be taken when confronting certain problem situations. Each decision implies the selection of one value over another. The values in question are loyalty, honesty, truthfulness, kindness, generosity, conformity, and impunitiveness. In an effort to encourage the respondent to become ego-involved in the situation, the respondent is asked in some items to supply the name of his best friend as a participant in the problem situation. Following are two sample items:

> You have just taken an important true-false examination in English. Your teacher has asked you to exchange papers so that you can grade each other's papers as she reads the answers aloud. You exchange papers with your best friend _____ who is seated near you. He slips you a note which reads, "Please change a few of my answers when they are incorrect. I *have* to get a passing mark on this test!"
>
> WHAT DO YOU THINK YOU *OUGHT* TO DO?
>
> _____A. Help your friend so that he will get a passing mark on the test.
>
> _____B. Mark his paper in the same way you would grade the paper of any other classmate.

In this item, alternative A is scored on the Loyalty scale, and B on the Honesty scale.

You and your classmates play a clarinet duet for the school assembly. There was much applause. Feeling rather pleased with her performance, your classmate says to a group of people you are standing with, "I guess I played it just about perfectly, didn't I?" You know that she squeaked a little on some of the high notes and that her timing was faulty in a number of instances.

WHAT DO YOU THINK YOU *OUGHT* TO DO?

_____A. Be generous and say to the person next to you, "She certainly was terrific today."

_____B. Say, "It was a good performance but not perfect. You'd better do some practicing on those high notes!"

On this item, alternative A is scored on the Generosity scale and B on the Truthfulness scale.

Farquhar and Payne (1963) have described the development of an instrument aimed at assessing relative preference for statements correlated with occupational motivation. Beginning with a set of eight alternatives describing high achievement motivation and eight describing low achievement motivation, they constructed a 64-item pair scale by combining high and low alternatives. Two sample items from the scale, the *Preferred Job Characteristics Scale,* follow:

I Prefer:
  1. A job where my opinion is valued, or
  2. A job with short working hours

I Prefer:
  1. A job which does not tie me down, or
  2. A job where I could decide how the work is to be done

In the first item, alternative 1 is the high-motivation alternative; and in the second, it is alternative 2.

ILLUSTRATIVE FORCED–CHOICE SELECTION ITEMS FOR THE AFFECTIVE DOMAIN OF THE TAXONOMY OF EDUCATIONAL OBJECTIVES

It was suggested in Chapter Three that the *Taxonomy of Educational Objectives* is a valuable source of ideas for test items. This is particularly true of ideas for affective measures, since valid and reliable materials in this area are so scarce. Items representing various levels of the Affective Domain follow. Each is keyed to a particular classification and objective in the Affective Domain Taxonomy.

1.1 Awareness

Objective: Awareness of works in literature.

Source: General Acquaintance Test in Literature (Chicago: Board of Examinations, University of Chicago, 1952), pp. 106–107.

Directions: The items in this test are arranged in sets of three, with five possible responses printed to the right of each group. For each item, blacken your Answer Sheet with the letter corresponding to the response that best completes the statement begun on the left. In no case will the same response be correct for more than one item within a single group of three. There is no objection to careful and intelligent guessing here.

1. In *Man and Superman* by Shaw (D)

2. In *The Emperor Jones* by O'Neill (B)

3. In *Winterset* by Anderson (A)

   A. the hero's father has been executed
   B. the hero had been a Pullman porter
   C. the hero is a white ruler of a South Sea island
   D. the hero finally becomes engaged to the heroine
   E. the hero is finally hanged

4. In *The Inferno* by Dante (B)

5. In *Don Quixote* by Cervantes (D)

6. In *Faust* by Goethé (A)

   A. the hero is accompanied by the devil
   B. the hero is accompanied by a poet
   C. the hero is accompanied by his father
   D. the hero is accompanied by a servant
   E. the hero is accompanied by an ambitious woman

2.3 Satisfaction in Responding

Objective: Pleasure in science activities.

Source: Adapted from *Interest Index; Test 8.2a* (Chicago: Evaluation in the Eight-Year Study, Progressive Education Association, 1939).

Directions: As you read each item below underline one of the four letters after the number of that item on the Answer Sheet.

Underline S if you feel you *do* get satisfaction from performing the activity.

Underline U if you are *uncertain* as to your reaction to performing the activity.

Underline D if you feel you *do not* get satisfaction from performing the activity.

Underline X if you have *never performed* the activity.

7. To experiment with plants to find out how various conditions of soil, water, and light affect their growth.

8. To study rock formations and to learn how they developed.

9. To visit an observatory to learn how astronomers study the stars.

10. To read about how distances to inaccessible places are measured, such as from the earth to the sun, the height of a mountain, etc.

11. To read about new scientific developments.

3.3 Commitment to a Value

Objective: Devotion to those ideas and ideals which are the foundation of democracy.

Source: Social Beliefs; Test 4.31 (Chicago: Evaluation in the Eight-Year Study, Progressive Education Association, 1944).

Directions: The statements in this test are expressions of opinions. They deal with unsettled questions, and *there are no right or wrong answers. Please express your point of view about them.* Indicate how you really feel about the issues expressed immediately after reading the statement. Do not pause too long on any one of them. Mark the Answer Sheet as follows:

A if you *agree* with the *whole statement.*

U if you are *uncertain* how you feel about the *whole statement.*

D if you *disagree* with the *whole statement.*

12. Freedom of speech should be denied all those groups and individuals that are working against democratic forms of government.

13. Negroes should not be allowed to fill positions involving leadership of white people.

14. The masses of the people have too little intelligence to vote wisely on important social issues.

4.2 Organization of a Value System

Objective: Development of dominant values.

Source: G. W. Allport, P. E. Vernon, and Gardner Lindzey, *Study of Values,* 3rd ed. (Boston: Houghton Mifflin, 1960). Copyright © 1960 by Houghton Mifflin Company. All rights reserved. Reprinted by permission of the publisher.

Directions: Each of the following situations or questions is followed by four possible attitudes or answers. Arrange these answers in the order of your personal preference by writing, in the appropriate box at the right, a score of 4, 3, 2, or 1. To the statement you prefer most give 4, to the statement that is second most attractive 3, and so on.

15. In your opinion, can a man who works in business all week best spend Sunday in
    a. trying to educate himself by reading serious books.
    b. trying to win at golf, or racing.
    c. going to an orchestral concert.
    d. hearing a really good sermon.

16. Viewing Leonardo da Vinci's picture, "The Last Supper," would you tend to think of it
    a. as expressing the highest spiritual aspirations and emotions.
    b. as one of the most priceless and irreplaceable pictures ever painted.
    c. in relation to Leonardo's versatility and its place in history.
    d. as the quintessence of harmony and design.

Comment: The profile obtained for this test is the basic datum for evaluation at 4.2. This profile consists of six fundamental values based directly upon the typology of Eduard Spranger: (1) Theoretical, (2) Economic, (3) Aesthetic, (4) Social, (5) Political, and (6) Religious.

5.1 Generalized Value Set

Objective: Respect for the worth and dignity of human beings.

Source: Problems in Human Relations Test. Cited in Paul L. Dressel and Lewis B. Mayhew, *General Education—Explorations in Evaluation* (Washington: American Council on Education, 1954), pp. 229–37. Reprinted by permission of the publisher.

17. Tom and Bob, who know each other only slightly, were double-dating two girls who were roommates. A sudden storm made it impossible to go to the beach as planned. Tom

suggested going to a movie. After making the suggestion, he realized Bob was without funds. As Tom, what would you do?
1. Pay for the movie.
2. Lend Bob money.
3. Leave it up to the girls.
*4. Get Bob to suggest something.
5. Apologize to Bob for making the suggestion.

18. Your social organization has pledged a student who is not liked by some of the members. One of your friends threatens to leave the school organization if this person is initiated. What would you do?
1. Talk to your friend.
2. Do not initiate the prospective member.
3. Get more members to support the prospective member.
*4. Vote on the prospective member.
5. Postpone the vote until the matter works itself out.

Scoring Rationale: The response marked with an asterisk is keyed to a point of view the authors of the instrument call "democratic."

GENERALIZED STANDARD SCALES

Using the equal-appearing intervals method, H. H. Remmers and his colleagues have developed a series of "standard scales." A generalized standard attitude scale is one that can be applied to any of a selected class of objects. The scale may be used to measure attitudes toward any given subject, for example, by inserting in the appropriate space the name of the subject. The statements in the scale remain the same and have the same values regardless of the subject chosen. A sample master scale developed by Remmers and Silance (1934) is presented below.[1] The scale values in parentheses following each item would not be included when the scale was duplicated for use.

A SCALE FOR MEASURING ATTITUDE TOWARD SCHOOL SUBJECTS

Form A

Directions:

Following is a list of statements about school subjects. Place a plus sign (+) before each statement with which you agree, and a minus sign (−) before each statement with which you disagree with reference to

---

[1] From H. H. Remmers and Ella Belle Silance, Generalized attitude scales. *Journal of Social Psychology* 5 (1934): 298–312. Reprinted by permission of the publisher.

each of the subjects listed at the left of the statements. Your score will in no way affect your grade in any course.

Name _____
      (You need not give your name if you prefer not to have your name
      known.)
Sex: male, female (underline one)

College subject you like best _____

College subject you like least _____

Age: ____

What occupation would you like best to follow? _____

_____

Science	English	Math	
			1. I hate this subject. (0.6)
			2. This subject is the most undesirable subject taught. (0.7)
			3. I detest this subject. (0.8)
			4. I look forward to this subject with horror. (1.0)
			5. This subject is disliked by all students. (1.3)
			6. It is a punishment for anybody to take this subject. (1.5)
			7. This subject is a waste of time. (1.6)
			8. This subject is based on "foggy" ideas. (2.1)
			9. I would not advise anyone to take this subject. (2.2)
			10. I have seen no value in this subject. (2.4)
			11. I have no desire for this subject. (2.5)

Science	English	Math	
			12. This subject reminds me of Shakespeare's play—"Much Ado About Nothing". (2.6)
			13. This subject is very dry. (2.8)
			14. This subject does not teach you to think. (2.9)
			15. I am not interested in this subject. (3.1)
			16. The minds of students are not kept active in this subject. (3.3)
			17. Mediocre students never take this subject, so it should be eliminated from schools. (3.4)
			18. I could do very well without this subject. (3.5)
			19. My parents never had this subject, so I see no merit in it. (3.6)
			20. This subject will benefit only the brighter students. (4.7)
			21. I haven't any definite like or dislike for this subject. (5.5)
			22. I am careless in my attitude toward this subject, but I would not like to see this attitude become general. (5.8)
			23. I don't believe this subject will do anybody any harm. (6.1)

Science	English	Math	
			24. This subject is a good pastime. (6.5)
			25. This subject is not a bore. (6.8)
			26. This subject saves time. (7.3)
			27. This subject is not receiving its due in public high schools. (7.6)
			28. I am willing to spend my time studying this subject. (7.7)
			29. This subject is O.K. (7.9)
			30. All lessons and all methods used in this subject are clear and definite. (8.1)
			31. This subject is a cultural subject. (8.3)
			32. All of our great men studied this subject. (8.4)
			33. This subject is a good subject. (8.5)
			34. This subject is a universal subject. (8.7)
			35. This subject teaches me to be accurate. (8.8)
			36. Any student who takes this subject is bound to be benefited. (8.9)
			37. This subject is very practical. (9.0)
			38. This subject develops good reasoning ability. (9.1)

Science	English	Math	
			39. This subject is profitable to everybody who takes it. (9.2)
			40. I really enjoy this subject. (9.4)
			41. This subject has an irresistible attraction for me. (9.6)
			42. This subject is of great value. (9.7)
			43. I love to study this subject. (9.8)
			44. I would rather study this subject than eat. (10.2)
			45. No matter what happens, this subject always comes first. (10.3)

Whereas in the Thurstone scales the statements are arranged in random order, Remmers' scales list them in order of increasing favorableness. This arrangement greatly decreases the time and labor involved in scoring without markedly affecting accuracy of measurement. The usual scoring procedure is to take the scale values for those statements with which the respondent agrees only and to summarize them in the form of a mean or median. In interpreting scores on Remmers' scale, one must remember that some error may be introduced by using the same scale values for an entire class of objects. In addition, the reported scale values were determined by post high-school and college students, although there is evidence of reasonable stability for the ordering of the statements. It is possible to shorten master scales by making a selection of statements, e.g., 20, representing various points along the continuum. The longer scale will, of course, provide better reliability.

THE PAIRED–COMPARISON METHOD

The paired-comparison method is one of the most flexible procedures for studying affective variables. The term *flexibility*, as used here, primarily involves the variety of affective learning outcomes that can be measured. The paired-comparison method can be applied in developing measures of interests, values, and attitudes. It is in the measurement of attitudes that the method has enjoyed its widest application. Basically, the method involves presenting the examinee a series of pairs of statements, practices, or whatever attitudinal object is being measured. Each statement is paired with every other statement. From each pair the respondent selects the alternative he prefers. The resulting scores, then, reveal a rank-order summary of his preferences. In addition, it is possible to determine the distances between statements. Scale values indicating the location of each statement on a favorable-unfavorable continuum can be derived. Representative statements may be selected to make up a refined attitude scale, a process that has two stages: first, statements are scaled; then this information is used to build an attitude-measuring instrument. Very refined preferential data are thereby gathered. The task can be time-consuming and tedious if a large number of statements (e.g., more than 20) are to be paired. It is advisable to use fifteen or fewer statements. Such refined data can be extremely useful in inventory development.

Rationale for the Method

The basic rationale for the paired-comparison technique is easily grasped. Suppose, in a forced-choice situation, that 80 percent of a group of students judge the study of mathematics to be more valuable than the study of English grammar. The remaining 20 percent obviously judge the study of English grammar to be more valuable. Suppose further that 55 percent—barely more than half—of the same judges perceive the study of English grammar to be more valuable than the study of American history. Logically, then, we should be justified in saying that the separation between mathematics and English grammar is considerably greater than the separation between English grammar and American history on the same scale. The scale might be termed "value of subject-matter courses," and we may then speak of distances along this scale as defined by the placement of various courses on it.

Some distances will be greater than others. The concept of comparative judgment—judgments of a "greater than" ($>$) and "less than" ($<$) variety—is implicit in this procedure. The theory and methods of comparative judgment were first described in detail and applied to psychological phenomena by Thurstone (1927a, b). Central to the paired-comparison method is the concept of *discriminal process*, which is a manifestation of an individual's reaction to a stimulus object. This reaction occurs when a subject is asked to make a judgment or evaluation of an activity, a person, an institution, or some abstract concept. Different people react in different ways to the same stimulus. Associated with each stimulus is a variety of reactions that may be represented by a number of points along a scale and are assumed to form a bell-shaped, or so-called normal, curve. Figure 8.1 illustrates the distributions of discriminal processes associated with stimulus i. The reaction to a given stimulus assumed to be aroused more frequently than any other is referred to as the *modal discriminal process*. This modal discriminal process, designated by $\bar{S}$ with a subscript, e.g., $\bar{S}_i$, is also called a *scale value*. It is the object of the paired-comparison method to allow us to derive estimates of the scale value associated with various stimuli so that a measuring instrument can be developed and applied to the assessment of affective variables.

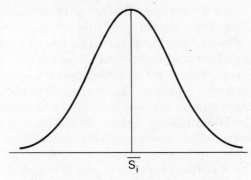

Psychological Continuum

FIGURE 8.1. Theoretical Normal Distribution of Discriminal Processes Evoked by Stimulus i about the Modal Discriminal Process S_i

An Illustrative Problem

Let us assume that we are interested in developing a measure of attitudes toward guessing on multiple-choice tests. If such an instrument were developed, we could perhaps use it to devise a correction-for-guessing formula that would yield more reliable and perhaps more valid scores on objective tests. It may also be interesting to know whether reliable individual differences in strength of attitudes toward guessing do exist. Based on the criteria for developing attitude statements described in Chapter Seven, seven statements describing a range of attitude from highly unfavorable (or cautious) behavior to favorable (or less cautious) behavior were written. These seven statements, arranged in a hypothetical order from most to least tendency to guess, are as follows:

1. Guessing raises my score more than it reduces it.
2. If I *can't* eliminate any choices in a question, I guess anyway.

3. If I could eliminate two out of five choices in a question, I would guess.

4. I guess more than most people on a difficult test.

5. If I could only eliminate one out of five choices in a question, I would omit it.

6. If I could eliminate three out of five choices in a question, I would not guess between the other two choices.

7. In general, I lose more points by guessing than I gain.[2]

Before we can administer these statements to individuals or groups of individuals, we must determine whether they in fact reflect varying degrees of favorableness toward guessing on multiple-choice tests. Scale values must be assigned to them. The law of comparative judgment, used in conjunction with the paired-comparison method, allows us to determine scale values by comparing every statement to every other statement in a set. A judgment on each pair of statements is made by a group of judges similar to those individuals to whom the resulting instrument will be administered. About 50 judges will usually suffice. Since each statement will be compared with every other statement, we will be asking the judges to make a total of 21 independent comparisons. The following expression can be used to determine the number of possible pairs in a group of n stimuli:

$$\text{Number of independent paired comparisons} = \frac{n(n-1)}{2}$$

where n = the number of stimuli or statements in a set.

We will illustrate the paired-comparison method with some hypothetical data from a group of 50 judges, all graduate students in education and psychology, to whom the following instructions were given:

> The following pairs of statements reflect either positive or negative attitudes toward the practice of *GUESSING ON MULTIPLE-CHOICE TESTS WHEN THERE IS A PENALTY FOR WRONG ANSWERS.*
>
> You are to read each pair and judge which of the statements, "1" or "2," is *MORE FAVORABLE* toward guessing (under penalty conditions). Indicate your selection on your answer sheet by marking space 1 for "Statement 1" or space 2 for

---

[2] Adapted from Barrie Wellens, *Validation of a guessing-tendency measure for predicting guessing behavior beyond the chance level on multiple-choice tests.* Unpublished doctoral dissertation, Syracuse University, 1957. Reprinted by permission of the author.

"Statement 2" for EACH PAIR. For example, if "b" is more favorable than "a" you would mark space 2.

Try to judge each pair of statements independently of all the other pairs. Do *NOT* respond in terms of your own agreement or disagreement with the statements—respond in terms of your judgment of which statement in each pair is more favorable toward guessing on a multiple-choice test with a penalty for wrong answers.

DO NOT OMIT ANY PAIRS.

Note that the judges are specifically instructed *not* to express their own attitudes toward the statements. We are interested at this point only in determining whether the set of statements in fact forms a scale. We are, however, tentatively, assuming a relatively unidimensional attitude domain. If we can accept our original set of statements, or can select an acceptable subset, we will administer the resulting scale to elicit individual attitudes. A standard IBM answer sheet is used to record the judges' choices.

Summarizing the Data

The first step in summarizing the data is to develop a frequency- or f-matrix, which describes the frequency with which each column statement is judged more favorable than each row statement. Such an f-matrix is illustrated in Table 8.1. The diagonal entries represent a

TABLE 8.1 A Frequency (f) Matrix Indicating the Frequency with Which Each Column Statement Was Judged More Favorable than a Row Statement By 50 Judges

Statement	1	2	3	4	5	6	7
1	25	21	17	19	9	6	2
2	29	25	21	18	13	8	5
3	33	29	25	20	21	14	9
4	31	32	30	25	23	17	14
5	41	37	29	27	25	21	18
6	44	42	36	33	29	25	24
7	48	45	41	36	32	26	25

comparison of each statement with itself, assumed to be n/2. Since we used 50 judges, n/2 is 25. Each frequency is then converted to a percentage, p, either by dividing each entry in Table 8.1 by 50 or by multiplying it by the reciprocal of 50 (1/50 = .02). Conversion of the frequencies in Table 8.1 to percentages is illustrated in Table 8.2.

Next, we sum the column entries in Table 8.2. It turns out in this

TABLE 8.2 A Proportion (p) Matrix (Corresponding to the f-Matrix of Table 8.1) Indicating the Proportion of Time That the Column Statement Was Judged More Favorable than a Row Statement by 50 Judges

Statement	1	2	3	4	5	6	7
1	.50	.42	.34	.38	.18	.12	.04
2	.58	.50	.42	.36	.26	.16	.10
3	.66	.58	.50	.40	.42	.28	.18
4	.62	.64	.60	.50	.46	.34	.28
5	.82	.74	.58	.54	.50	.42	.36
6	.88	.84	.72	.66	.58	.50	.48
7	.96	.90	.82	.72	.64	.52	.50
Sums	5.02	4.62	3.98	3.56	3.04	2.34	1.94

case that we guessed correctly about the ordering of the statements. This will, of course, not always be the case. It is advisable to rearrange the columns so that they are in rank order, keeping in mind that the interchange of any pair of columns requires a corresponding interchange of the pair of rows. For example, if we were to interchange columns 2 and 4, we would also interchange rows 2 and 4.

In order to obtain scale values using the law of comparative judgment, we must use a table of the normal curve. Such a table is provided in Appendix A. We convert each of the percentage entries in Table 8.2 to standard score values, z. (We ask the reader to accept on faith that this conversion is necessary.) The result of converting all p values to z values is summarized in Table 8.3. We now sum the column entries in

TABLE 8.3 A z-Matrix Giving the Normal Deviates Corresponding to the Proportions of Table 8.2

Statement	1	2	3	4	5	6	7
1	.000	−.202	−.412	−.305	−.915	−1.175	−1.751
2	.202	.000	−.202	−.358	−.643	−.994	−1.282
3	.412	.202	.000	−.253	−.202	−.583	−.915
4	.305	.358	.253	.000	−.100	−.412	−.583
5	.915	.643	.202	.100	.000	−.202	−.358
6	1.175	.994	.583	.412	.202	.000	−.050
7	1.751	1.282	.915	.583	.358	.050	.000
Sums	4.760	3.277	1.339	.179	−1.300	3.316	−4.939
Means	.680	.468	.191	.026	−.186	−.474	−.706
Mean + (.706)	1.386	1.174	.897	.732	.520	.232	.000
Rounded Means	1.4	1.2	.9	.7	.5	.2	.0

Table 8.3, and obtain a mean by dividing the sums by the total number of statements. These means are also summarized in Table 8.3. Statements with negative means are judged less favorable than those with positive scale values. By adding a constant to all the means, we can

express the entire rank ordering with positive values. The most convenient constant to add is the absolute scale value of the statement with the largest negative mean. This will make the scale value of the most unfavorable statement zero. This adjustment is reflected in the last row in Table 8.3. The adjusted means, rounded off to one significant decimal, are considered to be the attitude scale values. Scale refinement methods and techniques for checking internal consistency characteristics are described by Edwards (1957 b). To convert rounded means into a scale—say, from 0 to 100—the scale constructor should multiply each rounded mean by 100/1.4. It should be noted that the z value differences in any row between two columns represent an estimate of the difference in scale values. In Table 8.3 row 3 with columns 1 and 2, for example, we note that $2 - 3 = .202$ and $1 - 3 = .412$. Therefore $(.202) - (.412) = (2 - 3) - (1 - 3) = 2 - 3 - 1 + 3 = 2 - 1$. The numerical value $-.210$ is an estimate of distance statement 2 is from statement 1 on the attitude continuum. Stated another way, we could say that 1 should rank .210 scale values higher than 2. These estimates are repeated for all rows, and the average estimate is equal to the difference in means between columns 1 and 2.

Organizing, Administering, and Scoring the Instrument

We may use all of our attitude statements in our instrument if they do in fact scale the attitude in question—that is, if they fall on a continuum with reasonable distances between statements. If a large number of statements pile up at one end, we may question the scalability of the attitude. We might also select a subset of statements, each representing a different degree of favorableness toward the attitude. These should be selected so that a fairly wide range of scale values is represented. The statements are presented in random order to the target group of students whose attitudes toward guessing we are measuring. They are asked to indicate the statements they agree with and those with which they disagree (with the requirement that they indicate at least one). Their score will be the average (median or mean) of the scale values with which they agreed. A median or mean is computed for each member of the group. See Chapter Nine for a description of methods useful in computing the median and mean. Thus, if a student only checks items 4 and 5, his attitude-toward-guessing score would be .6.

THE METHOD OF EQUAL–APPEARING INTERVALS

The method of equal-appearing intervals was first described by Thurstone and Chave (1929). Like the scaling method of paired comparisons, the method of equal-appearing intervals requires the use of judges to provide data used in determining attitude scale values. Unlike the paired-comparison method, each statement is judged independently of the others in a set, allowing a large number of statements to be judged. It is assumed that a group of about 50 judges can arrange a series of statements in order (using eleven possible categories) from most to least favorable, with equal-appearing intervals of difference between adjoining statements.

The initial step in scaling is to collect a pool of statements that should reflect favorable, unfavorable, and neutral attitude positions. Each statement should be screened using the criteria for attitude statements described in Chapter Seven. A group of judges similar to the individuals to whom the final scale will be administered are asked to indicate the placement of each statement on an 11-point continuum. This may be accomplished either by physically arranging the statements in groups or by assigning ratings from 1 to 11. In the first procedure, each statement is typed on a separate card and placed by the judges in one of eleven piles labeled A through K. Only three reference points are labeled: unfavorable, neutral, and favorable. The element alphabetical categories can later be translated into an 11-point quantitative scale for determining scale values. Sometimes as few as seven or nine categories are used.

A	B	C	D	E	F	G	H	I	J	K

Unfavorable   Neutral   Favorable

In the other procedure, the statements may be duplicated on $8\frac{1}{2}" \times 11"$ paper with the 11-point continuum printed next to each statement on the continuum. It is important that the directions instruct the judge not to respond as he feels, but simply to indicate the placement of the statement with respect to its degree of favorableness toward the attitude object. If a judge places more than 20 percent of the statements in any given category, he is probably careless or unmotivated and should be eliminated from the analysis. We now have a series of statements rated on an 11-point continuum as many times as there are judges. Using the median rating, one scale value is determined for each item, and a measure of "agreement" among the judges is derived. Let us pursue a sample problem to illustrate these analyses.

An Illustrative Problem

Suppose we are interested in the general public's attitudes toward psychological testing. We have gathered a large number of statements reflecting varying degrees of favorableness toward this object. Following are seven sample statements:

1. Psychological testing is a highly objective method for judging individuals.

2. Psychological tests allow us to uncover facts about an individual we could not learn in any other way.

3. Psychological tests judge you more fairly than do human interviewers.

4. Psychological tests are the simplest means of evaluating pupil progress in the classroom.

5. Psychological tests are usually fun to take.

6. Psychological testing is an invasion of privacy.

7. Psychological tests should be placed under strict governmental control.

Determining Scale Values

We have obtained the cooperation of a representative sample of 50 members of the general public to provide judgments on each of the statements. A summary of their judgments of the above seven statements is given in Table 8.4. We have tallied the number of times (frequency = f) each statement was assigned to one of the eleven categories, and divided each frequency by 50 (the total number of judges) to obtain proportions (p). The third row for each statement in Table 8.4 is the cumulative proportion. This is simply the proportion of judgments in a given category plus the sum of all of the proportions below that category. The median of the distribution of judgments for each statement is taken as the scale value of the statement. If the data are arranged and summarized as they are in Table 8.4, the following formula for median may be applied:

$$\text{Scale Value (S)} = L + \left(\frac{.50 - \Sigma p_b}{p_w}\right) \qquad \text{(Equation 8.1)}$$

where S = the median or scale value of the statement
L = the lower limit of the interval in which the median falls (See Chapter Nine for a description of lower limits and meaning of median.)[3]
Σp_b = the sum of the proportions below the interval in which the median falls
p_w = the proportion within the interval in which the median falls.

---

[3] E.g., the real limits for a given category are assumed to extend one-half unit above and one-half unit below the category. The lower limit, then, for category 5 would be 4.5; for 6 it would be 5.5, and so on.

TABLE 8.4 Summary of Judgments About Attitudes Toward Psychological Testing Using the Method of Equal-Appearing Intervals

Statements		A 1	B 2	C 3	D 4	E 5	F 6	G 7	H 8	I 9	J 10	K 11	Scale Value	Q Value
1	f	0	0	1	1	2	4	4	6	11	12	9	9.14	2.63
	p	.00	.00	.02	.02	.04	.08	.08	.12	.22	.24	.18		
	cp	.00	.00	.02	.04	.08	.16	.24	.36	.58	.82	1.00		
2	f	1	0	1	2	2	4	6	7	9	11	7	8.75	3.08
	p	.02	.00	.02	.04	.04	.08	.12	.14	.18	.22	.14		
	cp	.02	.02	.04	.08	.12	.20	.32	.46	.64	.86	1.00		
3	f	0	0	1	2	4	6	7	10	9	7	4	8.00	2.91
	p	.00	.00	.02	.04	.08	.12	.14	.20	.18	.14	.08		
	cp	.00	.00	.02	.06	.14	.26	.40	.60	.78	.92	1.00		
4	f	1	2	4	6	6	10	8	6	3	2	2	6.10	3.16
	p	.02	.04	.08	.12	.12	.20	.16	.12	.06	.04	.04		
	cp	.02	.06	.14	.26	.38	.58	.74	.86	.92	.96	1.00		
5	f	2	3	4	5	6	8	6	7	4	3	2	6.13	3.80
	p	.04	.06	.08	.10	.12	.16	.12	.14	.08	.06	.04		
	cp	.04	.10	.18	.28	.40	.56	.68	.82	.90	.96	1.00		
6	f	3	5	8	11	10	8	3	1	1	0	0	4.32	2.50
	p	.06	.10	.16	.22	.20	.16	.06	.02	.02	.00	.00		
	cp	.06	.16	.32	.54	.74	.90	.96	.98	1.00	1.00	1.00		
7	f	3	7	10	13	11	3	2	1	0	0	0	3.88	2.16
	p	.06	.14	.20	.26	.22	.06	.04	.02	.00	.00	.00		
	cp	.06	.20	.40	.66	.88	.94	.98	1.00	1.00	1.00	1.00		

Sorting Categories

Substituting in Equation 8.1, we find the scale values for Statement 1 to be

$$S_1 = 8.5 + \left(\frac{.50 - .36}{.22}\right) = 8.5 + \frac{.14}{.22} = 8.5 + .64 = \underline{\underline{9.14}}$$

For Statement 2 the scale values would be:

$$S_2 = 8.5 + \left(\frac{.50 - .46}{.18}\right) = 8.5 + \frac{.04}{.18} = 8.5 + .22 = \underline{\underline{8.72}}$$

The scale values for all seven statements are described in Table 8.4.

Describing Variability among Judges

If the judges are in general agreement about the degree of favorableness reflected in a particular statement, their placements would show relatively little variability. It is assumed that a statement that shows relatively little variability is less ambiguous than one showing large variability. The measure of variability used with the equal-appearing interval method is the interquartile range, I.[4] The interquartile range is based on the fact that three points (the first, second, and third quartiles, or 25th, 50th, and 75th percentiles) will divide a distribution into four equal frequency areas. If two reference points, the 25th and 75th percentiles, are close together, then the middle 50 percent of the people are bunched close together. If they are far apart, the people are spread out. I is the range within which the middle 50 percent of the frequencies fall, and can be symbolized as follows:

$$I = P_{75} - P_{25} \qquad \text{(Equation 8.2)}$$

The 75th percentile may be obtained using the following equation:

$$P_{75} = L + \left(\frac{.75 - \Sigma p_b}{p_w}\right) \qquad \text{(Equation 8.3)}$$

Where P_{75} = the 75th percentile

L = the lower limit of the interval in which the 75th percentile falls

Σp_b = the sum of the proportions below the interval in which the 75th percentile falls

---

[4] The author wishes to express his appreciation to Dr. Carl J. Huberty of the University of Georgia for suggesting the symbol I to represent the interquartile range.

p_w = the proportion within the interval in which the 75th percentile falls

From the data in Table 8.4 for Statement 1 and Equation 8.3, P_{75} is calculated to be:

$$P_{75} = 9.5 + \left(\frac{.75 - .58}{.24}\right) = 9.5 + \frac{.17}{.24} = 9.5 + .71 = \underline{10.21}$$

The 25th percentile is calculated in a similar fashion:

$$P_{25} = L + \left(\frac{.25 - \Sigma p_b}{p_w}\right) \qquad \text{(Equation 8.4)}$$

Where P_{25} = the 25th percentile

L = the lower limit of the interval in which the 25th percentile falls

Σp_b = the sum of the proportions below the interval in which the 25th percentile falls

p_w = the proportion within the interval in which the 25th percentile falls

Again, using Statement 1 as an example, we can determine P_{25} to be:

$$P_{25} = 7.5 + \left(\frac{.25 - .24}{.12}\right) = 7.5 + \frac{.01}{.12} = 7.5 + .08 = \underline{7.58}$$

For Statement 1, I turns out to be

$$I = 10.21 - 7.58 = \underline{2.63}$$

The I values for all seven statements about psychological testing are given in Table 8.4. Other things being equal, e.g., scale values are about the same, we would select for our attitude scale those statements with small I values. Take, for example, the data for Statements 4 and 5 in Table 8.4. Their scale values are virtually the same, but the I values differ. We would probably select Statement 4 in preference to Statement 5 because of its smaller I value.

Selecting Statements, Administering, and Scoring the Attitude Instrument

In general, it is desirable to select about 20 statements for the final scale from a much larger pool representing gradations of favorableness of attitude (as indicated by scale values), with relatively small I values.

These statements are then arranged in random order (*without* the associated scale values) and presented to examinees with instructions to indicate with a circle or checkmark those they accept or agree with and those they reject or disagree with. An attitude scale score is obtained by calculating a median or mean of the scale values for the statements with which the individual agrees.

THE METHOD OF SUMMATED RATINGS (LIKERT SCALES)

Beginning with a set of attitude statements representing both favorable and unfavorable attitudes, we can develop a scale using less complex procedures than those required for the paired-comparison or equal-appearing intervals methods. Likert (1932) has shown that the assignment of integral (whole-number) weights to a set of response categories will yield scores that correlate very highly with those obtained from a Thurstone scale. The usual response categories are: strongly agree, agree, undecided, disagree, and strongly disagree. For those statements judged to be favorable toward the attitude object, weights of 5 for strongly agree, 4 for agree, 3 for undecided, 2 for disagree, and 1 for agree are assigned. For unfavorable statements, weights of 1 for strongly agree, 2 for agree, 3 for undecided, 4 for disagree, and 5 for strongly disagree are assigned. Thus, the higher the numerical score the more positive the attitude.

An Illustrative Problem

Following are seven statements, adapted from Glassey (1945), that might prove useful in developing a scale of attitudes toward education. Other subjects, e.g., reading, science, or social studies, could be substituted.

1. I am intensely interested in education.
2. Education does far more good than harm.
3. Education enables us to live less monotonous lives.
4. Sometimes I feel that education is necessary and sometimes I doubt it.
5. If anything, I must admit a slight dislike for education.
6. I dislike education because it means that time has to be spent on homework.
7. I go to school only because I am compelled to do so.

It is obvious that gradations of favorableness are reflected in these statements. We might even have a group of judges classify these statements as favorable, neutral, and unfavorable. If we can obtain, say, 80 percent agreement on their classification, we will have a basis for assigning scoring weights to the statements. We then administer the items to our target group and score according to the scheme outlined at the beginning of this section. We would assign high weights to agreement with favorable statements, and to disagreement with unfavorable statements. The neutral statements would not be scored but would serve as buffers. This process would be undertaken for a large pool of items.

Selecting Statements

The next step is to identify those statements that discriminate between individuals with very positive attitudes and those with unfavorable attitudes. The method used for selecting attitude statements is similar to the item-analysis procedures used in refining achievement tests (See Chapter Twelve). The procedure involves obtaining a total score on the instrument for each individual in the group. The top third of the scores is called the High Attitude group, and the bottom third is designated as the Low Attitude group. A good statement should, on the average, receive higher ratings from the High group than from the Low group. A table like Table 8.5 should be developed for each statement,

TABLE 8.5   Determination of Mean Differences in Ratings of Hypothetical High and Low Attitude Groups for Statement on Attitude Toward Education

Response Categories	Low Group			High Group		
	Weight	Frequency f	fX	Weight	Frequency f	fX
Strongly Agree	5	4	20	5	12	60
Agree	4	8	32	4	20	80
Uncertain	3	16	48	3	10	30
Disagree	2	14	28	2	6	12
Strongly Agree	1	8	8	1	2	2
Sums		50	136		50	184
Mean Rating		$\frac{136}{50} = 2.72$			$\frac{184}{50} = 3.68$	

and a mean rating calculated for the two groups. The larger the mean difference, the better the item. One must remember that the difference will sometimes favor the High group and sometimes the Low, depending upon whether the statement is favorable or unfavorable. The final scale is composed of those items with the greatest mean differences, keeping in mind that we want a full range of attitudes to be reflected. It would ideally include about 20–25 statements.

THE SEMANTIC DIFFERENTIAL TECHNIQUE

Another useful technique for assessing affective learning outcomes is derived from the work of Osgood, Suci, and Tannenbaum (1957). Based on the assumption that in written and spoken language the characteristics of ideas and things are primarily communicated by means of adjectives, considerable research has been undertaken to investigate the connotative meanings of concepts. The technique used in this research is the semantic differential, which is not a test procedure *per se* but a general method of obtaining ratings of concepts on a series of bipolar adjective scales. A page from a semantic differential might resemble the following:

LEARNING

FAST __:__:__:__:__:__:__ SLOW

GOOD __:__:__:__:__:__:__ BAD

WORTHLESS __:__:__:__:__:__:__ VALUABLE

QUIET __:__:__:__:__:__:__ ACTIVE

STRONG __:__:__:__:__:__:__ WEAK

UNPLEASANT __:__:__:__:__:__:__ PLEASANT

The respondent checks the blank on the continuum that corresponds to his feelings about the stimulus word. Any number of stimulus concepts might be used: people, objects, abstract concepts, practices, institutions, and the like. Osgood and his colleagues have identified three major dimensions of the meaning of concepts: *evaluation, potency,* and *activity*. Sample adjective pairs related to each of these dimensions are:

Evaluation: Good–Bad, Fair–Unfair
Potency: Strong–Weak, Heavy–Light
Activity: Fast–Slow, Active–Passive

The strongest dimension by far is the evaluative. It has been shown in hundreds of studies—in the United States, cross-culturally, and cross-nationally—to describe individuals' dominant feelings about ideas and objects. It is recommended that, in exploring affective learning outcomes, only the evaluative dimension be used.

Developing a Semantic Differential

The steps to be followed in constructing a semantic differential are as follows:

1. *Identify the concept(s) to be rated.* The number and type of concepts to be chosen will, of course, depend upon intent. It is best to select a

group of related concepts that can be viewed within the same frame of reference. The more homogeneous the set, the easier and more meaningful the contrasts. A group of concepts like *learning, teacher, school, study,* and *textbook* would constitute a relatively homogeneous set. A teacher may wish to investigate sentiments about the central concepts in a particular unit or course.

2. *Choose appropriate bipolar scales.* The choice of a set of scales should be dictated by relevance and representativeness. As was noted earlier, the semantic differential measures a concept's connotative meaning (its implications for the individual), not its denotative or descriptive meaning. One should *not* use adjectives, therefore, that provide physical descriptions (e.g., *rock:* Hard–Soft). In addition, the scales should be as representative as possible of the full range of sentiments likely to be associated with the concepts in question. Ideally, one would experimentally determine the scales most relevant to a given concept by trying out his own list and then perhaps undertaking a factor analysis. For a classroom teacher, this suggestion is impractical. A reasonable sample of evaluative scales has already been provided by Osgood, Suci, and Tannenbaum (1957). Following is a list of 28 adjective pairs that have been found to bear heavily on the evaluative dimensions of semantic scales:

Good–Bad	Beautiful–Ugly
Sweet–Sour	Clean–Dirty
High–Low	Calm–Agitated
Tasty–Distasteful	Valuable–Worthless
Kind–Cruel	Pleasant–Unpleasant
Bitter–Sweet	Happy–Sad
Empty–Full	Ferocious–Peaceful
Sacred–Profane	Relaxed–Tense
Brave–Cowardly	Rich–Poor
Clear–Hazy	Nice–Awful
Bright–Dark	Fragrant–Foul
Honest–Dishonest	Rough–Smooth
Fresh–Stale	Fair–Unfair
Pungent–Bland	Healthy–Sick

Consideration needs to be given to the difficulty level of the words. Obviously, students cannot use adjectives whose meanings they do not know.

3. *Design a response sheet.* Only one concept should appear on each page. The concept should be printed at the top of the page and the scales listed beneath. The polarity of scales should be alternated (e.g., good-bad, worthless-valuable). The ordering of scales on consecutive pages is fixed, but the order of concept presentation may be randomized. This latter suggestion, however, introduces difficulty in scor-

ing. Osgood has found that a seven-point scale is effective. One may use three-, five-, or even nine-point scales. For younger children, a five-point scale might be most suitable. Ordinarily, 10 to 15 adjective pairs would be sufficient for a group of about 10 related concepts. Subjects have no trouble, however, rating 20 concepts on 20 scales in an hour's time. The younger the group, the fewer concepts and scales should be used.

4. *Write instructions.* The cover sheet should include a general orientation to the task and perhaps a statement about why the data are being gathered. The significance of the scale positions should be spelled out, as well as the procedure for recording responses. It is also important to describe the attitude the examinee should take toward the task: highly motivated and candid, moving rapidly through the scales, expressing first impressions, making independent judgments of each adjective pair relative to the concept, and treating each concept independently. Some examinees, particularly younger ones, may experience some initial difficulty relating the adjective pairs to the concept. If this occurs, the students should be encouraged to proceed rather quickly and respond on the basis of first impressions. Do not try to explain the relation of an adjective to the concept, since this will probably invalidate the pupil's response. Elementary-school pupils typically view the semantic differential as a game and "play" it with vigor. The presentation of the task as a game can encourage freer responses from the pupils and thereby make for a more valid measure of the pupils' attitudes. For the very young, consideration might be given to oral administration, with the teacher reading the instructions, concepts, and pairs while the examinees read along with the teacher and respond.

An example of a relatively standard set of instructions for a semantic differential exercise follows:

The purpose of this activity is to measure the meanings of certain concepts by asking you to judge them against a series of descriptive scales. On each page you will find a different concept and beneath it a set of scales. You are to rate each concept on each of these scales.

Here is how you are to use the scales:

If you feel a particular concept is *very much* like one end of the scale, you should place your checkmark as follows:

PLEASANT X : ___ : ___ : ___ : ___ : ___ : ___ : UNPLEASANT
          1   2   3   4   5   6   7

or

PLEASANT ___ : ___ : ___ : ___ : ___ : ___ : X : UNPLEASANT
          1   2   3   4   5   6   7

If you feel a particular concept is *quite close* to one end of the scale (but not extremely), you should place your checkmark as follows:

RUGGED ___:_X_:___:___:___:___:___: DELICATE
        1   2   3   4   5   6   7

or

RUGGED ___:___:___:___:___:_X_:___: DELICATE
        1   2   3   4   5   6   7

If you feel a particular concept is *only slightly* like one end of the scale (but is not really neutral), you should place your checkmark as follows:

SHARP ___:___:_X_:___:___:___:___: DULL
      1   2   3   4   5   6   7

or

SHARP ___:___:___:___:_X_:___:___: DULL
      1   2   3   4   5   6   7

If you feel that the concept is *neutral* on the scale (that both sides of the scale are equally associated with the concept) or if the scale is completely irrelevant (unrelated to the concept), you should place your checkmark in the middle space.

HAPPY ___:___:___:_X_:___:___:___: SAD
      1   2   3   4   5   6   7

The direction toward which you check, of course, depends upon which of the two ends of the scale best describes your feeling about each concept.

Do not worry or puzzle over any one scale. It is your first impression of each concept that we want. On the other hand, please do not be careless because we want your true impressions. Do not try to remember how you checked similar items earlier in the scale. *Make each item a separate and independent judgment.*

Remember, you are judging the concept as *you* see it—not as we or others react.

Important: 1. Place your checkmarks in the middle of the spaces, not on the boundaries:

this   not this

___:___:_X_:___:___:___X___:

2. *Be sure to check every scale. Do not omit any.*

3. *Never put more than one checkmark on a single scale.*

5. *Score the scales and concepts.* In summarizing the responses quantitatively, the usual procedure is to assign values from 1 to 7 (or from 1 to whatever range of points is used) such that the interval closest to the adjective representing the negative pole (e.g., low evaluation) receives a 1 and the interval closest to the opposing adjective receives a 7. The successive integers represent gradations between these two points. An individual's score on each scale for each concept may be then computed in terms of the scale positions he has checked. If only the evaluative adjective pairs are used, a seven-point ten-scale differential for a single concept would yield a maximal "positive" score of 70 and a minimum score of 10. The responses obtained may be used to compare an individual's attitudes toward different concepts—for example, to a lecture on history versus a film. Similarly, one may compare two individuals' ratings of a given concept. Students are generally interested in their ratings relative to those of other members of the class. The semantic differential is a relatively nonthreatening task, and anonymity is therefore probably not required. In addition, the ratings of groups of people can be arranged in order to assess differences in attitude between groups, or toward various concepts within the group. The same concepts may also be rated at different points in time to assess changes in attitudes that take place as a function of some treatment or intervention.

FREE–RESPONSE AND OPINIONNAIRE METHODS

The opinionnaire is a frequently used polling method of gathering opinion and attitude data. The term *opinionnaire*, as opposed to questionnaire, is used intentionally, to suggest an emphasis on feelings rather than facts. The use of a well-constructed opinionnaire tends to systematize the data-gathering process and to help insure that the relevant questions are asked, and all important aspects of the problem surveyed. Unfortunately, opinionnaires are often haphazardly constructed, without proper concern for the phrasing of questions, the means of summarizing and analyzing data, or pilot testing or tryout of the schedule. Bledsoe (1972) suggests six criteria for a "good" opinionnaire:

1. Brevity.
2. Inclusion of items of sufficient interest and "face appeal" to attract the attention of the respondent and cause him to become involved in the task.
3. Provision for depth of response in order to avoid superficial replies.
4. Wording of questions neither too suggestive nor too unstimulating.
5. Phrasing of questions in such a way as to allay suspicion about hidden purposes and not to embarrass or threaten the respondent.

6. Phrasing of questions so that they are not too narrow in scope, allowing the respondent reasonable latitude in his responses.

Opinionnaires are generally of two types: the "closed" or precategorized type and the "open" or free-response type. The former type very closely resembles the forced-choice methods described earlier in this chapter. Rating scales are also frequently associated with the structured opinionnaire (see Chapters Four and Sixteen for further discussion of rating scales). It is recommended that the open-ended form of opinionnaire be adopted for classroom use. The use of such free-response questions allows the teacher to cover a wide variety of topics in an efficient manner. Analysis of the responses to free-response questions can, however, be quite time-consuming and difficult. In preparing opinionnaires, some general cautions should be observed (Sawin, 1969):

1. Spell out in advance the objectives, purposes, and specifications for the instrument. This task should be undertaken *before* questions are written.

2. Try to limit the length of the questionnaire (e.g., ten questions). If the student becomes impatient to finish, he is likely not to consider his answers carefully.

3. Make sure students understand the purpose of the opinionnaire and are convinced of the importance of responding completely and candidly.

4. If possible, use a sequence of questions. Green (1970) illustrates the advantages of this approach with a series of questions that could be used to stimulate attitudinal responses toward labor unions in a unit of a social studies course.

    a. How have labor-management relations been affected by unions?

    b. How have working conditions been affected by unions?

    c. What means, if any, should be used to control unions?

    d. What effects have unions had on the general economy of the country?

5. Make sure students are motivated to answer questions thoughtfully.

6. Control the administration of the opinionnaire so as to prevent students from talking with one another about the questions before answering them.

7. Urge students to express their own thoughts, not the responses they think the teacher wants.

8. Be sure the directions are clear, definite, and complete.

9. Urge students to ask about questions that are unclear to them.

10. If possible, try out the opinionnaire with other teachers or a couple

of students to identify and clear up ambiguous questions, difficult terms, or unclear meanings.

Content Analysis

A teacher will ordinarily undertake a content analysis of the responses to opinionnaire questions. *Content analysis* is a systematic, objective, and—ideally—quantitative examination of free-response material. In addition to examining opinionnaire responses, content analyses of textbooks, television broadcasts, essays, records of interpersonal interactions, plays, stories, dramas, newspaper articles, speeches, or propaganda materials may be undertaken.

Sawin (1969) and de Sala Pool (1959) have identified several steps in the content analysis:

1. *Identify the units for the purpose of recording results.* The specification of units, which requires great care, may be undertaken before beginning the analysis if the teacher knows what to expect, or after a sample of the responses has been examined. A unit is usually a single sentence, although any brief phrase that summarizes an idea, concept, feeling, or word will suffice.

2. *Identify the categories into which the units will be placed.* For example, the unit might be a sentence and the category a type of sentence, e.g., declarative, interrogative.

3. *Analyze all the content (or a representative sample) relevant to the problem.* A given piece of material could be sampled for a given student, or samples could be taken from a group of students.

4. *Seek to attain a high degree of objectivity.* The teacher may wish to complete an analysis or to put it aside and redo it (or a portion of it) later to check agreement of results. A comparison of the work of two teachers working independently could serve as another check on objectivity.

5. *Quantify the results, if at all possible.* The use of simple summary indices such as frequency counts and percents can be very helpful.

6. *Include a sufficiently large number of samples to insure reasonable reliability.* The larger the sample of material(s) analyzed, in general the greater the reliability.

An Illustrative Content Analysis

In an effort to evaluate the impact of an eight-week summer enrichment program for academically and artistically talented students, the author (Payne 1972) asked several questions like the following on a participant follow-up opinionnaire:

1. What contribution, if any, did the program make toward your developing a positive attitude toward learning?
2. How suitable were the instructional methods?
3. To what degree did the program influence your desire to attend college?
4. What do you feel were the most beneficial dimensions of the program?

A content analysis of the last question yielded the following results (with a sample of 50 subjects):

	Frequency	*Percent*
a. Contact with individuals with both different and similar interests.	34	68%
b. Freedom for independent and in-depth study.	12	24%
c. The high quality of teachers.	9	18%
d. The availability of cultural events, films, speakers, and the like.	8	16%
e. Freedom to broaden interests.	5	10%

Not only were relevant dimensions of the program identified, but a ranking of the importance of these dimensions also become possible. The fact that this information came from the participants themselves helps insure the validity of the responses. If precategorized responses had been used, we might have biased the respondents.

SUGGESTED READINGS

Beatty, W. H., ed. *Improving educational assessment and an inventory of measures of affective behavior.* Washington: Association for Supervision and Curriculum Development, 1969. Particularly valuable is the summary of scales in the second half of this book.

Cooper, C. R. *Measuring growth in appreciation of literature.* Newark, Delaware: International Reading Association, 1972.

Downie, N. M. *Fundamentals of measurement: Techniques and practices,* 2nd ed. New York: Oxford University Press, 1967. Chapter 16, "Appraisal of Attitudes," is a nontechnical survey of methods useful to classroom teachers.

Edwards, A. L. *Techniques of attitude scale construction.* New York: Appleton-Century-Crofts, 1957. A most readable and detailed presentation of six major methods of constructing attitude scales—paired comparisons, equal-appearing intervals, successive intervals, summated ratings, scalogram analysis, and the scale-discrimination technique.

Hartshorne, H., and May, M. A. *Studies in deceit.* New York: Macmillan, 1928.

Hartshorne, H., and May, M. A. *Studies in service and self-control.* New York: Macmillan, 1929.

Hartshorne, H., and May, M. A. *Studies in the organization of character.* New York: Macmillan, 1930. The studies of Hartshorne and May are among the most creative efforts ever made to develop performance measures of personality. The research resulting from the development of quantitative and objective methods in their Character Education Inquiry has had a lasting impact on assessment in the affective area.

Horrocks, J. E., and Schoonover, Thelma I. *Measurement for teachers.* Columbus, Ohio: Charles E. Merrill, 1968. Chapter 19 contains a summary of 29 different Thurstone-type scales.

Mager, R. F. *Developing attitude toward learning.* Palo Alto, Cal.: Fearon, 1968. Three principles that teachers can apply in nurturing favorable attitudes toward subject matter are described. Some information about assessing attitudinal outcomes is presented.

Mayhew, L. B. Measurement of noncognitive objectives in the social studies. In *Evaluation in social studies,* ed. H. D. Berg. Thirty-Fifth Yearbook of the National Council for the Social Studies. Washington: National Education Association, 1965. An informative and comprehensive overview of techniques for assessing affective variables, this essay also touches upon relevant research.

National Special Media Specialists. *The affective domain.* Washington: Communication Service Corporation, 1970. A resource book for media specialists concerned with the measurement and development of affective outcomes.

Nunnally, J. C., Jr. *Introduction to psychological measurement.* New York: McGraw-Hill, 1970. See Chapter 14, "Measurement of Sentiments," an excellent and comprehensive survey of methods.

Oppenheim, A. M. *Questionnaire design and attitude measurement.* New York: Basic Books, 1966. A step-by-step introduction to the design of questionnaires, surveys, and techniques of attitude-scale construction.

Osgood, C. E.; Suci, G. J.; and Tannenbaum, P. F. *The measurement of meaning.* Urbana, Ill.: 1957. A description of the development-and-research basis of the semantic differential technique.

Payne, S. L. *The art of asking questions.* Princeton, N.J.: Princeton University Press, 1951. An extremely useful guide to the phrasing of inventory, questionnaire, and survey items.

Pfeiffer, J. W., and Heslin, R. *Instrumentation in human relations training.* Iowa City: University Associates, 1973.

Raths, L. E.; Harmon, M.; and Simon, S. B. *Values and teaching.* Columbus, Ohio: Charles Merrill, 1966. Obviously, affective outcomes need to be developed before they can be assessed. This book provides examples of how a teacher can cultivate and build skills in the process of valuing.

Remmers, H. H. *Introduction to opinion and attitude measurement.* New York: Harper & Row, 1954. An outstanding book dealing with the topics of this chapter.

Remmers, H. H.; Gage, N. L.; and Rummel, J. F. *A practical introduction to measurement and evaluation.* New York: Harper & Row, 1965. See Chapter 10, an excellent introduction to attitude measurement oriented toward teachers.

Rokeach, M. *Beliefs, attitudes and values: A theory of organization and change.* San Francisco: Jossey-Bass, 1968. The author questions the vast research on attitudes and attitude change, and documents a need for a systematic and organized theory of values.

Shaw, M. E., and Wright, J. M., eds. *Scales for the measurement of attitudes.* New York: McGraw-Hill, 1967. An extensive collection of attitude scales, constructed by various researchers, that are unavailable from commercial publishers. Although the constraints of a particular assessment situation may preclude the use of an existing scale, many may be used as prototypes or modified. An excellent reference book.

Smith, F. M., and Adams, S. *Educational measurement for the classroom teacher,* 2nd ed. New York: Harper & Row, 1972. Illustrations of approaches to the measurement of literature appreciation, health attitudes, and music appreciation are included in Chapter 11.

Snider, J. G., and Osgood, C. E. *Semantic differential technique.* Chicago: Aldine, 1969. A sourcebook of basic studies of the origin, theoretical basis, methodology, validity, and specific uses of the semantic differential technique.

Thurstone, L. L. *The measurement of values.* Chicago: University of Chicago Press, 1959. A collection of 27 papers by a pioneer American psychologist and creator of many scaling and measurement innovations.

Walker, Deborah K. *Socioemotional measures for preschool and kindergarten children: A handbook.* San Francisco: Jossey-Bass, 1973.

IV
SUMMARIZING AND INTERPRETING TEST PERFORMANCES

9
DESCRIBING TEST PERFORMANCES

SUMMARY PREVIEW STATEMENTS

1. The study of statistics is important because the use of statistical methods:
   a. Facilitates the summarization and description of data.
   b. Assists in the interpretation of test scores.
   c. Is necessary to an adequate analysis of measuring instruments.
   d. Facilitates the decision-making use of test data.

2. A frequency distribution of test scores reveals the number of scores in each category along the score scale.

3. The frequency distribution facilitates examination of the shape of the distribution and, in particular, recognition of skewness or the tendency of scores to bunch up at the extremes of a distribution.

4. A percentile rank, which describes the percentage of scores at or below a given score (or the midpoint of a set of scores), is useful in interpreting individual performances.

5. A percentile rank is calculated by dividing the total number of scores (N) into the cumulative frequency at and below a given score (or midpoint), and multiplying the result by 100.

6. A percentile is a score point that divides a score distribution into fixed percentages or areas of the total distribution.

7. The median is that percentile (score point) that divides the total score distribution into two equal areas.

8. The First (Q_1), Second (Q_2), and Third (Q_3) Quartiles divide the distribution into four equal areas.

9. A distribution of scores that is asymmetrical may be characterized as skewed.

10. A positively skewed distribution has a high frequency of low scores and trails off to a low frequency of high scores.

11. A negatively skewed distribution has a high frequency of high

scores and trails off to a low frequency of low scores. Many achievement measures yield negatively skewed distributions.

12. The mean, or arithmetic average, is obtained by adding all the scores and dividing the sum by the total number of scores.

13. If the mean is larger than the median, it is likely that the distribution is positively skewed. Conversely, if it is less than the median the distribution is likely to be negatively skewed.

14. The variability (or spread) of a distribution of measures may be described by the variance (or its square root—the standard deviation), the inter- or semi-interquartile range, or the range (high score minus low score plus one).

15. The variance of a set of scores is calculated by adding the squared deviations of the scores (from the mean of all the scores) and then dividing the total by the number of scores.

16. The standard deviation is the square root of the variance.

17. The standard deviation can be estimated by dividing half the number of scores into the difference between the sums of the upper and lower one-sixths of the distribution of the scores.

18. In general, the greater the total number of scores, the greater the range of scores in standard deviation units.

19. The variability of scores is likely to be positively related to total test reliability, and to some extent to validity.

20. Standard scores represent methods of expressing test scores that have fixed means and standard deviations.

21. The basic standard score is the z score, which is calculated by dividing the standard deviation into the difference between a given raw score and the mean of all the scores.

22. A Z score is obtained by multiplying a z score by 10 and adding 50.

23. A T score is the same as a Z score when the scores are normally distributed.

24. The normal curve is an idealized theoretical (mathematical) bell-shaped curve that represents the distributions of some kinds of educational and psychological data, particularly when a large number of observations are involved.

25. The distribution of scores from classroom tests is rarely normal.

26. A College Board or CEEB standard score is obtained by multiplying the z score by 100 and adding 500.

27. Nonnormal distributions can be converted to normal distributions

by transforming all raw scores to percentile ranks and then entering a normal curve table, which gives z-score equivalents of the percentile ranks (see Appendix C).

28. Stanine standard scores are usually normally or sometimes non-normally distributed single-digit scores having a mean of approximately 5 and a standard deviation of approximately 2.

29. A correlation coefficient represents the degree of relation between a series of paired scores.

30. Correlation coefficients range from −1.00, indicating a perfect negative or inverse relationship, through .00, indicating the absence of relationship, to +1.00, indicating a perfect positive direct relationship.

31. When pairs of scores are expressed as z scores, the correlation coefficient is the average of the z-score products.

32. Correlation coefficients can be estimated from the differences between ranks of paired scores.

33. Examination of the degree of relationship in a set of paired scores is facilitated by the plotting of the pairs on a two-way grid (scatter diagram).

34. The more closely the plots of pairs of scores fall on a diagonal, the higher the correlation; the diagonal running from the lower left to upper right corners is positive, and that running from the upper left to lower right corners is negative, assuming the scores have been plotted low to high, left to right, and bottom to top of the scatter diagram.

35. Correlation methods are useful in studying test reliability and validity.

It is not the author's intent, nor is it possible, to develop the reader's statistical competencies to a high degree in this brief chapter. An effort will be made, however, to provide sufficient knowledge of and skill in elementary statistical procedures to facilitate the development, refinement, and interpretation of classroom tests. The statistical procedures to be described are applicable to such questions as "What is the typical score on this test?" "What is the average score?" "How variable or 'spread out' are the scores on this test?" "What are some methods useful in summarizing individual student scores?" and "How can I describe the relationship of scores on my test to scores on a standardized test that purports to measure the same variable?" In most instances, such topics as central tendency, variability, and correlation will be presented by describing and illustrating the commonly used indices. Short-cut procedures, subject to some error but useful in analyzing classroom tests, will also be described.

WHY STUDY STATISTICS?

Five of the many reasons why the study of statistics is important to the student of measurement will be briefly discussed.

First, and probably most important, the use of statistics greatly facilitates summarizing and describing large amounts of data about an individual student or group of students. Questions relating to average class performance and the spread of scores can be answered by application of appropriate statistical techniques.

Second, intelligent use of certain statistical procedures can be very helpful in interpreting test scores. Raw scores, e.g., scores indicating the number of correct responses on a test, are relatively meaningless in and of themselves. Raw scores need to be summarized and related to some meaningful reference point, e.g., the average score on a particular test for a local or nationally representative group, to have meaning for student, school administrator, or parent. Certain kinds of "derived scores," some of which will be described in this chapter, can profitably be used to communicate information about educational achievement.

Third, knowledge and comprehension of, and skill in using, certain statistical techniques are necessary for adequate analysis and evaluation of measuring instruments. Such test characteristics as reliability and validity can only be precisely assessed through the use of statistical methods.

Fourth, certain numerical facts, summarized in the form of statistical indices, aid in making decisions about, and evaluating, student achievement. The assignment of course marks is an example of an area in which knowledge of typical or average performance and the variability of scores can significantly influence judgments about, and the system used to report, individual student performances.

Last, as a kind of "extra added attraction," the study of statistics will allow the serious student to read with greater understanding research in his discipline, research on testing and measurement, and test manuals.

TABULATING DATA AND
FREQUENCY DISTRIBUTIONS

The first step an instructor ordinarily takes in analyzing the results of a test he has administered is to present a frequency distribution of the scores. Such a distribution is obtained by relating each test score to a number that indicates the frequency with which it occurs. In an ordinary classroom situation this can probably best be accomplished by listing the scores from high to low and tallying the number of times each occurs. It is sometimes desirable, when the class is large and the range of scores great, to group the scores into intervals of predetermined and uniform size. To determine the size interval to be used, it is suggested that the range of scores be determined (range = highest score minus lowest score plus one) and divided by some number between 10 and 20. This procedure is recommended because most experts feel that 10 to 20 class intervals are sufficient to summarize the data efficiently and yet neither grossly misrepresent the actual nature of the underlying distribution nor introduce excessive grouping errors in the statistics to be computed. This procedure has been followed with a set of 40 hypothetical scores on a seventh-grade American History test, and the results summarized in Table 9.1. This distribution of scores would be described as *negatively skewed*, i.e., there is a relatively high frequency of high scores, and the scores decrease in frequency toward the low or

TABLE 9.1 Illustration of Derivation of Frequency Distribution and Calculation of Percentile Ranks for 40 Hypothetical Scores on American History Test

Raw Scores on History Test									
49	36	25	17	41	39	29	21	40	35
37	33	35	14	26	32	44	40	45	31
35	42	33	38	1	36	36	28	34	4
28	32	24	16	12	31	38	38	27	30

(1)	(2)	(3)	(4)	(5)	(6)	(7)
Scores $(i = 3)$	Tally	Frequency	Cumulative Frequency	Percentile Rank	Cumulative Frequency to Midpoint	Percentile Rank of Midpoint
49–51	1	1	40	100	39.5	99
46–48		0	39	98	39.0	98
43–45	11	2	39	98	38.0	95
40–42	1111	4	37	93	35.0	88
37–39	1111	5	33	83	30.5	76
34–36	1111 11	7	28	70	24.5	61
31–33	1111 1	6	21	53	18.0	45
28–30	1111	4	15	38	13.0	33
25–27	111	3	11	28	9.5	24
22–24	1	1	8	20	7.5	19
19–21	1	1	7	18	6.5	16
16–18	11	2	6	15	5.0	13
13–15	1	1	4	10	3.5	9
10–12	1	1	3	8	2.5	6
7–9		0	2	5	2	5
4–6	1	1	2	5	1.5	4
1–3	1	1	1	3	.5	1

negative end of the score scale. Conversely, if one found a relatively high frequency of low scores, with the frequencies trailing off at the high or positive end of the score scale, the frequency distribution would be described as *positively skewed*. See Figure 9.1 for examples of both positively and negatively skewed distributions. Skewness, at a general level, is described in terms of the "tail" of the distribution. The fre-

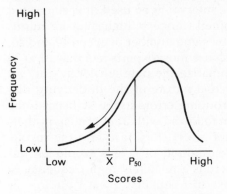

(a) Negatively Skewed Distribution

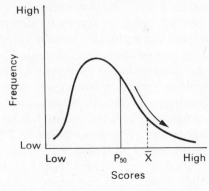

(b) Positively Skewed Distribution

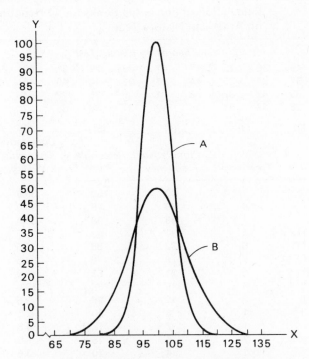

(c) Two Normal Distributions with Equal Means but
Unequal Standard Deviations (From Meyer 1967, p. 49)

FIGURE 9.1. Illustrative Frequency Distributions

quency distribution provides a teacher with a graphic picture of the performance of the group as a whole on a given test. The degree of skewness, in turn, *may* indicate something about the general difficulty level of the test for this group.

It should be noted, again, that for most classroom tests it is usually not necessary to group the scores.

RELATIVE POSITION—PERCENTILE RANKS

Raw test scores, as has been said, have relatively little meaning in and of themselves. It is not generally recommended that an instructor interpret an individual student's performance in terms of the proportion of the total number of test questions answered correctly. The primary difficulty here is that a test, being only a sample of behavior, could yield misleading interpretations if the "percent correct of total" procedure was employed, because other test samples might result in markedly different interpretations. Knowledge about the universe of behavior being sampled, the reliability of the test, and the difficulty levels of the items would need to be considered in making such an "absolute" type of test interpretation. We need, then, some method of deriving a score or number that will have meaning for an individual student. At the crudest level, rank in the group might be used, but the size of the group will obviously play a significant role in determining the meaning assigned to a particular rank (e.g., a rank of 3 in a group of 10 vs. a rank of 3 in a group of 1000). A derived score that has been found useful in describing individual student performance is the *percentile rank* (PR). A percentile rank is a number representing the percent of scores below a given score point. To calculate a percentile rank, one merely counts the number of scores below the given score, divides by the total number of students (N), and multiplies by 100. With reference to the data in Table 9.1, one could determine the PR for a score of 27 as follows:

$$\text{Percentile Rank} = \frac{cf_i}{N} \times 100 \qquad \text{(Equation 9.1)}$$

where cf_i = the number of cases below
the interval containing
the given score of interest

and therefore $PR_{27} = \frac{8}{40} \times 100 = \underline{\underline{20}}$

To facilitate the computation of percentile ranks, it is suggested that a *cumulative frequency* column be included in a summary data table. Such a column is calculated simply by adding successively the frequencies associated with each interval. Using the procedure just described, percentile ranks have been calculated for the hypothetical American History data in Table 9.1, and are listed in Column 5. A little thought about how we obtained the PRs should result in the realization that there is something wrong with our results. What we really have in Column 5 are the PRs for scores of 51, 48, 45, 42, etc., or the upper integral limits of each interval, not each individual score. With reference to our example, with a score of 27 we can see that the PR of 20 really stands for the scores of 25, 26, *and* 27, because we have grouped the data into intervals. There are methods of estimating the percentile ranks of scores that have been grouped into intervals (see, for example, Blommers and Lindquist, 1960, pp. 74–76), but these interpolative methods are outside the purview of this chapter. A reasonable compromise is to determine the percentile ranks for each of the midpoints of each of the intervals. In doing so we are assuming that the scores are evenly distributed in the interval and that the midpoint is representative of all the scores in the interval. We are assuming, then, that one-half of the scores are above the midpoint and one-half are below. Proceeding from this assumption, we can derive a new cumulative frequency column representing the cumulative frequencies from the midpoints of each interval by dividing in half the frequencies in each interval and adding that half-interval frequency to all the frequencies below. This new cumulative frequency column is found in Column 6 of Table 9.1. We now calculate the PRs in the usual way. For example, our new estimate for a PR for a score of 27 is

$$\text{Percentile Rank} = \frac{cf_{mi}}{N} \times 100 \qquad \text{(Equation 9.2)}$$
(from midpoint
of interval)

where cf_{mi} = the number of cases at or below the midpoint of the interval that contains the given score of interest

$$PR_{27} = \frac{9.5}{40} \times 100 = \underline{\underline{24}}$$

Discrepancies between the PRs calculated from the straight cumulative frequencies and the cumulative frequencies from the midpoints of the intervals will be noted in comparing Columns 5 and 7 of Table 9.1. In general, the larger the number of cases in an interval the larger the discrepancy between PRs. The PRs derived from the midpoint data are nevertheless reasonable values to use in interpreting test scores to individual students. Another reason for recommending that PRs be calculated from the midpoints of the intervals is that the possibility of a PR of 100 is eliminated. Telling a student that his score on the test had a

PR of 100 may result in the unfortunate misinterpretation of this PR as meaning that all items were answered correctly.

Another method for describing relative position in terms of standard deviation units will be described later in this chapter in the section on "Standard Scores."

THE TOTAL DISTRIBUTION—PERCENTILES

If we are interested in describing how an individual student performed, percentile ranks are useful derived scores. But how can we describe the overall performance of the group? If our focus is on the total distribution, *percentiles* (P_x) constitute useful descriptive reference points. A percentile is a score point below which a given percent of scores fall. The 50th percentile (usually referred to as the *median*), for example, is that score point above which 50 percent of the scores fall and below which 50 percent of the scores fall. Although related to each other, e.g., the percentile rank of a score of 27 is 28, and the 28th percentile is 27, PRs and P_xs summarize different characteristics of a distribution of scores and the methods of calculation differ. With PRs one begins with a score point and ends with a percent; with P_xs one begins with a percent and ends with a score point.

Before moving on to a discussion of how P_xs are calculated, one theoretical assumption about the data we work with must be examined. The data of education and psychology may be classified as either continuous or discrete. Discrete data are characterized by gaps on the score scale where no numerical values are possible, and are exemplified by such subjects as number of books in a library, size of family, and the like. Continuous data result from the measurement of continuous variables such as height, weight, intelligence, and school achievement. Although we generally use integral values (i.e., whole numbers) to report continuous data, the selection of units is really quite arbitrary. When data are grouped into intervals, we report for convenience's sake the *integral limits*, or the limits of the interval to the nearest unit involved. The *real limits* of a class or interval in a frequency distribution extend one-half unit on either side of the integral limits. The so-called integral limits are not really limits, but only the highest and lowest unit points within the interval. If one were to consider the interval 25–27 from Table 9.1, the real and integral limits would relate to each other in the following manner:

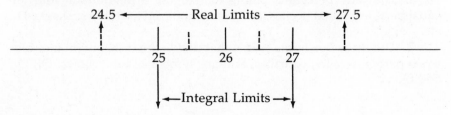

It should be noted that we do not change the size of the interval when moving from real to integral limits, and vice versa.

Any given percentile may be calculated by using the following formula:

$$P_x = L_x + \left(\frac{\frac{P_x N}{100} - cf_{L_x}}{fw_x}\right)i \qquad \text{(Equation 9.3)}$$

where

P_x = the percentile we are interested in calculating

L_x = the lower *real limit* of the interval containing P_x

$\dfrac{P_x N}{100}$ = the number of cases we wish to account for or describe

cf_{L_x} = the cumulative frequency up to the lower real limit of the interval containing P_x

fw_x = the frequency with which scores occur in the interval containing P_x

i = the size of the interval

Using Equation 9.1, we can calculate the 50th percentile (the median) from the data in Table 9.1, as follows:

$$P_{50} = 30.5 + \left(\frac{\frac{50(40)}{100} - 15}{6}\right) 3 = 32.99 \text{ or } \underline{\underline{33}}$$

One should become familiar with the procedure for calculating percentiles, not only because they are useful in describing one's own score distribution, but also because the norms of most standardized educational and psychological tests are reported in the form of percentiles.

Selected percentile points are worthy of special mention, because they are frequently referred to in test manuals and the measurement literature:

1. The nine percentile points that divide a distribution into ten equal parts are called deciles, and are symbolized as follows: D_1, D_2, D_3, etc.

2. The three percentile points that divide the distribution into four equal parts are called quartiles, and are symbolized as follows: Q_1, Q_2, and Q_3.

Identities such as the following should also be kept in mind:

$$\text{Median} = P_{50} = D_5 = Q_2$$
$$P_{25} = Q_1$$
$$P_{75} = Q_3$$

AVERAGE OR TYPICAL PERFORMANCE

We have already described one index of average performance, the median. The median is a useful statistic because it is relatively unaffected by extreme scores and therefore useful with skewed distributions. In most cases the best measure of "averageness" is the arithmetic mean, which is indexed by adding all scores and dividing the sum by the number of measures. Expressed as a formula

$$\overline{X} = \frac{\Sigma X}{N} \text{ or } \frac{\Sigma fX}{N} \qquad \text{(Equation 9.4)}$$

$\overline{X}$ = the symbol for the arithmetic mean

X = one observed score

fX = frequency of an observed score, if scores have been rank-ordered

Σ = "the sum of"

N = the total number of scores in the distribution

A procedure that allows for an efficient calculation of the mean, from grouped data such as we have in Table 9.1, involves "guessing the mean," and then coding the scores in the distribution around this "guessed mean." The guessed mean is sometimes referred to as the "arbitrary origin." Refer to Table 9.2 for an example of this procedure. We have guessed the mean to fall in the interval 31–33; more precisely, we have guessed it to be the midpoint of this interval, or 32. In practice it makes no difference where one guesses the mean will fall, since one will always obtain the correct answer, but some point in the middle of the distribution will keep the numbers small and more convenient to work with. We now code each of the intervals in the distribution by assigning deviation or "d" scores. This is done by subtracting the midpoint of the "0" interval and dividing by the interval size. We must assume that all intervals are the same size and that a "d" score is assigned to those intervals for which no scores were observed. Do not confuse "d" with "x," which is a deviation about the actual raw score mean $(x = X - \overline{X})$, and is sometimes used to derive indices of variabil-

TABLE 9.2   Illustration of Calculations of Mean and Standard Deviation with Coded Scores Using Hypothetical American History Test Data from Table 9.1

(1) Scores	(2) Midpoint of Interval	(3) Frequency	(4) d	(5) fd	(6) fd²
49–51	50	1	6	6	36
46–48	47	0	5	0	0
43–45	44	2	4	8	32
40–42	41	4	3	12	36
37–39	38	5	2	10	20
34–36	35	7	1	7	7
31–33	32	6	0	0	0
28–30	29	4	−1	−4	4
25–27	26	3	−2	−6	12
22–24	23	1	−3	−3	9
19–21	20	1	−4	−4	16
16–18	17	2	−5	−10	50
13–15	14	1	−6	−6	36
10–12	11	1	−7	−7	49
7–9	8	0	−8	0	0
4–6	5	1	−9	−9	81
1–3	2	1	−10	−10	100

Mean

$\overline{X} = G.\ M. + (i \times C)$

$C = \dfrac{\Sigma fd}{N} = \dfrac{-16}{40} = -.40$

$\overline{X} = 32 + (3)(-.40)$

$\overline{X} = 32 - 1.20 = 30.80$ or $\underline{\underline{31}}$

$N = 40$

Actual Standard Deviation

$\Sigma fd = -16$

$S = i\sqrt{\dfrac{\Sigma fd^2 - NC^2}{N-1}}$

$\Sigma fd^2 = 488$

$S = 3 \cdot \sqrt{\dfrac{488 - (40)(.16)}{39}} = 3 \cdot \sqrt{\dfrac{488 - 6.4}{39}}$

$i = 3$

$S = 3 \cdot \sqrt{\dfrac{481.6}{39}} = 3\sqrt{12.35} = 3(3.51) = \underline{\underline{10.53}}$

$C^2 = .16$

Estimated Standard Deviation

$\hat{S} = \dfrac{\Sigma X u_6^1 - \Sigma X L_6^1}{N/2} = \dfrac{302 - 86}{20} = \dfrac{216}{20} = \underline{\underline{10.8}}$

$1/6 \times 40 = 6.6$ or 7

ity: the variance and standard deviation. We next multiply the frequency by the d score, obtain the algebraic sum, and divide this sum by N. We now have what is, in essence, the mean of the coded scores, $(C = \Sigma fd/N)$. If that mean, i.e., C, came out to be zero, we would have guessed the mean correctly. Since we have been using coded scores, we must convert back to raw scores to obtain the mean of the distribution of grouped raw scores. The following conversion formula may be used:

$$\text{Raw Score Mean } (\overline{X}) = \text{G.M.} + (i)(C), \qquad \text{(Equation 9.5)}$$

where

$$\text{G.M.} = \text{the midpoint of the interval containing the guessed mean}$$

$$i = \text{the size of the interval}$$

$$C = \text{the mean of the coded scores or } \Sigma fd/N$$

It should be readily apparent from Table 9.2 how the mean is calculated from coded scores. It is interesting to note the discrepancy between the mean ($\overline{X} = 31$) and median ($P_{50} = 33$) of the distribution of hypothetical test scores. It will be recalled that we had described this frequency distribution as negatively skewed. Since the mean is sensitive to every score in a distribution, and since the median is essentially based on frequencies, one would expect a discrepancy between these two measures when the underlying distribution is skewed. Referring back to Figure 9.1, we find the general expected trend, with the mean larger than the median for positively skewed distribution, and the median larger than the mean when the scores are negatively skewed, as is the case with our distribution.

THE VARIABILITY OF PERFORMANCES

It should be apparent at this point that measures of central tendency (e.g., the mean and median) describe only one important characteristic of a distribution of scores. It is often highly desirable to describe how "spread out" or variable the scores in a distribution are. Whereas the mean and median are points on the score scale, a measure of variability must of necessity represent a distance along the score scale. Two reasonable reference points that describe distance along the score scale are the First Quartile (Q_1, or P_{25}) and the Third Quartile (Q_3, or P_{75}). The difference between these two score points, which describes the middle 50 percent of the scores, divided by 2 is a frequently used measure of variability called the semi-interquartile range (Q). Symbolically, it can be represented as follows:

$$Q = \frac{Q_3 - Q_1}{2} \qquad \text{(Equation 9.6)}$$

Using the data in Table 9.1 and Equation 9.3, we can determine Q_3 and Q_1 to be

$$Q_3 = 36.5 + \left(\frac{\frac{75(40)}{100} - 28}{5} \right) 3 = \underline{\underline{37.7}}$$

$$Q_1 = 24.5 + \left(\frac{\frac{25(40)}{100} - 8}{3} \right) 3 = \underline{\underline{26.5}}$$

$$Q = \frac{37.7 - 26.5}{2} = \underline{\underline{5.6}}$$

A more informative, refined, and sensitive statistic, useful in describing the variability of distributions of scores, is the standard deviation (S). The standard deviation, in essence, represents the "average amount of variability" in a set of measures, using the mean as a reference point. Strictly speaking, the standard deviation is the square root of the average of the squared deviations about the mean. The most elementary form of the standard deviation formula is

$$S = \sqrt{\frac{\Sigma f(X - \overline{X})^2}{N - 1}} \qquad \text{(Equation 9.7)}$$

It can be seen that the deviations (x) about the mean $(X - \overline{X})$ are the basic unit used to describe variability, and that the greater the variability the greater the standard deviation. Part c of Figure 9.1 shows two distributions in which the scores evidence different degrees of variability. The value of S will be larger for distribution B. The computation of the standard deviation and variance from raw scores can be facilitated through the use of the table of squares and square roots in Appendix B.

Why is the variability of a set of scores, and particularly the standard deviation of such scores, of interest? First, a measure of variability is descriptive. It reflects the degree of similarity in performances within groups of students. This will influence the interpretation of the scores both of individual students and the total group. Second, variability and the standard deviation are tied very closely to the concepts of reliability and validity. In general, the greater the variability of scores the greater the reliability. And again, in general, the greater the reliability the greater the *possibility* that an acceptable level of validity can be obtained. Third, the standard deviation is used to derive standard scores, which are in turn useful in both interpreting scores of individual examinees and combining data for decision-making purposes, e.g., assigning marks.

We saw earlier in this chapter how the use of coded scores could facilitate the computation of the mean. Instead of using the formula in Equation 9.7, which is rather inefficient if one is working with a large number of unique scores, to calculate the standard deviation, we can use the following formula:

$$S = i\sqrt{\frac{\Sigma fd^2 - NC^2}{N - 1}}$$ (Equation 9.8)

where

$\Sigma fd^2 =$ the sum of the product of multiplying each individual frequency by its squared coded score

$C^2 =$ a squared correction factor, $C = \dfrac{\Sigma fd}{N}$

$i =$ the size of the interval if the scores are grouped

$N =$ the number of scores.

This formula has been applied to our 40 hypothetical American History test scores, and the result is presented in Table 9.2 under the heading "Actual Standard Deviation." The obtained value of 10.53 describes what would probably be considered a moderately large amount of variability. Given the fact that this test contained 60 items and that $S = 10.53$, it is quite likely that the test will prove to be a reliable measure.

A short-cut method for estimating the standard deviation was originally suggested by W. L. Jenkins of Lehigh University and presented by Diederich (1964). This estimated standard deviation involves summing the raw scores in the upper one-sixth of the distribution, subtracting the sum of the raw scores for the lower one-sixth of the distribution, and dividing the result by half the total number of scores. Symbolically, the estimated standard deviation ($\hat{S}$) may be represented as follows:

$$\hat{S} = \frac{\Sigma X_{U\frac{1}{6}} - \Sigma X_{L\frac{1}{6}}}{N/2}$$ (Equation 9.9)

This formula has some intrinsic appeal for many because, of course, it does not involve extracting a square root. It should be noted, however, that the use of this approximation formula theoretically assumes a normal distribution and is therefore subject to additional errors when the curve is nonnormal. On the basis of extensive use of this estimate, informally reported by teachers and instructors, and brief research reports by Lathrop (1961) and McMorris (1972), it can be concluded that it is a robust statistic, i.e., violations of the assumptions underlying its use do not seriously affect its accuracy. Lathrop found, for example, that even when used with small and nonnormal distributions, Ŝ was a good approximation of S, with something like 3–5 percent error.

When we apply this formula to the data in Table 9.2 we find Ŝ to be 10.8, which corresponds very favorably with the actual standard of 10.53. It must be remembered that when working with scores grouped into intervals we use the midpoint of the interval to represent all of the scores in the interval. When obtaining the "sums," then, we must multiply the frequency of the interval by the midpoint. At this point one might ask what to do if one-sixth turns out to be part of a person. If, for example, we have, as we do in our example, 40 scores, a sixth of 40 (or .16 × 40) is about 6.6. To be accurate we should multiply .6 times the seventh score from the top and bottom and add it into the respective sum. In practice, since this procedure is an approximation, we can usually round to the next highest number.

RELATIVE POSITION—STANDARD SCORES

Standard scores are really nothing more than scores derived from the raw score distribution and expressed as deviations from the mean in terms of standard deviation units. They are preferred as measures of relative position, relative to percentile ranks, because they indicate an individual's position in a collection of scores with reference to the mean of the original group. Standard scores, then, contain more information than PRs. But the mean describes just one important characteristic of a distribution, and we need to take into account the variability of scores, which will significantly influence score interpretation. If, for example, a distribution of scores is quite homogeneous, the scores being very closely clustered about the hypothetical mean of 80, a score of 70 may represent an extremely low level of relative performance. On the other hand, if there is a large amount of variability it is likely that quite a few scores will be found to fall below 70, which now represents fairly typical performance. Scores, then, whose distributions have standard deviations and means of some standard value are known as standard scores. The operations by which raw scores are converted into standard scores are called transformations. We shall now discuss two kinds of standard score transformations that are frequently used in reporting test data.

Linear Transformations

The simplest type of standard score transformation is a linear one. A frequently used standard score system referred to in statistics is the z-score system. This type of score can be represented as follows:

$$z = \frac{X - \overline{X}}{S}$$

(Equation 9.10)

Again referring to the American History data in Table 9.2, we can see that a score of 42 would have a z score of +1.06:

$$z = \frac{42 - 30.80}{10.53} = +1.06$$

What does this mean? Telling an individual that his z score was +1.06 would indicate that his performance was above average—in fact, slightly more than one standard deviation above the mean—which may be more meaningful and informative than telling him that he had a PR 86. It is obvious from Equation 9.10 that if a student had a score equal to the mean his z score would be zero; if one standard deviation above or below, his z score would be +1.00 or −1.00. Generally, plus and minus three z-score units (a range of six standard deviation units) will describe the full range of scores in any distribution. For a distribution of scores for a classroom test, the range may be considerably less.

Some individuals have trouble keeping track of the "sign" of z scores and working with decimals. The former problem, and to some extent the latter also, can be overcome by using the following standard score conversion:

$$Z = 10 \left(\frac{X - \overline{X}}{S} \right) + 50$$

or

$$Z = 10(z) + 50 \qquad\qquad \text{(Equation 9.11)}$$

We now have a new system of standard scores, where the "standard" mean is 50 and the standard deviation is 10. Our raw score of 42 would now have a Z value of

$$Z = 10(+1.06) + 50 = 60.6 \text{ or } \underline{\underline{61}}$$

Both z scores and Z scores represent linear transformations. In other words, if the standard scores and corresponding raw scores were plotted as points with reference to a set of coordinate axes, the points would fall in a straight line. We have not changed the relationship of the scores or the shape of the underlying distribution. We have, in fact, subtracted a constant from each score and divided each difference by a constant.

Nonlinear Transformations

Classroom tests seldom yield so-called normal distributions. A normal distribution or curve, as illustrated in Figure 9.2, is a graphical

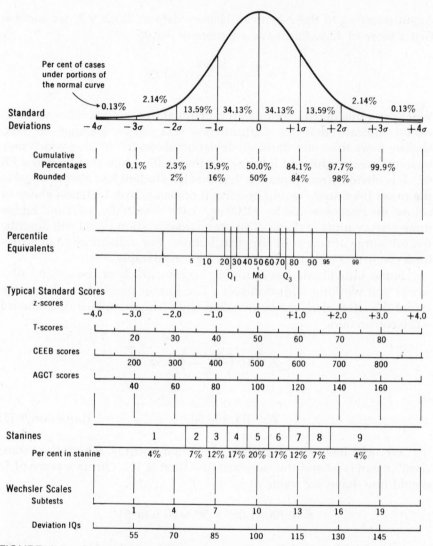

FIGURE 9.2. Relationships Between the Normal Curve, Percentiles, and Various Systems of Standard Scores

Source: *Test Service Bulletin* 48 (January 1955). Published by The Psychological Corporation.

plot of a particular mathematical function. One cannot tell just by "looking at" a distribution whether or not it is normal. The normal curve, however, has certain characteristics that have proven useful in working with test data, e.g., selected z score values define fixed percentages of scores. A system of standard scores has therefore been derived from the normal curve. These scores are called *T scores*. This system of standard scores is similar to Z scores in that the mean is 50 and the standard deviation is 10. We would find that the PRs for Z and T scores are the same only in the case of a "normal distribution." The term "normal distribution" is in quotation marks because there is no single normal curve, but a family or class of normal curves depending upon the mean and standard deviation of the underlying raw scores. Part c of Figure 9.1 shows two different normal curves. T scores can be derived for nonnormal distributions. One procedure involves actually changing the shape of the original raw-score distribution by an area transformation with the use of a table of the normal curve. One would look up the normal-distribution z score for given percentile rank values, and then use the transformation $T = 10(z) + 50$. Normalizing scores may be a reasonable thing to do if certain assumptions can be met. Many of the variables of education and psychology do in fact distribute themselves normally when based on large samples of individuals. Therefore, the normal curve may be a reasonable model for measurement. In addition, since the normal curve has certain characteristics that facilitate test interpretation, the use of a normal score transformation may be helpful. It should be noted that an individual with a T score of 50 will *not* have a raw score equal to the mean if the underlying distribution is not normally distributed, i.e., skewed.

Figure 9.2 describes the relationship among many systems of standard scores and a normal curve. Note particularly the percentile equivalents for various standard deviation points along the score scale.

Appendix C contains a table showing the relationships between T and z scores and percentile ranks when the original distribution of scores is "normal."

Two standard-score systems in Figure 9.2 are worthy of brief mention. The "standard nine" or *stanine* system of scores is increasing in popularity, particularly with publishers of standardized tests. It yields only nine possible values, which facilitates comprehension and interpretation, and is a normalized standard score. Its one drawback is that it groups together scores that might be quite different, assigning them the same stanine score, and therefore tends to mask individual differences. Stanines are actually defined in terms of standard deviation units. For example, a stanine of 5 includes those individuals who are within plus and minus .25 standard deviations of the mean.

College Entrance Examination Board or CEEB scores are also a frequently used and encountered type of standard score. This system, characteristic of the widely known Scholastic Aptitude Test, uses a score reporting system that avoids both negative numbers *and* decimals by arbitrarily setting the mean equal to 500 and the standard deviation to 100.

$$\text{CEEB Scores} = 100(z) + 500.$$

DESCRIBING RELATIONSHIPS

In testing we are frequently called upon to describe the relationship between two measures. The two measures might be scores by the same set of students on two different forms of the same test, thereby allowing us to describe reliability. Or they might be scores on a test, e.g., the College Board Achievement Test in French, and a criterion measure such as final exam scores in a first-year college French course, allowing us to describe the validity of the test.

Ideally, the first step in examining the relationship between two measures is to display the relationship or correlation graphically in the form of a scatter diagram. The procedure merely involves plotting the pairs of scores as dots on coordinate axes. Figure 9.3 is composed of six scatter diagrams showing varying degrees of relationship. Diagram *a* shows a perfect positive correlation where the highest X value (30) is associated with the highest Y value (22), the second highest X value (27) is associated with the second highest Y value (20), and so on down to the lowest X value (3) and the lowest Y value (4). Conversely, in diagram *b* we see a perfect inverse relationship between the scores, with the highest X score (30) associated with the lowest Y score (2) and so on. Both *a* and *b* represent perfect correlations; only the direction of the relationship is different, *a* being positive and *b* negative. Diagram *e* shows no consistent pattern between the measures. Two factors, then, are associated in correlation, *magnitude* (high to low) and *direction* (positive and negative), with the former generally the most important. The correlations of scatter diagrams *a–e* presented in Figure 9.3 are linear, i.e., have a tendency to follow a straight-line pattern. Curved-line relationships are, of course, possible (see diagram *f* in Figure 9.3). If one were examining the relationship between test anxiety and achievement-test performance, he might find that anxiety tended to be associated with *increased* performance up to a certain point, at which an increase in anxiety would be associated with *decreased* performance. One of the reasons for plotting scatter diagrams is to determine whether the relationship is linear or curvilinear and to get a "feel" for the data. The indices of correlation to be discussed in the remainder of this chapter are appropriate for linear relationships only, and the reader interested in curvilinear correlation procedures is referred to any number of standard texts (e.g., Ferguson 1966 and McNemar 1962).

After graphically examining a relationship, we come to the problem of describing it quantitatively. The most frequently used index of linear relationship is the Pearson product-moment correlation coefficient (r) which, in its simplest form, may be represented as follows:

$$r = \frac{\Sigma z_x z_y}{N},$$
(Equation 9.12)

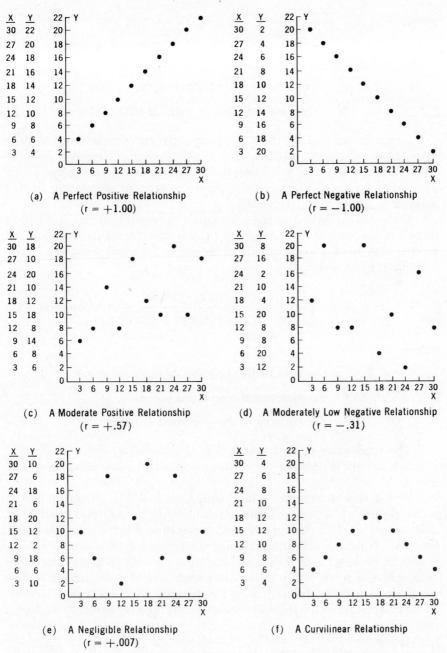

FIGURE 9.3. Scatter Diagrams Showing Various Degrees of Correlation

where

$$z_x \text{ and } z_y = \text{standard scores of the form } \frac{X - \overline{X}}{S}$$

$$\Sigma z_x z_y = \text{the sum of the product of the z scores}$$

$$N = \text{the total number of pairs of observations.}$$

Using Equation 9.12, then, requires converting each X and Y score to a standard score, specifically a z score, multiplying the pairs of corresponding z scores, summing the products, and dividing by N. An illustration of the calculation of a product-moment correlation in this manner is presented in Table 9.3.

If we are interested in the correlation between two measures for a large number of students, wish to bypass the calculation of standard scores, and have a desk calculator available, the following raw-score formula may be used:

$$r = \frac{N\Sigma XY - (\Sigma X)(\Sigma Y)}{\sqrt{[N\Sigma X^2 - (\Sigma X)^2][N\Sigma Y^2 - (\Sigma Y)^2]}}, \quad \text{(Equation 9.13)}$$

where

$$\Sigma XY = \text{the sum of the product of the raw scores}$$

$$u\Sigma X^2, \Sigma Y^2 = \text{the sums of the squared scores}$$

$$(\Sigma X)^2, (\Sigma Y)^2 = \text{the squares of the summed scores.}$$

The application of Equation 9.13 is also demonstrated in Table 9.3. We note identical results (within rounding error) using Equations 9.12 and 9.13.

Both direct and inverse relationships are possible. A correlation of +1.00 represents a perfect positive relationship between two variables, and one of −1.00 a perfect inverse or negative relationship. A correlation of .00 indicates the total absence of relationship between the scores. It should be emphasized that a correlation of −.68 indicates the same magnitude of relationship as does a correlation of +.68, and that they would be equally useful in making predictions. It is not true, however, that a correlation of .60 indicates twice as strong a relationship as does a correlation of .30, i.e., r is not directly proportional to the degree of correlation.

In calculating a correlation using Equation 9.12, we were essentially describing the relationship between X and Y in terms of an individual student's relative position on the two measures, expressed in standard score form. Correlation is invariant regardless of the units of measurement used. Earlier in this chapter we saw how ranks could also be used

TABLE 9.3   Illustration of Calculation of Product-Moment Correlation Between College Board French Test (X) and Final Exam Scores (Y) Using Standard Scores (z) and Raw Scores

Student	College Board Test (X)	Final Exam Score (Y)	z_x	z_y	$z_x z_y$	X^2	Y^2	XY
A	448	70	−.67	−1.0	.67	200704	4900	31360
B	572	80	.26	.0	.0	327184	6400	45760
C	763	98	1.70	1.80	3.06	582169	9604	74774
D	502	75	− .26	− .50	.13	252004	5625	37650
E	629	86	.69	.60	.41	395641	7396	54094
F	345	72	−1.44	− .80	1.15	119025	5184	24840
G	525	68	− .09	−1.20	.11	275625	4624	35700
H	417	70	− .90	−1.00	.90	173889	4900	29190
I	327	66	−1.58	−1.40	2.21	106929	4356	21582
J	518	84	− .14	.40	− .06	268324	7056	43512
K	654	94	.88	1.40	1.23	427716	8836	61476
L	780	97	1.83	1.70	3.11	608400	9409	75660
M	528	85	− .07	.50	− .03	278784	7225	44880
N	409	78	− .96	− .20	.19	167281	6084	31902
O	644	83	.80	.30	.24	414736	6889	53452
Σ	8061	1206			13.32	4598411	98488	665832
X̄	537	80						
S	133	10						

Correlation Using z Scores

$$r = \frac{\Sigma z_y z_y}{N}$$

$$r = \frac{13.32}{15} = \underline{\underline{.89}}$$

Correlation Using Raw Scores

$$r = \frac{N\Sigma XY - (\Sigma X)(\Sigma Y)}{\sqrt{[N\Sigma X^2 - (\Sigma X)^2][N\Sigma Y^2 - (\Sigma Y)^2]}}$$

$$r = \frac{15(665832) - (8061)(1206)}{\sqrt{[15(4598411) - (8061)^2][15(98488) - (1206)^2]}}$$

$$r = \frac{9987480 - 9721566}{\sqrt{[68976165 - 64979721][1477320 - 1454436]}}$$

$$r = \frac{265914}{\sqrt{[3996444][22884]}} = \frac{265914}{\sqrt{91,454,624,496}}$$

$$r = \frac{265,914}{302,414} = \underline{\underline{.88}}$$

to represent relative position. There is an efficient procedure for correlating two sets of scores that uses only ranks. It is called the Spearman Rank Difference or Rank Order correlation:

$$\rho = 1 - \left(\frac{6(\Sigma D^2)}{N(N^2 - 1)}\right)$$

(Equation 9.14)

where

$$\Sigma D^2 = \text{the sum of the squared differences in ranks}$$
(the number 6 is a constant value)

$$N = \text{the number of ranked pairs of scores.}$$

The procedure merely involves assigning a rank of "1" to the highest score on each variable, "2" to the next highest, and so on. Rankings are completed separately for the two variables being correlated. In the case of tied scores, averaged ranks are assigned. For example, if four examinees all had scores of 25 on the same test, and were tied for the ranks of 8, 9, 10, and 11, an average rank would be assigned—in this situation, 9.5 (8 + 9 + 10 + 11)/4. After the ranking has been completed (note that we cannot have more ranks than people and that the algebraic sum of the differences in ranks is zero), the differences in ranks are squared, summed, multiplied by 6, and substituted in Equation 9.14. This was accomplished on the same College Board and Exam scores of Table 9.3, and the calculations are summarized in Table 9.4. The rank difference correlation of .83 compares favorably with the product-moment correlation of .89. The rank differ-

TABLE 9.4 Illustration of Calculation of Spearman's Rank Order Correlation with Hypothetical College Board (X) and French Final Exam (Y) Scores from Table 9.3

Student	(1) College Board Score (X)	(2) Exam Score (Y)	(3) Rank of X Score	(4) Rank of Y Score	(5) D $R_x - R_y$	(6) D² $(R_x - R_y)^2$
A	448	70	11	12.5	−1.5	2.25
B	572	80	6	8	−2	4
C	763	98	2	1	1	1
D	502	75	10	10	0	0
E	629	86	5	4	1	1
F	345	72	14	11	3	9
G	525	68	8	14	−6	36
H	417	70	12	12.5	− .5	.25
I	327	66	15	15	0	0
J	518	84	9	6	3	9
K	654	94	3	3	0	0
L	780	97	1	2	−1	1
M	528	85	7	5	2	4
N	409	78	13	9	4	16
O	644	83	4	7	−3	9

$$\rho = 1 - \frac{6(\Sigma D^2)}{N(N^2 - 1)} \qquad \Sigma D = 0$$
$$\Sigma D^2 = 92.5$$

$$\rho = 1 - \frac{555}{3360}$$

$$\rho = 1 - .17$$

$$\rho = \underline{\underline{.83}}$$

ence *tends* to be a conservative (lower) estimate of relationship than the product-moment, unless a large number of ties tend to inflate the obtained coefficient. The Spearman correlation, because of its relative accuracy and computational ease, is recommended for use by the classroom teacher as an adequate correlational index in analyzing his tests. How correlational procedures can be applied in evaluating a test will be described in Chapter Eleven.

SUGGESTED READINGS

Clarke, R. B.; Colardarci, A. P.; and Caffrey, J. *Statistical reasoning and procedures.* Columbus, Ohio: Charles E. Merrill Books, 1965. A good source for the nonmathematically-oriented student.

Downie, N. M., and Heath, R. W. *Basic statistical methods,* 2nd ed. New York: Harper & Row, 1965. A readable text oriented toward those working with test data.

Edwards, A. L. *Statistical methods for the behavioral sciences.* New York: Holt, Rinehart and Winston, 1961. The treatment of the various correlation procedures available to the student of measurement is a strong point of this text.

Guilford, J. P. *Fundamental statistics in psychology and education,* 4th ed. New York: McGraw-Hill, 1965. A standard and comprehensive reference work in the area of statistics, this volume considers the basic concepts of inferential and descriptive techniques and has separate chapters on reliability, validity, and norms.

Weinberg, G. H., and Schumaker, J. A. *Statistics: An intuitive approach.* Belmont, Cal.: Wadsworth, 1962. An introductory treatment of statistical concepts oriented toward the mathematically unsophisticated.

Young, R. K., and Veldman, D. J. *Introductory statistics for the behavioral sciences.* New York: Holt, Rinehart and Winston, 1965. This text combines programmed learning with the usual discussive and expository approach.

The following brief volumes are highly condensed presentations of descriptive statistical topics. All use the "programmed learning" method and would be useful for a quick overview or review.

Amos, J. R.; Brown, F. L.; and Mink, O. G. *Statistical concepts: A basic program.* New York: Harper & Row, 1965.

Bradley, J. S., and McCleland, J. N. *Basic statistical concepts: A self-instructional text.* Fair Lawn, N.J.: Scott, Foresman, 1963.

McCollough, Celeste, and Van Atta, L. *Statistical concepts: A program for self-instruction.* New York: McGraw-Hill, 1963.

McCollough, Celeste, and Van Atta, L. *Introduction to descriptive statistics and correlation: A program for self-instruction.* New York: McGraw-Hill, 1965.

Townsend, E. A., and Burke, P. J. *Statistics for the classroom teacher: A self-teaching unit.* New York: Macmillan, 1963.

10
INTERPRETING TEST PERFORMANCES

SUMMARY PREVIEW STATEMENTS

1. Test performances may be interpreted in light of absolute standards, relative averages, or test content.

2. Interpretations of scores on most standardized tests should be limited to the relative (normative) performances of representative groups.

3. Normative data may be expressed in the form of raw scores, standard scores (z, Z, T, CEEB scores or stanines), percentile ranks, age scores, or grade scores.

4. The value of any set of normative data rests primarily on the nature and number of students and schools represented.

5. Percentile rank and standard score norms have direct interpretability if the national sample matches the local group in terms of relevant demographic and educational characteristics.

6. A grade equivalent is the average raw test score for a particular grade.

7. Among other problems, grade equivalent norms suffer from the following shortcomings:
   a. A given grade equivalent does not mean the same thing for each student who receives it, whether the student is in the same class or grade, or is above or below it.
   b. Most grade norms are based on the untenable assumption of uniform growth throughout the year, and therefore use ambiguous units of measurement.
   c. Most grade norms discount the learning or loss of learning that occurs over the summer months.
   d. Extrapolated (estimated) grade norms are open to many misinterpretations.
   e. Grade norms should not be considered standards.

    f. The value of grade norms depends on the match between curriculum and test content.

    g. Extreme grade equivalents are difficult to interpret.

8. Age norms are based on average test scores at various age levels.

9. It is highly desirable to develop local test norms.

10. Expectancy norms for achievement tests can be developed by relating test scores to ability measures or relevant external criteria.

11. Published test norms should be:
    a. Clearly described.
    b. Expressed as standard scores and percentile ranks.
    c. As up-to-date as possible.

12. Profiling achievement test scores in various subject areas from the same battery allows for the identification of individual student and class strengths and weaknesses.

13. Percentile bands corresponding to the standard error of measurement should be used when profiling test scores.

14. In interpreting profiles, consideration should be given to the elevation, scatter, and shape of the profile.

15. In interpreting test scores to students, the teacher should carefully consider the potential psychological impact of such scores and the many related factors that bear meaning.

16. A student has a right to an interpretation of his score on any test.

17. In interpreting and reporting scores to the public, care should be taken to:
    a. Explain the purpose of the tests.
    b. Avoid the use of composite scores for each school.
    c. Prepare a tabular and narrative summary.
    d. Avoid implying that norms are standards.
    e. Take into account the many economic and demographic variables that influence test scores.

This chapter focuses on the problem of deriving meanings from scores primarily on standardized tests. Many of the ideas and suggestions it offers can, however, be applied by the classroom teacher to his own tests.

The meaning of a given test score is not readily apparent, no matter what type of test or student is involved. There are two general approaches to the derivation of meaning from a test item, score, or set of scores. One may use the approach to be described in Chapter Thirteen to derive an *absolute* interpretation of the test performance in light of specific objectives. A more *relative* approach involves contrasting a given performance with that of a known reference group—a summary of the performances of a classroom, all classrooms in a school, a school system, state, region, or national sampling of students. We will focus here on local norms (usually restricted to a school system or smaller unit) and national norms like those used in conjunction with standardized tests available from commercial publishers.

Normative data, usually in the form of derived scores, may be expressed as raw scores, standard scores (z, Z, T, CEEB scores, and stanines), percentile ranks, age scores, or grade scores. The first three of these means of expressing test scores were described in Chapter Nine. If a criterion-reference framework was used to develop a test, the interpretation of a given individual's score as a percentage of the total possible correct answers would not be too misleading. It is imperative, however, that all the objectives be spelled out, that a reasonably narrow area of achievement be measured, and that the population of items (of which the test is a sample) be made explicit. Such a percentage interpretation should only be used as a quick benchmark for judging achievement. Tests are fallible, particularly classroom tests, and the samplings of behaviors they represent are limited. It would be more reasonable to relate a given raw score to other performances in the classroom. We could convert the raw scores to standard scores or percentile ranks and then interpret a given performance in terms of variance from the average or position (percentage) relative to the other performances.

PERCENTILE RANK NORMS

Percentile ranks can be used to express local or national normative data, and are particularly useful with classroom tests. The process merely requires developing a frequency distribution and calculating a percentile rank for each raw score according to the procedures outlined in Chapter Nine. Given that an individual has a raw score equivalent to a percentile rank of 64, we can say that his performance is as good as or better than those of 64 percent of the people with whom we are contrasting it. The use of percentile ranks is suggested because they are readily understood by almost everyone and can be used with many types of tests and distributions of scores. That the percentile rank depends on the frequency distribution creates a danger in interpretation. This danger involves the fact that the units used to express percentile ranks are not equal to raw-score units (except in the unlikely occurrence of a rectangular distribution, i.e., a distribution in which each observed score has the same frequency of occurrence). The difference in raw-score units between percentile ranks of 84 and 88 is *not* equal to the difference between the percentile ranks of 50 and 54. We have, then, an interpretation based only on a ranking of individuals, without regard to differences between ranks. Because of the unequal units, percentile ranks should not be averaged (unless one wishes to describe average percentile ranks). The point is that the mean percentile rank is not equal to the percentile rank of the mean.

An illustration of the method used to read percentile ranks from norm tables for a subtest of the *Stanford Achievement Test* is presented in Figure 10.1. The procedure is relatively straightforward. Each raw-score

Test: SAT Hypothetical Sub Test: Standardization				
Variable I Grade 5			II Grade 6	

	%ile	1	5 10 20 30 50 70 80 90 95 99
30-31		100	
28-29	100	98	
26-27	99.7	95	
24-25	99	89	
22-23	98	82	
20-21	95	73	
18-19	91	64	
16-17	84	53	
14-15	75	43	
12 13	63	33	
10-11	50	24	
8-9	35	15	
6-7	20	8.3	
4-5	8.3	3.2	
2-3	2.1	.7	
0-1	.2	.1	
			1 5 10 20 30 50 70 80 90 95 99
			Percentile Scale

FIGURE 10.1. Schematic Illustration of Determination of Percentile Norm Lines for Grades 5 and 6 on Intermediate II Level of Stanford Achievement Test

distribution (for Grade 5 and Grade 6 separately) was plotted on a normal percentile chart, a smooth curve fitted to the points, and the percentile rank corresponding to each score was read. For Grade 5 a raw score of about 11 would have a percentile rank of 50, but for Grade 6 a raw score of about 17 would be needed for the same percentile rank. In other words, the 50th percentile for Grade 5 is 11, and for Grade 6 it is 17.

STANDARD SCORE NORMS

As was the case with percentile ranks, standard scores can be used to express either local or national normative data. They are very effective with classroom tests. Standard scores have an advantage over percentile ranks in that they are a direct reflection of the raw score with regard both to size of unit and to shape of distribution. In addition, they are on a "standard scale" with fixed mean and standard deviation, which allows us to manipulate them mathematically with greater confidence. The reader is referred to Appendix C for a table showing the relationship between T and z scores, and percentile ranks when the underlying distribution is normally distributed.

GRADE NORMS

Grade score norms involve the calculation of grade scores or grade equivalents. A grade equivalent of a given raw score is the grade level of those students whose median (or mean) is the same as that particular raw score. If the median score of a group of seventh-graders is 54, all raw scores of 54 would have grade equivalents of 7.0. Decimal numbers are usually used, the first digit representing the school year and the second the month in a ten-month school year.

A sample of grade norms from the *Stanford Achievement Test* are presented in Table 10.1. These norms are expressed as grade scores. To arrive at a grade equivalent, one need only place a decimal to the left of the final digit. For example, a grade score of 45 is the same as a grade equivalent of 4.5 (or the fifth month of the fourth school year). In addition, Table 10.1 provides the corresponding percentile ranks and stanine scores for given grade scores. Grade scores are derived in a separate process. A chart like Table 10.2 is developed for each subtest of the SAT. Tables 10.1 and 10.2 are used together to arrive at an interpretation. Given a raw-score total correct of 37 on the Word Meaning subtest, we find a grade score of 78 on Table 10.2. This grade score is the same as a grade equivalent of 7.8. The grade score can be seen in Table 10.1 to have a percentile rank of 64 and a stanine of 6.

TABLE 10.1 Sample Grade Norms for Intermediate II Level of Stanford Achievement Test (Grade 7, September through December)

Sta-nine	%ile Rank	Word Mean.	Para. Mean.	Spell.	Lang.	Arith. Comp.	Arith. Concepts	Arith. Appl.	Social Studies	Science	%ile Rank	Sta-nine
						GRADE SCORES						
9	99	129	120	125	120	117	124	122	123	121	99	9
	98	121	117	122	117	112	118	119	119	118	98	
	96	115	115	118	114	105	111	115	117	116	96	
8	94	110	112	115	111			111	114	113	94	8
	92	105	109	112	108	100	103	106	112	110	92	
	90	100	106	108	107				110	107	90	
	89	96			105	96	95				89	
7	88	93	104	105	104			101	107	104	88	7
	86		100	102	102	91	88				86	
	84	90			100			96	104	100	84	
	82		96	97	98				100		82	
	80	88		92	97	86	85	91		96	80	
	78		92		95				96		78	
	77			88	93					92	77	
6	76	85	87		90	84	82	86	90		76	6
	74			85	88					88	74	
	72	83	84		86	82	80		86		72	
	70		82	82	84			83	83	85	70	
	68	80		80	82				81		68	
	66		80		80	79	78	80		81	66	
	64	78	78	78	79				79		64	
	62				77	77			77	78	62	
	60	76	77	76	76		76	77			60	
5	58		75	75	75				76	75	58	5
	56	75			74	74	73	74	74		56	
	54	73	73	73	73					72	54	
	52		72		72				72		52	
	50	71	71	71	71	71	71	71	71	71	50	
	48		70	70	70		70		70	69	48	
	46	69	69		69	68		68	68	67	46	
	44		67	68	67		68		66		44	
	42	67	66	67	66	66		66	65	66	42	
	40				65		66				40	
4	38	66	65	66	64	65		65	64	64	38	4
	36		64	64	63		65		63	62	36	
	34	64	62	63	62	63		63	62		34	
	32	62	61		61		63			60	32	
	30		60	62	60	62		61	61		30	
	28	60	59	60	58	60	61		60	58	28	
	26	59	57	59	57			59	59	57	26	
	24				56	59					24	
	23	57	56	57	55		59	57	58	56	23	
3	22		54		54	58			56		22	3
	20	56	53	56	53	56	56	56	55	54	20	
	18	54	52	54	51				54	52	18	
	16		50	53	50	54	54	54	53	50	16	
	14	52	49	51	48			51	52	49	14	
	12	51	48	50	46	52	52		51	47	12	
	11	49	47	48	45			49	50	46	11	
2	10	47	46	47	44	50	49	46	49	44	10	2
	8	46	44	45	41	48		44	48	43	8	
	6	42	42	44	38	46	46	42	45	42	6	
	4	41	39	41	35	44	43	40	43	39	4	
1	2	38	34	37	32	38	40	36	40	36	2	1
	1	33	30	33	29	36	36	34	37	34	1	

TABLE 10.2   Conversion of Raw-Score Number Correct to Grade Score on Intermediate II Word Meaning Subtest of Stanford Achievement Test

No. Right	Grade Score	No. Right	Grade Score
1	20	25	59
2	23	26	60
3	25	27	62
4	27	28	64
5	29	29	66
6	30	30	67
7	32	31	68
8	33	32	69
9	35	33	71
10	36	34	73
11	38	35	75
12	39	36	76
13	41	37	78
14	42	38	80
15	44	39	83
16	46	40	85
17	47	41	88
18	49	42	90
19	51	43	95
20	52	44	100
21	54	45	105
22	55	46	110
23	56	47	118
24	57	48	129

Source: Reproduced from Stanford Achievement Test, copyright © 1964 by Harcourt Brace Jovanovich, Inc. Reproduced by special permission of the publisher.

Because they are expressed in terms of the units around which schools are organized, grade equivalents are ordinarily easily understood. In addition, they lend themselves to the plotting of achievement profiles in various subject areas, thus allowing for examination of a given pupil's strengths and weaknesses.

Flanagan (1951) has noted a number of the problems encountered in interpreting grade equivalents:

1.   It is incorrect to say, for example, that a sixth-grader who achieves a grade equivalent of eight on a test is performing at eighth-grade level. He has been taught and tested on sixth-grade material, not eighth-grade material. Rather, he performs as would the typical eighth-grader taking *his* test.

2.   Grade norms assume uniform growth throughout the year, which is not the case within or across subject areas or grades. A grade score of 3.0 might yield a percentile rank of 40 on a reading subtest and a percentile rank of 20 on a math subtest of a survey achievement battery. The

units of measurement are ambiguous. This lack of uniformity in scaling is well illustrated by Figure 10.2. The curve represents a plot of grade equivalent scores and test raw scores, which obviously depart from a straight-line relationship. Caution, then, must be used in interpreting a given individual's score on different subtests and assessing growth. In other words, a change of three score points may result in a variable change in grade scores, depending on the raw scores involved.

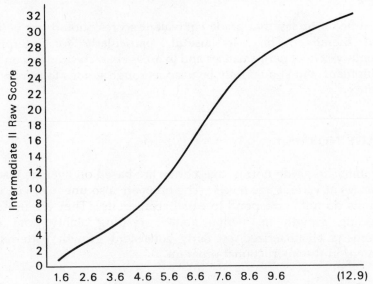

FIGURE 10.2. Relationships between Grade and Raw Scores on Arithmetic Concepts Subtest of Stanford Achievement Test

Source: Reproduced from Stanford Achievement Test, copyright ©
1966 by Harcourt Brace Jovanovich, Inc. Reproduced by special permission of the publisher.

3. It is impossible to test at all grade levels. Therefore, a great many grade equivalents are based on extrapolated values, which tend to be nothing more than educated guesses.

4. The procedures used to determine grade equivalents tend to exaggerate the significance of small differences in raw scores because of customarily large within-grade variability.

5. There is a danger that, because of the correspondence between the label *grade equivalent* and the way the schools are organized, teachers will come to consider the grade equivalent a standard for performance. Such a misinterpretation attests to lack of knowledge of local objectives and individual differences.

6. A score on any achievement test is a function of the treatment of the

subject matter in the curriculum. An assumption of uniformity for test standardization is unwarranted.

7. Extremely high or low grade equivalents are difficult to interpret due to the lack of reliable measurement at the extremes of any score scale.

8. Most norms tables are based on a ten-month school year, and thus ignore the gains or losses of proficiency that occur during the summer months.

Suffice it to say that grade equivalent scores should not be interpreted literally. They are useful, particularly for interpreting elementary-school performances and in areas characterized by continual development, but should only be used as rough guides to level of performance.

AGE NORMS

Similar to grade norms, age norms are based on average test performances at various age levels. The units are also unequal, i.e., equal age units do not correspond to equal score units. They are useful for expressing growth in mental ability, reading ability, and other phenomena characterized by fairly consistent growth patterns and treatment in the instructional program.

LOCAL NORMS

Local norms are more valuable for many purposes than are those provided by test publishers. Due to the idiosyncrasies of the local curriculum, student body, community needs, and teacher characteristics, national norms may not be representative of the local instructional situation. Local school personnel must then develop their own reference data. Generating test data and summarizing them in the form of percentile ranks and standard scores would be most helpful, particularly for achievement test results. Some test manuals provide guidelines for the development of local norms. In addition, many test publishers will provide a norming service for a nominal fee.

EXPECTANCY NORMS

It is unreasonable to interpret performance on a test without reference to other relevant variables. For an achievement test, one relevant variable is student ability. Many test publishers therefore provide for the dual standardization of achievement and scholastic aptitude (or intelligence) tests. The correlation between achievement and aptitude measures is determined, and using the aptitude score an expected achievement performance can be predicted. In this manner a student may be judged to be under- or overachieving in a particular subject. The expectancy table is one form in which these data are expressed (see Chapter Eleven for a description of expectancy tables).

Another example of an expectancy interpretation of a test score is found in the procedures suggested for use with the *Readiness Skills* measures associated with the *Gates-MacGinitie Reading Tests*. This test, intended for use in Kindergarten and Grade 1, is made up of eight subtests: Listening Comprehension, Auditory Discrimination, Visual Discrimination, Following Directions, Letter Recognition, Visual-motor Coordination, Auditory Blending, and Word Recognition. All of these skills have been found to be important in the teaching of reading, but not to the same degree. The appropriate weights for each subtest were determined through the application of multiple regression techniques in order to provide the best prediction of later reading achievement. Multiple regression is like the correlation procedures examined in Chapter Nine, but instead of two variables, e.g., a test score and a criterion, there are several predictors and a single criterion. After the tests are scored they are entered on a score record. A sample score record for a first-grade student is shown in Figure 10.3.

The raw scores are converted to stanines, according to the appropriate tables. The stanines are multiplied by the standard weights previously shown to approximate best the importance of each subtest in later reading achievement. The relative importance of each subtest is shown on the score record; Letter Recognition is the most and Word Recognition the least important. The weighted scores are summed to yield a Total Weighted Score (TWS) and converted to a Readiness Standard Score (RSS). Conversion to the RSS is accomplished through the use of a table like Figure 10.4.

Total Weighted Scores are ordinarily used when evaluating general reading readiness and making decisions about the organization of classes. In making comparisons among children, both the RSS (a normalized standard score) and the Readiness Percentile Score (a percentile rank) are used. For example, the TWS of 62 in Figure 10.3 yields an RSS of 48. The mean of the RSSs is 50, with a standard deviation of 10. Thus this individual is 0.2 standard deviation below the average. In addition, his TWS of 62 is equivalent to a percentile rank of 42, which means he did as well as or better than 42 percent of the first-grade children in the normative sample. The teacher may use such test information to work with students individually or to form groups aimed at developing the competencies required for effective reading instruction.

SCORE RECORD				
Subtest	Raw Score	Stanine	Weight	Weighted Score
I. Listening Comprehension	14	5	1	5
II. Auditory Discrimination	13	3	2	6
III. Visual Discrimination	20	6	2	12
IV. Following Directions	11	6	2	12
V. Letter Recognition	13	6	3	18
VI. Visual-Motor Coordination	13	6	1	6
VII. Auditory Blending	6	3	1	3
Total Weighted Score				62
	Readiness Standard Score			48
	Readiness Percentile Score			42
VIII. Word Recognition	9	5		

FIGURE 10.3.   Sample Score Record

Source: Reprinted by permission of the publisher from Gates-MacGinitie *Reading tests readiness skills teacher's manual* (New York: Teachers College Press, copyright 1968 by Teachers College, Columbia University), p. 15.

Total Weighted Score	Readiness Standard Score	Readiness Percentile Score
*		
20	29	2
21	30	2
22	30	2
23	31	3
⋮	⋮	⋮
38	37	10
39	38	12
40	38	12
41	39	14
42	39	14
43	40	16
44	40	16
45	40	16
46	41	18
47	41	18
48	42	21
49	42	21
50	43	24
51	43	24
52	44	27
53	44	27
54	44	27
55	45	31
56	45	31
57	46	34
58	46	34
59	47	38
60	47	38
61	48	42
62	48	42
63	48	42
64	49	46
65	49	46
66	50	50
67	50	50
68	51	54
69	51	54
70	52	58
71	52	58
⋮	⋮	⋮
89	64	92
90	65	93
91	66	95
92	68	96
93	69	97
94	70	98
95	71	98
96	72	99
*		

FIGURE 10.4. Portion of Grade 1 Readiness Standard Score and Percentile Norms

Source: Reprinted by permission of the publisher from Gates-MacGinitie *Reading tests readiness skills teacher's manual* (New York: Teachers College Press, copyright 1968 by Teachers College, Columbia University), p. 20.

CRITERIA FOR PUBLISHED NORMS

A test manual should provide a comprehensive description of the procedures used in collecting normative data. Among the essential and desirable characteristics of normative data are the following (American Psychological Association, 1966):

1. Normative data should be described so clearly that a potential user can readily judge the relevance of the norms for his testing purposes.

2. Normative data should be reported in the form of standard scores and percentile ranks.

3. If grade norms are provided, provision should be made for conversion of grade equivalents to standard scores and percentile ranks.

4. With each test revision and/or renorming, relationships between new and old norms should be described and equivalency tables provided.

5. Normative data should be published at the same time as the test.

6. Every effort should be made by the publisher to keep his norms as current as possible.

7. The publisher should point out the importance of establishing local norms, and procedures useful in doing so.

8. Descriptive data (e.g., measures of central tendency and variability) should be reported for the normative sample(s).

9. In addition to norms, tables showing the expectation a person who achieves a given test score has of attaining or exceeding some relevant criterion score should be provided.

10. Sufficient information should be provided on such variables as numbers of schools, sex, number of cases, geographic location, age, educational level, and the like, so that it can be determined whether a set of norms are in fact representative of the population they are claimed to represent.

11. Sampling procedures should be spelled out in detail.

12. Normative data should be reported only if the associated reliability and validity data are also available.

13. The testing conditions under which the normative data were obtained should be specified.

14. If profiling of different subtests is suggested, the relevant normative data should be comparable, i.e., gathered on the same population(s).

INTERPRETING PROFILES

Some publishers of multiscore instruments suggest that the scores be profiled to aid in interpretation. Such a graphic representation facilitates the examination of relative highs and lows, strengths and weaknesses, and positive and negative tendencies. For technical reasons differences between scores, particularly in batteries whose subtests focus on similar outcomes, are unreliable. Therefore, great caution must be exercised in interpretation. Treating small differences (which are likely to be chance differences) as significant can only lead to erroneous decisions. This point can be illustrated with reference to the sample score record for the Gates-MacGinitie Readiness Skills test in Figure 10.3. The publisher notes in the manual that the difference between a stanine of 5 on one subtest and 6 on another is very likely due to chance. The difference between Auditory Discrimination and Auditory Blending (stanine of 3), and the subtests with stanines of 5 or 6 are one standard deviation or larger in size. These differences are reliable for this test and may be considered of importance for instruction.

One way to overcome the problem of interpreting differences in scores on the same profile is to rely on *percentile bands.* These bands are illustrated by the shaded areas in Figure 10.5, which is a sample student profile for the *Sequential Tests of Educational Progress.* It can be seen that the scores are plotted not as points but as bands. Percentile bands correspond to the obtained score plus and minus one standard error of measurement (a measure of reliability—see Chapter Eleven for a discussion of the standard error of measurement). These bands represent the ranges within which we can be reasonably sure of finding the student's "true" performance. If the bands for two different tests do *not* overlap, we can feel reasonably confident that the performances are different enough to warrant further consideration.

Three major types of information in score profiles need to be taken into account during interpretation. The *level* or *elevation* of the profile, which may be thought of as an individual's average score on all tests represented in the profile, must be considered. Second, *scatter* or *dispersion* should be examined. Scatter involves the extent to which an individual varies throughout the subtest. One measure of scatter is the standard deviation of scores for an individual on the different tests. A third characteristic of a score profile is the *shape*, which reveals the particular points at which the individual has high or low scores. A simple ranking of subtests from high to low on the profile should provide the necessary information. It should be noted that we are basically considering ways of "looking at" a profile. Obviously, some subtests are more important than others for any given purpose.

TEST USAGE AND INTERPRETATION, AND STUDENT ANXIETY

There is no doubt that the examinee feels tension and anxiety before, during, and after a testing experience. This is particularly true if the test is of great consequence to the examinee. Midterms and finals,

Name _Lawrence_ _Albert_ _E._
  Last   First   Middle
School _Midtown H.S. (1)_ Grade or Class _11_
Age _16_ _2_ Date of Testing _Fall_ _1957-58_
   Years Months   Fall or Spring   Year

Norms Used

☑ Publisher's   ☑ Fall   Grade or Class _11_
☐ Local   ☐ Spring   Other _____
                                _____

Ⓒ Copyright 1957, All rights reserved

Cooperative Test Division Ⓔ Ⓣ Ⓢ Educational Testing Service · Princeton, N.J. · Los Angeles 27, Calif.

Here you can profile a student's percentile ranks on as many as six tests in the STEP series. In order for your comparisons between the areas to be valid, all tests included should be administered within a period of 4 or 5 months.

Recording. Directions for recording information and drawing percentile bands on the PROFILE form are included in each STEP MANUAL FOR INTERPRETING SCORES. Consult the manuals for the tests used.

Interpreting. To compare a student's performance on one of the tests in the STEP series with that of students in the norms group used, note the unshaded parts of the column above and below the percentile band. For example, if the Listening percentile band is 24-36, you know that 24 per cent of students in the norms group score lower than this student and 64 per cent score higher. In other words, this student's Listening performance is below average with respect to the norms group.

To compare a student's standings on any two tests in the STEP series, the following rules apply:

1. If the percentile bands for any two tests overlap, there is no important difference between the student's standings on those two tests.
2. If the percentile bands for any two tests do *not* overlap, standing represented by the higher band is really better than standing represented by the lower band.

Examples: According to local norms, a student's percentile bands for three tests are

Mathematics (2A)	50-62
Social Studies (2A)	60-71
Science (2B)	41-52

Bands for Mathematics and Social Studies overlap; there is no important difference between the student's standings in these two areas. The same is true of Mathematics and Science. However, bands for Science and Social Studies do not overlap; the student's standing in Social Studies is higher than his standing in Science.

More detailed discussions of interpretations are contained in each STEP MANUAL FOR INTERPRETING SCORES.

D37R25

FIGURE 10.5. Sample Student Profile

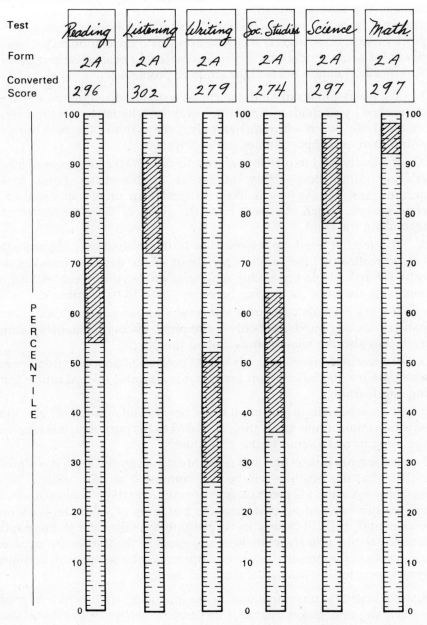

college entrance exams, and scholarship qualifying exams are examples of tests likely to evoke considerable test anxiety potentially harmful to the student. In the classroom situation, improper uses of tests can damage the teacher-student relationship. The misuse of tests stems primarily from two sources (Lennon 1954): (1) misunderstanding of the proper role of tests, and (2) failure to appreciate the emotional problems posed for some children by any ego-threatening evaluation procedure. Specifically, Lennon notes eight kinds of problems:

1. If a teacher looks upon the norm on a standardized test as a goal to be reached by all children, and criticizes those who fail to meet this rigid standard, the pupils will quite naturally come to think of tests as hurdles rather than as stepping stones to development.

2. If a teacher in interpreting test results fails to take into account other relevant information—ability differences, health status, home background, and the like—he is likely to render an unjust appraisal of a child's work, which may well have the effect of discouraging or antagonizing the child.

3. If a teacher overemphasizes tests in the evaluation program, and fails to realize that they cover only a part of the desired outcomes, he runs the risk of placing undue emphasis on certain objectives and of confusing the pupil as to what he is supposed to be learning.

4. If a teacher habitually uses test results as bases for invidious comparisons among pupils, not only is the pupil-teacher relationship damaged, but also the relationships among the pupils.

5. If a teacher berates or scolds a child because of poor performance on a test, he may be building up unfavorable attitudes toward future testing and learning.

6. If a teacher fails to let a pupil know how he did on a test, or give him any indication of how the testing is related to his purposes, it is hard for the pupil to make sense of the procedure.

7. If a teacher is insecure, and feels threatened by the tests, it is almost certain that this attitude will be communicated to the children. If a school or system-wide program is in operation, in the planning of which the teacher has had no part, and the purposes of which he does not understand, he is obviously in no position to make clear to the pupils how the testing is likely to do them any good. If the test results are used as a means of appraising teacher competence, the temptation becomes very strong for the teacher to teach for the tests.

8. If a teacher is unsympathetic to a testing program in which he must participate, and makes slighting or sarcastic reference to "these tests that we have to give again," he is certainly engendering a poor attitude on the pupil's part; even young pupils are shrewd enough to sense,

however vaguely, that by such behavior the teacher is abdicating his rightful position.[1]

Such commonsense procedures as returning test papers as soon as possible, discussing test items with the entire class, and demonstrating to the class the uses of test information will help to develop proper student attitudes and a healthy perspective on the place and value of testing in the instructional program. There is no substitute for respect of the individual student and his needs and desires.

INTERPRETING AND REPORTING TEST RESULTS TO THE PUBLIC

Because of their considerable interest and investment in education, members of the general public need to be apprised of student progress and achievement. The most efficient way of communicating information on performance is probably the use of standardized test scores. Despite their shortcomings, the results derived from standardized tests constitute an immediately understandable summary of student performances. It is imperative that public reports of test scores be carefully presented and explained. Hawes (1972) has summarized several guidelines for reporting test results to the public:

1. *Prepare the public and press for the impending report.* A briefing session should be held to discuss the intent of administering the tests and their use.

2. *Introduce the results with an explanation of test content.* A series of scores is in and of itself relatively meaningless. A description of the content of the tests will help communicate their value to individual students, the schools, and the public.

3. *Prepare a tabular summary of the results for general release.* Breakdowns accompanied by descriptions of such factors as full score ranges, medians, socioeconomic background of the school population, and sex differences will help convey a clearer picture of the results. Consideration might be given to ways of reporting results for special samples and to comparative and growth data.

4. *Avoid the use of composite scores for each school.* Composite scores invite invidious comparisons between schools, and are open to misinterpretation and misuse. The use of composite scores in-house is, however, defensible.

---

[1] R. T. Lennon, Testing: Bond or barrier between pupil and teacher. *Education*, September 1954: 38–42. Reprinted by permission of the publisher.

5. *Avoid reporting grade equivalents.* The danger of using grade equivalents has been discussed. If possible, report percentiles by grades.

6. *Avoid implying that norms are standards.* One should emphasize that normative data are references and benchmarks. A more informative approach is to cite growth data over time (assuming the same tests are involved).

7. *For school-by-school release, report factors influencing test score meaning.* There are many relevant "input factors." Ability level of the student body, teacher turnover rate, per-pupil cost factors, socioeconomic base of the school population, average class size, pupil-teacher ratios, teacher salaries, minority enrollment, pupil mobility, average daily attendance, average years teaching experience, and educational level of the teachers are some of the variables that help to account for a school's test results. Any innovative approach—a large number of open classrooms, for example—should be acknowledged, because it influences curriculum and in turn affects test results.

8. *Provide an overall summary of the results.* It is better for the local educational agency to prepare the summary than to allow those less informed about tests to make possibly damaging interpretations. Emphasis should be on the broad significance of the results for the community, particularly regarding planning and the need for innovative programs.

The interpretation of test scores—whether to individual students, colleagues, parents, or members of the community in general—requires careful preparation and a thorough understanding of what test scores mean, what influences them, and how they can be used. It is a demanding task.

SUGGESTED READINGS

Angoff, W. H. Scales, norms, and equivalent scores. In *Educational measurement*, 2nd ed., ed. R. L. Thorndike. Washington: American Council on Education, 1971. Chapter 15 is the most comprehensive single source for the developer of norms. Although quite technical in places, it contains much of value for the user of norms as well.

Lyman, H. B. *Test scores and what they mean.* Englewood Cliffs, N.J.: Prentice-Hall, 1963. An excellent overview of the many ways in which test scores may be reported. The emphasis on the interpretation of scores is a strong point of the book.

Thorndike, R. L., and Hagen, Elizabeth. *Measurement and evaluation in psychology and education,* 3rd ed. New York: John Wiley & Sons, 1969. Chapter 7, "Norms and Units for Measurement," contains a comprehensive and readable discussion of issues related to test interpretation.

Davis, F. B. *Educational measurements and their interpretation.* Belmont, Cal.: Wadsworth, 1964. Clear if somewhat technical issues are discussed in Chapter 8, "The Interpretation of Individual Test Scores"; Chapter 9, "The Interpretation of Group Scores"; and Chapter 10, "The Measurement of Change."

Gronlund, N. *Measurement and evaluation in teaching,* 2nd ed. New York: Macmillan, 1971. Chapter 15 contains an educationally oriented discussion of the interpretation of test scores and use of norms.

Miller, D. M. *Interpreting test scores.* New York: John Wiley & Sons, 1972. This self-study programmed book contains most of the basic information necessary for initial approaches to test interpretation.

V
INSTRUMENT REFINEMENT

11

ASSESSING RELIABILITY AND VALIDITY

SUMMARY PREVIEW STATEMENTS

1. Educational and psychological tests must always be considered fallible measuring instruments due to the influence of many kinds of errors, primarily involving sampling of behaviors, examinee instability, and scoring.

2. Unsystematic errors, e.g., guessing, fluctuate both within and between testing situations and primarily tend to reduce test reliability.

3. Systematic errors—e.g., the extension of test administration time, yielding inflated scores—are consistent and primarily tend to affect test validity.

4. Test validity should be viewed in terms of the intent of testing and the use(s) to which the data are to be put.

5. A test is not valid or invalid in general, but with respect to a particular criterion in a particular situation with a particular group.

6. Content validity involves how well the items on a test sample a defined universe of tasks.

7. The chief problem in establishing criterion-related validity is defining and securing a reliable measure of the criterion.

8. Criterion-related validity involves the ability of a test to predict, usually through the use of correlational procedures, an individual's status in relation to some relevant criterion.

9. Construct validity involves the degree to which we are able to infer from a test score whether or not an individual possesses some hypothetical trait or characteristic.

10. Content validity relies on the proper delineation of the behaviors to be assessed and can be judged in light of the table of specifications.

11. Expectancy tables are useful in the interpretation of criterion-related validity.

12. Construct validity can be examined, usually on intelligence and personality measures, by noting:
    a. Differences between groups assumed or known to differ in relation to the construct or trait in question.
    b. Changes in performances as a result of treatment related to the construct.
    c. Correlations with other reliable and valid measures of the construct.
    d. The degree to which the items on the test tend to measure the same thing.
    e. The factors that influence the test-taking performance itself.

13. Test reliability generally involves consistency in measurement with different sets of items, examinees, examiners, occasions, or scorers.

14. In general, if a test is valid it is also reliable; however, the converse is not always true.

15. Test-retest reliability requires administering the same test on two different occasions and correlating the results.

16. Equivalent-forms reliability is established by correlating scores on two forms of a test constructed from the same table of specifications.

17. Internal-consistency reliability can be estimated by correlating the scores on two halves of a test and applying the Spearman-Brown formula, one of the Kuder-Richardson formulas, or one of a number of other estimating formulas.

18. Length, objectivity, and the mental functions measured are three factors that significantly influence test reliability.

19. Kuder-Richardson reliability coefficients estimated from speeded tests tend to be spuriously inflated.

20. Estimating internal-consistency reliability with Kuder-Richardson formula 21 requires only knowledge of the mean, variance, and number of items, if the items are dichotomously scored.

21. If the range of item difficulties on a test is large, Kuder-Richardson formula 21 may yield a low reliability estimate reflecting lack of item homogeneity.

22. The standard error of measurement is a general estimate of the magnitude of unsystematic errors expressed in actual test-score units.

23. Multiplying the standard deviation of the test scores by the square root of the difference between the reliability coefficient and 1 will provide an estimate of the standard error of measurement.

24. In general, tests composed of items that measure similar content or mental functions tend to have higher reliabilities than those that measure dissimilar functions.

We have thus far considered some of the basic steps in developing a test. The learning outcomes to be measured have been identified, data-gathering procedures specified, items written, the instrument administered, and scores summarized. It is time now to step back and examine how well the job has been accomplished. We must seek answers to the questions "Does the test measure what I want it to measure?" and "Does the test measure consistently?" The former question relates to *validity* and the latter to *reliability*. Most test experts consider reliability an aspect of validity. Problems relating to the (1) definitions, (2) methods of estimating, and (3) factors influencing validity and reliability will be considered in this chapter. Although our discussion of these two highly important test characteristics will be aimed at the individual who is actually engaged in test development, any individual involved in selecting, administering, and interpreting tests must be thoroughly familiar with these concepts in order to make intelligent and meaningful use of test results.

THE CONCEPT OF ERRORS IN MEASUREMENT

Most tests developed by behavioral scientists yield quantitative descriptions of individuals. In general, we are less concerned with the scores themselves than with what they represent and the characterizations they provide.

Our testing hopes, however, are rarely completely realized. For example, if we administer a test today, wait three weeks, and administer it again, it is highly unlikely that an individual would obtain the same score on both occasions. Another example is a situation in which we are interested in predicting how well a particular high-school student will perform in college. We have results from a scholastic aptitude test and know how scores on it relate to grades during the first semester of the freshman year. On the basis of a test score we predict a C average, only to find that our student achieves a B average. Errors are obviously involved in both situations—errors in measuring and errors in estimating (or predicting).

It was noted in Chapter Nine that two statistical indices useful in describing the variability of a set of scores are the standard deviation and the square of the standard deviation, the variance. What contributes to these indices of variation? Obviously, primary contributors are true individual differences in the trait or skill measured by the test. Such factors as reading ability, memory, the physical condition of the examinee or testing room, and the form of the item may also differentially affect the individuals taking the test, causing their scores to be higher or lower than they should be.

Errors may be meaningfully categorized as *unsystematic* or *systematic*. Unsystematic sources of variation are those factors whose effects are orderless, show no consistent pattern, and fluctuate from one testing occasion to the next. Motivation to perform well on an achievement test, for example, could differentially influence individuals on the same or different occasions. In addition, such factors as variation in attention to the test task and guessing could act as unsystematic sources of error. Systematic effects are those whose influences are the same for an individual on different testing occasions, or for all examinees on the same occasion. If, for example, the test administrator does not rigidly adhere to the time limits specified in the directions for a speeded test and allows every examinee an extra five minutes, scores would be spuriously inflated. The extra time influences the scores in a way that, although constant in the situation, changes the meaning of the scores. Such factors as learning, training, forgetting, fatigue, and growth can function as systematic sources of errors, in some cases increasing and in others decreasing the scores that would have resulted under error-free conditions. One of the limitations of the systematic vs. unsystematic classification is that it is not mutually exclusive. In other words, a given factor, e.g., the physical condition of the testing room, may be systematic in one situation (e.g., the exposure of all examinees to the same poor lighting conditions) and unsystematic in another (e.g., different testing room in a test-retest situation).

The problems associated with controlling and assessing the effects of unsystematic errors are problems of determining reliability. On the other hand, the use of a variety of experimental procedures to determine the extent to which a test is affected by constant errors reflects on the validity of a test.

DEFINING AND ASSESSING VALIDITY

The concept of constant error, as it relates to test validity, implies that there exists some standard or standards for evaluating the presence or absence of such errors. Criteria must be identified, constructed, and collected by the test developer, or sometimes by the user, in order that judgments about validity may be made. The nature of the criteria used to evaluate the validity of a test will in turn be dictated by the purposes of developing and using the test. Three rather broad aims or purposes of testing have been identified (American Psychological Association 1966):

1. *"The test user wishes to determine how an individual performs at present in a universe of situations that the test situation is claimed to represent.* For example, most achievement tests used in schools measure the student's performance on a sample of questions intended to represent a certain phase of educational achievement or certain educational objectives." The type of validity described here is generally referred to as *content* validity.

2. *"The test user wishes to forecast an individual's future standing or to estimate an individual's present standing on some variable of particular significance that is different from the test.* For example, an academic aptitude test may forecast grades, or a brief adjustment inventory may estimate what the outcome would be of a careful psychological examination." Validity defined in this way is called *criterion-related* validity.

3. *"The test user wishes to infer the degree to which the individual possesses some hypothetical trait or quality (construct) presumed to be reflected in the test performance.* For example, he wants to know whether the individual stands high on some proposed abstract trait such as 'intelligence' or 'creativity' that cannot be observed directly. This may be done to learn something about the individual, or it may be done to study the test itself, to study its relationship to other tests, or to develop psychological theory." We are here concerned with the *construct* validity of a test.

The type of validity information gathered will, of course, depend upon the use to be made of the test results. Using the broadly defined test-use categories, three types of validity have been defined. However, the method employed to determine validity could form the basis for an alternative classification. Thorndike and Hagen (1961) have proposed such a classification, distinguishing between types of validity that (a) are primarily dependent upon a rational analysis of the test and its items, and those that (b) rely on empirical and statistical evidence.

Content Validity

In general, content validity is evaluated on the basis of a rational analysis of the item content. Take, for example, an educational achievement test. Validity would be assessed by the professional judgments of an instructor in light of the instructional objectives of a particular class or school. The instructor would seek an answer to this question: How adequately do the items of this test measure the objectives, in terms of both subject matter and cognitive skills, that I want them to measure? Content validity rests on the specification of the universe of behavior to be sampled. For a standardized achievement test, this specification might take the form of a statement in the test manual summarizing the textbooks or subject-matter experts consulted or the course syllabi reviewed. For an informal classroom test, the universe might be defined in terms of a table of specifications developed by the teacher.

Criterion-Related Validity

To establish a claim for criterion-related validity, however, one must draw upon statistical or experimental data. These data are usually presented in the form of correlation coefficients. Means, standard deviations, or other descriptive indices derived from groups known to differ on the variable being measured are occasionally brought to bear on validity claims. The chief problem in using correlational techniques to establish validity involves the identification of an acceptable criterion. The criterion must be external to the test and provide a direct measure of the variable in question. If one were interested in the variable "academic success during the freshman year in college," a criterion measure might be a grade-point average or score on a comprehensive examination. A test estimating either of these criteria might then be developed and experimentally administered to a group of high-school seniors. Later their scores would be correlated with grade-point averages or exam scores obtained at the end of their freshman year in college. If the correlation is high (e.g., +.80), we would conclude that the test has a high degree of criterion-related validity and could be used confidently to make predictions.

In addition to correlation indices, a useful way of summarizing criterion-related validity data is in an *expectancy table*. An expectancy table is a two-way grid that relates test and criterion scores. A simple expectancy table relating scores on the Sentences subtest of the *Differential Aptitude Test* and grades in a Rhetoric course for 100 freshman females is presented in Table 11.1. The left-hand portion of the table summarizes the entries from a bivariate frequency distribution or scatter diagram similar to those described in Chapter Nine. In the right-hand portion of the table, each cell frequency has been converted to a percentage based on the total number of tallies in its row. These data might be interpreted as follows: of the 23 freshman women who took the course in Rhetoric and had test scores between 50 and 59, 39 percent (or 9 individuals) received a grade of C, 35 percent (or 8) received Bs, and 26 percent (or 6) received a grade of A. Not one of the students with a score of 50 or more obtained a grade lower than C, but since only three women scored this low, this generalization is somewhat risky. We might, then, use this expectancy-table information to predict the performance of women who take this course in the future.

TABLE 11.1 Expectancy Table Relating DAT *Sentences* Scores to Grades in Rhetoric for 100 College Freshman Females *(Correlation = .71)*

Total No.	Number Receiving Each Grade					Test Scores	Percent Receiving Each Grade					Total Percent
	F	D	C	B	A		F	D	C	B	A	
1					1	80–89					100	100
5				1	4	70–79				20	80	100
22			3	14	5	60–69			14	63	23	100
23			9	8	6	50–59			39	35	26	100
22		3	13	6		40–49		14	59	27		100
16	1	3	9	3		30–39	6	19	56	19		100
8	1	4	3			20–29	13	50	37			100
2		2				10–19	100					100
1		1				0–9	100					100
100	2	13	37	32	16	$\overline{X} = 48.58$						
						$S = 15.20$						

Source: Reprinted from A. G. Wesman, Expectancy tables: A way of interpreting test validity. *Test Service Bulletin* 38 (1949): 12. Published by the Psychological Corporation.

The situation is applicable to either the predictive or concurrent use of tests, depending on the amount of elapsed time between the collection of test scores and criterion data and the purpose for which the scores are intended. With regard to the concurrent use of criterion-related validity data, one might be interested in answering a general question such as: "Can I substitute this test score for a more elaborate and expensive criterion measure?" Here the test scores and criterion data would be gathered at the same time and correlated.

Construct Validity

Construct validity is investigated through the use of rational analytic, statistical, and experimental procedures. If a researcher is developing a measure of test anxiety, he would want to be confident that the items in his instrument represent a reasonable sample of the kinds of anxiety responses that a student might make in a testing situation and that the scores on his instrument change when anxiety is experimentally manipulated. Experimental manipulation might be accomplished by administering the instrument under stressful and non-stressful conditions using different instructions. An analysis of the scores would ideally reveal differences in the expected direction, as a function of the two types of experimental instructions.

Construct validity involves the "psychological meaningfulness" of a test score, i.e., the degree to which certain theoretical or explanatory constructs can account for item responses and test performances. It is generally relevant where no single criterion is available or acceptable in defining the variable or trait of interest.

The specific techniques employed to provide evidence of construct validity are varied, and in many instances are limited only by the creativity and ingenuity of the investigator. The logic of construct validity parallels the application of the scientific method. The development or use of theory (or a nomological net) that interrelates various elements of the construct under investigation is central (Cronbach and Meehl 1955). Hypotheses based on a theory are derived and predictions made about how the experimental test scores should relate to specified variables. These predictions may involve hypothesizing a positive or negative relationship. For example, we would want our measure of test anxiety to correlate positively with a second measure of test anxiety, but not with intelligence. The hypotheses are now subjected to experimental verification. Cronbach and Meehl (1955) suggest five types of evidence that might be assembled in support of construct validity. These have been succinctly stated by Helmstadter (1964) as follows:

Group differences. Samples of individuals assumed or demonstrated to differ on the variable under investigation would be predicted to exhibit differential performance. Data gathered in this way are essentially cross-sectional.

Changes in performance. Longitudinal studies might be undertaken to show changes over time or occasions for the same group. One would expect, for example, that scores on an achievement test would rise as students progress through a course.

Correlation. Obviously, a test should be positively correlated with another test that purports to measure the same variable, and show no correlation with measures of entirely different variables. The convergent-discriminant validity notion of Campbell and Fiske (1959) follows logically here from the experimental methods of similarities and differences suggested by Cronbach and Meehl (1955) in their classic discussion of construct validity.

Internal consistency. Internal consistency involves interitem correlations, i.e., the degree to which items measure the same thing. Whether internal consistency should be high or low depends on one's theory and predictions about it.

Studies of the test-taking process. What does the examinee do when he takes a test? What mental processes are involved in responding to the items? Does the form of the test and its items seem to make a difference? These are some of the questions that should be investigated.

It should be obvious that the three types of validity discussed above are not independent. Content validity, for example, must usually be present before criterion-related validity can be demonstrated. Establishing construct validity requires data derived and used in establishing both content and criterion-related validity. Also, we have implied that the demonstration of content validity is primarily a subjective process. But if we consider the content validity of a classroom test, for example, to be defined in terms of instructional objectives and curriculum, we should be able to demonstrate validity empirically by contrasting the performances of subjects who are course-sophisticated and those who are course-naive. Such a procedure would surely indicate whether or not exposure to the content and instruction of a particular course makes any difference in test performance. This procedure has been advocated by Ebel (1956) and applied successfully by Krouskopf (1964). Cronbach (1971) has also suggested that one examine content validity empirically by correlating scores from two forms of the same test, both developed from the same content domain. A combination construct validity-reliability procedure, then, can help us understand and demonstrate content validity. Suffice it to say that there is no single way to estimate validity, because the kind of evidence desired depends on the projected use of the results. A test, then, is not valid or invalid in general, but in relation to the purposes for developing and using it.

It is a cliché of measurement that a test must be reliable before it can be valid. In a very real sense, however, validity is not strictly a characteristic of the instrument but of the *inference* that is to be made from the test scores derived from the instrument. We need primarily to be concerned with the validity of the interpretation we make from test results (Cronbach 1971).

DEFINING AND ASSESSING RELIABILITY

We have noted that the influence of unsystematic errors in measurement is the problem with which the determination of reliability is concerned. In fact, we will define the reliability of a test as *the degree to which the test and its scores reflect true or nonerror variance.* In other words, we may define the reliability of a test and its scores as the degree to which they are influenced by unsystematic factors. Reliability will be represented symbolically as r_{tt}.

One need only reflect briefly on possible sources of variability to realize the tremendous variety of factors that may influence test scores. Some sense of this variety can be gained from a brief examination of Table 11.2. Part of the variance within a set of scores can be attributed to lasting and general traits (Category I of Table 11.2). Almost any test performance will depend on such general characteristics, which are persistent for most individuals. They are clearly systematic, and should be

TABLE 11.2 Possible Sources of Variance in Performance on a Particular Test

I. *Lasting and general characteristics of the individual*
   A. Level of ability on one or more general traits, which operate in a number of tests
   B. General skills and techniques of taking tests
   C. General ability to comprehend instructions

II. *Lasting but specific characteristics of the individual*
   A. Specific to the test as a whole (and to parallel forms of it)
      1. Individual level of ability on traits required in this test but not in others
      2. Knowledges and skills specific to particular form of test items
   B. Specific to particular test items
      1. The "chance" element determining whether the individual does or does not know a particular fact (Sampling variance in a finite number of items)

III. *Temporary but general characteristics of the individual* (Factors affecting performance on many or all tests at a particular time)
   A. Health
   B. Fatigue
   C. Motivation
   D. Emotional strain
   E. General test-wiseness (partly lasting)
   F. Understanding of mechanics of testing
   G. External conditions of heat, light, ventilation, etc.

IV. *Temporary and specific characteristics of the individual*
   A. Specific to a test as a whole
      1. Comprehension of the specific test task (insofar as this is distinct from IB)
      2. Specific tricks or techniques of dealing with the particular test materials (insofar as this is distinct from IIA 2)
      3. Level of practice on the specific skills involved (especially in psychomotor tests)
      4. Momentary "set" for a particular test
   B. Specific to particular test items
      1. Fluctuations and idiosyncrasies of human memory
      2. Unpredictable fluctuations in attention or accuracy, superimposed upon the general level of performance characteristic of the individual

V. *Variance not otherwise accounted for (chance)*
   A. "Luck" in the selection of answers by "guessing"

Source: R. L. Thorndike, *Personnel selection.* New York: John Wiley and Sons, 1949, p. 73. Reprinted by permission of the publisher.

treated as such in any sequence of operations designed to estimate reliability (Thorndike 1949). Thorndike considers systematic factors as "true" characteristics of the individual. Categories II, III, and IV may be considered true or error variance, depending upon the reliability-estimating technique. Category V will always be considered as error variance.

It is interesting to note that a national committee of testing experts has concluded that "the estimation of clearly labeled components of error variance is the most informative outcome of a reliability study, both for the test developer wishing to improve the reliability of his instrument and for the user desiring to interpret test scores with maximum understanding. The analysis of error variance calls for the use of appropriate experimental design" (American Psychological Association 1966). Cronbach *et al.* (1963, 1970) have recently explicated a theory labelled "generalizability" that adheres very closely to this conception of reliability.

We shall now examine four approaches to the estimation of test reliability: (a) test-retest, (b) equivalent form, (c) split-test, and (d) Kuder-Richardson methods. The headings used to describe these methods parallel those presented by Ghiselli (1964).

Reliability Determined from Repetition of the Same Test

This technique simply involves administering the same form of a test to the same examinees on two or more occasions and correlating the scores. There is usually a significant delay between administrations. Since the same form of the test is used on both occasions, lasting-general and lasting-specific factors are considered true variance, and temporary-general and temporary-specific are considered error. This method has the advantage of requiring only one form of a test, and the distinct disadvantage of being significantly influenced by practice and memory. In addition, the test-retest method may cause an interaction between the test and examinee, particularly when used with personality inventories. Having taken the inventory once may have caused him to introspect, which might result in significant score changes the second time the inventory is administered. Some testing experts claim that the test-retest method is an estimate of the reliability *not* of the instrument but of the examinee. It must nevertheless be conceded that such information is useful within a specific testing situation. One could not expect, for example, to estimate future behavior if scores on the prediction test did not hold up over time.

Reliability Determined from Equivalent Forms of a Test

In order to determine reliability in this way one must, of course, have two forms of the test. The items on each form must be parallel in terms of the content and the mental operation required to respond to the items. In developing equivalent forms, the test developer must begin with a complete and detailed set of specifications. Such a blueprint would ideally specify item type, difficulty level, content coverage, and the like. In a real sense the correlation of equivalent forms serves to monitor the consistency and ability of the item writer. More important, however, this correlation serves as a check on the sampling from the universe of behaviors in question. There is no particular reason to believe that any given set of 35 vocabulary items is superior or inferior to any other set. If we find a high degree of response consistency over forms of the test, however, we will have greater confidence in the sampling of items, i.e., greater confidence that the samples of items accurately represent the universe from which they were drawn.

Application of this reliability-estimating procedure merely involves administering two forms of the same test to the same group, and correlating the scores. Referring to Table 11.2, we can see that the variances considered true or error depend upon the interval between testings. Categories I and IIA will be treated as systematic (or true) variation. Categories IIB and IVB, in addition to V, will be treated as unsystematic or error. Categories III and IVA will be treated as true if the retesting is immediate, e.g., same day, and as error if there is a delay of several weeks or more between testings. The latter procedure is generally recommended.

Reliability Determined from Comparable Parts of a Test

Both reliability-estimating techniques described above require two test administrations. Several methods have been devised to estimate reliability from a single administration of a test. Although practical, single-administration estimating procedures have the disadvantage of designating and treating the sources of variance in Categories III and IV of Table 11.2 as systematic, and therefore probably yield an inflated estimate of reliability as compared with equivalent forms. The procedures usually involve splitting a test in half and using information derived from the half-tests, in terms of either a correlation or variance, to estimate the reliability of the full-length test. The four bases used most frequently for splitting a test in half are (a) random halves, (b) top and bottom halves, (c) "equivalent" halves, and (d) odd and even halves. The last two methods are worthy of special consideration. The "Equivalent halves" approach is probably the most desirable of the split-test procedures for estimating reliability. In a sense, it parallels the equivalent-forms method. The determination of equivalence requires that a matching of pairs of items be undertaken, guided by the original test blueprint or table of specifications. After the test is administered, a score for each of the equivalent halves is derived. A more efficient procedure that yields very similar results, at least for a teacher-made test, is the odd-even method. Here again, two scores are derived for each examinee, one from the odd-numbered items and one from the even. This procedure has been followed with sample data from a ten-item test administered to 25 subjects, whose results are summarized in Table 11.3.

At this point the determination of reliability may take either of two directions. Let us look first at a correlational procedure for estimating

TABLE 11.3 Hypothetical Data Used in Estimating Reliability from the Single Administration of a Test

Student	Odd Items					Even Items					Odd Score	Even Score	Total Score
	1	3	5	7	9	2	4	6	8	10			
A	+	0	+	0	+	+	0	+	+	0	3	3	6
B	+	0	0	0	0	+	0	+	0	0	1	2	3
C	+	+	+	+	0	+	+	+	+	+	4	5	9
D	0	+	+	0	0	0	+	0	+	0	2	2	4
E	0	+	+	+	0	+	+	0	0	0	3	2	5
F	+	0	0	0	0	0	0	0	0	0	1	0	1
G	+	+	+	+	0	+	+	0	+	0	4	3	7
H	+	0	+	+	0	0	+	+	0	0	3	2	5
I	+	0	0	0	0	0	+	0	0	0	1	1	2
J	+	+	+	+	+	+	+	+	+	+	5	5	10
K	+	0	+	0	0	+	+	0	+	+	2	4	6
L	+	+	+	0	+	+	+	+	0	+	4	4	8
M	0	0	0	0	0	0	0	0	0	0	0	0	0
N	+	+	0	+	0	0	+	+	+	+	3	4	7
O	+	+	+	+	+	+	+	+	+	0	5	4	9
P	+	+	0	0	0	+	+	+	+	+	2	5	7
Q	+	+	+	0	0	+	+	0	0	0	3	2	5
R	+	0	0	+	0	+	0	+	0	0	2	2	4
S	+	0	0	0	+	+	0	0	0	0	2	1	3
T	0	0	0	0	0	+	0	0	0	0	0	1	1
U	+	+	0	+	+	+	+	+	0	0	4	3	7
V	+	+	0	0	0	+	+	+	0	0	2	3	5
W	0	+	0	0	0	+	0	0	0	0	1	1	2
X	+	+	0	0	+	+	0	+	0	+	3	3	6
Y	0	+	0	+	0	0	+	0	0	+	2	2	4
Nc	19	15	11	10	7	18	16	13	9	8			
p	.76	.60	.44	.40	.28	.72	.64	.52	.36	.32			
q	.24	.40	.56	.60	.72	.28	.36	.48	.64	.68			
pq	.18	.24	.25	.24	.20	.20	.23	.25	.23	.22			

$\overline{X}_o = 2.48$ $\overline{X}_e = 2.56$ $\overline{X}_x = 5.04$ $\Sigma pq = 2.24$

$S_o^2 = 1.85$ $S_e^2 = 2.09$ $S_x^2 = 6.84$

$S_o = 1.36$ $S_e = 1.45$ $S_x = 2.62$

reliability from half-test scores. We would first determine the Pearson product-moment or Spearman rank-order correlation between the odd and even halves of the test. (The reader may wish to refresh his memory about rank-order correlation by referring to Table 9.4.) For our example, the rank-order correlation was found to be .752. This correlation describes the relationship between scores on the halves of the test, but we are interested in the full-test reliability. We must, therefore, put the test back together. Application of the Spearman-Brown formula allows us to estimate the full-length test reliability. The general form of the Spearman-Brown formula is as follows:

$$r_{tt} = \frac{nr}{1 + (n - 1)r}$$ (Equation 11.1)

where

  n = the number of times the test is to be lengthened

  r = the original test reliability or correlation.

In our example, we are trying to determine the full-test reliability if the length of the test were doubled. Equation 11.1 could be rewritten as follows:

$$r_{tt} = \frac{2r_{oe}}{1 + r_{oe}}$$ (Equation 11.2)

where

  r_{oe} = the correlation between the odd and even halves of the test,

with r_{oe} = .752

$$r_{tt} = \frac{2(.752)}{1 + (.752)} = \frac{1.504}{1.752} = \underline{.86}$$

Assuming that most reliability coefficients over .70 are within an acceptable range, our obtained estimate of .86 would allow us to use this hypothetical test with a relatively high degree of confidence.

The Spearman-Brown formula, as expressed in Equations 11.1 and 11.2, really describes the effect of lengthening the test on reliability. Generally, as we increase the number of items we increase reliability. This assumes that the items added are equivalent to the original items in terms of functions measured, difficulty level, and the like. One additional assumption of Equation 11.2 is that the standard deviations of the two halves of the test are equal. Cronbach (1951) has shown that violation of this assumption will lead to an overestimate of reliability. Although the overestimation is not extremely large—not more than 5 percent when one variance is 50 percent as large as the other—some error is introduced. Because of this tendency to overestimate, the relative inefficiency of rank-order correlation procedures with large groups, and the need to use the Spearman-Brown formula, a more direct method of estimating reliability from the halves of a test is suggested. The following calculating formula, first described by Flanagan (1937) should be used:

$$r_{tt} = 2\left(1 - \frac{S_o{}^2 + S_e{}^2}{S_x{}^2}\right), \qquad \text{(Equation 11.3)}$$

where

$S_o{}^2$ and $S_e{}^2$ = the raw score variances on the odd and even halves of the test respectively,

and $\qquad S_x{}^2$ = the variance of total test raw scores.

Application of this formula to the data in Table 11.3 yields the following results:

$$r_{tt} = 2\left(1 - \frac{1.85 + 2.09}{6.84}\right) = \underline{\underline{.85}}$$

Our reliability estimate is almost identical to that derived by Equation 11.2, because the variances are not very discrepant. Equation 11.3 is really an estimate of the degree of equivalence between the two full-length tests, which are as similar as are the two halves of one test. It therefore represents for some test experts a very reasonable estimate of reliability. Equation 11.3 is useful not only because of the less restrictive assumptions underlying its use, but also because the variances involved in the formula may be estimated using the approximation formula of a standard deviation presented in Chapter Nine (see Equation 9.9 and Table 9.2).

Reliability Determined from Item Data

Intuition suggests that if one wants to determine whether or not the items in a test measure the same thing, he should examine item scores as well as examinee scores. A reliability-estimating procedure of Kuder and Richardson (1937, 1939) does just this. The usual formula assumes, however, that the items in the test (1) are scored right or wrong, (2) are not significantly influenced by speed, and (3) measure a common factor. The last assumption is of critical importance when estimating the reliability of a classroom test. In many instances, such tests are not homogeneous with respect to content and/or learning outcome measured. Therefore, caution must be exercised in applying either of the two Kuder-Richardson formulas described below. The most frequently used Kuder-Richardson formula, Number 20, can be expressed as follows:

$$r_{tt} = \left(\frac{k}{k-1}\right)\left(\frac{S_x^2 - \Sigma pq}{S_x^2}\right),$$ (Equation 11.4)

where

k = the number of items in the test

p = proportion of examinees answering item correctly (or the proportion responding in a specified direction)

q = 1 − p

S_x^2 = the variance of the total test raw scores.

Calculation of the term pq can be facilitated through the use of columns 1 and 3 of the table in Appendix A. The term p or q can be entered in column 1 and the term pq read directly from column 3. The term pq represents the variance of an item. It is assumed that items that measure the same thing will have fairly homogeneous difficulty levels and, therefore, variances. In addition, it will be seen in Chapter Twelve that if items all have difficulty levels of about 50 percent a test will tend to be maximally reliable. The use of the correction factor k/k − 1 we ask the reader to accept on faith. Note, however, that if we have a small number of items, say 10, the correction can be relatively large as compared to a situation in which we have 80 items. Applying Equation 11.4 to the hypothetical data in Table 11.3, we find that:

$$r_{tt} = \left(\frac{10}{10-1}\right)\left(\frac{6.84 - 2.24}{6.84}\right) = (1.11)(.67) = \underline{.74}$$

This value is noticeably lower than any other we have seen thus far. The discrepancy might be attributed to overestimation by the other methods or underestimation by KR_{20} because of failure to meet assumptions. Inasmuch as KR_{20} is a very precise method, i.e., it considers actual item variances, it will be the accepted value. Since the item variances of classroom tests tend to be relatively similar, we may be able to shortcut the actual calculation of the item variances. This can be done by using Kuder-Richardson formula Number 21. The use of this formula assumes that the items all have the same difficulty level. KR_{21} is written:

$$r_{tt} = \left(\frac{k}{k-1}\right)\left(1 - \frac{\overline{X}(k - \overline{X})}{kS_x^2}\right),$$ (Equation 11.5)

where

$$k = \text{the number of items on the test}$$

$$\overline{X} = \text{the mean of the total test raw scores}$$

$$S_x{}^2 = \text{the variance of the total test raw scores.}$$

Knowing only the number of items, mean, and variance (which can be approximated from Equation 9.9), we can calculate a reasonably precise estimate of reliability. Again using the data in Table 11.3, we find that:

$$r_{tt} = \left(\frac{10}{10-1}\right)\left(1 - \frac{5.04(10-5.04)}{10(6.84)}\right) = \underline{\underline{.70}}$$

This reliability estimate, although close, is less than that derived from Equation 11.4 (KR_{20}). Such will be the case unless all of the items in the test are of the same difficulty level.

Using Lord's finding that the standard error of measurement computed from KR_{20} is very close to a linear function of the square root of the number of items (1959), Saupe (1961) has derived some very efficient estimates of KR_{20} reliability. One of these, which he labels $R_{20}{}'$, can be expressed as follows:

$$R_{20}{}' = \left(\frac{k}{k-1}\right)\left(1 - \frac{.20k}{S_x{}^2}\right) \qquad \text{(Equation 11.6)}$$

Now all we need to know is the number of items and variance and we can estimate reliability with a high degree of efficiency and accuracy—if the number of items and the variance are reasonably large. This brief formula yields an estimate of reliability very close to those made above:

$$R_{20}{}' = \left(\frac{10}{10-1}\right)\left(1 - \frac{.20(10)}{6.84}\right) - \underline{\underline{.79}}$$

Drawing upon the theoretical and empirical work of Lord (1959) and Saupe (1961), Cureton *et al.* (1973) have provided another method of estimating internal consistency reliability that is useful to the classroom teacher. Their formula reads as follows:

$$r_{tt} = 1 - .043k\left(\frac{N}{\Sigma X_{U_6^1} - \Sigma X_{L_6^1}}\right)^2 \qquad \text{(Equation 11.7)}$$

Where k = total number of dichotomously scored items on test

N = total number of subjects about whom we have data

$\Sigma X_{U\frac{1}{6}}$ = the sum of the total scores for individuals in the upper one-sixth of the distribution

$\Sigma X_{L\frac{1}{6}}$ = the sum of the total scores for individuals in the lower one-sixth of the distribution

The reader will recall that use was made of the terms $\Sigma X_{U\frac{1}{6}}$ and $\Sigma X_{L\frac{1}{6}}$ in estimating standard deviation in Chapter Nine.

Using the data in Table 11.3, we find that Equation 11.7 gives us an estimate close to the others we have calculated:

$$r_{tt} = 1 - .043(10)\left(\frac{20}{36 - 6}\right)^2 = \underline{\underline{.81}}$$

One-sixth of N is 3.3, but because this is too few individuals upon which to base an estimate we rounded to 4.

Faced with all these formulas, which one should a teacher select to analyze his tests? Since most of the formulas presented in this section on reliability have been shown by the author (Payne 1963) to yield highly similar results, the decision will probably be based on familiarity with the formulas, computational ease, form of the data, or nature of the test. Taking all these factors into account, we recommend Flanagan's formula (Equation 11.3). It has the advantages of relative ease of calculation and the fact that items need *not* be scored right or wrong —making it applicable to essay tests—to justify its use.

FACTORS INFLUENCING RELIABILITY AND VALIDITY

In addition to the intrinsic factors already identified as influencing test or criterion reliability, and thus validity, two additional factors need to be considered: group heterogeneity and speededness.

Heterogeneity refers to the range of talent or individual differences represented in the group with which reliability and/or validity studies are undertaken. It is logical that if a standard deviation is small we will not be able to discriminate reliably among members of a homogeneous group. We have described reliability in terms of the influence of error. Assume a specified amount of unsystematic error, and assume further that with error constant we find that Group A has a large standard deviation and Group B a small standard deviation. If we estimate reliability by correlating two forms of a test, we would find that Group A has the larger reliability coefficient, while the amount of error is the same for both groups. Another example would be the selection for a job of only the top 20 percent of applicants based on a test score and the correlation of these scores with some job proficiency criterion (e.g., supervisors' ratings). The resulting validity coefficient would, of necessity, be low because of the restricted range of individual differences represented in the group. We need a method for expressing the reliability of a test independent of variability. This can be accomplished by using the *standard error of measurement* (S_{em}):

$$S_{em} = S_x\sqrt{1 - r_{tt}} \qquad \text{(Equation 11.8)}$$

The standard error of measurement theoretically represents an estimate of the standard deviation of the (unsystematic) errors obtained in repeated sampling with parallel forms of a test with the same subjects. In addition to serving as an index of reliability independent of group variability, the S_{em} may be used to assist in interpreting test scores. The individual's score may then be conceived of as a band or interval rather than a point. A frequently used procedure is to establish "reasonable limits" (plus and minus), corresponding to two or three times the S_{em}, around an observed score. Let us consider a practical situation in which the use of the standard error of measurement can facilitate decisionmaking with a test. As a college admissions officer, you have required all applicants to take the Great Aptitude Test. You intend to select the freshman class, other things being equal, from the top half of the ability distribution. The "cutoff score" corresponds to a score of 70. Karen has a score of 65. On the basis of her academic record and recommendations, she appears to be someone who could greatly benefit from a college education. Because her test score did not equal or exceed the cutoff score, should she be rejected? No! We know that tests are fallible, i.e., not perfectly accurate. Some errors of measurement are always present, and these errors sometimes cause scores to be higher or lower than they should be. We need to take into consideration, then, the error of measurement in interpreting Karen's score. We might ask, "Is it possible that Karen's *true* score is higher than the cutoff point on the admissions test?" Such a question assumes that an observed test score is composed of some true ability plus some error. Our task is to specify and evaluate the error component of the test score. Let us assume that our Great Aptitude Test has a standard deviation of 20 and a reliability of .75. Using Equation 11.8, we find that S_{em} is equal to 10. If we establish reasonable limits of $2S_{em}$ around her observed score (65 plus and minus 20), we note that it would be quite possible for Karen to obtain a score above the cutoff score if tested again. We are, therefore, justified in including Karen in the pool of applicants from which we wish to select the freshman class. A useful reference is presented in Table 11.4. This table, from an article by Ricks (1956), presents the standard errors of measurement (Equation 11.8) for selected combinations of standard deviation values and reliability coefficients. For most

TABLE 11.4   Standard Errors of Measurement for Given Values of Reliability Coefficient and Standard Deviation

SD	Reliability Coefficient					
	.95	.90	.85	.80	.75	.70
30	6.7	9.5	11.6	13.4	15.0	16.4
28	6.3	8.9	10.8	12.5	14.0	15.3
26	5.8	8.2	10.1	11.6	13.0	14.2
24	5.4	7.6	9.3	10.7	12.0	13.1
22	4.9	7.0	8.5	9.8	11.0	12.0
20	4.5	6.3	7.7	8.9	10.0	11.0
18	4.0	5.7	7.0	8.0	9.0	9.9
16	3.6	5.1	6.2	7.2	8.0	8.8
14	3.1	4.4	5.4	6.3	7.0	7.7
12	2.7	3.8	4.6	5.4	6.0	6.6
10	2.2	3.2	3.9	4.5	5.0	5.6
8	1.8	2.5	3.1	3.6	4.0	4.4
6	1.3	1.9	2.3	2.7	3.0	3.3
4	.9	1.3	1.5	1.8	2.0	2.2
2	.4	.6	.8	.9	1.0	1.1

Source: *Test Service Bulletin* 50 (1956). Published by the Psychological Corporation.

purposes it will be sufficiently accurate if the table is entered with values nearest the actual ones.

In addition, there exist correction formulas that may be used to estimate the potential influence of the range of individual differences on reliability and/or validity coefficients. These are outside the scope of this book, but the interested reader is referred to Ghiselli (1964) for detailed presentations of the theory and application of these formulas, and of the concept of standard error of measurement. The main point here is that there does not exist for any test, even standardized tests, a single standard index of reliability or validity, and that it is necessary in most instances to assess these test characteristics each time the test is used.

It was noted early in Chapter One that one of the bases that might be used to classify a test is the extent to which speed influences scores. At one extreme are pure speed tests, whose items are easy and all of approximately equal difficulty. At the other extreme are power tests. The items in a power test are generally arranged in increasing order of difficulty. Perfect scores on power tests are unlikely even with the most generous time limits. The selection of a reliability-estimating technique will be influenced by the extent to which speed affects the scores. A test user or developer must first decide whether he wants speed of response to have a significant influence on the scores, and then select an appropriate reliability-estimating technique. The possible spurious influence of speed can best be illustrated by examining the use of split-half reliability-estimating techniques with a pure speed test. The maximum difference between the odd and even scores would be one, assuming that if an item is attempted it will be answered correctly. The half-test scores would obviously be highly correlated and an overestimated reliability would result. The appropriate procedure would be to use equivalent forms, or perhaps separately timed halves.

The concepts of validity and reliability are of paramount importance in educational and psychological measurement. If the analysis of a test does not reveal an acceptable amount of both, we cannot have confidence in the use of the test to evaluate and make decisions about students.

SUGGESTED READINGS

Ahmann, J. S., and Glock, M. D. *Evaluating pupil growth*, 4th ed. Boston: Allyn and Bacon, 1971. Students desiring an excellent review of the interaction of reliability and validity in and with educational measurement are referred to Chapters 9 and 10 of this widely used text.

Anastasi, Anne. *Psychological testing*, 3rd ed. New York: Macmillan, 1968. Good introductory treatments of reliability and validity can be found in Chapters 4, 5, and 6. In addition to presenting the essentials of the concepts, Anastasi stresses interpretation.

Cronbach, L. J. Test validation. In *Educational measurement*, 2nd ed., ed. R. L. Thorndike. Washington: American Council on Education, 1971. See Chapter 14. Intended for the intermediate and advanced student, this chapter contains the latest thinking on the topic by one of the nation's foremost experts. Rather than approaching the validation of the test *per se*, Cronbach describes methods useful in validating interpretations of data arising from specified procedures.

Ghiselli, E. E. *Theory of psychological measurement*. New York: McGraw-Hill, 1964. Chapters 8 and 9 contain a recent summary of the theories of reliability.

Helmstadter, G. C. *Principles of psychological measurement*. New York: Appleton-Century-Crofts, 1964. Chapters 4, 5, and 6 contain some of the most readable discussions of content, criterion-related, and construct validity available. The presentations are simultaneously brief and technically correct.

12

ANALYZING ACHIEVEMENT
ITEM CHARACTERISTICS

SUMMARY PREVIEW STATEMENTS

1. Item-analysis techniques are among the most powerful tools a teacher can use to improve the quality of classroom tests.

2. Item analyses are undertaken to select the best items, identify faulty items, and detect individual or class learning difficulties.

3. Item analysis generally involves an examination of item difficulty, item discrimination, and, if multiple-choice items are used, distractor effectiveness.

4. Item difficulty (p) can be indexed by the proportion of examinees who respond correctly or in a particular direction.

5. Item difficulty can be estimated from the proportion (or percent) of the combined high-scoring and low-scoring thirds of the total distribution of scorers responding correctly to the item.

6. Item difficulties will range from 0 to 100 percent.

7. Item discrimination (D) can be indexed by subtracting the number of low-scoring students (the lower one-third of the total score distribution) from the number of high-scoring students (the upper one-third), and dividing the difference by the number that represents one-third of the total group.

8. The range of D is from -1.00 to $.00$ to $+1.00$.

9. To examine distractor effectiveness for multiple-choice items, the responses to each alternative for the high and low groups are inspected separately.

10. Item-difficulty values should generally fall in the range from 30 percent to 70 percent if the intent is to maximize the measured differences between individuals.

11. Item-discrimination values should be as large as possible if the intent is to maximize the measured differences between individuals.

12. In general, the greater the number of items with high discrimination values the higher the internal-consistency reliability of the test.

13. Items with extremely high or low difficulty indices should be examined closely for possible structural or content defects or ambiguity.

14. Examining the mean scores on individual essay items separately for high- and low-scoring students can provide useful information on discrimination.

15. Plotting the responses of each student to each item in terms of correctness (+ = right, − = wrong) can help identify individual student or class strengths and weaknesses.

16. If criterion-referenced measures are used, items with higher difficulty values are likely to be found.

17. The concept of item discrimination has relatively little value in the criterion-referenced use of tests.

18. If items are eliminated from a test because of poor difficulty or discrimination indices, they should be replaced with other items measuring the same objectives.

19. Developing an item file will assist the teacher in refining test items and provide considerable flexibility in test development.

Item-analysis techniques are among the most valuable tools a classroom teacher can apply in attempting to improve the quality of his achievement tests. The use of even the most elementary item-analysis procedures can bring about a remarkable improvement of classroom instruments. The methods discussed in this chapter will be aimed primarily at improving measures of the norm-referenced variety. Further consideration will be given to item-selection techniques relevant to criterion-referenced tests and items in Chapter Thirteen.

Item analyses are conducted for four general purposes: (1) to select the best available items for the final form of a test; (2) to identify structural or content defects in the items; (3) to detect learning difficulties of the class as a whole, identifying general content areas or skills that need to be reviewed by the instructor; and (4) to identify for individual students areas of weakness in need of remediation.

There are three main elements in an item analysis. One is examination of the *difficulty* level of the items, i.e., the percentage of students responding correctly to each item in the test. Another is determination of the *discriminating* power of each item. Item discrimination in its simplest form usually, but not always, refers to the relation of performance on each item to performance on the total test. For a classroom test, item discrimination is generally indexed by the number of high-scoring individuals (based on total score) responding correctly versus the number of low-scoring individuals responding correctly.

A third element in item analyses, if multiple-choice or matching items are used in the test, is examination of the effectiveness of the distractors (foils, or alternative answers). Again, data derived from the high and low scorers are used. But now the complete response patterns associated with all the alternatives in each item are studied, rather than just the correct answer.

Many sophisticated item-analysis procedures are available. The more mathematically complicated and rigorous techniques are beyond the scope of this book, and the reader is referred to the presentations by Davis (1951, 1952) and Guilford (1954) for expanded treatments of the topic, particularly with regard to useful correlational procedures.

PREPARING DATA FOR ITEM ANALYSIS

Preparing data for the item analysis of a classroom test generally involves counting the number of individuals in high- and low-scoring groups who answer each item correctly. This count can be accomplished by a show of hands in class or by examination of the answer sheets. An efficient show of hands approach has been outlined by Diederich (1964) and is recommended if the class is relatively small and sufficient time is available. In general, the following steps are followed in gathering and recording data for an item analysis:

1. *Arrange the answer sheets in order from high to low.* This ranking is usually based on the individual's total score on the test. An item analysis of data derived from high and low scorers (based on total score) is referred to as an internal item analysis. If an external criterion is used (e.g., another test that is supposed to measure the same thing as the one under analysis), the item analysis is referred to as an external item analysis. The total score on the test is the most satisfactory criterion on which to base a ranking of individuals for an analysis of a classroom test.

2. *High- and low-scoring groups are identified.* For purposes of item analysis, these two extreme sets of examination papers are called crite-

rion groups. Each subgroup will generally contain from 25 to 50 percent of the total number of people who took the test. The goal is to include enough people in the criterion groups to justify confidence in the results, and yet keep the criterion groups distinct enough to insure that they represent different levels of ability. Kelley (1939) has shown that maximally reliable item discrimination results will be obtained when each criterion group contains 27 percent of the total. Thus, in undertaking an item analysis on a classroom test, between 25 and 33 percent represents a reasonable size for the criterion groups. The high and low groups, however, should contain the same number of individuals.

3. *Record separately the number of times each alternative was selected by individuals in the high and low groups.*

4. *Sum the number of correct answers to each item made by the combined high and low groups.*

5. *Divide the total number of correct responses by the maximum possible, i.e., the total number of students in the combined high and low groups, and multiply the result by 100.* This percentage is an estimate of the *difficulty index.* Some test constructors allow items to be omitted, and students inadvertently omit items. If all individuals have not attempted all items, item-difficulty indices should be obtained by dividing the total number of correct responses by the number of individuals who attempted the item. On speeded tests, omitted items in the middle of the test should probably be considered wrong, but those at the end should be considered omitted.

6. *Subtract the number of correct answers made by the low group from the number of correct answers by the high group.*

7. *Divide this number* (the difference, H − L) *by the number of individuals contained in the subgroup (i.e., the number in the high [or low] group).*

This decimal number is the *discrimination index.*

Sample item data and the resulting indices derived from the procedures described above are presented in Table 12.1. These data refer to four hypothetical multiple-choice items answered by different classes (thus producing fluctuating numbers of cases in the high and low groups). The procedure for deriving indices of difficulty and discrimination can, of course, be used profitably with two-choice (e.g., true-false), matching, or any number of multiple-choice objective item types. Further, the concepts of difficulty and discrimination may be applied in evaluating more subjective item types, e.g., completion and, with some difficulty, essay items.

The reader may now legitimately ask how these data can be used to improve his test. The following three sections will consider the use of item-analysis data in improving the quality of a classroom test.

TABLE 12.1   Sample Item-Analysis Data Derived from Four Hypothetical Multiple-Choice Items

Group	Group	Group Size	Response Alternatives[1]					Total No. Correct (H and L)	Difficulty Index	(H−L)	Discrimination Index
			1	2	3	4	5				
Item 1	High	12	0	11	0	1	0				
								20	83%	2	+.17
	Low	12	2	9	1	0	0				
Item 2	High	25	2	2	20	1	0				
								26	52%	14	+.56
	Low	25	5	8	6	2	4				
Item 3	High	16	2	2	8	2	2				
								6	19%	−2	−.13
	Low	16	4	3	4	1	4				
Item 4	High	30	20	3	2	1	4				
								28	47%	12	+.40
	Low	30	8	1	8	9	2				

[1]Underlined numbers indicate correct answers.

USING INFORMATION ABOUT ITEM DIFFICULTY

An item's difficulty level is important because it tells the instructor something meaningful about the comprehension of, or performance on, material or tasks contained in the item. Referring to Item 1 in Table 12.1, one can see that the item is easy (estimated difficulty index = 83%). Note here an apparent paradox, namely, that the higher the value of the difficulty index the easier the item. This paradox is comprehensible when we recall that the difficulty index represents the percentage of the total number of respondents answering the item correctly. In other words, there is an inverse relationship between the magnitude of the index and what it purports to represent. In any event, an instructor might be justified in concluding that with respect to Item 1, nearly everyone had command of the material. Extremely high difficulty indices, however, may indicate a structural defect in the item. The data for Item 1 may have been obtained from the following item:

Item 1. Among the major contributors to low reliability are:

1. an inappropriate time limit.
*2. inadequate samplings of content and individuals.

---

* Keyed as correct.

3. lack of content heterogeneity in the test.
4. differential weighting of alternatives in scoring each item.
5. poor lighting in the testing room.

Upon examination of the content and structure of the test, it is obvious that a grammatical clue exists. The stem calls for a plural response, and the only plural response is "2"—which in this case happens to be the correct answer. A student who noticed this clue could respond correctly to the item without knowing the answer. This irrelevant clue could alone account for the high difficulty index, particularly where the low group is concerned. The lesson here is obvious. In selecting items for a test, consideration of content alone or item analysis data alone can be very misleading. Both factors need to be considered in accepting items for the final form of the test.

The difficulty index described in this chapter is only an estimate of the "real" difficulty level of an item. It is based on the responses of only the high- and low-scoring groups. The middle groups, usually from 50 to 33 percent of the total, have been eliminated. It is assumed, and has been found true in practice, that approximately half of the middle group will score like the high group and half like the low group. The index is only an estimate from another standpoint. Guessing may be a factor on any test item, particularly if the item is quite difficult. Each item should theoretically be corrected for guessing. For a classroom test, however, this scoring refinement is probably unnecessary.

A number of authorities have shown that if a test is composed entirely of items at the 50 percent difficulty level, it is possible for it to be maximally reliable or, more precisely, to evidence maximum internal consistency. In other words, items at the 50 percent level allow for item-discrimination indices to obtain their maximum possible value: unity. In a sense median difficulty may be viewed as a necessity but not a sufficient condition for acceptable discrimination. It may be desirable, however, to include in the test items that are fairly easy (those at the beginning of the test for psychological reasons) or fairly difficult (those measuring highly complex learning outcomes). When these types of items are included in the test, generally lowered (internal consistence) reliability estimates will be obtained. Cureton (1966) has shown this to be particularly crucial if Kuder-Richardson Formula 20 is used. A paradox is evident. If an instructor uses the *Taxonomy of Educational Objectives* as a framework for instruction and measurement, the resulting test will of necessity reflect a range of item-difficulty indices. This will result in lower Kuder-Richardson reliabilities, despite the fact that it represents a desired state of affairs. Two recommendations should help ameliorate the problem. First, limit the range of item difficulties, e.g., between 30 and 70 percent. Second, interpret the Kuder-Richardson reliabilities derived from classroom tests with caution. Whereas we generally desire Kuder-Richardson values above .85 for published tests of achievement, aptitude, and intelligence, on a single classroom test .70 might be considered acceptable. In addition, it is assumed that other data will be gathered, so that the reliability of the composite score used to make a final decision will reach a higher and more acceptable level.

A useful application of item-analysis data is to develop a chart that relates student performance on each item (correct = +, incorrect = 0) and the content of the item. A sample chart for five students and four items is presented below. It is apparent that the concept of reliability could be profitably reviewed. In addition, several areas in need of

Item Content	*Student*				
	S_1	S_2	S_3	S_4	S_5
Use of table of specification	+	+	0	0	+
Computing mean	+	0	0	+	+
Definition of reliability	+	0	+	0	0
Interpreting correlation coefficient	+	+	0	+	+

review for individual students have been highlighted by reproducing the responses of each examinee to each item. When the class and number of items are large, the sheer mechanics of recording responses can be quite laborious. The benefits that accrue to both student and instructor can, however, be substantial. In such cases, items with similar content could be grouped together. Another interesting variation is to refer back to the original table of specifications, particularly if the *Taxonomy of Educational Objectives* was used to develop it, and use the corresponding behavior categories instead of content categories.

USING INFORMATION ABOUT ITEM DISCRIMINATION

Item discrimination has been defined as the degree to which an item differentiates the high achievers from the low achievers. A perfect positively discriminating item would be answered correctly by all of the high group and none of the low group; the discrimination index would then be +1.00. If all of the low group and none of the high group responded correctly, the index would be −1.00. In a sense, we might interpret the discrimination index as the correlation of the item with the total test score. Extreme values are almost never observed on a classroom test. Items in the middle range of positive discrimination are usually found in practice.

The data reported in Table 12.1 for Item 2 were obtained from the following item:

Item 2.   A teacher proposes the following objective for a course in Fine Arts: "The pupils should be able to understand and appreciate good music." The principal drawback to this objective, from a measurement standpoint, is that it is a

1. general objective.
2. student objective.
*3. nonbehavioral objective.
4. teacher objective.
5. compound objective.

This item is "sound" from a number of standpoints. The "middle difficulty level" criterion has been met, with an index of 52 percent. In addition, it discriminates between the high and low groups, as indicated by the index of +.56. The item is structurally sound and measures a desirable outcome, namely, the ability to apply knowledge about objectives in a new situation. Another possible explanation for the good discrimination is that the alternatives contain plausible but incorrect answers.

In general, all items in a test of relative achievement should discriminate positively. This assumes that we are striving for an additive scale, in which item scores are summed, and that we want each item to make a positive contribution. It is also assumed that we are interested in developing a test of relative achievement, as opposed to a mastery test, in which all items do not necessarily need to meet an internal-discrimination criterion. It is usually assumed in developing a classroom test that high positive total scores will be correlated with more knowledge and skill.

An instructor will occasionally find a negatively discriminating item such as the following (refer to Table 12.1 for appropriate item-analysis data):

Item 3.   Which of the following alternatives best summarizes the limitations of the *Taxonomy of Educational Objectives*?

1. For the most part it is written in nonbehavioral terms.
2. It deals with "inferred" rather than "real" behavior.
3. It may restrict our thinking only to the categories of the *Taxonomy*.
4. The categories of the *Taxonomy* are not mutually exclusive.
*5. All of the above are limitations of the *Taxonomy*.

This item, answered correctly by more of the low group than the high group, is apparently ambiguous. One possible source of ambiguity is the nature of the task. In essence, the student is required to make a value judgment. Most students apparently do not possess enough information to make an appropriate judgment. The use of "all of the above," though correct in the instructor's eyes, may have contributed to the difficulty of the task (difficulty index = 19 percent) and made responding to the item easier for the low than the high group. Students in the low group may have been able to identify correctly two of the "limitations" and therefore been drawn to answer 5. It is difficult to speculate about the line of thinking followed by the high group. The item obviously does not work well and should be rewritten or discarded.

Another point is raised by the data on Item 3. It was found that discrimination for this item was low, as was the difficulty index. In general, extremely difficult or extremely easy items will show very little discrimination.

An instructor will select items for the final or a future form of his test that have the highest discrimination indices and measure the desired outcomes of instruction. Ebel (1965a) suggests that items with discrimination indices below +.40 could benefit from rewriting, and that those below +.20 should be improved or discarded.

EXAMINING DISTRACTOR EFFECTIVENESS

An *ideal* item, at least from a statistical item-analysis standpoint, is one that all students in the high group answer correctly and all students in the low group miss. In addition, the responses of the low group should be evenly distributed among the incorrect alternatives. Again, however, this rarely happens in practice. The situation illustrated by Item 4 is frequently encountered:

Item 4. The primary purpose of using a "table of specifications" in achievement test development is to:

*1. help insure that each objective will be given the desired relative emphasis on the test.
2. show the students the content to be covered by the test.
3. translate statements of objectives from nonbehavioral, to behavioral terms.
4. translate ultimate into immediate objectives.
5. show the students what to study for.

Again referring to the item-analysis data in Table 12.1, it can be seen that, despite appropriate levels of difficulty and discrimination, the item can be improved. First, the responses of the low group are not evenly distributed among the incorrect alternatives. Also, answers 2 and 5 have a particularly low frequency of selection, and are therefore not contributing much to the item. In fact, they are making a negative contribution, because more members of the high group than the low group are selecting them. The low frequency of selection of 2 and 5 might be accounted for by their content. They are very similar, and relative to the stem are implausible. They should be replaced or eliminated because they just take up reading time. Incidentally, there is nothing sacred about the practice of providing four or five alternative answers for all multiple-choice items. Tversky (1964), as we have noted previously, has shown mathematically that the use of three alternatives for each question will maximize the discriminability, power, and information yielded per unit of time. This makes intuitive sense; we all know how hard it is to invent consistently "good" fourth and fifth distractors. They frequently turn out to be merely space fillers.

EFFECTS OF ITEM ANALYSIS ON RELIABILITY AND VALIDITY

It has been suggested that items in the middle range of difficulty that show a high degree of discrimination should be selected for the final form of a test. Such a procedure helps insure that the test has a high degree of internal-consistency reliability because items that are highly correlated with the total score are likely to be highly correlated with each other. This procedure assumes that an instructor has the opportunity to pretest his items. Very frequently, however, this opportunity does not present itself. Two alternatives are available.

The first requires rescoring of the test *after* the item analysis has been completed. Although bad items cannot be rewritten, poor items can be eliminated. The analyzed and rescored test should be more reliable than the original. A large number of items cannot, of course, be eliminated. If this were allowed to happen, many of the important learning outcomes would not be measured, and the content validity of the test would be lowered. The rescoring procedure must be used with caution. Informal studies by the author have indicated, in addition, that the correlations between original and rescored tests run in the high +.90s, suggesting essentially unchanged ranking.

The second and more desirable alternative to pretesting is to select items from a file set up over a period of time. When a particular item is used, the resulting item-analysis data is recorded on a card. Such data is accumulated until the instructor has weeded out most of the poor items, and can select items with a greater degree of confidence. The availability of an item file provides a great deal of flexibility for an instructor. It allows, for example, parallel forms of a test to be assembled with comparative ease. Another justification for developing an item file is that a teacher usually has small samples of students on whom to try out the items. This limitation can be overcome by accumulating information on each item. The comparability of the groups and testing conditions is important in accumulating data. Such a subtle factor as the position of an item on a test may also be of significance. Item-analysis data, then, must be considered "relative," meaning that an instructor cannot expect an item to function in exactly the same way on two or more occasions.

LIMITATIONS OF ITEM ANALYSES

In addition to the limitations of small sample size and the possibility of reduced content validity, several other cautions should be noted.

Some experts suggest that internal item analyses should be completed only on tests that measure essentially the same mental functions. For a classroom achievement test, which generally deals with heterogeneous learning outcomes, item-analysis techniques like those described in this chapter should be considered crude devices for refining the test. If for no other reason, an instructor should conduct an item analysis to force himself to look critically at the measurements he is using to make important decisions about students.

Item-analysis techniques are not directly applicable to essay tests, although information related to mean performance on each item might have diagnostic significance for an instructor.

Another limitation of item-analysis data relates to its use in a diagnostic manner. It has been suggested that, by building a chart relating each student's response to each item, evaluations could be made of either individual or class strengths and weaknesses. One must be cautioned that such evaluations are based on limited information that may call into question the reliability of judgments. Even when items are grouped on the basis of content or outcome (comprehension, recall of knowledge, application, and the like), only a few samples of behavior are available for analysis. Chance could therefore play an important role, at least for individual analyses, in determining the consistency and validity of a performance on a given item. As we increase the number of samples of behavior, we also increase the likelihood that we can have confidence in the results. The problem of attempting to base diagnoses on limited item information is not peculiar to classroom tests and practices. Many commercial test publishers erroneously encourage their clientele to make specific subject-matter judgments on the basis of item data. Decisions like these should be based on many sources of data, which may include the results of a diagnostic test (see Chapter Fourteen) developed specifically to aid in guiding remediation.

SELECTING ITEMS FOR CRITERION–REFERENCED MEASURES

It will be noted in Chapter Thirteen that, since most criterion-referenced measures are used in conjunction with mastery learning and individualized instruction programs, difficulty is encountered in selecting the "best" items for a test. If everyone masters the material and the test items are tied very closely to specific objectives, nearly everyone should do well on all the items. Therefore, it might be reasonable to expect and select items at about the 80 percent level of item difficulty, if instruction has been effective. It is imperative that students who participate in the item analysis of measures for use in criterion-referenced situations *have already worked through the material* being tested. It might be advisable for the reader to refer to the suggestions by Cox and Vargas (1966) and Popham (1971) concerning some approaches to item selection for criterion-referenced measures.

Finally, the instructor should be warned about being blinded by statistics. Item-analysis data suggest the kinds of learning that have taken place and the items that are in need of repair. The final decision about an item must be made by considering not only item-analysis data but also the content and structure of the item and the nature of the group being tested.

DEVELOPING AN ITEM DATA FILE

Teachers are encouraged to develop a file of test items. Recording items on 3″ × 5″ or 5″ × 8″ cards and accumulating data on their difficulty and discrimination over several administrations allows for the refinement and improvement of classroom tests. Such a file has the advantages of:

1.   Encouraging the teacher to undertake an item analysis as often as is practical.

2.   Allowing for accumulated data to be used to make item analyses more reliable.

3.   Providing for a wider choice of item format and objectives—in other words, greater flexibility in test construction.

4.   Facilitating the revision of items and suggesting ideas for new items.

5.   Facilitating the relation of the test item and its objective to the table of specifications.

6.   Facilitating the physical construction and reproduction of the test, because each item is on a separate card.

7.   Accumulating a large enough pool of items to allow for some items to be shared with students for study purposes.

A test item file has the disadvantages of:

1.   Requiring a great deal of clerical time.

2.   Inhibiting creative test-construction efforts on the part of the teacher by allowing for access to ready-made items.

3. Providing the opportunity for the file of items to dictate the content of instruction.

These negative factors can influence a teacher's measurement practices, but the overall advantages of an item file certainly outweigh them.

A sample item-analysis data card suitable for objective items from classroom tests is presented in Table 12.2. Table 12.3 contains an item-

TABLE 12.2   Sample Item-Analysis Data Card

(FRONT)

Item No.: 37 Topic: Trade barriers Level: Comprehension—Junior High Cell: 14 Objective: 14	Reference: Farquhar's *Introduction to Economics,* rev. ed., 1971, pp. 201–214.

Item 3.   A tariff may be defined as a tax on
       *1. imported goods.
        2. money brought into the country.
        3. exported goods.
        4. imported cats and dogs.	

(BACK)

Item No.: 37				Test: Midterm Class: 7th		
Options	Upper Third	Lower Third	Upper Third	Lower Third	Upper Third	Lower Third
*1	15	8				
2	0	3				
3	3	3				
4	2	1				
5						
Omits	0	0				
Difficulty	58%					
Discrim- ination	.35					
Date	2/14/63					
Class Size	60					
Comments						

TABLE 12.3   Sample Item-Analysis Card from 1961 Standardization of Stanford Achievement Test

BATTERY: Intermediate II FORM: 1 TEST: Arithmetic Concepts ITEM: No. 18	Percent each option			
	Grade	4	5	6	7

<table>
<tr><td rowspan="6">BATTERY: Intermediate II
FORM: 1
TEST: Arithmetic Concepts
ITEM: No. 18

What is the value
of N if $\frac{N}{25} = \frac{80}{100}$?

a. 50 b. 2½ *c. 20 d. 80</td><td colspan="4" align="center">Percent each option</td></tr>
<tr><td>Grade</td><td>4</td><td>5</td><td>6</td><td>7</td></tr>
</table>

		Percent each option			
BATTERY: Intermediate II FORM: 1 TEST: Arithmetic Concepts ITEM: No. 18 What is the value of N if $\frac{N}{25} = \frac{80}{100}$? a. 50 b. 2½ *c. 20 d. 80	Grade	4	5	6	7
	N	150	350	330	200
	a	15	12	5	4
	b	20	13	10	6
	*c	32	50	69	75
	d	20	19	12	9

Source: Reproduced from Stanford Achievement Test, copyright © 1964 by Harcourt Brace Jovanovich, Inc. Reproduced by special permission of the publisher.

analysis card used in the 1961 standardization of the *Stanford Achievement Test*. The item analyzed in Table 12.3 was considered a good one and was included in the final version of the test. In addition to meeting an acceptable discrimination criterion, determined by another analysis, the item shows a grade progression in the percentage of pupils answering it correctly (see alternative c).

This chapter has only hinted at the many potential uses of item-analysis data. Study of the Suggested Readings will give additional perspective on this very valuable technique.

SUGGESTED READINGS

Ahmann, J. S., and Glock, M. D. *Evaluating pupil growth*, 4th ed. Boston: Allyn and Bacon, 1971. Chapter 6, "Appraising Classroom Achievement Tests," contains one of the most informative discussions of item-analysis techniques available. Many examples and uses are illustrated.

Davis, F. B. Item analysis techniques. In *Educational measurement*, ed. E. F. Lindquist. Washington: American Council on Education, 1951. A moderately technical presentation of methods of examining difficulty and discrimination. The problem of correcting for guessing is considered in detail, as are ideas for organizing a test item file.

Ebel, R. L. *Essentials of educational measurement*. Englewood Cliffs, N.J.: Prentice-Hall, 1972. Chapter 14, "How to Improve Test Quality Through Item Analysis," is a very readable discussion of the underlying rationale and procedures for analyzing items on a classroom test.

Henryssen, S. Gathering, analyzing, and using data on test items. In *Educational measurement*, 2nd ed., ed. R. L. Thorndike. Washington: American

Council on Education, 1970. Chapter 5 is a comprehensive overview of practical and technical issues, emphasizing statistical concerns. Comparable in coverage to Davis' article, this essay also summarizes recent developments and thinking.

Katz, M. Improving classroom tests by means of item analysis. *Clearing House,* 35 (1961): 265–269. Presents detailed instructions for a useful method of analyzing classroom achievement test items.

Lange, A.; Lehmann, I. J.; and Mehrens, W. A. Using item analysis to improve tests. *Journal of Educational Measurement* 4 (Summer 1967): 65–68. The procedures outlined in this chapter are illustrated in this brief article.

VI
OTHER SOURCES AND USES OF ASSESSMENT DATA

13

THE DEVELOPMENT AND APPLICATION OF CRITERION–REFERENCED MEASURES

SUMMARY PREVIEW STATEMENTS

1. Criterion-referencing focuses primarily on the use to which a test is to be put.

2. Each item in a test used in a criterion-referenced way represents a performance objective stated in behavioral terms.

3. Criterion-referenced measures are primarily used to assess individuals and the effectiveness of treatments.

4. Scores from criterion-referenced measures are directly interpretable in light of the objectives they measure, and ideally have immediate implications for the instructional program and quality of student progress.

5. It would be unusual for an assessment program to be devoted exclusively to the use of criterion-referenced measures.

6. As opposed to *norm-referenced* measures, which assess interindividual differences and uses in selection situations, criterion-referenced measures are frequently characterized by:
   a. Low variability of total test scores across individuals.
   b. A large proportion of items that are relatively easy if the material has been mastered.
   c. Relatively low item discrimination.
   d. High reliance on a wide variety of item types, particularly performance measures.
   e. High reliance on content-validity methods to establish claims that the items and test measure what we want them to measure.
   f. Relatively low reliability.

7. Criterion-referenced measures can be used to place an individual within a learning sequence, diagnose individual student and class

achievement, monitor individual and class progress, evaluate curricula, and group students for instructional purposes on the basis of content achievement.

One of the recent trends in educational assessment is the rebirth or, perhaps more correctly, rekindled interest in criterion-referenced measures. Although the idea of basing a series of test items on specific performance criteria has existed since the turn of the century, not until the advent of mastery learning and individualized curricula was proper attention paid to this use of test scores. A criterion-referenced measure is one that is used to identify an individual's status with respect to an established standard of performance (Popham and Husek 1969). The standard of performance is usually a highly refined behavioral objective describing expected pupil changes and the conditions and criteria under which these changes can be exhibited. It is not possible to distinguish a criterion-referenced measure from a norm-referenced measure merely by looking at it; the differences show up in the use made of the scores (Simon 1969). The interpretation of scores—relative for norm-referenced and absolute for criterion-referenced—is the major difference between these two approaches to assessment. The two kinds of measures could be envisioned on a continuum whose poles might be characterized as "Interpretation Tied to Specific Objectives" and "Interpretation Tied to Relative Performances." It is quite possible for a criterion-referenced measure to be used in a norm-referenced way, but is less likely for the converse to be true.

Following is a set of criterion-referenced items (Cox and Graham 1966):[1]

Objective	Sample Test Items
The student is able to:	
1. Recognize numerals from 1 to 10.	1. 1 2 3 4 "Draw a circle around the 2."

---

2. a. Determine which numeral comes before or after another numeral.
   b. Determine which of two numerals is the largest or smallest.

2. a. 10 8 5 2
   "Draw a circle around the number that comes just after 7."
   b. 7 5
   "Draw a circle around the larger numeral."

3. Discriminate between +, −, =, ≠.

3. + − = ≠
   "Draw a circle around the sign which means to add."

4. a. Add two single-digit numerals with sums to 10, vertically.
   b. Add two single-digit numerals with sums to 10, horizontally.

4. a.   5
       + 4
   b. 3 + 1 =

5. a. Add two single-digit numerals involving carrying, horizontally.
   b. Add two single-digit numerals involving carrying, vertically.

5. a. 8 + 3 =
   b.   7
       + 8

6. a. Add three single-digit numerals involving carrying, vertically.
   b. Add three single-digit numerals involving carrying, horizontally.

6. a.   1
         8
       + 4
   b. 7 + 3 + 2 =

7. a. Place one- and two-digit numerals in a column so they could be added.

   b. Determine which columns of numerals is written so it could be added.

7. a. 15   16   2
   "Place these numerals in a column so they could be added."
   b. 15   15   15
      16   16   16
       2   2   2
   "Draw a circle around the column which is written so it could be added."

8. Add 2 two-digit numerals without carrying.

8.   20
   + 11

9. Add 2 three-digit numerals without carrying.

9.   215
   + 723

10. Add 2 two-digit numerals with carrying.

10.   58
    + 36

This set of test items is interesting because it illustrates a potentially valuable application of criterion-referenced measures. These ten objective-item pairs are sequenced—that is, item 8 builds upon the knowledge and skills elicited by items 1 through 7. The total score on such an instrument has direct interpretability. Given a total score on a scaled measure, the instructor can discern which items an individual answered wrong. On a norm-referenced test, this is usually impossible. The application of the idea of analyzing learning sequences and hierarchies has been well illustrated by Gagné (1967).

DEVELOPING CRITERION–REFERENCED MEASURES

Mayo (1970) has noted that the development of criterion-referenced measures closely parallels that of a traditional achievement test. In the development of the usual classroom test—or standardized test, for that matter—four general steps are followed (see Chapters One and Four for a more complete overview):

1.   Specification of expected student performance outcomes.
2.   Construction, identification, collection, or adaptation of measuring methods appropriate to each outcome.
3.   Selection of those post-tryout items that yield maximum discrimination against an internal criterion and are answered correctly by an average of about 50–60 percent of the students.
4.   Establishment of guidelines for interpreting the scores against normative standards.

The first two steps are applicable to the development of criterion-referenced measures. Adjustments are, however, required in the final two steps. Inasmuch as criterion-referenced measures focus on an individual's performance on a set of tasks, discrimination—defined as the capacity of an item to distinguish between groups of more and less knowledgeable individuals—is not an applicable concept. We do hope that an individual will learn as he progresses through the educational experience. Therefore, Cox (1971) has suggested an index of discrimination based on the relative proportions of students passing an item at the beginning and at the conclusion of a unit or course as the best indication of its effectiveness. One might expect an item on a mastery test to have a difficulty level as high as 85 percent at the conclusion of instruction, whether it be self-administered or teacher-directed.

With regard to interpretation of the resulting scores, it is sufficient to note that the meaning of an individual's score is derived from an examination of his skills or knowledge relative to his deficiencies. What is proposed is a kind of diagnostic interpretation. Assuming no deficiencies in the items, a criterion-referenced measure is a directly relevant sample of student behavior.

DIFFERENCES BETWEEN CRITERION–REFERENCED AND NORM–REFERENCED MEASURES

Several of the differences between criterion-referenced and norm-referenced measures are briefly summarized below. The differences are in most cases matters of degree rather than kind.

Dimension	Criterion-Referenced Measures	Norm-Referenced Measures
1. Intent	Information on degree to which absolute external performance standards have been met	Information for relative internal comparisons
	Description of maximum performance by individuals, groups, and treatment	Comparisons of individuals, particularly when high degree of selectivity is required.
2. Directness of measurement	Great emphasis	Lesser emphasis
3. Variability among scores	Relatively low	Relatively high
4. Difficulty of items	Items tend to be easy, but with some range	Item difficulty localized around 50 percent
5. Item type	Great variety, but less reliance on selection-type items	Variety, but emphasis on selection-type items
6. Discriminating ability of item	Not emphasized	Greatly emphasized
7. Methods of establishing validity	Reliance on content validity	Emphasis on criterion-related validity.

Dimension	Criterion-Referenced Measures	Norm–Referenced Measures
8. Emphasis on reliability	Focus on reliability of domain sampling; therefore internal consistency of some interest	Greater concern with parallel form and test-retest estimates of performance stability
9. Influence of guessing	Can be of consequence	Generally not a problem
10. Importance of which items are missed	High	Emphasis on number of missed items
11. Necessity for maintaining security of test items	Relatively low	Relatively high
12. Area of education best served	Instruction	Guidance Selection Grading

Several of these distinctions need further explanation.

The variability of the scores is probably the single most important technical difference between the two approaches to measurement. Since criterion-referenced measures are most frequently used in mastery-testing situations, an individual who attempts an item representing an objective he has seriously worked toward is highly likely to answer it correctly. His total score is likely to be high, as are the scores of the total group. Therefore, variability among scores is likely to be low. Unfortunately, variability is a characteristic of scores that is highly related to the traditional indices of instrument quality and accuracy. These indices are, therefore, considerably less relevant to criterion-referenced measures than to norm-referenced measures.

One of the chief objectives in writing items for norm-referenced measures is to make them as discriminating as possible. By controlling for such factors as discriminability among alternative answers and vocabulary, one attempts to maximize discrimination and thereby increase variability. By contrast, the writer of criterion-referenced items is interested solely in making the item measure the objective in the most direct way.

Since the items in a criterion-referenced measure represent a set of objectives, they should be correlated. A measure of internal consistency (see Chapter Eleven) is appropriate here. The old problem of variability, however, presents itself. We should probably reduce our standards of acceptable reliability to about .50 to accommodate the lowered variability.

Items that do not discriminate between more and less knowledgeable or skillful students need not be eliminated from a criterion-referenced test if they reflect an important learning outcome (see Chapter Twelve). Cox (1971) has reported the results of a study he conducted with Vargas demonstrating that, in a pre-posttest situation, an index based on subtraction of the percentage of pupils who passed an item on the pretest from the percentage who passed the item on a posttest provided information useful in identifying pretest items of diagnostic significance. Some of these items would have been overlooked if traditional item-analysis methods had been used.

Since we hope that individuals will achieve instructional objectives as a result of their educational experiences, we might expect an item on a criterion-referenced test to be answered correctly by a greater proportion of them after instruction than before it; if the instruction is successful, the proportion answering correctly should be high. Such indices of change in difficulty and absolute level of difficulty can be useful in assessing instructional effectiveness but should not be used to judge the adequacy of the item itself, as would be the case with norm-referenced tests. The quality of an item on a criterion-referenced test is a function of the degree to which it matches the objective and is directly interpretable with reference to it. Panels of expert judges could be employed to help make these item-objective evaluations.

Methods of assessing validity that employ correlation are generally inapplicable to criterion-referenced measures due to lack of score variability. Instead, the test developer must rely on logical but subjective analysis of the match between item and objective (see the discussion of content validity in Chapter Eleven.

STANDARDIZED CRITERION–REFERENCED MEASURES

As the idea of criterion-referenced measures takes hold in the schools, there will evolve a demand for standardized measures. As has been noted, a considerable amount of time must be devoted to generating test items, particularly when criterion-referenced items are required. Each objective must be represented by at least one, and preferably several, items. Selecting a standardized criterion-referenced test is equally as demanding, if not more so, than selecting any achievement test. The critical question is "Do these items measure the objectives I wish to assess?" With a standardized criterion-referenced measure, one at least has the advantage of a list of the objectives being measured. The teacher must evaluate this list in light of his classroom instruction and expected outcomes.

Descriptions of two recently published standardized criterion-referenced tests follow. One might well ask what makes a standardized criterion-referenced test standardized. Since no norms are involved, its chief characteristics are probably (1) the care given the development of objectives, (2) the potential uniformity of administrations with regard to directions, scoring, and so forth, and (3) the care given to refining the instrument through item and reliability analyses. (See Chapters Eleven and Twelve for consideration of these topics.)

Prescriptive Reading Inventory (PRI)[2]

PUBLISHER: California Test Bureau/McGraw-Hill

PURPOSE: To serve as a diagnostic criterion-referenced measure of individual student reading behavior, and to provide information that can be used to reinforce, remediate, or supplement reading development.

RANGE AND ADMINISTRATION TIME: Four test levels span the grade range 1.5–6. Each level requires four 45-minute sessions.

COST (pkg/35): Red, green and blue machine-scorable $18.30; orange book (Grades 4–6) $10.60.

CONTENT: An analysis of five basal reading programs yielded 1248 reading behaviors and related study skills. From this list 90 behaviors in seven categories (Recognition of Sound and Symbol, Phonic Analysis, Structural Analysis, Translation, Literal Comprehension, Interpretive Comprehension, and Critical Comprehension) were selected. A given objective may be included in one or all four levels. Following are some sample objectives, items, and suggested classroom activities from the PRI:

OBJECTIVE: Phonic Analysis

When given familiar printed words, the student can demonstrate knowledge of consonant substitution by choosing from specified initial or final consonants to make new words. (Consonant Substitution)

---

[2] From Prescriptive Reading Inventory. Reproduced by permission of the publisher, CTB/McGraw-Hill, Del Monte Research Park, Monterey, CA 93940. Copyright © 1972 by McGraw-Hill, Inc. All rights reserved. Printed in the U.S.A.

SAMPLE ITEMS

Find the questions by the cats. Look at the first cat. Read the word beside the cat. Now cross out the first letter in the word. Look at the letters across from the word. One of them can take the place of the letter you crossed out and make a new word. Fill in the circle by that letter.

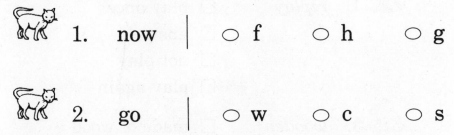

Find the first rabbit. Read the word beside the rabbit. Now cross out the last letter in the word. Look at the letters across from the word. One of them can take the place of the letter you crossed out and make a new word. Fill in the circle by that letter.

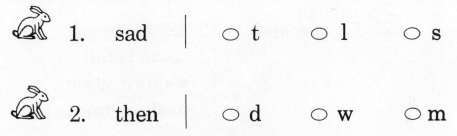

SAMPLE SUGGESTED CLASSROOM ACTIVITIES

   2. Consonant Substitution
      a. Individual children spin wheels to choose consonants to sub-stitute for specific phonetic parts.
      b. Divide a group of children in half. Let one half make cards beginning with initial consonants or consonant blends, and the other half make cards with corresponding ending word parts from a list which has been given to them. Give an oral word and have the children with the appropriate cards come to the front of the room and form the word.

OBJECTIVE: Structural Analysis

The student can demonstrate knowledge of affixes and root words by choosing the correct definition for certain affixed words. (Affixes and Root Words)

SAMPLE ITEMS

Find the rabbit at the top of the page. Read the underlined word beside the rabbit. Now look at the answers. One of the answers tells what the underlined word means. Mark the answer.

1. *replay*
- ☐ play once
- ☐ answer
- ☐ not play
- ☐ play again

3. *wooden*
- ☐ made of wood
- ☐ one who would
- ☐ full of wood
- ☐ not woody

7. *spoonful*
- ☐ full of spoons
- ☐ spoon is full
- ☐ wants a spoon
- ☐ made of spoons

SAMPLE SUGGESTED CLASSROOM ACTIVITY

18. Affixes and Root Words
   a. Place sentences and/or phrases on a board with spaces provided for an affixed word. Give each student a card with either a root word or an affix (based on root words and affixes necessary to fill spaces provided). Have student match root words to sentences. Student holding the root word card will indicate which affixes will make a word to fit the sentence; the student holding the affix card will indicate correctness of response.

COMMENT: It is too early to judge the value of this instrument. It looks promising. The publisher has gone to some lengths to provide aids to help the teacher make maximum use of the test results. Among these aids are:

Individual diagnostic maps. A display for each student of those reading behaviors he has mastered, those he has not mastered, and those in need of review.

Individual study guides. A prescription for each student of those pages in his reading materials that give the best instruction on the behaviors he has not mastered. The objectives of the PRI are keyed to a large number of widely used reading programs.

Class diagnostic map. Similar to the individual diagnostic map but serves as class summary.

Class grouping report. A listing of students in the class according to their shared deficiencies.

Tests of Achievement in Basic Skills—MATH (TABS)[3]

PUBLISHER: Educational and Industrial Testing Service

PURPOSE: To provide a criterion-referenced measure of mathematics achievements commonly expected of students in a modern comprehensive school.

RANGE AND ADMINISTRATION TIME: Grades 7–9 (Level C, two parallel forms). Approximately one hour.

COST (pkg/35): $7.50

CONTENT: Each form of this power test contains 64 machine-scorable items, each related to an explicit performance objective. The items are grouped into three sections: Arithmetic Skills, Geometry; Measurement Application; and Modern Concepts. Following are some sample objectives and items:

OBJECTIVE	ITEM
8. Given two two-digit integers, with unlike signs, the student must correctly subtract one from the other.	8. Subtract $(-93) - (+62)$ F -155 G $- 31$ H $+ 31$ J $+155$

OBJECTIVE	ITEM
35. The student must correctly divide two literal expressions.	35. Simplify $$\frac{X^2Y^2}{XY}$$ A XY B 1/XY C X^3Y^3 D X + Y
47. Given a volume or a weight, and a price per volume or weight, the student must correctly determine a total unit price.	47. 16 ounces of rice costs 12 cents. $3\frac{1}{2}$ pounds of rice costs how much? A 32 cents B 42 cents C 56 cents D 84 cents
56. The student must convert any whole number less than 500 from base 2 to base 10, base 5, or base 8.	56. $101_{\text{base } 2} = ?_{\text{base } 10}$ F 3 G 4 H 5 I 6

COMMENT: The publisher, in addition to encouraging the user to evaluate the results in light of the local instructional situation, provides national data for comparative purposes. This is an example of a test that can be used in either a criterion-referenced or a norm-referenced manner. As part of the reporting service, the teacher may receive an Individual Right Response Record and a Class Right Response Summary. The publisher also makes available an individualized mathematics program keyed to the TABS.

POSSIBLE APPLICATIONS OF CRITERION–REFERENCED MEASURES

As has been noted, the rekindled interest in criterion-referenced measures is partially a response to the evaluation of mastery learning and individualized instruction. It is not surprising, then, to find the major applications of criterion-referenced measures in these areas. At least eight general uses for criterion-referenced measures can be identified:

Placement in a Learning Continuum

The major function of a criterion-referenced measure used as a placement test is to provide a general profile of an individual's performance on a variety of work units. Lindvall and Cox (1969), for example, show how a mathematics placement test can be used to locate individuals differentially within a series of mathematic units variously labeled Numeration, Place Value, Addition, Subtraction, and so on. The challenge to the test constructor is to gather as much relevant information as possible in the most efficient manner. Placement tests should probably be administered at the beginning of the school year or at the outset of a new extended learning sequence.

Diagnosis of Individual Student Achievement

Perhaps the best use of a criterion-referenced measure is as a diagnostic tool. Used in this way, it should allow a student to "test out" of a particular unit. If his performance does not merit this, the resulting information will allow him and the instructor to identify areas in need of further study.

Monitoring of Individual Student Progress

The periodic administration of a criterion-referenced test similar in comprehensiveness to the previously described placement tests should facilitate monitoring of student progress. Such a periodic check may also have a motivational function for the student. These measures might serve as the basis for end-of-unit examinations. Both monitoring and placement measures are broader in coverage and objectives than are specific diagnostic measures.

Diagnosis of Class Achievement

Diagnostic tests may be applied on a classwide basis in the same way in which they are employed with individual students. Areas in which a majority of the students appear to be encountering problems might serve as focal points for remediation and for the planning and development of special remedial units.

Monitoring Class Progress

Again, individual student data could be aggregated for an entire class to provide the teacher and administration with a picture of group progress.

Evaluation of Curricula

Criterion-referenced measures might profitably be used to evaluate a limited-scope curriculum. Accumulated data could be used to assess the progress of students toward a specified set of objectives. Competing programs utilizing comparable objectives but different instructional approaches could be compared. By comparing growth data, for example, for a series of objectives and items on a year-to-year basis, or comparing the growth rates of different groups in a given year, important evaluative data could result.

A relatively recent methodological innovation called item-person sampling might be employed in such studies of program (rather than student) performance. If, for example, a limited amount of examination time is available and a considerable number of objectives need to be assessed, item-person sampling or matrix sampling could be employed. Rather than requiring all individuals to respond to all items, subsets of items could be answered by subsets of individuals. Since the focus is on the program, rather than on individual student performance, all students need not answer all questions. Assume, for example, a 40-item criterion-referenced test covering an entire unit, and 80 students. We can randomly divide the 40 items into five eight-item tests, and the 80 students into five 16-person groups. Each group of 16 students takes a different eight-item test. All objectives are covered, and when the data are aggregated we have a comprehensive picture of the effectiveness of the entire program. For more information on the subject of item-person sampling, see Cronbach (1963b), and Lord (1962).

Project and Program Evaluation

It may well be that the most significant application of criterion-referenced measures is the evaluation of innovative educational programs and projects. The use of criterion-referenced tests in the National Assessment of Educational Progress represents an application on a national scale. Programs built on the "accountability concept," e.g., performance-contracting projects, represent another area in which criterion-referenced items and instruments can provide informative data.

Grouping on the Basis of Content Achievement

Some schools may wish to group or track students on the basis of ability in particular subject-matter areas. Criterion-referenced measures might be an excellent basis for such grouping.

A MINOR CONTROVERSY

Criterion-referenced measures are intended to measure what, not how much, the student has or has not learned. Although originally limited to relatively simple learning outcomes, criterion-referenced measures are now beginning to be applied to complex objectives.

A minor controversy surrounds the use of criterion-referenced measures. Ebel (1971), for example, has argued that criterion-referenced measures have limited applicability to the day-to-day classroom setting because (1) such measures do not tell us all we need to know, or perhaps the most important things we need to know, about student learning; (2) it is difficult to base criterion-referenced measurement on meaningful criteria of achievement; and (3) the mastery learning on which criterion-referenced measures focus represents only one classroom methodology used a small percentage of the time. One might add, however, that this percentage is increasing every year.

In response to these alleged limitations, Block (1971) has suggested that (1) criterion-referenced measures, although they do not "tell all," provide relevant information on the excellence or deficiency of an individual's performance; (2) the cost of development in teacher time and effort is not as great as Ebel supposes, particularly in regard to the generation of objectives; and (3) the time spent on developing skills in the schools is greater than Ebel assumes, and criterion-referenced measures are particularly well suited to assessment in these areas. It should be noted that the application of computer technology to the assembly of tests has been refined and that most of the technical problems have been worked out.[4]

Suffice it to say that criterion-referenced measures are different, at least their uses are relatively individualistic. They should take their rightful place in the educational assessor's library. They can provide information not readily available from other sources and can be used to supplement but not supplant existing methodology.

SUGGESTED READINGS

Airasian, P. W., and Madaus, G. F. Criterion referenced testing in the classroom. *Measurement in Education* 3 (May 1972): 1–8.

Block, J. H., ed. *Mastery learning: Theory and practice.* New York: Holt, Rinehart and Winston, 1971. A useful little paperback summarizing major issues. The papers by Airasian (on evaluation), Bloom (on affective outcomes), and Carroll (on measurement problems) are well worth reading.

---

[4] See, for example, Computer assisted test construction. *Educational Technology* Volume 13, No. 3 (March 1973).

Davis, F. B. Criterion referenced measurement. *TM Report Number 12*, 1972. Published by ERIC Clearinghouse on Tests, Measurement, and Evaluation.

Educational Records Bureau. *Proceedings of the Thirty-Fifth Annual Conference of Educational Records Bureau.* Greenwich, Conn.: ERB, 1970. The papers by Davis, Ebel, and Nitko are an excellent introduction to the promise and the problems inherent in the criterion-referenced approach to measurement.

Lindvall, C. M., and Cox, R. C. The role of evaluation in programs for individualized introduction. In *Educational Evaluation: New Roles, New Means,* ed. R. W. Tyler. Chicago: University of Chicago Press, 1969.

Mayo, S. T. Mastery learning and mastery testing. *Measurement in Education* 1 (March 1970): 1–4.

Popham, W. J., ed. *Criterion-referenced measurement.* Englewood Cliffs, N.J.: Educational Technology Publications, 1971. A collection of highly relevant and readable papers. The best single source available.

Popham, W. J., and Husek, T. R. Implications of criterion-referenced measurement. *Journal of Educational Measurement* 6 (1969): 1–9.

14

ASSESSING COGNITIVE LEARNING OUTCOMES WITH STANDARDIZED ACHIEVEMENT TESTS

SUMMARY PREVIEW STATEMENTS

1. Standardized achievement tests are carefully developed and tested on usually large and representative student populations.

2. The term *standardization* usually refers to the uniform and controlled conditions required for administration and scoring, and sometimes to the availability of normative data.

3. Standardized achievement tests are usually based on extensive analyses of common educational outcomes.

4. Refined item-selection procedures and test analyses characterize standardized measures.

5. Standardized tests are used to:
   a. Direct curricular emphases.
   b. Provide educational guidance.
   c. Stimulate learning activities.
   d. Direct and motivate administrative and supervisory efforts.

6. As compared to classroom proficiency tests, standardized achievement tests are:
   a. Less responsive to local instructional objectives.
   b. More reliable.
   c. More likely to reflect an even balance of item difficulty levels.
   d. More likely to include discriminating items.
   e. Likely to be accompanied by normative data.

7. Achievement survey batteries provide an overview of the major instructional thrusts in primary, elementary, and secondary schools and colleges in such areas as language arts, mathematics, social studies, science, reading, and study skills.

8. Survey battery subtests have the advantage of being standardized on the same populations.

9. Specific subject or area tests provide detailed coverage of limited topics in such areas as chemistry, history, economics, foreign languages, and the like.

10. The diagnostic achievement tests usually applied in the fields of elementary reading and arithmetic:
    a. Provide very detailed analyses of student strengths and weaknesses.
    b. Have items that are tied to specific instructional objectives.
    c. Have scores with direct implications for actual remedial procedures.

11. Information about standardized tests can be secured primarily from:
    a. Buros' *Mental Measurements Yearbook*.
    b. Test reviews in professional journals.
    c. Test manuals, specimen sets, and publishers' catalogues.

12. Among the factors that must be considered in selecting a standardized achievement test for possible use are:
    a. Level and appropriateness of content.
    b. Cost.
    c. Copyright date.
    d. Adequacy of administration and scoring directions.
    e. Adequacy of reliability and validity data.
    f. Adequacy of suggested interpretive guides and normative data.

13. In establishing a schoolwide assessment system, one must consider the following factors:
    a. School educational philosophy and objectives.
    b. The use to which the data are to be put.
    c. Communication and security of results.
    d. Scheduling of tests.
    e. Evaluation of the testing program.
    f. Achievement of cooperation from teachers, administrators, students, and members of the community.

14. Schoolwide assessment systems must be responsive to the needs of students, teachers, and society.

In attempting to measure and evaluate the results of learning, an instructor may use either instruments he constructs himself or tests available from a commercial publisher. The usual choice is to use a classroom test because it is more likely to reflect accurately the instructional program of a particular teacher and class. There are instances, however, when the use of a standardized test may be desirable, if not preferable.

This chapter briefly surveys the major types of standardized achievement tests. It would be impossible, and probably unnecessary, to describe and evaluate all the achievement tests that are available. Therefore, representative tests will be discussed in some detail, and common characteristics identified. The chapter will discuss the location and evaluation of information on standardized tests, and the establishment of an assessment system.

USES OF STANDARDIZED ACHIEVEMENT TESTS

Achievement has been defined as the extent to which specified instructional objectives are attained. Achievement tests, then, provide evidence about a student's status or level of learning. They may deal with knowledge of facts and principles as well as the ability to apply them in complex and usually lifelike situations.

Achievement tests hold a relatively unique position among the many types of educational and psychological tests. Measures of intelligence, personality, and the like deal with "constructs." We hypothesize and infer the presence of the construct from the responses to the instrument. Thus we have only indirect evidence of its nature. In assessing an achievement behavior, we attempt to measure a sample of the behavior itself; the evidence is therefore more direct.

Achievement-test data may be applied in a variety of ways by teachers, principals, and other administrative and supervisory personnel. Walter W. Cook has identified fifteen major functions served by achievement tests (Cook 1951, p. 36). According to Cook, achievement tests:

Direct curriculum emphasis by:

1. Focusing attention on as many of the important ultimate objectives of education as possible.

2. Clarifying educational objectives to teachers and pupils.

3. Determining elements of strength and weakness in the instructional program of the school.

4. Discovering inadequacies in curriculum content and organization.

Provide for educational guidance of pupils by:

5. Providing a basis for predicting individual pupil achievement in each learning area.

6. Serving as a basis for the preliminary grouping of pupils in each learning area.

7. Discovering special aptitudes and disabilities.

8. Determining the difficulty of material a pupil can read with profit.

9. Determining the level of problem-solving ability in various areas.

Stimulate the learning activities of pupils by:

10. Enabling pupils to think of their achievements in objective terms.

11. Giving pupils satisfaction for the progress they make, rather than for the relative level of achievement they attain.

12. Enabling pupils to compete with their past performance record.

13. Measuring achievement objectively in terms of accepted educational standards, rather than by the subjective appraisal of teachers.

Direct and motivate administrative and supervisory efforts by:

14. Enabling teachers to discover the areas in which they need supervisory aid.

15. Affording the administrative and supervisory staff an overall measure of the effectiveness of the school organization and of the prevailing administrative and supervisory policies.

The foregoing functions are those primarily served by comprehensive batteries. Such batteries have limited value in planning the instructional programs of individual students or identifying individual strengths and weaknesses. They are useful in making intraindividual and interindividual comparisons across broad subject-matter areas and identifying areas in which more focused testing would prove informative.

A COMPARISON OF INSTRUCTOR–MADE AND STANDARDIZED TESTS

Ideally, one would not expect instructor-made and standardized achievement tests to differ significantly in quality. In practice, however, this is not the case. Because of time pressures and limited resources, a classroom teacher cannot consistently produce the kinds of measuring instruments he might prefer. The major differences between the two types of test have been succinctly summarized by Gronlund (1965) and are presented in Table 14.1. The most outstanding differences involve the availability of normative data useful in interpreting scores and the learning outcomes measured. The standardized test is likely to cover a broad spectrum of content taught over a fairly long

TABLE 14.1 Comparative Advantages of Standardized and Informal Classroom Tests of Achievement

	Standardized Achievement Tests	Informal Achievement Tests
Learning Outcomes and Content Measured	Measures outcomes and content common to majority of United States schools. Tests of basic skills and complex outcomes adaptable to many local situations; content-oriented tests seldom reflect emphasis or timeliness of local curriculum.	Well adapted to outcomes and content of local curriculum. Flexibility affords continuous adaptation of measurement to new materials and changes in procedure. Adaptable to various size work units. Tend to neglect complex learning outcomes.
Quality of Test Items	General quality of items high. Written by specialists, pretested and selected on basis of effectiveness.	Quality of items is unknown unless test item file is used. Quality typically lower than standardized because of limited time and skill of teacher.
Reliability	Reliability high; commonly between .80 and .95, frequently above .90.	Reliability usually unknown; can be high if carefully constructed.
Administration and Scoring	Procedures *standardized;* specific instructions provided.	Uniform procedures possible but usually flexible.
Interpretation of Scores	Scores can be compared to norm groups. Test manual and other guides aid interpretation and use.	Score comparisons and interpretations limited to local school situation.

Source: N. E. Gronlund, *Measurement and evaluation in teaching* (New York: Macmillan, 1965), p. 223. © copyright, Norman E. Gronlund, 1965. Reprinted by permission of the publisher.

instructional period. Both types of tests are aimed at school-learned information and skills, but they differ in degree of specificity. The standardized test, based on the pooled judgments of leading subject-matter experts, represents a collection of implied educational objectives and provides an informative picture of overall educational progress across schools and classes.

The two types of tests also differ with respect to certain statistical qualities. The standardized test is likely to have a better balance of item-difficulty levels, more discriminating items, and higher reliability. This is not to say that teacher-made tests cannot achieve a high level of quality, but it does require a considerable expenditure of time and effort.

Teacher-made tests seldom have accompanying norms. They typically test 20 to 40 students and are used to make intraclass comparisons. Again, this is not to say that teachers cannot develop meaningful normative data. The use of the same tests and items over several semesters or years allows for the opportunity to accumulate valuable distributions of scores. Most testing experts agree that local norms should also be developed for standardized tests.

TYPES OF STANDARDIZED ACHIEVEMENT TESTS

There are three general types of standardized achievement tests. The first is the *survey battery*, which consists of a group of individual subject-matter tests designated for use at particular levels. The second category is the *specific subject* or area test. The third category is the *diagnostic* test, which is usually administered when a survey battery or specific subject test indicates a substandard performance. Its purpose is to diagnose the area or areas of weakness so that remedial instruction may be instituted. Following are brief discussions of these three categories of standardized achievement tests, accompanied by descriptions of representative tests of each type.

Survey Batteries

Comprehensive survey achievement batteries are the mainstay of school testing programs, providing valuable information about the effectiveness of various instructional programs. The last two or three decades have seen a significant improvement in the quality of achievement batteries, particularly in regard to the learning outcomes measured and the quality of normative data made available to facilitate interpretation.

The content of a battery will, of course, vary according to the level of student achievement being measured. Table 14.2 suggests the range and variety of educational achievements that can be measured with the six batteries of the *Stanford Achievement Tests* (Kelley *et al.* 1964, 1965). There is a general trend toward an increase in the range of content coverage as one moves up the grade scale, and a tendency throughout to measure comprehension rather than recall of specific facts.

A distinct advantage of the survey battery over a series of individual subject-matter tests from different publishers is its simultaneous standardization of all subtests. Scores on individual subtests can thus be considered comparable, since the normative data were derived from the same population.

Some appreciation for the magnitude of the job of developing a standardized survey battery can be gained from a brief survey of the process of preparing the 1964 edition of the *Stanford Achievement Tests* for the batteries covering Grades 1 through 9. After careful review of the

TABLE 14.2 Content of the Six Batteries of the Stanford Achievement Tests

Content	Battery					
	Primary I (Grades 1–2)	Primary II (Grades 2–3)	Intermediate I (Grades 4–5)	Intermediate II (Grades 5–6)	Advanced (Grades 7–9)	High School (Grades 9–12)
Word Reading	x					
Vocabulary	x					
Arithmetic	x					
Science and Social Studies Concepts		x				
Word Study Skills	x	x	x			
Spelling	x	x	x	x	x	x
Paragraph Meaning (Reading)	x	x	x	x	x	x
Word Meaning		x	x	x		
Language (English)		x	x	x	x	x
Computation		x	x	x	x	
Arithmetic Concepts		x	x	x	x	
Arithmetic Applications			x	x	x	
Science			x	x	x	x
Social Studies			x	x	x	x
Numerical Competence						x
Mathematics						x

content and grade coverage of the 1953 edition, consultation with subject-matter experts, and review of appropriate courses and textbooks, the authors developed test specifications or "blueprints." Items were then written and edited by four different groups of individuals. The experimental forms of the test, which contained a total of approximately 15,000 questions, were pretested on 49,000 pupils in 19 school systems. Approximately 40 percent more items were tried out than were projected for the final forms of the test. The items selected (1) met the original content specifications, (2) were characterized either by an increasing percentage of correct answers at each grade level or high item-discrimination indices, and (3) were of appropriate difficulty. A total of 264 school systems representing all 50 states and over 850,000 students were involved in the final standardization and norming. Normative data were reported as grade equivalents, percentile ranks, and stanines. To facilitate interpretation of the *Stanford* scores, expectancy tables relating grade scores and IQs derived from the Otis Quick-Scoring Mental Ability Tests are provided. This dual standardization of measures of achievement and capacity represents a highly desirable trend in the development of standardized tests.

Illustrative Survey Batteries

Following are some brief descriptions of selected survey batteries widely used in the public schools. They represent well the variety of batteries available from commercial publishers. Only general information about ranges of application, cost, and total administration times is summarized. All batteries can be hand- or machine-scored. All publishers offer a scoring service, which is probably cheaper than a comparable local service. In addition, elaborate reporting services are available at nominal costs. An instructor seriously considering a given test would, of course, wish to examine a specimen set purchasable from the publisher, and would seek out such other sources of information as the test catalogue, test manual, and reviews in Buros' *Mental Measurements Yearbook* (MMY). To give the reader the flavor of the *MMY* reviews, critical comments about selected batteries have been excerpted from the *Seventh MMY*.

TITLE: **Adult Basic Learning Examination (ABLE)**

AUTHORS: Bjorn Karlsen, Richard Madden, and Eric F. Gardner

LEVELS AND SCORES AVAILABLE: Three achievement grade levels:
I—1–4; II—5–8; III—9–12

Six scores: vocabulary, reading, spelling, arithmetic (computation, problem solving), total

COPYRIGHT YEARS: 1967–1971

NUMBER OF FORMS: Two

COST OF BOOKLETS: $17.00–$17.50 for 35 tests

TESTING TIME: 145–250 minutes

PUBLISHER: Harcourt Brace Jovanovich

CRITICAL COMMENTS:[1] Appears promising for the purposes for which it was developed. Nouns appear to be overemphasized

---

[1] Based on reviews by A. N. Hieronymus, Edward B. Fry, and James W. Hall, *Seventh mental measurements yearbook* (Highland Park, N.J.: Gryphon Press, 1972).

(on Level I Form A, 32 of 50 vocabulary words are nouns). Reading test items do not recognize the multifaceted nature of reading comprehension. The reading tests do not represent the kind of reading adults do. Very little attention is given to writing skills: only spelling is tested, to the exclusion of capitalization, punctuation, and usage skills. No empirical data on the published forms of the ABLE are provided. Questions about normative data are raised and local norms (grade norms based on children's performance) are encouraged. Most appropriate use is in research on the effectiveness of various adult-education programs. In terms of reliability, the weakest tests are Vocabulary and Arithmetic Problem Solving.

TITLE: **California Achievement Tests (CAT),** 1970 Edition

AUTHORS: Ernest W. Tiegs and Willis W. Clark

LEVELS AND SCORES AVAILABLE: Five subtests in reading; mathematics and language available separately.

COPYRIGHT YEARS: 1957–1970

NUMBER OF FORMS: One

COST OF BOOKLETS: $9.00–$14.50 for 35 tests

TESTING TIME: 171–212 minutes in 3 sessions

PUBLISHER: McGraw-Hill/California Test Bureau

TITLE: **Comprehensive Tests of Basic Skills (CTBS)**

LEVELS AND SCORES AVAILABLE: Grades 2.5–12
Subtests: reading, arithmetic, language and study skills

COPYRIGHT YEARS: 1968–1970

NUMBER OF FORMS: Two

COST OF BOOKLETS: $10.40 or $12, depending on level, for 35 tests

TESTING TIME: 238–257 minutes in four sessions

PUBLISHER: McGraw-Hill/California Test Bureau

CRITICAL COMMENTS:[2] The most glaring weakness of CTBS is the lack of validity data. No empirical relationships with external measures (e.g., grades, teacher's ratings, other achievement tests) are reported. More reliability data are needed; preliminary data suggest satisfactory consistency, though perhaps little differentiation among subtests.

The battery covers the important skills, particularly at the elementary-school level. There is some question about the relative ease of subtests for the upper grade within each level. The battery is easy to administer and causes few problems for the examinee.

The strongest point of the battery is the emphasis it places on using tests to plan, evaluate, and improve instruction and help individual students learn, rather than just ranking students.

The CTBS is one of the better recent batteries to appear on the commercial market. To acquaint the reader with the content of the test, the following sample items are reprinted from Form Q–Level 3 (Grades 6, 7, and 8).[3]

Reading—Vocabulary

DIRECTIONS:
For each item on the next two pages, choose the word in dark print that has the *best* meaning for the underlined word. Mark on your answer sheet the space that goes with the letter of the meaning you choose.

SAMPLE ITEMS:
Read the first Sample Item below and see how the right answer is marked on your answer sheet.

---

[2] Based on reviews by J. Stanley Ahmann, Frederick G. Brown, Peter A. Taylor, and Verna White, *Ibid*.
[3] From Comprehensive Tests of Basic Skills, Form Q, 3. Reproduced by permission of the publisher, CTB/McGraw-Hill, Del Monte Research Park, Monterey, CA 93940. Copyright © 1968 by McGraw-Hill, Inc. All rights reserved. Printed in the U.S.A.

allow him

  A give

  B let

  C follow

  D leave

Now do the next Sample Item and mark the answer on your answer sheet.

start the game

  F win

  G forget

  H begin

  J stop

Reading—Comprehension

DIRECTIONS:

Read each selection and do the items following it. Be sure you choose only the _best_ answer for each item. Mark on your answer sheet the space that goes with the letter of the answer you choose.

SAMPLE ITEMS:

Read the first Sample Item below and see how the right answer is marked on your answer sheet.

Following directions means the same as

  A following instructions

  B doing it your own way

  C listening to the teacher

  D asking questions

Now do the next Sample Item and mark the answer sheet.

Be sure you mark

  F a good answer

  G many answers

  H all the answers

  J the best answer

Language—Mechanics and Language-Expression

DIRECTIONS:

Some phrases in the letter and story on the next two pages are underlined and numbered. The underlined phrases might contain a mistake in punctuation. For each underlined phrase, three other possible ways of punctuating it are listed at the bottom of the page. Choose the answer that uses the best punctuation and mark the space that goes with its letter on your answer sheet. If the punctuation in the underlined phrase is best as it is, mark the space that goes with the letter for "Best as it is."

SAMPLE ITEMS:

Read the first Sample Item below and see how the correct answer is marked on your answer sheet.

He likes ^I<u>cake—ice</u> cream, and candy.

   I A cake. Ice

     B cake, ice

     C cake ice

     D Best as it is

Now do the next Sample Item and mark the answer on your answer sheet.

Do you like to play ^{II}<u>ball;</u>

   II A ball

      B ball.

      C ball?

      D Best as it is

In the stories on this page and the next page, each sentence is divided into four underlined parts. If there is a mistake in capitalization in one of these parts, mark the space on your answer sheet that goes with the letter of that part. If there is *no* mistake in capitalization, mark the space on your answer sheet that goes with "None."

In the Sample Item below, the name "carol" should begin with a capital letter, so the correct answer is D.

   A My three

   B friends are

C named Ann,

D carol, and Sue.

E None

In the next two stories, each numbered blank shows that one or more words are missing. Find the number of the item below that matches in the blank. Choose the word or words in the item that fit correctly in the blank. Then mark on your answer sheet the space that goes with the letter of the answer you choose. Read this Sample Item.

We $\underset{\text{—}}{\overset{\text{III}}{}}$ now going to the circus.

   III A is

        B am

        C are

        D was

C is the correct answer because "are" fits correctly in the sentence.

Language—Spelling

DIRECTIONS:
In each item on the next page, there are four spelling words and the word "None." In some items, one word is not correctly spelled. In others, all of the words are correctly spelled. If there is a word that is misspelled, mark on your answer sheet the space for the letter that is in front of that word. If all the words are correctly spelled, mark on your answer sheet the letter that is in front of the word "None."

SAMPLE ITEMS:
Read the first Sample Item below and see how the correct answer is marked on your sheet.

    A horse

    B slow

    C pound

    D speling

    E None

Now do the next Sample Item and mark the answer on your answer sheet.

F heavy

G kwick

H cloud

J maybe

K None

Arithmetic—Computation

DIRECTIONS:

On the next four pages, the word above each column will tell you to add, subtract, multiply, or divide. Use scratch paper to do your work. Mark on your answer sheet the space that goes with the letter of the answer you think is correct.

SAMPLE ITEMS:

Do the Sample Item in the first column below and see how the correct answer is marked on your answer sheet.

Now do the Sample Item in the next column and mark the answer on your answer sheet.

Addition		*Subtraction*	
	A 4		A 1
8	B 6	3	B 6
+4	C 8	−2	C 23
	D 12		D 32

Arithmetic—Concepts and Arithmetic—Applications

DIRECTIONS:

Read each item in the next two tests and choose the answer you think is correct. Mark on your answer sheet the space that goes with the letter of the answer you think is correct. Use scratch paper to do your work.

SAMPLE ITEMS:

Do the first Sample Item below and see how the correct answer is marked on your answer sheet.

What should be next in this series:
8, 10, 12, ____?

A 11
B 13
C 14
D 16

Now do the next Sample Item and mark the answer on your answer sheet.

Which fraction means the *same* as one-half?
F 1/8   G 1/4   H 1/3   J 1/2

Study Skills—Using Reference Materials and Study Skills —Using Graphic Materials

DIRECTIONS:

On the next page there are three library catalog cards that give you many kinds of information about books. Use the cards at the top of the page to do the items about library cards. Mark on your answer sheet the space that goes with the letter of the answer you think is right.

SAMPLE ITEMS:

Read the first Sample Item below and see how the right answer is marked on your answer sheet.

J	Baker, Nina
92	Henry Hudson; illus. by
H 885b	George Fulton. Alfred A. Knopf, Inc., c1958 140 p., illus.

What information about the book is on the first line?

A the name of the book

B the date the book was published

C the name of the writer

D the number of pages in the book

Now do the next Sample Item and mark the answer on your answer sheet.

Who published the book?

F Nina Baker

G Alfred Knopf

H Henry Hudson

J George Fulton

TITLE: **Iowa Tests of Basic Skills (ITBS)**

AUTHORS: E. F. Lindquist, A. N. Hieronymus, and others

LEVELS AND SCORES AVAILABLE: Grades 3–9

Five Scores: vocabulary, reading comprehension, language skills, work-study skills, and mathematics skills

COPYRIGHT YEAR: 1971

NUMBER OF FORMS: Two

COST OF BOOKLETS: $1.20 per complete booklet

TESTING TIME: 60–80 minutes per subtest (V & R combined)

PUBLISHER: Houghton Mifflin

TITLE: **Iowa Tests of Educational Development (ITED)**

AUTHORS: E. F. Lindquist and Leonard S. Feldt

LEVELS AND SCORES AVAILABLE: Grade 9–12

Ten scores: understanding of basic social concepts, general background in natural sciences, correctness and appropriateness of expression, ability to do quantitative thinking, ability to interpret reading materials in social studies, ability to interpret reading materials in natural sciences, ability to interpret literary materials, general vocabulary, subtotal, and use of sources of information

COPYRIGHT YEARS: 1942–1963

NUMBER OF FORMS: Two

COST OF BOOKLETS: $2.40 for 20 tests

TESTING TIME: 60–75 minutes per subtest in full-length version

PUBLISHER: Science Research Associates

CRITICAL COMMENTS:[4] The ITED is one of the most widely used and excellent measures of achievement ever designed. The manual presents high-quality normative data. Some experts have experienced concern about the meaning of battery profiles and intraindividual differences. The total battery takes considerable administration time. The ITED is one of the few tests that focuses on higher-order mental abilities, rather than facts and knowledge. There exists less than optimal documentation of validity claims.

TITLE: **Metropolitan Achievement Tests (MAT)**

LEVELS AND SCORES AVAILABLE: Grades K–13

Depending on level, scores are available in various combinations for reading, word analysis, language arts (spelling, language, study skills), social studies (study skills, vocabulary, information), mathematics (computation and concepts, analysis, and problem solving), and science (concepts and understanding, information)

COPYRIGHT YEARS: 1931–1971

NUMBER OF FORMS: Two

COST OF BOOKLETS: $9.50–$13.90 for 35 tests

TESTING TIME: 120–316 minutes in three–eight sessions

PUBLISHER: Harcourt Brace Jovanovich

CRITICAL COMMENTS:[5] The Metropolitan Achievement Tests' greatest utility seems to be for guidance or as a general survey of com-

---

[4] Based on reviews by Ellis B. Page and Alexander G. Wesman, *Seventh mental measurements yearbook* (Highland Park, N.J.: Gryphon Press, 1972).
[5] Based on reviews by Elizabeth Hagen and Frank B. Womer, *Ibid.*

petencies at the beginning of the secondary-school program. It has an above-average manual for interpretation. The item types used to measure proficiency in spelling and language are limited, and poor learners are measured inadequately. On the strength of the data presented, it is reasonable to suppose that most of the tests are adequately reliable. Some appear questionable, particularly the social studies skills subtest in the Intermediate Battery and certain of the language subtests in the Advanced Battery. The content of the high-school battery has not changed in 10 or 15 years, and there seems to be little reason for a secondary school to consider using it. The test shows its age. The normative sample is adequately described. The authors give only very general information on the materials and methods used to develop specifications for the test. A specific shortcoming exists in the reliability data for the test of Mathematical Analysis and Problem Solving.

TITLE: **SRA Achievement Series**

AUTHORS: Louis P. Thorpe, D. Welty Lefever, and Robert A. Naslund

LEVELS AND SCORES AVAILABLE: hand- and machine-scored editions—two levels (grades 1–2, 2–4) multilevel editions—three levels (grades 4.5–6.5, 6.5–8.5, 8.5–9).

Depending on level, scores are available in various combinations for reading (vocabulary, verbal-pictorial association, language perception, comprehension), language arts (capitalization, punctuation, grammatical usage, spelling), arithmetic (concepts, reasoning, computation), social studies, science, and optional work study skills.

COPYRIGHT YEARS: 1954–1969

NUMBER OF FORMS: Two

COST OF BOOKLETS: $4.35–$8.85 for 25 tests

TESTING TIME: 320–365 minutes in four–seven sessions

PUBLISHER: Science Research Associates

CRITICAL COMMENTS:[6] Comparability of the two forms, both in content and difficulty, has been achieved to a greater than usual

_____

[6] Based on reviews by Miriam M. Bryan and Fred M. Smith, *Ibid*.

degree. The reading tests make no effort to measure speed of reading comprehension or flexibility in adjusting speed to suit different purposes; the reading selections are all of considerable length. Shorter selections would offer a wider variety of content without restricting the diversity of questions. In the arithmetic reasoning subtest the situational approach is used, causing some interlocking of questions: an erroneous answer to a question dealing with the selection of arithmetic process may result in an erroneous answer to a question requiring computation. The social studies test emphasizes recall of information at all levels. Teachers need to examine the battery to determine the extent of its content validity for their school.

TITLE: **Stanford Achievement Tests (SAT)**

AUTHORS: Truman L. Kelly, Richard Madden, Eric F. Gardner, Herbert C. Rudman, Jack C. Merwin, and Robert Callis

LEVELS AND SCORES AVAILABLE: K–12

See Table 14.2 for subtest scores available

COPYRIGHT YEARS: 1923–1970

NUMBER OF FORMS: Four (two for high school)

COST OF BOOKLETS: $8.00–$16.50 for 35 tests

TESTING TIME: 90–350 minutes in five to seven sessions

PUBLISHER: Harcourt Brace Jovanovich

CRITICAL COMMENTS:[7] The format of the individual tests in the SAT battery is excellent. The user is not given any direct empirical evidence of the stability of the individual tests on the entire battery; empirical validity data are completely lacking. No interbattery correlation matrix is given. There is a lack of reliability data on the entire battery. No test-retest studies or reliability figures for comparable forms are reported.

The tests in the *High School Basic Battery* do not appear adequate for (a) use in curriculum evaluation (except as item norms are

---

[7] Based on reviews by Peter F. Merenda, Robert L. Wright, Georgia S. Adams; and Gerald C. Helmstadter, Elizabeth Hagen, and William A. Mehrens, *Ibid*.

used), (b) measurement of intraindividual differences, or (c) study of individual student gains from year to year. The tests have a high ceiling and may prove most useful to high schools many of whose students are aiming for college. Additional data on reliability should be provided. More information on the process of content selection, as well as correlations with other widely used achievement batteries, should be provided.

The *Stanford Early School Achievement Test's* norm data are minimal but sufficient. Reliability data are average. The test's biggest weakness is that teachers will not understand how to interpret and use the data. It can be used to assess kindergarten programs whose objectives and content are similar to those appraised by the test. The authors state that SESAT is not a "readiness test"; however, if a first-grade program is based on the assumption that students have mastered the skills appraised by SESAT, the results might be useful in determining whether children should be placed in the first-grade program.

TITLE: **Tests of Academic Progress (TAP)**

AUTHORS: Dale P. Scanell, Oscar M. Haugh, Alvin H. Schild, William B. Reiner, Henry P. Smith, and Gilbert Ulmer

LEVELS AND SCORES AVAILABLE: Four—grades 9, 10, 11, 12

Seven scores: social studies, composition, science, reading, mathematics, literature, total

COPYRIGHT YEARS: 1964–1966

NUMBER OF FORMS: Two

COST OF BOOKLETS: $1.14 per booklet

TESTING TIME: 370 minutes in three sessions

PUBLISHER: Houghton Mifflin

CRITICAL COMMENTS:[8] Examination of items using Bloom's *Taxonomy* indicates that all subtests except social studies measure higher-order abilities, i.e., interpretation, comprehension, evaluation, and application of principles. The social studies subtest

---

[8] Based on a review by C. M. Lindvall, *Ibid*.

probably includes too many items measuring only knowledge. Within each content area, the authors have attempted to base items largely on abilities developed in relatively basic courses. Users of TAP must interpret the results of the tests in light of the courses taken by the students tested. Interpretation of results on these high school tests to parents and students is not the same as for elementary-school test batteries for which all pupils have had relatively equivalent course preparation. The tests lend themselves better to diagnosis, i.e., of the extent to which pupil performance is in keeping with amount of course work. The manuals for the test provide little information on validity. The user must assume responsibility for determining the validity of TAP in terms of the projected use of results and the specific abilities he wishes to measure. The manual does provide an extensive breakdown of the content covered by the items. Reliability data are available only for Form 1. Standardization procedures are equivalent to those of other major test publishers. If these tests are used with care and judgment, they can be quite valuable in counseling and in assessing an academic program.

TITLE: **Wide Range Achievement Test (WRAT),** revised edition

AUTHORS: J. F. Jastak, S. R. Jastak, and S. W. Bijou

LEVELS AND SCORES AVAILABLE: Two, ages 5.0 to 11.11, 12.0 and over

Three scores: spelling, arithmetic, reading

COPYRIGHT YEARS: 1940–1965

NUMBER OF FORMS: One

COST OF BOOKLETS: $3.75 for 50 tests

TESTING TIME: 20–30 minutes

PUBLISHER: Guidance Associates

CRITICAL COMMENTS:[9] This test poses a persistent problem of differentiation between "intelligence" and "achievement." The author reports a "general" factor from a "clinical factor analysis"

---

[9] Based on reviews by Jack C. Merwin and Robert L. Thorndike, *Ibid*.

which accounts for 28 percent of the variance of each of the three scores, and five group factors which the authors say "may be conceived of as true personality variables" (e.g., Group Personality Factor I, labeled "Verbal" and said to be unrelated to intelligence, is reported to carry 30 percent of the variance of the reading score and 24 percent of the variance of the spelling score). Reviewers seriously question the labeling of this test as an "achievement" test. A user can make comparisons with the norms provided, but their meaning is questionable because the identity and nature of the groups serving as bases for score interpretation are far from clear. All parts of the test are timed, and the word-pronunciation test is discontinued after a specified number of failures. This procedure tends to inflate split-half reliabilities, and causes one to discount startling values reported. The validity of the test is seriously questioned. The author states that "it is acceptable practice to use criteria of internal consistency . . ." and that "validity can be determined only by the comparison of one test score with those which measure entirely different abilities." It is hard to reconcile these statements with each other or with the usual concepts of test validation. This test may have some value in a clinical or research setting in which individuals of such diverse ability or background are tested that one cannot predict the appropriate level of test in advance, and needs to make a quick estimate of each person's general level of ability and educational background. One would hesitate to recommend it for other purposes.

Specific Subject Tests

Individual tests on special topics do not differ significantly from the kinds of subtests found in most survey batteries. They do differ in depth of coverage. The specific test contains more items and covers more aspects of a topic than does a subtest from a battery purporting to measure the same material. There are, in addition, many specialized tests on topics not commonly covered by batteries, e. g., economics, trigonometry, physics, chemistry.

The primary reason for using individual tests, as opposed to battery subtests, is that they provide detailed accounting. Specific tests are generally administered after an unusual student performance is noted on one or more subtests of a survey battery.

Illustrative of the kind of specific subject-matter tests available is the *Nelson Biology Test* (Nelson 1965), which measures the extent to which important educational objectives have been attained by students in typical high-school biology courses. Normative data are available on more than 3500 students, for both of the two forms. In addition, the publisher has responded to the recent movement for curriculum reform in science by providing separate norms for students using Biological Science Curriculum Study materials. One outstanding characteristic of this test is that it attempts to measure learning outcomes according to the scheme suggested by the *Taxonomy of Educational Objectives*. Table 14.3 is a summary table of specifications for this test; this is precisely the type of information an instructor needs if he is to evaluate the test intelligently for possible use with his students. Such a table facilitates study of the degree of correspondence between the test and the local curriculum. Obviously, the teacher also will need to examine specific items.

It is generally recommended that specific subject tests such as the *Nelson* be used to supplement teacher-made tests, which are undoubtedly more responsive to specific objectives of instruction. The opportunity to evaluate overall local student performance against a national sampling of students has, nevertheless, much to recommend it.

Illustrative Subject Area Tests

Brief descriptions of six more specific subject tests follow. Again, only general characteristics of the tests are described. The critical comments are excerpted from reviews in Buros' *Seventh Mental Measurements Yearbook* (Buros 1972).

TITLE: **Anderson-Fisk Chemistry Test**

AUTHORS: Kenneth E. Anderson and Franklin G. Fisk

LEVELS AND SCORES AVAILABLE: Grades 10–13

    Total score only

COPYRIGHT YEARS: 1950–1966

NUMBER OF FORMS: Two

COST OF BOOKLETS: $8.70 for 35 tests

TESTING TIME: 50 minutes

PUBLISHER: Harcourt Brace Jovanovich

TABLE 14.3 Classification of Items in the *Nelson Biology Test*

OBJECTIVES:	Knowledge				Understanding				Application				Total			
	Form E		Form F		Form E		Form F		Form E		Form F		Form E		Form F	
	# of Items	% of Form	# of Items	% of Form	# of Items	% of Form	# of Items	% of Form	# of Items	% of Form	# of Items	% of Form	# of Items	% of Form	# of Items	% of Form
CONTENT:																
Living Things																
Characteristic Cellular and Molecular Structure, Classification, and Grouping	6	9	6	9	7	10	8	12	5	8	4	6	18	27	18	27
Life Processes																
Human Health and Functions	5	8	4	6	5	8	4	6	1	2	2	3	11	18	10	15
Plant and Animal Life	1	2	3	5	6	9	3	5	2	3	1	2	9	14	7	12
Life Cycles, Reproduction, Heredity, Biological History	2	3	4	6	4	6	5	8	8	12	8	12	14	21	17	26
Ecological Relationships																
World Biome, Natural Resources, and Conservation	2	3	1	2	4	6	5	8	1	2	1	2	7	11	7	11
Methodology and Research																
Experimental Reasoning Procedures, Terminology					1	2			5	8	6	9	6	9	6	9
Total	16	25	18	28	27	41	25	39	22	35	22	35	65	100	65	100

Note: Percents subject to rounding error.

CRITICAL COMMENTS:[10] The content of this test, intended for a variety of chemistry programs, represents a good compromise. According to Bloom's *Taxonomy,* 45 percent of the items are in the "application" category; the remaining items are evenly divided between the two lower levels. The content is drawn almost exclusively from the body of chemical knowledge, paying virtually no attention to the scientific processes by which this body of knowledge was acquired. With the exception of a lack of information on special aspects of the test, the reliability information is satisfactory and the procedures are adequately described. There is no explanation of the selection of schools or the extent of selective participation by school districts, factors that greatly attenuate the meaningfulness of the reference-group data. The norms are somewhat misleading, however, in that they are based on a hypothetical population with a mean Otis I.Q. of 105, artificially low for high-school chemistry students.

TITLE: **Crary American History Test,** revised edition

AUTHOR: Ryland W. Crary

LEVELS AND SCORES AVAILABLE: Grades 10–13

Total score only

COPYRIGHT YEARS: 1950–1965

NUMBER OF FORMS: Two

COST OF BOOKLETS: $8.70 for 35 tests

TESTING TIME: 50 minutes

PUBLISHER: Harcourt Brace Jovanovich

CRITICAL COMMENTS:[11] The test covers American history from the colonial period to the recent past. Items focusing on different periods are juxtaposed. The test is useful only at the end of a course, unless used as a pretest. It is of little use in identifying strengths or weaknesses. The survey nature of the test makes it inappropriate for measuring achievement in courses that focus

---

[10] Based on reviews by William R. Crawford and Ronald D. Anderson, *Ibid.*
[11] Based on a review by Richard E. Gross, *Ibid.*

on a particular era. Too many of the questions emphasize simple recognition or recall. As a result, this test fails to address the emerging purposes of the new social studies, such as process and inquiry competencies, assessment of key concepts, and the ability to generalize that results from a grasp of the structure of the discipline. Another weakness is the failure to include items acknowledging the social conflict and urban unrest of the 1960s. A new edition should reflect changing concerns.

TITLE: **Cummings World History Test,** revised edition

AUTHOR: Howard H. Cummings

LEVELS AND SCORES AVAILABLE: Grades 9–13

Total score only

COPYRIGHT YEARS: 1950–1966

NUMBER OF FORMS: Two

COST OF BOOKLETS: $8.70 for 35 tests

TESTING TIME: 50 minutes

PUBLISHER: Harcourt Brace Jovanovich

CRITICAL COMMENTS:[12] This multiple-choice test offers DK (don't know) as a guessing distractor. In experimental tryout, students used this choice increasingly as items increased in difficulty; in actual testing, however, students tend to guess rather than use distractors. No provision is made for guessing; if guessing penalties were provided for, the distractor would serve a more useful function. The present form of the test allows an astute student to increase his score by ignoring the DK option. The test has two major failings in the realm of content: (1) it fails to provide the student with any opportunity to exercise such skills as application, analysis, synthesis, and evaluation—all legitimate objectives of social studies—and (2) it fails to measure important affective objectives of world history instruction. Item tryout and standardization were carried out simultaneously. It would have been pref-

---

[12] Based on reviews by John Manning and William J. Webster, *Ibid.*

erable to undertake the two processes separately, using a new sample for standardization. Unfortunately, the conclusive evidence for equivalence—the correlation between the two forms —is not available. Close scrutiny is recommended to insure that the facts tested are those considered important in the user's world history program.

TITLE: **Missouri College English Test (MCET)**

AUTHORS: Robert Callis and Willoughby Johnson

LEVELS AND SCORES AVAILABLE: Two, grades 12–13

Three parts: Part 1 requires the examinee to determine whether each of 60 underlined sentences in a group of themes contains an error in the mechanics of expression, i.e., capitalization, grammar, punctuation, or spelling; Part 2 asks the student to decide which of four sentences best expresses an idea; Part 3 asks the examinee to indicate the order in which a series of sentences should be arranged.

COPYRIGHT YEARS: 1964–1965

NUMBER OF FORMS: Two

COST OF BOOKLETS: $7 for 35 tests

TESTING TIME: 50 minutes

PUBLISHER: Harcourt Brace Jovanovich

CRITICAL COMMENTS:[13] In Part 1, most of the errors tested are of an elementary sort that continually plague teachers of composition. The student is expected to recognize a standard of formal correctness that may be somewhat unrealistic. Some items involve proofreading, which depends too much on visual acuity. In Part 2, the distractors are awkward, and include ungainly sentences that a good editor would never approve. In Part 3, one is unsure what is being tested and doubts that it has much to do with the ability to organize one's own sentences. The authors make the

---

[13] Based on reviews by John B. Carroll and Clarence Derrick, *Ibid*.

common mistake of reporting split-half reliability coefficients without pointing out that they may be inflated because of seededness (the authors claim that this is a power test, i.e., the 90-item test can be completed in 40 minutes by a vast majority of college freshmen). The test's diagnostic usefulness is limited by (1) a relatively small number of items pertaining to each category of error, and (2) the major effort required to obtain diagnostic information from the answer sheets. Those who want a test that puts less emphasis on mechanics and more on stylistic matters and diction should look elsewhere.

TITLE: **Pimsleur Spanish Proficiency Tests**

AUTHOR: Paul Pimsleur

LEVELS AND SCORES AVAILABLE: First- and second-level courses in grades 7–12, or first and second semesters in college

Four scores: listening, speaking, reading, writing

COPYRIGHT YEAR: 1967

NUMBER OF FORMS: Two

COST OF BOOKLETS: Each subtest costs $7.50 per test tape, $7.40–7.50 for 35 tests

TESTING TIME: 25–45 minutes for each subtest

PUBLISHER: Harcourt Brace Jovanovich

CRITICAL COMMENTS:[14] The test's chief shortcoming is the overlap of abilities measured by the separate tests. This situation arises because the framework dictates that the four skills be tested independently, creating a problem of validity for all the tests and of reliability for the speaking and writing subtests. In Part 1, Listening Comprehension, it is possible for the student to read ahead before he listens. A greater problem is that Part 1 emphasizes visual perception so heavily that the student who has been taught by an intensive audiolingual approach is at a distinct

---

[14] Based on reviews by Gino Parisi and E. E. Bilyeu, *Ibid.*

disadvantage. Throughout the tests there is an overemphasis on knowledge of vocabulary, even where comprehension is being measured. The problem is particularly evident in the Listening and Reading Comprehension tests. Particularly excellent are the Writing Proficiency tests and the Fluency portions of the Speaking tests.

TITLE: **Test of Economic Understanding (TEU)**

LEVELS AND SCORES AVAILABLE: high school and college

Total score only

COPYRIGHT YEARS: 1963–1964

NUMBER OF FORMS: Two

COST OF BOOKLETS: $5.95 for 25 tests

TESTING TIME: 50 minutes

PUBLISHER: Science Research Associates

CRITICAL COMMENTS:[15] Overall, the TEU falls short of meeting its stated primary purpose of providing standards for the evaluation of instruction. It lacks the requisite scope and depth to be sensitive enough for that purpose. The test appears to sample the student's comprehension rather than his ability to apply and analyze economic concepts and principles. The data on reliability and validity indicate that the test can be used with reasonable confidence in individual evaluation. However, content validity must ultimately be judged by the teacher in relation to his own objectives. Testwiseness is likely to influence scores, but only slightly. The development of the test shows careful regard for modern criteria of excellence in development and standardization. An uncommon feature of the manual is a lengthy section intended to guide discussion of items in each form of the test. This can create a problem over time: teachers may begin to teach the answers too specifically, and students may learn answers without understanding them.

---

[15] Based on reviews by Edward J. Furst and Christine H. McGuire, *Ibid*.

Diagnostic Tests

Diagnostic tests are usually administered after a period of instruction, sometimes to a group but usually individually, to identify learning weaknesses in a detailed and analytical way, with a view to remediation. The use of an achievement battery to identify students who demonstrate inadequate learning is generally recommended. A standardized diagnostic test can then be used to (1) identify for the student and instructor the types of errors being made, (2) make the instructor aware of the important elements, difficulties, and subject and skill sequences in the learning process, and (3) suggest remedial procedures. A substantial amount of diagnostic testing to obtain even more detailed information about pupil difficulties makes use of informal teacher-made devices and direct observation of behavior.

In addition to exhibiting the usual characteristics required of a test (e.g., reliability, validity, and objectivity), diagnostic tests should: (1) be tied to specific curricular objectives and expected learning outcomes; (2) include items that directly measure and analyze specific functions or emphasize selected mechanical aspects of learning; (3) suggest specific remedial procedures for the errors indicated by responses to specific items; and (4) cover reasonably broad integrated learning sequences. Hayward (1968) has suggested three critical questions that need to be asked when selecting a diagnostic reading test, and that are generalizable to any diagnostic test:

1. Does the test measure the necessary component skills, and do the subscores represent meaningful areas for providing remedial instruction?
2. Are the subscore reliabilities sufficiently high (above .90) for individual application?
3. Are the intercorrelations among the subscores sufficiently low (below .65) to warrant differential diagnosis?

Unfortunately, most of the diagnostic tests available do not meet even minimal criteria. There is a lack of efficient high-quality instruments that may be used diagnostically in program planning. Many achievement batteries attempt to serve as both survey instruments and diagnostic tests. The general procedure is to provide between five and ten subject scores and an item-by-item breakdown of the individual subject scores. Such a breakdown is too general and based on too few items to be considered a reliable procedure; although of some value when used as an initial screening, such an analysis should not form the basis for instruction. It might be fairer to say that diagnostic tests differ from survey and specific subject-matter tests in the degree of refinement with which they measure achievement, than to say that they measure different kinds of achievement.

Diagnostic tests usually cover either arithmetic skills or reading. A brief description of two representative diagnostic tests should illustrate the general approach to developing diagnostic tests and the kinds of information they yield.

The **Stanford Diagnostic Arithmetic Test (SDAT)** (Beatty, Madden and Gardner 1966) is one of the best, if not the best, available diagnostic arithmetic tests. Two forms (W and X) are available at two levels (Grade 2–middle of Grade 4, and latter part of Grade 4–middle of Grade 8). The subtests at Level One of the SDAT are as follows:

Concepts of Numbers and Numerals
A. Number Systems, Counting
B. Operations
C. Decimal Place Value

Computation
A. Addition
B. Subtraction
C. Multiplication
D. Division

Number Facts
A. Addition
B. Subtraction
C. Multiplication
D. Division

The entire test is designed to diagnose specific weaknesses in working with numbers. The 192 items of Level One in the SDAT, which require about 205 minutes of testing time and six sittings, must be hand-scored with a strip-key. SDAT scores can be converted to grade scores or stanines (based on a standardization population of approximately 8000 cases) if desired. The primary application of the test must, however, be on an individual, class, or local school level. The manual contains general guidelines for use of the results to make individual and class analyses.

The **Diagnostic Reading Scales** (Spache 1968), developed by George D. Spache, are a series of articulated and integrated tests providing standardized evaluations of oral and silent reading skills and auditory comprehension. Specifically, measures of the following variables may be obtained:

1. Word recognition.
2. Word analysis.
3. Oral reading.

4. Silent reading.
5. Auditory comprehension.

and the following specific phonic skills:

6. Consonant sounds.
7. Vowel sounds.
8. Consonant blends.
9. Common syllables.
10. Blends.
11. Letter sounds.

The test, then, yields rather a detailed analysis of reading proficiency. The author and publisher suggest that the scales can be used effectively with normal and retarded readers at the junior and senior high-school levels.

Although the reliability data provided in the manual are a little less extensive than might be desired, the validity data are quite impressive, at least by comparison to other available diagnostic reading tests. Validity data should reflect the effect of remediation on scores, include correlations with other tests, and, most importantly, describe the sampling from relevant domains in terms of content validity relative to the reading process.

LOCATING INFORMATION ABOUT TESTS

It would be impossible to list, let alone critically evaluate, all those tests that might be of interest to a particular instructor or administrator. A potential user needs information bearing on such questions as (1) What types of tests are available that will yield the kinds of information I am interested in? (2) What do the "experts" say about the tests I am interested in? (3) What research has been undertaken on this test? (4) What statistical data relating to validity and reliability are available for examination? and (5) With what groups may I legitimately use this test? Thorndike and Hagen (1961, p. 208) suggest that the answers to these and many other relevant questions may be found in one or more of the following resources:

1. Buros' *Mental Measurements Yearbooks.*
2. Test reviews in professional journals.
3. Test manuals and specimen sets.
4. Text and reference books on testing.
5. Bibliographies of tests and the testing literature.
6. Educational and psychological abstract indexes.
7. Publishers' test catalogues.

Three additional sources should be mentioned:

8. *Tests in Print: A Comprehensive Bibliography of Tests for Use in Education, Psychology and Industry.* Published by the editor of the *Mental Measurements Yearbooks,* this volume contains listings of 2126 tests in print in 1961. A new edition was published in 1973 (Highland Park, N.J.: The Gryphon Press).

9. *Test Collection Bulletin.* This quarterly digest describes the holdings and recent acquisitions of the Test Collection at Educational Testing Service, Princeton, New Jersey.

10. *CSE Elementary,* and *CSE—ECRC Preschool Kindergarten Test Evaluations.* Published by the UCLA Center for the Study of Evaluation, these publications rate major tests at these two levels on such factors as validity, appropriateness, usability, and technical excellence.

Of the ten resources listed above, the first three are probably the most immediately informative. These three sources will be discussed in turn, highlighting the types of information that each will provide.

The Mental Measurements Yearbooks

Probably the most useful sources of information about tests are the *Mental Measurements Yearbooks,* edited by Oscar K. Buros. Up-to-date and comprehensive bibliographies, test reviews, and book reviews are published in the *Yearbooks,* seven of which have been published to date. Buros' goal was to develop in the potential user and publisher a critical attitude toward tests and testing, facilitate communication, and in general bring about a significant increase in the quality of published tests. Specifically, Buros wanted the *Yearbooks* "(a) to provide information about tests published as separates throughout the English-speaking world; (b) to present frankly critical test reviews written by testing and subject specialists representing various viewpoints; (c) to provide extensive bibliographies of verified references on the construction, use, and validity of specific tests; (d) to make readily available the critical portions of test reviews appearing in professional journals; and (e) to present fairly exhaustive listings of new and revised books on testing, along with evaluative excerpts from representative reviews which these books receive in professional journals." The *Yearbooks* have made a significant and lasting contribution toward these ends.

Some sense of the extensiveness of the *Yearbooks* can be gained from a brief look at the contents of the two-volume, almost two-thousand page *Seventh Yearbook* (Buros 1972). The Tests and Reviews section includes extensive listings for 1,157 tests, 798 test reviews by 439 reviewers, 181 excerpted test reviews from 39 journals, and 12,372 references for specific tests. A breakdown of the tests by type follows:

Tests by Major Classification in *Seventh*
Mental Measurements Yearbook

Classification	Number	Percentage
Vocations	181	15.6
Personality	147	12.7
Miscellaneous	129	11.1
Intelligence	121	10.5
Reading	102	8.8
Mathematics	96	8.3
Science	80	6.9
Foreign Languages	75	6.5
English	55	4.8
Social Studies	53	4.6
Speech and Hearing	38	3.3
Achievement Batteries	36	3.1
Sensory-Motor	20	1.7
Fine Arts	14	1.2
Multi-Aptitude	10	0.9
Total	1,157	100.0

Buros has also published summaries of the reviews of published reading tests (1969) and personality tests (1970).

Test Reviews in Journals

Despite the fact that such authoritative comprehensive sources as the *Yearbooks* are available, it is often difficult to locate recent data on either new or old tests. Test reviews are periodically carried by the following journals: the *Journal of Counseling Psychology*, the *Personnel and Guidance Journal*, *Contemporary Psychology*, *Perceptual and Motor Skills*, *Professional Psychology*, the *Journal of Special Education*, *Measurement and Evaluation in Guidance*, and the *Journal of Educational Measurement*. This last journal carries approximately a third of the test reviews published yearly. In addition, Summer and Winter issues of *Educational and Psychological Measurement* contain "Validity Studies" sections where relevant research data are reported.

An Illustrative Test Review

The **Content Evaluation Series** is a set of achievement measures aimed at assessing end-of-year progress in Grades 7, 8, and 9. Copyrighted in 1968 by Houghton Mifflin, the Series contains six tests:

Language Ability, Composition, Literature, Mathematics, Earth Science (Grades 8 and 9 only), and Physical Science (Grades 8 and 9 only). The tests can be machine- or hand-scored and require approximately 40 minutes of administration time per test. The Combined Language Arts Tests cost $15.00 for 35 booklets, the Mathematics Test $7.20 for 35 booklets, and the Science Tests $11.00 for 35 booklets. Following is a review, by Margaret Fleming of the Cleveland Public Schools, of the Content Evaluation Series:[16]

Innovative content and item format distinguish the Language Ability and Composition Tests, the most promising of the six tests in the new Content Evaluation Series. Using a "situation and what to do" motif, both instruments sample creatively some Language Arts areas new to standardized tests. These and their companion tests have been intentionally designed for an educational level bridging the traditional top limit of grade 8 for elementary grades and the lower limit for secondary grades, grade 9. It would appear that the series has accomplished its purpose in this regard.

The Language Ability Test focuses on understanding of the structure of basic English and use of standard sentence patterns as indicators of language maturity. Criteria for judging maturity levels have been drawn from traits of superior student and adult writers identified in the research of Loban and Hunt. The Composition Test departs from content found in traditional writing skills instruments—usually identification of conventions drawn from various grammar systems. Rather, it samples production of effective composition according to key rhetorical principles—invention, organization, and style.

Although the format of these tests demands careful reading of directions and questions, reading difficulty appears to be in an appropriate range for this educational level. An average grade level of fifth and sixth grade was obtained after applying the Dale and Chall formula to the reviewer's random sample of four 100-word passages for these tests.

While the third Language Arts instrument of the series, the Literature Test, adheres to a more conventional question-answer format, its content is directed toward interpretation of literary elements and identification of literary devices. This emphasis on appreciation of literary elements rather than of comprehension components, the hallmarks of typical literature tests, is a good direction for standardized tests at this educational level.

---

[16] Reprinted from the Fall 1970 issue of the *Journal of Educational Measurement*, Volume 7, No. 3. Copyright © 1970 by the National Council on Measurement in Education, East Lansing, Michigan. Reprinted by permission of the author and publisher.

The three additional tests, Mathematics, Earth Science, and Physical Science, are more traditional in item design. The Mathematics content, drawn from the contemporary approach in mathematics, emphasizes conceptual rather than computational elements. Pupils are required to sift out mathematical meanings embedded in language problems in the majority of items. The Science tests reflect current science curricula at this educational level by focusing on the separate areas of Physical Science and Earth Science rather than combining these subjects in an omnibus instrument. Both the Science and Mathematics Tests present a wider range of reading levels than the Language Arts Tests. An average level of fifth and sixth grade was found, however, in four random samples of materials in each test.

DIRECTIONS FOR ADMINISTRATION

Directions for the CES, printed with helpful color coding, are well-written and complete. The CES manuals are thorough in emphasizing the need for careful advance planning of test programs. Suggestions for dealing with realities in the school situation—handling of materials, preparation of answer sheets, and room arrangements—are sound.

It is encouraging, too, to find at least one short paragraph about the teacher's role for motivation of students for test-taking. It would have been an even greater convenience for users if the more adequate discussion found in the Technical Manual, "Preparation for CES Test Administration," had been included in the Teachers' Manuals.

RELIABILITY

Reliability coefficients are reported from a sample of 400 papers per grade. Obtained by the split-half method and corrected by the Spearman-Brown formula for the length of the test, coefficients ranged from .74 to .95. Four coefficients dropped below .80. These were for Earth Science (Grade 8) with .74, Physical Science (both Grades 8 and 9) with .77, and Mathematics (Grade 7), .79.

Standard errors of measurement for both raw and standard scores are listed for all tests at all grade levels. Unfortunately, limited explanation is supplied in the Technical Manual and Teachers' Manuals about the use of this information. In view of general tendencies by educators to fixate on test scores without recognition of the nature of the "band of error" in score numbers, this limitation is regrettable.

VALIDITY

The usual references to content validity are noted in the Technical Manual. Though textbooks, courses of study, expert opinion, and standards employed throughout the country in curriculum content are cited as sources for test content, specific sources are not identified. This information would assist educators in judging the appropriateness of the tests for their school situations, particularly in view of the fact that these are end-of-year achievement tests.

Criterion-related validity, as one would anticipate in view of the recent development of the CES, is presented in terms of only one study, which uses expectancy tables of 178 to 187 cases to report the relationship of three Language Arts Tests with final marks in English. The suggestion that standardized test scores should be bases for final marks is a vulnerable educational practice today when criticisms about use of tests as sole criteria for educational advancement have been raised by the public. Hopefully, teachers would use test scores from survey achievement tests as one of many elements in determining final marks for pupils.

While no information about construct validity is furnished directly in the Technical Manual, intercorrelations are provided to demonstrate the extent to which the six achievement tests overlap. Correlations are generally higher for the Language Arts Tests (in the .70 range) than between these tests and Mathematics or Science. These data indicate relatively discrete areas are being measured by the instruments.

NORMS

Schools have become particularly sensitive to comparisons to be made as a result of test norms. Norms, therefore, are subject to closer scrutiny than ever before. The CES was standardized using 27 schools from 21 districts representing 17 states. Sample requirements were identical to those used in Project Talent, but were not always actualized. An overrepresentation of rural northeast communities (less than 5,000 population) and underrepresentation of urban southeast communities (5,000 to 249,999 population) as well as rural west communities (less than 5,000 population) occurred. As they stand, the norms appear to represent a one-out-of-three ratio of rural to urban population. With projections that three out of four persons now live in larger metropolitan areas, a wider use of metropolitan area schools appears appropriate for tests in the 1970's if norms are to reflect "national" characteristics.

No information is presented about the chronological age range or scholastic aptitude levels of pupils represented in the norms group. Nor does the manual supply information about the organizational patterns of the schools involved, the particular Science or other curricula followed in norms schools, the socio-economic indices of the school communities, or item difficulty data. It would have been helpful to know what percentage of pupils in each grade finished all items so that one might gauge the influence of time limit on the tests. These omissions are considered major weaknesses for valid interpretation of test scores obtained on the CES.

MATERIALS

Much of the material contained in the Technical Manual might have been combined with the Teacher's Manuals, thereby increasing utility of interpretative materials and reducing cost for this series. The manuals also lack the all-important answer key. Presently, MRC hand-scoring masks must be purchased separately.

Though MRC-style answer sheets with their notoriously small oval spaces are the only type presently available, test booklets generally present a readable, convenient format. One would recommend, however, reprint of page 7 of the Language Arts Booklet where the single column arrangement suddenly shifts into a double column format.

INTERPRETATIVE INFORMATION

Standard scores, in addition to stanines and percentiles, have been provided for the CES series. Omission of grade equivalent scores is a positive move toward more meaningful interpretation of pupil performance. The standard score system allows comparison of scores from different subject areas and grades, which is usually inappropriate with grade equivalent scores. Stanines also help to erase that "indelible" aura of specific grade scores by their reference to a band of performance. Explanation of the relationship of stanines and percentiles could have been improved by a graphic representation of the score model, the normal curve, as well as adjective designations for each stanine.

Diagnostic possibilities for CES results are emphasized in the manuals. Discussions generalize that results can indicate areas of strength and weakness as well as vocational directions in which a student may be especially gifted. In cases of survey achievement tests such as these, where there has been extensive rather than intensive sampling of skill areas, it is erroneous to suggest that item response records for individual pupils will be reliable enough for diagnostic use. There should have been more emphasis on the use of item response information to identify group or class weaknesses.

The most complete item classifications are found in the Language Arts Tests. This information might have been improved, however, if a grid arrangement had been used to pull content and skills together with the cluster of items representing each.

A composite chart combining subject matter with skills and abilities data is also needed to improve the interpretation of results of the Science Tests. The item classification for Mathematics uses a gross outline which does not identify the particular operation involved in the content sampled. More definitive arrangement of content will be necessary if teaching prescriptions are to be developed from the results of the Mathematics Test. The manuals should emphasize that item response records are likely to be obtained only through use of scoring services. Such information is typically a deluxe option in scoring services.

SUMMARY

The CES generally accomplishes its purpose in providing content appropriate for a "junior high" educational level. While two of the Language Arts Tests in the series represent innovative approaches to content and item design, omissions in norms and validity information and some incomplete item classifications limit the potential usefulness of CES at this point in time.

Test Manuals and Specimen Sets

After preliminary decisions have narrowed the field, it is a good idea to obtain specimen sets from publishers. Such a set usually contains a copy of the test questions, scoring key, answer sheets, examiner's manual, and occasionally a technical manual. The sets, available at a nominal cost, should be ordered on official school or institution letterhead stationery, because most publishers attempt to insure that their materials are distributed to qualified individuals only, in order to maintain security. If there is any question about the qualifications required for the purchase of a particular test, one should consult the publisher's catalogue.

The test manual is the most informative and readily accessible source of information about a specific test. Directions for administering and scoring the test; statistical information about validity, reliability, and norms; a description of the test's development; and suggestions for interpreting and using the test results constitute the usual content of the manual. The reviewer should remember, however, that the publisher has a vested interest, and all tests should be evaluated critically.

SELECTING AN ACHIEVEMENT TEST

After informally reviewing several tests in a particular area and making a preliminary decision about the purpose of testing and the projected uses of the test data, the instructor would profit from a detailed examination of two or three tests. A form and a set of evaluative questions that have been found useful in judging a test for possible use in schools are reprinted below. The first eight categories are essentially descriptive, but nevertheless important. For example, such factors as the affiliation of the author and the copyright date bear no such significant criteria as credibility, authenticity, and recency. The outline presented here is an adaptation and expansion of an outline originally developed by Cronbach (1960, pp. 147–153).

In undertaking a "critical analysis," one will consult many sources. The reader is referred to pages 336–343 for information on identifying references. In addition, it would be well worthwhile for the test evaluator to refer to *Standards for Educational and Psychological Tests and Manuals* (American Psychological Association 1966) for assistance in identifying minimally acceptable criteria for many of the variables described in this outline. It is usually a good idea to record the comments, evaluations, and sources consulted during the review process.

Outline for Critical Analysis of a Standardized Achievement Test

1. Title — Note complete and exact title of test.

2. Author — A brief summary of professional affiliations and credentials would be informative.

3. Publisher — Some publishers are more reputable than others. Check with experts in testing.

4. Copyright Date — Note dates of first publication and each revision.

5. Level or Group for whom Test Is Intended — Such factors as age, grade, and ability level need to be considered. What background does the author presuppose for examinees? Is the test available at different levels? If so, which ones?

6. Forms of the Test — What forms of the test are available? If the forms are not essentially the same, major differences should be mentioned and evaluated. What evidence is presented on equivalence of forms?

7. Purpose and Recommended Use — Summarize the use of the test recommended by the author.

8. Dimensions of Areas that the Test Purports to Measure — Give a brief definition or description of the variables involved. If the test has a great number of scales (or scores), as do the *California Achievement Tests,* it may be necessary simply to mention the subscores and highlight only the group or distinctive scores.

9. Adminis-
   tration
   Describe briefly. The median time required to complete the test should be indicated. If parts of the test are timed separately, note how many "starting points" are necessary. Are the directions easy for the test administrator to follow and the test-takers to comprehend? Is special training required for valid administration? Is the test largely self-administering? Are there objectionable features?

10. Scoring
    Scoring procedures should be described very briefly. Is the test planned and organized so that machine-scored answer sheets can or must be used? Is a correction for guessing justified and/or applied? (Refer to the discussion of guessing in Chapter Four.)

11. Source of
    Items
    Where did the author get the items? What criteria did he use in item selection? Are some items taken from other tests? If so, which ones?

12. Description
    of Items
    (Format
    and Con-
    tent)
    Briefly describe the major types of items used. Attention should be given to *item form* (e.g., multiple-choice, analogy, forced-choice) and *item content* (e.g., culture-free symbols, nonsense syllables, food preferences, occupational titles). How many response categories are there? Note a typical example of the major type(s) of item used. It is imperative that the actual items be evaluated in light of the questions a teacher would ask of the data.

13. Statistical
    Item
    Analysis
    Was an item analysis made to determine item discrimination and difficulty? What were the results? What criteria were used to select items for the final form(s) of the instrument? What analytic techniques were used?

14. Method
    and Results
    of Valida-
    tion Re-
    ported by
    Publisher
    and Author
    For most tests this topic is related to categories 11, 12, and 13. One must ask, "What was done to make the test valid and useful?" Some tests are validated by expert judgment, some by an external criterion, and so on. What has the author done to demonstrate the validity of the test? What correlations with other tests does he present? Has he used an external criterion to evaluate the usefulness of the scores? This section should deal with data other than those obtained in the construction of the test. What specific "predictions" could one make from an individual's test score on the basis of the validity data presented?

15. Validity as   This is in many respects *the* crucial evaluative crite-
    Determined rion. The recent literature should be consulted, and
    by Others   studies briefly summarized.

16. Reliability   State briefly how reliability was determined. Report
    interesting or unusual data on reliability. Was relia-
    bility computed separately for each subgroup or part
    of the test?

17. Norm   How many were involved? How were they selected?
    Group(s)   Are separate norms available for each group with
    whom one might wish to compare an individual's
    score, i.e., norms for each sex, age level, curriculum
    major, occupation?

18. Interpreta- How are scores expressed? (Percentile ranks, stan-
    tion of   dard scores, grade scores?) What is considered a
    Scores   "high" score? a "low" score? How are these scores
    interpreted? What significance do they have in view
    of the answers to category 10?

19. Major   What assumptions are examined and what questions
    Evaluations are raised in Buros' *Mental Measurements Yearbooks?*
    by   What do measurement textbooks say about the test?
    Experts

20. Cost Fac-   The initial cost of booklets and answer sheets should
    tors   be considered, as well as such factors as cost of scor-
    ing, reusability of booklets, and availability of sum-
    mary and research services.

21. Distin-   What are the outstanding features of this test, its con-
    guishing   struction, and its use? Note both desirable and unde-
    Charac-   sirable features.
    teristics

22. Overall   How well do such factors as validity, reliability, stan-
    Evaluation dardization, and item content coincide with the in-
    tended use of the test?

How should the information in these twenty-two categories be weighted? No universal answer can be given, since the selection of a particular test or battery will depend upon the individual needs of specific instructors or schools. The purpose of testing must be foremost in the mind of the test evaluator. Such questions as "What specific information is needed?" and "How will the test data be interpreted and used?" are highly significant. Questions relating to validity, reliability, and the representativeness of the normative data should be critically reviewed and heavily weighted in the final decisions if the test is to be used in a norm-referenced way. (See Chapter Thirteen.)

The critical evaluation of a standardized achievement test is a time-consuming and relatively involved process. But considering the kinds of decisions that will be made about students and programs as a result of such tests, the expenditure of effort is more than justified.

ESTABLISHING A SCHOOL–WIDE ASSESSMENT SYSTEM

If educators are truly concerned with the "total student." it is imperative that a comprehensive assessment system be established. The term *assessment* is used intentionally, in preference to *testing* because most schools have testing programs to meet accreditation requirements. The data from such programs are usually filed away and never benefit student, teacher, or administration. The backbone of an assessment system can, however, be the testing program. It needs to be supplemented with periodic assessments of such untraditional variables as student attitudes toward school and learning, classroom environment, parental attitudes, and teacher values. The cost of a schoolwide program is not inconsequential, and may be as much as several dollars per student per year. The potential benefit to the student, school, and society justifies the cost. Data from a comprehensive program can be used to (1) improve the instructional program, (2) facilitate curriculum revision, (3) assist in educational and vocational counseling, (4) help the administrative staff appraise the overall impact and effectiveness of the educational program, and, most importantly, (5) help the individual examine his progress and strengths.

Designing a Program

The design of a school-wide program has at least nine major phases:

1. Classification of the school's philosophy and purpose in establishing the system. Answers are sought to the question "What information is desired?"

2. Solicitation of staff cooperation and involvement in program development.

3. Communication to all faculty of the nature, extent, and purpose of the assessment program.

4. Designation of those who will use and have access to the information.

5. Determination of the manner in which information will be used.

6. Designation of responsibilities for the execution of the program.

7. Stimulation of financial and moral support for the program.

8. Provision for the administrative machinery for reevaluation of the program.

9. Interpreation of the program to the community. (See Chapter Ten.)

The last phase is particularly critical as the general public becomes increasingly involved in setting school policies and monitoring the educational process.

An Illustrative Testing Program

The standardized testing portion of the assessment system might resemble the program outlined in Table 14.4, from Mehrens and

TABLE 14.4 A Typical School Testing Program

Grade	Kind of Test
K	Reading Readiness
1 or 2	General Intelligence or Scholastic Aptitude
4	Achievement Battery
5	Achievement Battery
5	General Intelligence or Scholastic Aptitude
6	Achievement Battery
7	Achievement Battery
8	Multifactor Aptitude Test
10	Achievement Battery
11	General Intelligence or Scholastic Aptitude
9, 10, 11, or 12	Interest Test

Source: Adapted from Mehrens and Lehmann 1969, p. 273.

Lehmann (1969). It is generally recommended that testing take place in the fall. Data derived from a fall test administration should have maximum usefulness throughout the school year, if for no other reason than that it is recent. In addition to measures of achievement and scholastic aptitude (which are considered minimal), such other types of measures as special aptitude, various types of interest, value, attitude, and personality inventories should be made available. Obviously, there is no single program like that outlined in Table 14.4 that will suffice for all schools. Different objectives and needs require different tests and patterns of administration.

Criteria for an Effective Program

Traxler (1950) has presented a set of fifteen criteria that can be employed in examining the effectiveness of an assessment system. These criteria, in the form of "critical questions," are as follows:

1. Is the program comprehensive?

2. Does the program include all the students in the school?

3. Are the tests given at regular intervals?

4. Are the tests administered at times of the year that maximize their usefulness?

5. Are the tests in the school's testing program comparable?

6. Do the tests used agree with the objectives and the curriculum of the school?

7. Are the specific tests carefully chosen?

8. Are the tests carefully administered to each group?

9. Are the tests scored accurately?

10. Are the test results interpreted in terms of appropriate norms?

11. Are the test results quickly disseminated to teachers and counselors in understandable terms?

12. Are the test results recorded on individual cumulative record forms?

13. Is a definite attempt made to relate the test scores to other kinds of information?

14. In addition to the regular testing program, is there provision for special testing as needed?

15. Does the school have an in-service program for educating teachers in the use of test results?

SUGGESTED READINGS

Adams, Georgia Sachs (in consultation with T. L. Torgerson). *Measurement and evaluation in education, psychology and guidance.* New York: Holt, Rinehart and Winston, 1964. Chapter 5, "Application of the Principles of Measurement in the Selection of Tests"; Chapter 13, "The Place of Standardized Achievement Tests in the Improvement of Instruction"; and Chapter 14, "Educational Diagnosis," are highly recommended.

Ahmann, J. S., and Glock, M. D. *Evaluating pupil growth,* 4th ed. Boston: Allyn and Bacon, 1971. Chapter 11 is an excellent discussion of general and special achievement tests. The process of standardization is neatly summarized, and discussions of representative tests are illustrated with sample items. In addition, Chapter 16 describes the establishment of a schoolwide program of evaluation.

Bauernfeind, R. H. *Building a school testing program.* Boston: Houghton Mifflin, 1963. This book provides an overall picture of the processes involved in developing a comprehensive and integrated testing program and presents informative discussions of basic measurement principles and factors in test interpretation.

Findley, W. G., ed. *The impact and improvement of school testing programs* (62nd Yearbook of the National Society for the Study of Education). Chicago: University of Chicago Press, 1963. This high-quality reference work contains 12 chapters contributed by the country's leading testing experts.

Gerberich, J. R.; Greene, H. A.; and Jorgensen, A. J. *Measurement and evaluation in the modern school.* New York: David McKay, 1962. Part 5, "Measuring and Evaluating in the School Subjects," contains 11 chapters devoted to the major subject-matter areas, e.g., reading, arithmetic and mathematics, foreign languages, business education, biological and physical sciences, industrial arts and home economics, and so on.

Katz, M., ed. *Selecting an achievement test: Principles and procedures,* 2nd ed. Evaluation and Advisory Service Series pamphlet no. 3. Princeton: Educational Testing Service. This 34-page booklet provides a succinct summary of the major variables that must be considered in selecting an achievement test.

Mehrens, W. A., and Lehmann, I. J. *Standardized tests in education.* New York: Holt, Rinehart and Winston, 1969. This excellent paperback reference book contains a comprehensive survey of aptitude, achievement, interest, personality, and attitude measures. The coverage of achievement tests is particularly informative and valuable.

Nunnally, J. C. *Educational measurement and evaluation.* New York: McGraw-Hill, 1964. Part III of this excellent textbook contains three chapters covering the construction and use of the various types of achievement tests.

Thorndike, R. L., and Hagen, Elizabeth. *Measurement and evaluation in psychology and education,* 2nd ed. New York: John Wiley and Sons, 1961. Chapter 8, "Where to Find Information about Specific Tests," and Chapter 11, "Achievement Tests," are informative.

15

ASSESSING AFFECTIVE LEARNING OUTCOMES WITH STANDARDIZED INSTRUMENTS

SUMMARY PREVIEW STATEMENTS

1. The major standardized measures of affective learning outcomes useful to the classroom teacher focus on academic interests, motivation, attitudes, and values.

2. In using standardized measures of affective learning outcomes, one should be careful to:
   a. Insure that the instrument and instructional objectives are in harmony.
   b. Have a qualified professional direct the administration, scoring, and interpretation.
   c. Respect the privacy of individual students.
   d. Explain to the students the reason for using a particular measure.
   e. Insure that all students receive an interpretation of their scores.
   f. Respect the security and confidentiality of student scores.
   g. Draw upon all relevant nontest information in interpreting a test score.
   h. Exercise caution in interpreting out-of-date test scores.
   i. Examine carefully the characteristics of any norm group selected for reference purposes.
   j. Select a measure at an appropriate reading and experience level.

3. Profiling scores on multiscore affective inventories is a useful aid to interpretation.

4. The critical reviews of standardized measures in Buros' *Mental Measurements Yearbooks* should be consulted when selecting a particular test.

5. Standardized affective measures can be used in the classroom as stimuli for learning units.

6. Examination of study habits and attitudes is a valid use of selected standardized affective measures.

7. Standardized affective tests have a variety of research uses.

Although limited in quantity, and to some extent in quality, standardized measures of affective learning outcomes are available for classroom use. This brief chapter will describe some of these measures, focusing on academic interests, motivation, attitudes, and values. General personality inventories are outside the scope of this book, and will not be considered. Reference to any number of standard texts (e.g., Allen 1958; Bass and Berg 1959; Cronbach 1970; Horst 1968, and Kleinmuntz 1967) should provide the interested reader with a wealth of information on personality measurement procedures. In addition, Buros' *Personality Tests and Reviews* (1970) is the best single source on commercially available instruments of the type discussed here.

SOME CONCERNS AND CAUTIONS IN USING STANDARDIZED AFFECTIVE MEASURES

Before considering specific instruments, some general statements on potential problems encountered in their use are in order. The following list of concerns and cautions was influenced by Cottle (1968).

1. As is the case with standardized achievement and aptitude tests, one must be sure that the objectives, item content, and scores of the instrument are consistent with those of the user. Otherwise, gross misassessment may result.

2. The administration, scoring, and interpretation of such measures should be handled directly by, or under the guidance of, a trained and competent professional.

3. Respect for the privacy and integrity of the examinee is imperative. *Affective inventories should be voluntary.* The right of an individual to refuse should be honored.

4. It is imperative that the intent of administering a particular test be explained in full to the student. The projected use of the results should also be described. Such a description and the attendant discussion should help to promote rapport, insure seriousness of intent, and arouse examinee motivation.

5. It is generally advisable to encourage an examinee to record his

initial response to an item. Such a procedure will tend to elicit "typical" reactions. Extended deliberations tend to create confusion in the mind of the respondent.

6. If possible, a graphic procedure (e.g., a profile) should be used to report the scores. This is a particularly informative approach if a multi-score instrument is being used.

7. Inspection of single items should be discouraged because they tend to lack reliability.

8. During interpretation, the respondent should be provided a copy of the description of the results from scoring the instrument.

9. If answer sheets are sent to a scoring service, it should be requested to return them with the reported scores or profiles. Spot-checking for scoring errors is always desirable.

10. The private nature of an affective inventory precludes discussion of a particular score or set of scores with anyone but the examinee. However, summary statistics based on group data, in the form of means or standard deviations, are legitimate material for open discussion.

11. Profiles on scores should be regarded as held in trust for the individual or the institution. They should be released only to professionally competent persons with a legitimate right to access.

12. The reading level of the inventory must be appropriate to the individual or group being tested. Oral administration might be considered.

13. If norms tables are to be used to assist score interpretation, it is imperative that they be appropriate to the group tested and the administration procedure used.

14. If possible, any unusual reaction to the testing situation or to a specific item by an examinee should be recorded at the time of testing.

15. Because of the variability of affective behaviors, caution should be exercised in accepting and/or interpreting scores on inventories administered more than three to six months previous.

16. Probably most important of all, an interpretation should never be based solely on a single test score or set of scores from the same instrument. Nontest data must be used to put the scores in perspective and assist in the confirmation or contravention of an interpretation.

ILLUSTRATIVE STANDARDIZED MEASURES IN THE AFFECTIVE DOMAIN

Following are descriptions of three general classes of affective measures—(1) academic interests and motivation, (2) general and academic attitudes, and (3) values—that might be useful to the classroom teacher. The critical comments on selected tests are excerpted from reviews in Buros' *Seventh Mental Measurements Yearbook* and the *Journal of Educational Measurement*.

STANDARDIZED MEASURES OF ACADEMIC INTERESTS AND MOTIVATION

TITLE: **College Interest Inventory (CII)**

AUTHOR: Robert W. Henderson

LEVELS AND SCORES AVAILABLE: Grades 11–16

> Sixteen scores: Agriculture, Home Economics, Literature and Journalism, Fine Arts, Social Science, Physical Science, Biological Science, Foreign Language, Business Administration, Accounting, Teaching, Civil Engineering, Electrical Engineering, Mechanical Engineering, Law, Total

COPYRIGHT YEAR: 1967

NUMBER OF FORMS: One

COST OF BOOKLETS: $20.00 for 25 tests

TESTING TIME: 30 minutes

PUBLISHER: Personal Growth Press

CRITICAL COMMENTS:[1] This inventory, proposed as a tool useful in academic counseling aimed at exploring curricular but occupationally-related choices, is based on an interesting premise. This premise is that a combination of forced and free-choice methodology should yield the most valid interest measurement. Data supplied by the author and publisher are suggestive but far from conclusive.

> *Administration and Scoring.* This inventory is virtually self-administering. Directions lead the respondent to select at least one but not more than five choices from each group of fifteen items. There are forty-five such blocks with each being concerned with either (a) a course of study, (b) occupation, or (c)

---

[1] This review by the present author is reprinted from O. K. Buros, ed., *Seventh mental measurements yearbook* (Highland Park, N.J.: Gryphon Press, 1972), pp. 1408–1409. Reprinted by permission of the editor.

a behavior activity or task associated with a course of study or occupation.

Responses are recorded on an IBM 805 answer sheet for hand scoring. No provision is made for machine scoring. Such lack of efficiency must surely detract from the wide application of this device. Hand scoring is facilitated by transparent keys.

Validity. Validity of the CII relates to the question, "Do the scores on this instrument in fact reflect the interests they purport to measure?" A tentative "probably" must be the answer to this question at this stage of development. Basically, validity was established by use of contrasted groups criterion-keying methodology. Items which discriminated those college juniors and seniors who indicated an intent to follow a particular vocation closely connected with a particular curriculum (e.g., C.P.A. for Accounting) and students in general were selected from an original pool of 100 items. This is surely an acceptable practice. Its application here may be open to question on two counts. First, there is a question of voiced intent and actual entry into the particular occupations or even successful completion of the course of study. Second, the criterion group sample sizes were severely restricted in size, sometimes being as small as 16.

Interscale correlations support the relative independence of the fifteen curricular groupings. These, for the most part near-zero correlations, can partially be accounted for as an artifact of the forced-choice methodology.

Obviously, more validity data are needed. One would be interested in data on academically-successful high scorers, for example, or follow-up data related to professed interest and field of entry.

Reliability. Internal consistency (corrected split-half) within curriculum groupings is excellent. The lack of stability data is unfortunate.

Interpretation. Test interpretation is facilitated by the use of a profile sheet which contains indications of the means of the criterion groups as well as a shaded area corresponding to the score range for the middle 70 percent of that group, and the mean scores for the "college students in general" on a particular scale. Percentile ranks can be approximated from the profile chart. Only 12 ranks, however, are provided for guidance of the approximations.

The counselor is more or less left to his own devices with regard to using the test information with clients. Some general suggestions are made and some probing questions presented. The test undoubtedly can provide a valuable function by serving as a "springboard" in initiating student self-appraisal and establishing a counseling relationship. It would be extremely helpful if a kind of casebook were provided potential users. Such a reference could suggest ways in which CII data may be used with particular types of students.

Summary. The CII in its present form should probably be considered to be a preliminary or experimental edition. As new data are incorporated into a new manual and the essential recommendations of the *Standards for Educational and Psychological Tests and Manuals* are emphasized, concern about the psychometric properties of the CII will lessen. The basic problem with the CII during its current infancy is lack of validity data. If for no other reason than this, its many competitors, chiefly the *Strong Vocational Interest Blank*, must be preferred.

TITLE: **Educational Interest Inventory (EII)**

AUTHOR: James E. Oliver

LEVELS AND SCORES AVAILABLE: Grades 11–13

Scores are available for both males and females on Literature, Music, Art, Education, Communication, Physics, Chemistry, Botany, Zoology, Sociology, History and Political Science, Psychology, Economics, Mathematics; for males only on Business Administration, Engineering, Industrial Arts, Agriculture, and Earth Science; for females only on Secretarial Arts, Library Arts, Nursing, and Home Economics.

COPYRIGHT YEARS: 1962–1970

NUMBER OF FORMS: Two—A (Men) and B (Women)

COST OF BOOKLETS: $.50 each

TESTING TIME: 40–45 minutes

PUBLISHER: Educational Guidance

TITLE: **School Apperception Method (SAM)**

AUTHORS: Irving L. Solomon and Bernard D. Starr

LEVELS AND SCORES AVAILABLE: Grades K–9

Students are encouraged to construct stories in response to pictorial stimuli relating to relations with teachers, principals, and schoolmates; attitudes toward school work; anger, aggression, and other aspects of the total school environment.

COPYRIGHT YEAR: 1968

NUMBER OF FORMS: One

COST OF BOOKLETS: $10.00 for a set of 22 cards and manual

TESTING TIME: 30–45 minutes

PUBLISHER: Springer Publishing Company

CRITICAL COMMENTS:[2] The SAM belongs in the projective tradition of personality assessment. It is a projective instrument designed to be situationally relevant to schools. Three explicit claims are made for the SAM: (1) stimuli are situationally relevant to the school (one can question the extent to which the pictorial stimuli depict typical school problems); (2) the very content of the stimuli assures school-oriented associations (norms are not presented to document this claim); and (3) responses provide data on which trained personnel can formulate hypotheses for school decisions (this claim avoids explicit quantitative standards against which the SAM should be assessed). There is little evidence that the stimuli represent typical school problems—norms are totally lacking, and reliability and validity are unsubstantiated. It is recommended that auxiliary information be used with the SAM. For school testing purposes, SAM is probably better than other thematic techniques. Outside of use by experienced professional psychologists, its application should be restricted to research.

TITLE: **School Interest Inventory (SII)**

AUTHOR: William C. Cottle

LEVELS AND SCORES AVAILABLE: Grades 7–12

Total score only

COPYRIGHT YEARS: 1959–1966

NUMBER OF FORMS: One

---

[2] Based on reviews by Willard E. Reitz and Norman D. Sundberg, *Ibid*.

COST OF BOOKLETS: $.33 per test

TESTING TIME: 20–30 minutes

PUBLISHER: Houghton Mifflin

CRITICAL COMMENTS:[3] The validity of the SII is not extensively investigated in the manual. Stability reliability for decisionmaking about pupils was established only for a short time period. The user should not bother with the recommended weighted scoring system. No norms are presented, the student's relative standing within his own school being recommended as a method of interpretation. The nonapplicability of a number of items to some students is a weakness. The predictive strength of the instrument compared with such other available measures as attendance, previous grades, and counselor and teacher opinion, is unconsidered. No mention is made of the test content nor of its relationship to other reference variables. One is left with the feeling that significant information regarding school dropout-proneness may be buried in the instrument, unrevealed by the total score. Evidence presented by Goodwin (1969), however, is quite supportive of the SII as a predictive instrument.

TITLE: **School Motivation Analysis Test (SMAT),** research edition

AUTHORS: Arthur B. Sweney, Raymond B. Cattell, and Samuel E. Krug

LEVELS AND SCORES AVAILABLE: Ages 12–17

Forty scores: four motivation scores (unintegrated, integrated, fatal, difference-conflict) for each of six drives (assertiveness, mating, fear, narcissism, pugnacity-sadism, protectiveness) and each of four sentiments (self-sentiment, super-ego, school, home)

COPYRIGHT YEARS: 1961–1970

NUMBER OF FORMS: One

COST OF BOOKLETS: $15.00 for 25 tests

---

[3] Based on reviews by Gene V. Glass and Leonard V. Gordon, *Ibid*.

TESTING TIME: 50–60 minutes

PUBLISHER: Institute for Personality and Ability Testing

STANDARDIZED MEASURES OF GENERAL AND ACADEMIC ATTITUDES

TITLE: **California Life Goals Evaluation Schedules (CLGES)**

AUTHOR: Milton E. Hahn

LEVELS AND SCORES AVAILABLE: Ages 15 and over

Ten scores: esteem, profit form, power, leadership, security, social service, interesting experiences, self-expression, independence

COPYRIGHT YEARS: 1966–1969

NUMBER OF FORMS: Two—consumable form D–S, reusable form D–M

COST OF BOOKLETS: $11.50 for examiner's kit of 25 tests

TESTING TIME: 30–45 minutes

PUBLISHER: Western Psychological Services

CRITICAL COMMENTS:[4] This test is still in its experimental phase, and norms, reliabilities, and validities are tentative. Different norms are used for males and females. The norms are tentative based on relatively small samples (Ns of 309 and 363). Regarding content validity, the author acknowledges that "whether or not the 15 items in each schedule comprise an adequate sampling of the concept involved must be determined by further use and research," and that "only clues to predictive validity are available." Meager data on reliability are presented (reliabilities for scales range between .71 and .86). Considerable attention is given to interpretation, mostly in terms of guidelines for future research. It is suggested that CLGES normally be administered in conjunction with other tests and interviews. Generally speak-

---

[4] Based on a review by Robert W. Lundin, *Ibid*.

ing, the present data are too limited in occupational groups to make broad generalizations. Opportunities exist for research using various socioeconomic, ethnic, and religious groups, as well as people with different political leanings and occupations.

TITLE: **Demos D Scale: An Attitude Scale for the Identification of Dropouts (DDS)**

AUTHOR: George D. Demos

LEVELS AND SCORES AVAILABLE: Grades 7–12

Five attitude scores: teachers, education, peers and parents, school behavior, total

COPYRIGHT YEARS: 1965–1970

NUMBER OF FORMS: One

COST OF BOOKLETS: $7.50 for 25 tests and manual

TESTING TIME: 15–40 minutes

PUBLISHER: Western Psychological Services

CRITICAL COMMENTS:[5] The primary purpose of the DDS is to determine verbalized opinions which reflect attitudes presumably related to dropping out of school. . . ." These responses *may be* related to dropping out of school; however, the author has not adequately demonstrated such a relationship. It is necessary to go beyond the fact that students do respond to the items in assessing the reliability. Similarly, not a single validity coefficient is presented. No norms are provided; however, there are tables of means for each of the 29 items and the total inventory. Two methods of score interpretation are available: (1) scores may be compared to standardization groups (though there is no information about score distribution), or (2) the examiner may interpret a score in terms of the probability of a student dropping out. The meaningfulness of the expectancy tables is open to serious question. The fundamental psychometric data needed to evaluate the extent to which the device achieves what is claimed

---

[5] Based on reviews by John R. Brown and Leonard V. Gordon, *Ibid*.

for it are simply not presented. The DDS has very little to recommend it for any professional purpose. Its use in research at the local level may, however, prove profitable.

TITLE: **Study Attitudes and Methods Survey (SAMS)**

AUTHORS: William B. Michael, Joan J. Michael, and Wayne S. Zimmerman

LEVELS AND SCORES AVAILABLE: Grades 9–16

Six factor dimensions: academic interest–love of learning, academic drive–conformity, study methods, study anxiety, manipulation, alienation toward authority

COPYRIGHT YEARS: 1972

NUMBER OF FORMS: One

COST OF BOOKLETS: $9.50 for 25 tests

TESTING TIME: 50–55 minutes

PUBLISHER: Educational and Industrial Testing Service

TITLE: **Survey of Study Habits and Attitudes (SSHA)**

AUTHORS: William F. Brown and Wayne H. Holtzman

LEVELS AND SCORES AVAILABLE: Grades 7–12, 12–14

Seven scores: study habits (delay avoidance, work methods, total), study attitudes (teacher approval, education acceptance, total), total

COPYRIGHT YEARS: 1953–1967

NUMBER OF FORMS: Two

COST OF BOOKLETS: $3.50 for 25 tests

TESTING TIME: 20–25 minutes

PUBLISHER: Psychological Corporation

CRITICAL COMMENTS:[6] The SSHA is recommended for use as a (a) screening instrument, (b) diagnostic instrument, (c) teaching aid, and (d) research tool. A major weakness is that scores can be manipulated by the student at will. The SSHA's usefulness as a research tool is severely limited by its susceptibility to faked scores. The SSHA has been carefully devised and has satisfactory reliability (test-retest reliabilities after 4- and 14-week intervals vary from .83 to .94); there is statistical evidence for some of the least important aspects of validity (low correlation efficients between SSHA and aptitude tests, high correlations between SSHA and grades). Its use as a predictor is unwarranted, and subscale scores should be interpreted with caution. Additional research is needed to justify SSHA's use as a screening or diagnostic instrument. Nonetheless, it is a good teaching aid and will be useful to students who are frank in their responses. (Form C is an improvement over the earlier edition in that one set of norms is applicable to both sexes.) To facilitate the interpretation of scores, a very useful diagnostic profile, a copy of which is exhibited in Figure 15.1, has been developed.

STANDARDIZED MEASURES OF VALUES

TITLE: **Differential Value Profile (DVP)**

AUTHOR: Walter L. Thomas

LEVELS AND SCORES AVAILABLE: College

Six scores: aesthetic, humanitarian, intellectual, material, power, religious

COPYRIGHT YEARS: 1963–1969

NUMBER OF FORMS: One

COST OF BOOKLETS: $.15 per test

TESTING TIME: 30–45 minutes

PUBLISHER: Combined Motivation Education Systems

---

[6] Based on reviews by Carleton B. Shay, Martin J. Higgins, Albert E. Roark, and Scott A. Harrington, *Ibid.*

CRITICAL COMMENTS:[7] The DVP is designed for use with college students and measures six value clusters defined "by factor analyses." Internal consistency (KR_{20} coefficients range from .76 to .88) and test-retest (correlations vary between .83 and .94) reliability estimates are presented in the manual. There are two kinds of validational evidence: (1) ten judges scaled items and achieved fair to good agreement, and (2) a validation study was undertaken with college freshmen from church-related and public colleges. Thus the DVP provides stable, internally consistent, face valid measures of six well-known value clusters. However, the items are somewhat offensive to the test-wise students of today, and the practical utility of this inventory for research in education and guidance remains to be demonstrated.

TITLE: **Survey of Personal Values (SPV)**

AUTHOR: Leonard V. Gordon

LEVELS AND SCORES AVAILABLE: Grades 11–16 and adults

Six scores: practical mindedness, achievement, variety, decisiveness, orderliness, goal orientation

COPYRIGHT YEARS: 1964–1967

NUMBER OF FORMS: One

COST OF BOOKLETS: $4.50 for 25 tests

TESTING TIME: 15–20 minutes

PUBLISHER: Science Research Associates

CRITICAL COMMENTS:[8] The *Survey of Personal Values* is an interesting addition to the realm of personality assessment which has long been dominated by *Study of Values*. Reliability is adequate but incomplete (long-term reliability must be presumed). There is no single, observable criterion against which the SPV scales can be validated. To criticize the negative intercorrelations of scales is unjustified (ipsative scored scales will intercorrelate negatively on the average). The long, arduous process of determining what

---

[7] Based on a review by Robert Hogan, *Ibid.*
[8] Based on a review by Gene V. Glass, *Ibid.*

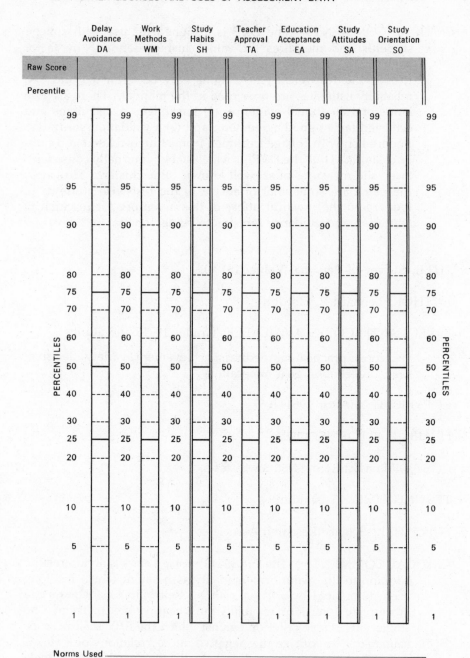

FIGURE 15.1. Diagnostic Profile for Survey of Study Habits and Attitudes

Name _____
              Last   First

School _____ Date _____

Age _____   Sex _____   Form of SSHA_____

Circle Grade or Year in School:

    High School: 7 8 9 10 11 12   College: Fr. Soph. Jr. Sr.

Profiling Your SSHA Scores

To find out how you did on each scale of this survey, look at the numbers in the row marked "Percentile." Your percentile on each scale shows your relative standing in the group of people described on the "Norms Used" line at the bottom of the chart. For example, if your norms group is college freshmen and your percentile on the TA scale is 45, it means that 45 percent of the freshmen received lower scores than yours on the TA scale, while 55 percent of them received higher scores. Thus, your percentile tells where you rank in comparison with others in your norms group.

You can complete your profile by making a heavy line across each column at the level which corresponds to your percentile rank on that scale. For example, if your percentile rank on the DA scale is 65, make a heavy line across the DA column halfway between 60 and 70. Draw a line corresponding to your percentile rank for all seven scales.

Then start at the horizontal line you have drawn and black in each column up to or down to the 50th percentile line. Since the 50th percentile line represents the score made by the middle student of your group, the vertical bars above that line on your profile show those scales on which you have scored higher than the middle student and the bars below that line show the scales on which you scored lower.

What Your SSHA Scores Mean

High scores on SSHA are characteristic of students who get good grades; low scores tend to be characteristic of those who get low grades or find school work difficult. Therefore, your scores on the SSHA scales can indicate your strengths and weaknesses in the areas measured by the survey, and also help to predict future academic achievement.

What the SSHA Measures

(DA) DELAY AVOIDANCE—your promptness in completing academic assignments, lack of procrastination, and freedom from wasteful delay and distraction.

(WM) WORK METHODS—your use of effective study procedures, efficiency in doing academic assignments, and how-to-study skills.

(TA) TEACHER APPROVAL—your opinions of teachers and their classroom behavior and methods.

(EA) EDUCATION ACCEPTANCE—your approval of educational objectives, practices, and requirements.

(SH) STUDY HABITS combines the scores on the DA and WM scales to provide a measure of academic behavior.

(SA) STUDY ATTITUDES combines the scores on the TA and EA scales to provide a measure of scholastic beliefs.

(SO) STUDY ORIENTATION combines the scores on the SH and SA scales to provide an overall measure of study habits and attitudes.

SPV scales measure has only begun. Its norms are skimpy. Immediate dissemination and use are not recommended pending further analysis and reporting of additional data—the SPV should be viewed as a research instrument.

TITLE: **Study of Values, A Scale for Measuring the Dominant Interests in Personality (SV),** 3rd edition

AUTHORS: Gordon W. Allport, Philip E. Vernon, and Gardner Lindzey

LEVELS AND SCORES AVAILABLE: Grades 10–16 and adults

COPYRIGHT YEARS: 1931–1970

NUMBER OF FORMS: One

COST OF BOOKLETS: $4.50 for 35 tests

TESTING TIME: 20 minutes

PUBLISHER: Houghton Mifflin

DESCRIPTION: The following brief description of the six varieties of personal values is excerpted from the 1960 manual of the *Study of Values:*[9]

1. *The Theoretical.* The dominant interest of the theoretical man is the discovery of *Truth.* In the pursuit of this goal he characteristically takes a "cognitive" attitude, one that looks for identities and differences; one that divests itself of judgments regarding the beauty or utility of objectives, and seeks only to observe and to reason. Since the interests of the theoretical man are empirical, critical and rational, he is necessarily an intellectualist, frequently a scientist or philosopher. His chief aim in life is to order and systematize his knowledge.

2. *The Economic.* The economic man is characteristically interested in what is *Useful.* Based originally upon the satisfaction of bodily needs (Self preservation), the interest in utilities develops to embrace the practical affairs of the business world. . . . This type is thoroughly "practical" and conforms well to the pre-

---

[9] From G. W. Allport, P. E. Vernon, and G. Lindzey, *A study of values,* 3rd ed. (Boston: Houghton Mifflin, 1960). Reprinted by permission.

vailing stereotype of the average American business man. . . .
The economic man wants education to be practical and regards
unapplied knowledge as waste.

3. *The Aesthetic*. The aesthetic man sees his highest value in *Form*
and *Harmony*. Each single impression is enjoyed for its own
sake. He need not be a creative artist, nor need he be effete; he is
aesthetic if he but finds his chief interest in the artistic episodes of
life. . . .

4. *The Social*. The highest value for this type is love of people. In
the *Study of Values* it is the altruistic or philanthropic aspect of
love that is measured. The social man prizes other people as
ends, and is therefore himself kind, sympathetic, and unselfish.
He is likely to find the theoretical, economic, and aesthetic attitudes cold and inhuman.

5. *The Political*. The political man is interested primarily in *power*.

6. *The Religious*. The highest value of the religious man may be
called *Unity*. He is mystical, and seeks to comprehend the cos-
mos as a whole, to relate himself to its embracing totality.

To facilitate the interpretation of SV scores, a profile is provided
on the back of the test booklet. This profile is illustrated in Figure
15.2.

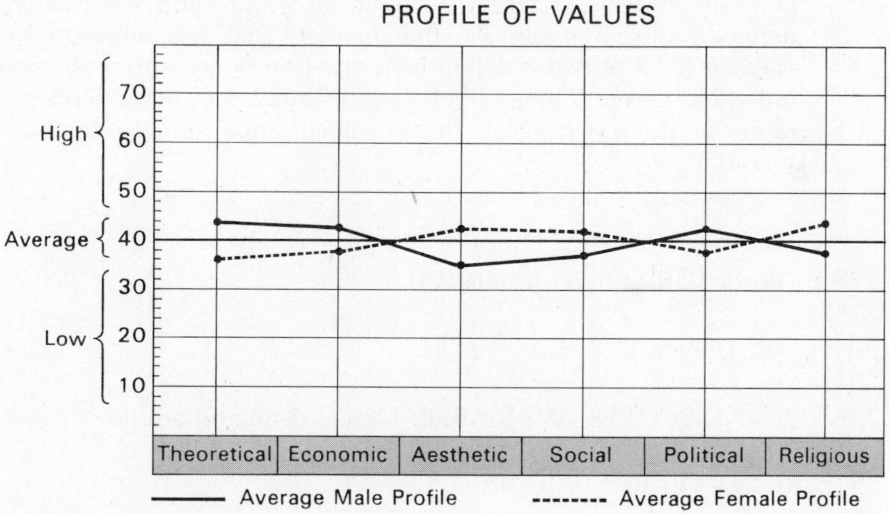

PROFILE OF VALUES

FIGURE 15.2. Profile of Values from the Allport-Vernon-Lindzey Study of
Values

CRITICAL COMMENTS:[10] In an early review in the *Mental Measurements Yearbook*, Gage cited the criticism that the SV content confounds interests and values. Mowrer has amplified this point by noting that the word "values" is "an essentially useless term, . . . which verges on meaninglessness, and certainly lacks power and precision."

The theoretical base of the SV—Spranger's types—has been questioned by many experts for four basic reasons: (1) traits (variables of choice) reside in people, while types have a fictional flavor; traits appear veridical while types seem nominal; (2) psychologists have tried to assess the universe of trait terms, while few have studied the taxonomy of personalities; (3) no attempt is made by the authors to explicate the logic of ideal types; and (4) psychologists tend to associate type concepts with fuzzy thinking. Two further theoretical issues raised by the test are (1) the degree to which value scores are related to nontest variables in a manner consistent with type theory and (2) the adequacy of Spranger's types as a taxonomy of personality. The types as described in the SV have two shortcomings: (1) an air of stuffy respectability, and (2) a pervasively middle-class flavor.

In spite of several problematic features—ipsative scoring and the associated difficulties of interpreting correlations of subscales between persons, a restricted range of usage, and the poorly defined nature of "values"—the *Study of Values* is a surprisingly viable test. It provides dependable and pertinent information on individual cases. In addition, the steadily mounting bibliography on the test suggests that it will continue to be useful as a research device.

TITLE: **Work Values Inventory (WVI)**

AUTHOR: Donald E. Super

LEVELS AND SCORES AVAILABLE: Grades 7–16 and adults

COPYRIGHT YEARS: 1968–1970

NUMBER OF FORMS: One

COST OF BOOKLETS: $15.00 for 100 tests

---

[10] Based on a review by Robert Hogan, *Ibid.*

TESTING TIME: 10–20 minutes

PUBLISHER: Houghton Mifflin

DESCRIPTION: The author and publisher of the WVI suggest two approaches to interpretation. The first relies on a relative score interpretation; the various scale scores are compared to determine the individual's relative emphases on values. The two or three values ranked highest and lowest should receive greatest attention. A second type of interpretation requires the conversion of raw scores to appropriate percentile ranks.

The major values measured by the WVI are as follows:

1. *Altruism*. Associated with work that enables one to contribute to the welfare of others.

2. *Aesthetic.* Associated with work that permits one to make beautiful things and contribute beauty to the world.

3. *Creativity*. Associated with work that permits one to invent new things, design new products, or develop new ideas.

4. *Intellectual Stimulation*. Associated with work that provides for independent thinking and learning how and why things work.

5. *Achievement*. Associated with work that gives one a feeling of accomplishment in doing a job well.

6. *Independence.* Associated with work that permits one to work in his own way and as fast or as slowly as he wishes.

7. *Prestige*. Associated with work that gives one standing in the eyes of others and evokes respect.

8. *Management.* Associated with work that permits one to plan and assign work for others to do.

9. *Economic Returns*. Associated with work that pays well and enables one to have the things he wants.

10. *Security*. Associated with work that assures one of a job even in hard times.

11. *Surroundings*. Associated with work that is carried out under pleasant conditions.

12. *Supervisory Relations.* Associated with work that is carried out under a supervisor who is fair and with whom one can get along.

13. *Associates.* Associated with work that brings one into contact with fellow workers whom he likes.

14. *Way of Life.* Associated with work that permits one to choose the kind of life he likes and be the type of person he wishes to be.

15. *Variety*. Associated with work that allows one to do different types of jobs.

CRITICAL COMMENTS:[11] The present inventory consists of only 45 items, three in each of the 15 scales. The manual is unusually well-written. However, brevity and directness have been achieved at the cost of questionable reliability and a format that may not adequately standardize test responses. While the tables of norms are good and the interscale analyses excellent, reliability needs further confirmation, correlations with other tests must be computed for the up-to-date form of the test, and no data have yet been collected for the evaluation of predictive validity. The test does seem to measure what it is supposed to; however, users of the WVI must confront the question "What do these work value scores mean?"

SUGGESTED USES OF STANDARDIZED AFFECTIVE MEASURES

The uses of affective measures to be discussed in this section deal primarily with the *Survey of Study Habits and Attitudes* (SSHA), *Study of Values* (SOV), *School Interest Inventory* (SII), and *Work Values Inventory* (WVI).

Applications of standardized affective tests fall into five general categories: (1) classroom application, (2) screening and selection, (3) counseling, (4) research, and (5) program evaluation.

Classroom Applications

The imaginative classroom teacher can create many situations in which the use of affective measures makes a real contribution to the instructional program. The *Work Values Inventory* (WVI), for example, could be used on a pre- or post-basis to assess changes in work values associated with a unit on the "world of work," or the WVI itself could be used as a starting-point in exploring various occupations. It might be helpful to have students estimate their scores before taking the test, and then compare these estimates with the test results. Individual student scores or class means could then be compared with selected normative data. The study of vocations could be stimulated by this method; discussion might revolve around known differences between occupational groups. It could be noted, for example, that on the WVI psychiatrists score significantly higher than lawyers, CPAs, and engineers on Al-

---

[11] Based on reviews by Ralph F. Berdie, David V. Tiedeman, and John W. French, *Seventh mental measurements yearbook* (Highland Park, N.J.: Gryphon Press, 1972).

truism; and that teachers score higher than psychologists on Security. The entire class or small groups could examine in detail how various occupations relate to scores on the WVI.

If a teacher is particularly concerned about the work habits of his students, the SSHA might be used to explore possible difficulties.

Inasmuch as the personnel offices of businesses and industries frequently administer tests of various dimensions of personality to prospective employees, classroom experience with an inventory should help students prepare for this experience. Practice on similar tests usually results in reduced anxiety in a formal assessment setting.

Screening and Selection

The *School Interest Inventory* is an instrument that illustrates well the sensible use of an affective measure. It is suggested that the SII be used on an intrainstitutional basis, so that a student's scores are compared only to those of other individuals in the same school. It will be recalled that the SII is used to identify potential dropouts. Students in the seventh or eighth grade could be administered the SII, and their scores ranked from highest to lowest within grade and sex. (Higher scores indicate a greater probability of the student's dropping out of school.) Using any number of criteria, e.g., a cutoff score of 25 or above or selection of the top 20 percent, one could identify students who might benefit from counseling. Counselees could consider the possibility of continuing in the same or another course of study, or explore vocational and social adjustments that do not require a high-school diploma. The counselor or teacher may also wish to set up "rap groups" in which personal, social, or vocational problems could be explored. Obviously, the use of a test as a screening instrument should be undertaken in conjunction with other relevant data. School achievement records, at-tendance, teachers' opinions, and age relative to school grade need to be considered.

Personnel managers frequently find that affective measures are useful in the hiring and placement of special classes of employees, and that scores may be related to job success. It is imperative when an affective measure is used in this manner that its relevance be demonstrable.

Counseling

Perhaps the major uses of standardized affective measures involve counseling. The value of such measures to stimulate a student to "look at himself" cannot be overestimated. The test can be used as a starting-point to help establish rapport in the counseling interview. Asking the student to predict his scores and then comparing his prediction with the actual results can be beneficial. The SSHA diagnostic profile is very useful in this kind of activity; it is illustrated in Figure 15.1. Descriptions of the various subscores can also be used as a basis for discussion. Student involvement in the actual task of profiling is recommended. Readers interested in the use of test scores in counseling are referred to books by Goldman (1961) and Meyering (1968).

Research

There are numerous fields of research using affective measures that might prove of interest to the educator. The authors of the *Study of Values*, for example, note that it has been used to research the following topics:

1. Differences in the scores of those in different college majors and occupational, religious, ethnic, and nationality groups.
2. Changes in values over time, and as functions of specific training and educational experiences.
3. Relationships with other attitude-, interest-, and cognitive-style measures.
4. Relationships between friendship choice and sociometric status.

Program Evaluation

Another area in which affective measures are achieving great popularity is program evaluation. As was noted in Chapter One, curriculum evaluation is receiving increased attention from educational measurement and assessment experts and consultants. Most state and federal educational programs require the assessment of affective variables, and local school systems are also becoming conscious of these important outcomes. Measures of such variables as attitude toward school, respect for self, and appreciation of artistic efforts are illustrative of educational product-and-process outcomes in a comprehensive evaluation system. The self-concept is a personal attribute that is given considerable attention in program evaluation. In addition to Buros' *Seventh Measurements Yearbook*, the reader is referred to an excellent review of available measures by Wylie (1961).

SUGGESTED READINGS

Aiken, L. R. Jr. *Psychological and educational testing.* Boston: Allyn and Bacon, 1971. Chapter 8 contains a good introduction to the issues and representative methods of assessing interests and attitudes.

Anastasi, Anne. *Psychological testing,* 3rd ed. New York: Macmillan, 1968. Chapter 18 of this excellent text provides a brief survey of interest and attitude measures.

Berkowitz, L. *The development of motives and values in the child*. New York: Basic Books, 1969. The author summarizes recent findings on cultural, religious, social-class, and familial influences on the development of morality and motivation to achieve.

Evans, K. M. *Attitudes and interests in education*. London: Routledge and Kegan Paul, 1965. A brief review of the significant studies and methodologies used to investigate relationships between educational attitudes and interests on the one hand, and achievement, teaching, self-assessments, and reactions to authority on the other.

Jacob, P. E. *Changing values in college: An exploratory study of the impact of college teaching*. New York: Harper and Row, 1957. A report on the results of an extensive survey of college courses and their impact on student attitudes.

Mehrens, W. A., and Lehmann, I. J. *Standardized tests in education*. New York: Holt, Rinehart & Winston, 1969. See Chapter 4 for an introduction to a variety of noncognitive measures.

Morris, C. *Varieties of human value*. Chicago: University of Chicago Press, 1956. This book presents the theory, methodology, and results of a study of five major value dimensions of "the good life."

Thorndike, R. L., and Hagen, Elizabeth. *Measurement and evaluation in psychology and education*, 3rd ed. New York: John Wiley & Sons, 1969. Chapter 12, "Questionnaires and Inventories of Self-Appraisal," touches on topics considered in this chapter.

16

ASSESSING AFFECTIVE, PERFORMANCE, AND PRODUCT OUTCOMES BY DIRECT OBSERVATION

SUMMARY PREVIEW STATEMENTS

1. Observational techniques may be used to assess a variety of learning outcomes expressed as feelings, performances, or products.

2. The potential advantages of observational methods over paper-and-pencil measures are that they:
   a. Are uniquely adaptable to certain learning outcomes.
   b. Are useful in assessing applications in real-life activities.
   c. Supplement other data sources.
   d. Can provide both quantitative and qualitative information.

3. The difficulties of making valid and reliable observations derive from:
   a. Preobservation knowledge and psychological set on the part of the instructor.
   b. Failure to see isolated bits of behavior in the total context of the setting.
   c. Confusion of description and interpretation.

4. Observational methods may be used to study:
   a. Individual and/or group behavior.
   b. Instructional procedures and their influences.
   c. Student products and procedures.
   d. A variety of psychomotor and interpersonal behaviors.

5. Considerable care must be exercised in developing the wide variety of instruments, such as numerical and graphic rating scales and checklists, used to record the results of observations.

6. Rating scales should probably be limited to ten points or less of gradation for each characteristic.

7. Anecdotal records of significant behavioral incidents can greatly enhance teacher understanding of student behavior and achievement, and thus increase the relevance of parent conferences and instructional planning.

8. Anecdotal records should:
   a. Be brief but complete.
   b. Be limited to single behavioral incidents.
   c. Describe "what happened."

9. The observation and recording of student-teacher interaction can contribute invaluable data to the understanding of instructional effectiveness.

10. Flanders' "interaction analysis system" is composed of ten categories describing the classroom verbal environment.

11. An interaction analysis of the sequence of student and/or teacher verbal behaviors can be used to determine the extent of an instructor's direct and indirect influence.

12. Examination of student-student interaction through the application of sociometric techniques allows for an analysis of the classroom social structure.

13. Sociometric methods may be used to examine student preferences for project, seat, work, or recreational partners.

14. Sociometric choice making should be limited to clearly defined real-life situations and should allow for mutual choices.

15. Sociometric data may be examined to identify stars, isolates, rejectees, neglectees, cliques, and cleavages so that the teacher may work with them.

16. Sociometric data may be summarized in the forms of sociograms or sociomatrices.

17. Student evaluations of teacher effectiveness are a source of valuable classroom data.

18. The key to the assessment of student performances and skills is the simulation of the criterion behavior.

19. The four major types of simulation tasks are situation tests, in-basket tests, work sample tests, and problem-solving games.

20. The development of simulation performance tasks involves:
    a. Analysis of the desired or criterion behavior.
    b. Identifying and selecting for study the most crucial elements to be observed.

    c. Providing directions and materials for the student.

    d. Recording the results of the simulation.

21. Performance, process, and procedure objectives may be considered ends in themselves.

22. The performances of students in such subject fields as music, vocational education, physical education, art, drama, public speaking, and science can be effectively studied through the use of rating scales and checklists.

23. Student products may also be validly assessed through the use of rating scales and checklists.

24. The key to the valid and reliable assessment of both performances and products is the specification of the expected criterion behavior.

    Most of the myriad possible achievement outcomes in our schools and classrooms can be assessed with formal paper-and-pencil devices. This is particularly true of learning outcomes that involve knowledge, verbal and thinking skill development, comprehension, and intellectual problem solving. In addition, it is becoming increasingly apparent that many affective outcomes can be assessed with paper-and-pencil measures, providing data useful for both student and teacher. But this is not the whole story. It is difficult at best to approach the assessment of proficiency in many skill areas and in situations in which personal-social development is emphasized. The best approach to assessing behavioral changes is direct observation of those behaviors. We need to know not only whether a student knows what to do, but also whether he can do it. The assessment of behaviors and outcomes in lifelike and realistic (as opposed to the classroom atmosphere) situations can supply us with some of the most valid data for decisionmaking.

ADVANTAGES OF OBSERVATIONAL METHODS

    The use of observational methods has been slighted in most school assessment situations, probably because of the difficulty of developing and applying the techniques. There are, however, many advantages to observation (Bonney and Hampleman 1962; Green 1970):

1. Observational methods allow us to gather data, particularly about

social-emotional-personal adjustment, in valid and reliable and precise ways not possible with more traditional methods.

2.   Observational methods allow us to test an individual's ability to apply information in lifelike situations.

3.   Because of the similarity between the testing situations and the setting in which the skills and knowledges are likely to be used, we find that observational measures tend to have higher predictive validity than do many other methods of predicting successful job performance.

4.   Observational methods are easily adapted to a variety of settings, tasks, and kinds of individuals, at all age and educational levels.

5.   Observational data can serve as an invaluable supplement to achievement and ability data available from other sources.

6.   Observation provides both qualitative and quantitative data.

7.   The use of data from a variety of sources results in a more reliable overall assessment.

8.   The fact that observations take place in natural settings enhances their integration into the total instructional program and allows the instructor to use observation as part of the teaching process.

DISADVANTAGES AND DIFFICULTIES OF OBSERVATIONAL METHODS

Observing students is a difficult task. Many factors influence what a teacher perceives and how his observations are reported. Training and experience are the prime contributors to the development of effective observational skills. There are a number of pitfalls that both experienced and inexperienced observers need to avoid (Prescott 1957, p. 100; Cronbach 1963a):

1. *Faculty knowledge.* Armed with misinformation and mistaken ideas about human development and behavior, a teacher can distort observational records and the resulting interpretations.

2. *Uncritical acceptance of data.* Failure to distinguish between fact and opinion and the acceptance of rumors can lead to distortion of facts.

3. *Failure to prespecify objectives.* Obviously, if we don't know what we are looking for, we may observe irrelevant behavior.

4. *Conclusion-leaping.* Drawing inferences from a single incident and failing to consider contraindicating data can lead to faulty conclusions.

5. *Failure to consider situational modifiers.* Behaviors result from many influences, and observations must take context into account. A single behavior may have two or more antecedents.

6. *Making false inferences from unreliable data.* The tendency to

generalize from too limited a sampling of behaviors, and to make judgments on the basis of a few incidents, is a common pitfall.

7. *Failure to distinguish behaviors.* In most modern classrooms many activities take place simultaneously. It is difficult to distinguish relevant from irrelevant behavior.

8. *Failure to recognize personal expectations.* Teachers must realize that their observations will be colored by their own expectations, preferences, biases, and psychological needs.

9. *Failure to record observations accurately.* Observations should be recorded when they occur, or immediately afterward. Otherwise, selective forgetting may operate to reduce the validity of the report. There is a tendency to forget things that conflict with our own beliefs and expectations more readily than those that coincide with them.

10. *Excessive certainty.* Inferences from observations should be considered tentative and hypothetical until corroborative evidence is obtained.

11. *Oversimplification.* One should guard against assigning a single cause to a single behavior; behavior has multiple determinants.

12. *Emotional thinking.* We tend to give disproportionate weight to incidents that have had a disturbing effect on us.

13. *Substitution fallacy.* There is a tendency to substitute an observed behavior for a desired objective—for example, substituting teacher behavior (process) for the criterion of pupil performance. Observing shop work or physical education, one may tend to substitute "how students do something" for the quality of the product. This pitfall suggests the danger of giving such variables as "student-teacher interaction" or "group participation" the status of ultimate criteria.

APPLICATIONS OF OBSERVATIONAL DATA

Despite the pitfalls to be avoided in collecting observational data, such data can make a number of very valuable contributions to the improvement of the teaching-learning situation (Michaels and Karnes 1950). Observational data may be used to study:

1. Group responsibility.
2. Group participation.
3. Attitudes toward subject matter.
4. Individual student interaction with the group.
5. Individual student and teacher interaction.
6. Teacher and class interaction.
7. Individual student achievement.
8. Class achievement.

9. Unanticipated but related outcomes.
10. Individual students in light of instructional hypotheses.
11. Teaching techniques.
12. Personal and academic problem areas.

Observational methods are particularly useful in studying an individual's manipulative and psychomotor skills. In addition, opportunities to gather data in naturally occurring or contrived situations are limited only by teacher creativity. Interpersonal relationships can be observed and objectively summarized. Observation is a means of monitoring important outcomes, particularly those dealing with application skills, without encroaching on instructional time or disrupting the class. The presence of an outside observer may, however, inhibit the "naturalness" of the situation.

The application of observation data in assessing interpersonal relationships and performance skills will be treated in detail later in this chapter.

USING RATING SCALES TO RECORD OBSERVATIONAL DATA

Rating scales not unlike those developed by the method of summated ratings, described in Chapter Eight, are frequently used to record the results of observations. They may be easily applied in collecting self-observation or self-report data. The three scales most frequently used in educational settings are numerical, graphic, and checklist. These types of scales are efficient in respect both to the amount of time required to complete them and to the number of individuals who can be rated. Moreover, they do not require sophisticated raters and are relatively easily constructed. On the other hand, rating scales are all too often based on undifferentiated gross impressions and susceptible to conscious or unintentional distortion.

Numerical Scales

Numerical scales generally take the form of a sequence of defined numbers. The definitions of the numbers might be in terms of degree of favorableness, frequency, pleasantness, or agreement with a statement. Color or odor, for example, might be rated as:

5—Most pleasant.
4—Moderately pleasant.
3—Neutral.
2—Moderately unpleasant.
1—Most unpleasant.

Guilford (1954) cautions against using negative numbers or defining the end categories so extremely that no one will select them. It is probably a good idea to create more categories than one actually intends to use so as to maximize discrimination. One might, for example, use a scale like the following:

4—Always.

3—Usually.

2—Sometimes.

1—Never,

combining categories 1 and 4 for analytic purposes. Research seems to indicate that, depending upon the nature of the task and the sophistication of the rater, from 7 to about 20 categories may be used. With checklists, as few as two categories (e.g., present-absent) can be used reliably.

The definitions of the numbers in a numerical scale allow for semantic confusion. This problem is well illustrated by a study by Simpson (1944), who asked a population of high-school and college students to indicate what certain terms connoted for them. For example, does the term "often" mean 65 times in 100 (or even less) or 85 times in 100? A selected sample of Simpson's results is presented in Table 16.1. It is

TABLE 16.1 Meanings Assigned to Selected Frequency Terms Used in Rating Scales

Term	Average of Midpoint Ranges Assigned	Range of Middle 50% of Assignments
Always	99	98–100
Very Often	88	80–93
Usually	85	70–90
Often	78	65–85
Generally	78	63–85
Frequently	73	40–80
Rather Often	65	45–80
Sometimes	20	13–35
Occasionally	20	10–33
Seldom	10	6–18
Rarely	5	3–10

Source: Adapted from Simpson, 1944.

obvious that individuals define terms very differently. Such differences undoubtedly serve to lower both the validity and the reliability of ratings. Simpson did find, however, that there were no appreciable differences between the sexes in the interpretation of frequency terms. One possible method of overcoming the problem of variable definitions is to specify the frequency to be assigned to each rating term. The following scheme might be used:

>5—Almost always (86 to 100 percent of time).
>
>4—Generally (66 to 85 percent of time).
>
>3—Frequently (36 to 65 percent of time).
>
>2—Sometimes (16 to 35 percent of time).
>
>1—Rarely (0 to 15 percent of time).

Although this procedure allows for some latitude in interpretation, it provides raters a common frame of reference.

Graphic Scales

Another popular rating format is the graphic scale, which is ordinarily a straight line—sometimes vertical but usually horizontal—adorned with various verbal cues to the rater. Guilford (1954) presents the following example of a graphic scale:

Is the student a slow or quick thinker?

Extremely Slow	Sluggish Plodding	Thinks with Ordinary Speed	Agile-Minded	Exceedingly Rapid

The rater is free to place a checkmark anywhere along the scale. In scoring, we might superimpose equal-interval categories (perhaps using a ruler) and assign numerical weights, e.g., the midpoint between Agile-Minded and Exceedingly Rapid might be weighted 5, and so on. This procedure is similar to the scoring method suggested for the semantic differential technique described in Chapter Nine. Another scoring approach involves the use of a ruler to measure the distance between one of the end categories and the checkmark. The suggestion of precision in such a procedure is probably not justified. One should avoid using extremely long lines, which tend to produce a clustering of ratings; the resulting increase in reliability is so slight that the extra work involved is unjustified. It is probably also a good idea to determine the location of the "high" or "good" end of the scale randomly, e.g., it might be on the right for one characteristic and on the left for another.

Graphic rating scales are simple and easy to administer, and can be intrinsically interesting.

An illustration of some of the many forms that a graphic rating scale may take has been presented by Guion (1965), and reproduced in Figure 16.1. The form of such a scale may range from simple (A and B) to fairly structured (I). Increased structuring better defines the task for the rater. The optimal number of rating points is probably seven to nine.

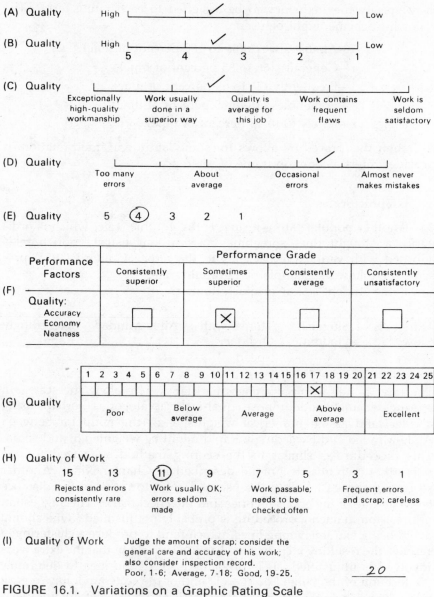

FIGURE 16.1. Variations on a Graphic Rating Scale

Generally, one should provide more rating categories than he intends to measure so as to offset possible respondent bias and respondent sets. It is not unusual to select an odd number of points (E) so that the "average" will have a central position on the scale, yielding maximum discrimination. An even number of points can sometimes be used profitably, particularly if they are collapsed for scoring, e.g., using a four-point scale (Never, Sometimes, Usually, and Always) to gather data, but scoring dichotomously. Some raters find it easier to make judgments when numerical point scales (B) are converted to verbal scales (C). However, an additional interpretation problem is thus introduced: the possibility that raters will read different meanings into the verbal cues. In any event, rating scales used with care and intelligence can yield very meaningful data. They are particularly adaptable to assessing products and performances.

Checklists

Another popular method of recording the results of observations is the checklist. Checklists can be used by relatively naive raters and tend to make complex judgments unnecessary. It is imperative, however, that the categories be as clear and precise as possible. The developer of a checklist would be well advised to use behavioral terms if at all possible. Checklists may be used to assess:

1. Which instructional objectives or skills have been met or mastered.
2. Student interests, hobbies, problems, preferred reading matter, radio or television programs, and the like.
3. Student behavior in a variety of settings.
4. Conformity to prescribed sequences of steps in task performance.
5. Student products.

Bonney and Hampleman (1962) cite the following example of a checklist used by an industrial arts teacher to identify the unsatisfactory items in a woodwork product before it goes to the finishing room.

Unsatisfactory Items in Woodwork Product

____ 1. Knots	____12. Operation Missing
____ 2. Lack of Filling	____13. Veneer Discolored
____ 3. Core or Glue	____14. Veneer Split
____ 4. Joint Shrinkage	____15. Rounded Edges
____ 5. Veneer Sand-through	____16. Exposed Glue
____ 6. Glaze or Burnish	____17. Coarse Sanding
____ 7. Loose Veneer	____18. Grain and Color of Veneer
____ 8. Tear-outs	
____ 9. Rough Machinery	____19. Damage
____10. Warpage	____20. Open Joints
____11. Dimensions	

An individual's "score" on the checklist may simply be the number of items checked or not checked, or a standard for an acceptable product may be established. If some elements of the checklist are more important than others from an instructional standpoint, differential weights might be applied. A range of three possible values would probably suffice.

There is a tendency on the part of some raters to use too many or too few items in a checklist. This response set can be combatted by requiring a fixed number of checks by the rater. Whether or not to use this technique will, of course, depend upon the nature and intended use of the checklist.

THE DEVELOPMENT AND USE OF ANECDOTAL RECORDS

An anecdotal record is a description of what an individual does or says. It describes in concrete detail the situation in which the action or comment occurs, and what others present do or say. Randall (1936), who is credited with the development of the anecdotal record concept, defines it as a

> . . . record of some significant item of conduct, a record of an episode in the life of the student, a word picture of the student in action; the teacher's best effort at taking a word snapshot at the moment of the incident; any narrative of events in which the student takes such part as to reveal something which may be significant about his personality.

The main thrust of the anecdotal record is to record social and emotional facets of a pupil's growth and adjustment. Records can also be made of other dimensions of relevant classroom or extraclassroom behavior. In general, the anecdotal record contributes to better understanding of individual students. Collected over a period of time, anecdotal material can provide a longitudinal view of a student's growth and patterns of change.

A sample anecdotal record is presented in Table 16.2. The kinds of information summarized in the anecdotal record could probably not be gathered in any other way.

Possible Uses of Anecdotal Material

The rich behavioral information collected in anecdotal form can be used in many ways (Jarvie and Ellingson 1940), some of which are listed below:

1.   Anecdotal records may supplement data gathered in other ways to assess progress toward a set of objectives.
2.   Anecdotal records may suggest aspects of the curriculum that need

TABLE 16.2   Illustrative Anecdotal Record

Date: 9/17/74   *Student's Name:*   Libby

Observer: Wilma (Student Teacher)

Description of Incident:

The fifth-grade class was working on a social studies display which involved the construction of models of many different kinds of homes common to different nationalities and countries. Libby was asked to work with Stella, a black girl, to build, study, and make a class report on a typical South American home. At first Libby was upset about the assignment and asked to be allowed to work with one of her friends, another white girl. When the teacher insisted that she carry out the first assignment she began her project quite reluctantly. As her work progressed, her interest in the country and in working with Stella became overtly enthusiastic.

Comment:

It appears that Libby has gained more than a knowledge of other lands and customs from this project. Libby has begun to work through some of her feelings regarding other races, and apparently is becoming more accepting and less fearful as a result of her experience.

---

to be reviewed or revised for particular students, or may suggest beneficial remedial activities.

3.   Such data are useful in parent-teacher conferences to pinpoint specific areas of concern.

4.   Anecdotal data can increase the teacher's insight into new students' strengths and weaknesses.

5.   Many of the incidents reported in anecdotal form could be useful to school counselors, and teachers should make every effort to share them with counselors and other teachers to whom they are relevant.

6.   Certain anecdotal records may have implications for vocational guidance, and communication with educational and business personnel outside the school. Care should be taken to respect the security of such material and release it only in confidence.

Suggestions for Generating and Improving Anecdotal Records

Barker and Wright (1954) and Gronlund (1971) have made several suggestions for the development and improvement of anecdotal records. They emphasize the desirability of:

1. Determining in advance what is to be observed and being alert to unusual behavior.

2. Reporting only the "what" and "how" of the subject's actions and interactions with others.

3. Describing in detail the scene at the beginning of each period of observation.

4. Reporting in sequence each step in the course of every action by the subject.

5. Allowing no overlap between factual description and interpretation of the incident(s).

6. Observing and recording sufficient material to make the report meaningful and reliable.

7. Recording the incident during or as soon after the observation as possible.

8. Restricting a given record to a single incident.

9. Recording both positive and negative incidents.

10. Collecting a number of anecdotes on a given student before attempting to make inferences.

11. Gaining practice in writing anecdotal records.

12. Establishing a plan for obtaining periodic systematic anecdotal samples.

OBSERVING AND RECORDING STUDENT–TEACHER INTERACTION

Classrooms are characterized by continual student-teacher interaction, the quantity and quality of which strongly influences the quantity and quality of learning. It is only within the last several decades that we have attempted to describe classroom interaction systematically; previously, exchanges between teacher and student were difficult and expensive to classify and record. Recent advances in the development of observational systems (Simon and Boyer 1970; Medley and Mitzel 1963; Murray 1970; Amidon and Hough 1967) have greatly facilitated the collection of interaction data.

Most systems of observation tend to focus on *process* variables —those variables related to behaviors, moves, or strategies aimed at enhancing learning. It is hoped that research will eventually reveal which strategies are most effective with which kinds of students, teachers, and objectives. It was noted in Chapter One that educational assessment is concerned not only with relationships between inputs and outputs, but also with the nature of transactions within the classroom. Observational systems, particularly Flanders' interaction analysis method (Amidon and Flanders 1963), provide us with techniques for studying these transactions. Teachers are interested in learning about discrepancies between their intended objectives and actual practices. Data from observations and tape recordings of class sessions, summarized in a systematic way, can reveal what actually happens.

Flanders' interaction analysis system—which provides for the collection of data on the degree of teacher directedness, student talk, and identification of periods of silence and confusion—is a very valuable tool in the hands of a skilled observer. Flanders' system (a description of which is presented in Table 16.3) implicitly assumes that the indirect approach is generally preferable. There are, however, many instructional needs that can only be approached directly. Flanders (1964) has noted that interaction analysis

.consists simply of observing, recording, and counting events as they occur. The usefulness of such a simple procedure will depend on congruence between the purpose of observing and the nature of the categories. Thus the proper application of interaction analysis be-

TABLE 16.3   Summary of Categories for the Flanders System of Interaction Analysis in Its Regular Ten-Category Form

Teacher Talk	Indirect Influence	1. Accepts Feeling: accepts and clarifies the feeling tone of the students in a non-threatening manner. Feelings may be positive or negative. Predicting or recalling feelings are included. 2. Praises or Encourages: praises or encourages student action or behavior. Jokes that release tension, not at the expense of another individual, nodding head or saying "um hm" or "go on" are included. 3. Accepts or Uses Ideas of Student: clarifying, building, or developing ideas or suggestions by a student. As teacher brings more of his ideas into play, shift to category five. 4. Asks Question: asking a question about content or procedure with the intent that a student answer.
	Direct Influence	5. Lecturing: giving facts or opinions about content or procedure; expressing his own ideas, asking rhetorical questions. 6. Giving Direction: directions, commands, or orders to which a student is expected to comply. 7. Criticizing or Justifying Authority: statements intended to change student behavior from non-accept to acceptable pattern; bawling someone out; stating what he is doing; extreme self-reference.
Student Talk		8. Student Talk—Response: talk by students in response to teacher. Teacher initiates the contact or solicits student statement. 9. Student Talk—Initiation: talk by students which they initiate. If "calling on" student is only to indicate who may talk next, observer must decide whether student wanted to talk. If he did, use this category.
		10. Silence or Confusion: pauses, short periods of silence and periods of confusion in which communication cannot be understood by the observer.

Source: N. A. Flanders, *Teacher influence, pupil attitudes, and achievement.* Coop. Res. Monograph No. 12, OE 25040 (Washington: U.S. Government Printing Office, 1965).

gins by identifying the purposes of observation clearly and then designing a set of categories that fits the purposes. Only rarely will an existing set of categories be appropriate.

Ideally, teachers should design their own interaction analysis systems to be highly relevant to their own objectives and instructional procedures. Flanders' system, however, has been shown to be quite adaptable to a variety of settings. Ordinary procedure requires a teacher to visit a colleague's classroom (teachers can record sessions on video- or audiotape and undertake their own analyses) and record the sequence of behavior taking place every three seconds for a given period of time. The ordinary rate is about 20–25 observations per minute. Observation continues until a new activity begins, and the observer shifts to a new set of objectives. Obviously some training, experience, and practice are required to produce accurate data. Training films and packages are available.

The sequences of categorical behaviors recorded are analyzed as pairs. The following activities and codes are illustrative of the process (Amidon and Flanders 1963):

Activity	*Category* (See Table 16.3)
1. Students settle in seats.	10
2. Teacher: "Boys and girls, please open your social studies books to page 5."	6
3. Students search for book and page.	10
4. Teacher: "Jimmy, we are all waiting for you."	7
5. Teacher: "Jimmy, please turn your book·to page 5."	6
6. Teacher: "I know some of you had trouble with this material yesterday, but I'm sure we will find it interesting today."	1
7. Teacher: "Has anyone had a chance to think about what we discussed yesterday?"	4
8. Jeff: "I thought about Asia."	
9. Teacher: "Good, I am glad you mentioned that."	2
10. Teacher: "If I understand you completely you are suggesting . . ."	3
	10

Pairs of numbers are now tabulated on a matrix, the first number as a row entry and the second as a column entry. A·sample matrix for the foregoing codes is presented in Table 16.4. Thus, 10–6 is recorded in the cell formed by Row 10 and Column 6. The second pair, 6–10, belongs in Row 6 and Column 10, and so on.

Recorded in this fashion, data indicate both how often each type of behavior occurs (see the Totals in Table 16.4) and the sequence in which it occurs. From this information an observer can accurately reconstruct a general pattern of "cause and effect." A teacher can determine how direct or indirect his approach is by comparing the number of times his actions fall in Categories 1–4 (Indirect) and in 5–7 (Direct). He can check pupil responses to each of his actions by noting the frequency with which it is followed by behavior in Category 8 or 9. For example, pupil-initiated responses are probably more often prompted by indirect than by direct teacher behavior, and thus that behavior in Category 3 as a reaction to pupil response encourages even more pupil participation, particularly that in Category 9. In addition, comparison of Categories 2 and 7 reveals a teacher's relative use of criticism and praise. Sequences of Categories 3 and 9 indicate a teacher's ability to build on a pupil's remarks or to evoke pupil-initiated statements. Research indicates that in the average classroom someone is talking about two-thirds of the time. Two-thirds of this time it is the teacher who is talking; and two-thirds of the time a teacher is talking he is using direct influence. On

TABLE 16.4   Sample Interaction Analysis Matrix*

					Second Digit of Pair						
	Categories	1	2	3	4	5	6	7	8	9	10	Total
	1				1							1
	2			1								1
	3										1	1
	4								1			1
First Digit of Pair	5											0
	6	1									1	2
	7						1					1
	8		1									1
	9											0
	10						1	1				2
	Total	1	1	1	1	0	2	1	1	0	2	10

* Note: See Table 16.3 for a description of the categories.

the average, two-thirds of an observational session is devoted to recording teacher talk (Categories 1–7) and a little less than one-third focuses on Categories 5 through 7.

OBSERVING AND RECORDING STUDENT–STUDENT INTERACTION: SOCIOMETRIC TECHNIQUES

Sociometric techniques are methods of studying complex interpersonal relationships in social settings. The social structure of the classroom is composed of many different types of relationships, which are worthy of study for many reasons. Students who feel comfortable with their peers are likely to utilize their academic abilities more fully than those who are uncomfortable. Research evidence suggests that students who have at least several good friends in the class are likely to enjoy better mental health and learn more effectively than pupils who have few friends or are actively disliked. Gnagey (1960), for example, has shown that the social structure of the classroom interacts with teacher behavior to influence not only students' perceptions of their teacher, but their learning as well. Gnagey demonstrated experimentally that individuals, particularly males, who identify with highly influential defiant students learn less than those who identify with influential but submissive class members. Support was found for the hypothesis that a deviant's defiance of a teacher so disrupts the expectations of the other students that they learn fewer facts from a film presentation than those who see the deviant submit. Thus it behooves a teacher, in the interests of maintaining classroom control and enhancing learning, to examine patterns of influence and identification within the classroom. There is also a relationship between being liked and having positive feelings about oneself and favorable attitudes toward school. Sociometric data can also be used to study:

1. Optimal organizational patterns for effective classroom groups.
2. The social adjustment of students.
3. The social structure of student groups.
4. The influence of school and classroom practices and innovations on students' social relations.

In summary, it can be said that the study of social relationships has implications for student achievement, as well as personal adjustment. Teachers should do everything possible to enhance the emotional support pupils receive from their peers.

Collecting Sociometric Data

It is probably a good idea to limit the number of choices to five or less when posing a sociometric question to students. Students may be asked who they would prefer as:

1. Luncheon partners.
2. Seatmates.
3. Partners on a project.
4. Fellow committee members.
5. Laboratory partners.
6. Recreational partners.

The teacher may also wish to know which student the class members perceive as:

7. Most or least cooperative.
8. Most or least influential.
9. Best or worst student(s).
10. Most or least personally liked.

It is probably *not* a good idea to ask students to respond to a question eliciting active rejection (e.g., "Who would you definitely not like to sit near during class?"). Such a question tends to stimulate feelings of dissension and resentment among class members.

Directions for sociometric questions like the following might be used:

Name _____ Date _____ Class _____

We are going to need committees to work on a _____ project. Each of you knows with whom you enjoy working most. These may be the same persons with whom you work in other classes, or they may be different. Put your name at the top of the page. Opposite the number "1" below, put the name of the boy or girl with whom you would most like to work, opposite "2" your second choice, and opposite "3" your third choice. I will keep all of these choices in mind and try to arrange the committees so that everyone will be with one or more of the three people named. No one will see your choices except me. You may choose a boy or girl who is absent today if you want to. Write down the last name as well as the first so that I will be sure to know whom you mean. We will probably get started on the project in about six weeks.

It is extremely important that the confidentiality of responses be respected.

In choosing a stimulus situation (e.g., work group, seating partner), Gronlund (1959) cautions us to make sure that the situation:

1. Is clearly defined.
2. Is an activity or situation with which the group is familiar.
3. Is an activity or situation in which the group will have a genuine opportunity to become involved.
4. Is general enough not to require specific skills or knowledges.
5. Is based on relationships that are strong, fundamental, and relatively permanent.

6. Allows for reciprocal choice and mutual association among group members.

Summarizing Sociometric Data

Before discussing sample sociometric data, we need to consider briefly some common sociometric terms. Following are some selected terms, their definitions, and symbolic representations:

Term	Definition	Representation
Star	A student who receives a large number of choices, or a number larger than chance. In three choice situations, better than chance is 7; in four choice situations, it is 8; in five choice situations, it is 9 (Bronfenbrenner 1945).	
Mutual choice	Students who choose each other.	
Isolate	A student who receives no positive choices (e.g., student C).	
Rejectee	A student who is actively rejected by group members (if rejection data are gathered).	
Neglectee	A student who receives very few positive choices (e.g., student C).	
Sociometric clique	A number of individuals who choose each other but make very few choices outside the group.	
Sociometric cleavage	A lack of sociometric choices between two or more subgroups, e. g., boys and girls.	

Figure 16.2 is a summary of sociometric data gathered from 22 students at Cedar Creek School, who were asked to identify three classmates with whom they would most like to work on a project. The matrix of Figure 16.2 represents the usual initial step in tabulating sociometric data. The choices of all individuals quizzed (N) are tabulated in an N × N matrix, with the names recorded in the same order, beginning at the top left-hand corner, across the top and down the left-hand margin of the matrix. A choice is usually indicated by a plus sign (+), rejection by a minus sign (−), and a mutual choice by a circled plus sign (⊕). Thus, if student 7 chooses student 10, a "+" is placed in the cell formed by the intersection of Row 7 and Column 10. Several facts are immediately obvious from an examination of Figure 16.5. Two individuals can be identified as "stars": students 10 and 15. These individuals are quite popular with their classmates. Harriet (student 17) is an isolate. It also appears that the girls like Gil. Students 3, 5, 16, 18, and 22 are neglectees.

It is argued by some authorities that the complex structure of the group is obscured by relying on a simple summary representation such as that in Figure 16.2. Some suggest that a *sociogram*—a graphic picture of the social relations among group members—better represents sociometric data. Males are usually symbolically differentiated from females in the sociogram. The plotting of a sociogram like Figure 16.3 (based on the data in Figure 16.2) will probably have to be undertaken several times to reduce the crossing of lines sufficiently to present an uncluttered picture. Placements will have to be arranged and rearranged to depict interrelationships as clearly as possible. Some experts prefer the *target sociogram,* which uses four concentric circles. The stars are placed in the innermost circle, and the isolates in the outermost ring. The ring next to the innermost circle might contain individuals who receive more choices than they give (or more than the mean number of choices per student), and the next-to-outer ring students who make more choices than they receive (or who receive less than the mean number of choices per student).

Forsyth and Katz (1946) have suggested an alternative to the sociogram which they call the *sociomatrix*. The development of a sociomatrix requires rearranging the rows and columns of the original summary-data matrix so that the structure of the group becomes more readily apparent. In the first step, the rows and columns of any two students with a mutual choice are shifted to the top left-hand corner of the matrix. Next, mutual choices with the original two are shifted to the upper left-hand corner. After all mutual choices have been positioned, a search is made for those who choose or are chosen by one of the mutual-choice students. The process of rearrangement is continued on the principle that anyone chosen by at least half the members of the subgroup may be added to it. When no further persons can be found satisfying this criterion, the subgroup is considered complete.

Person Chosen

		1	2	3	4	5	6	7	8	9	10	11	12	13	14	15	16	17	18	19	20	21	22
1.	Gloria S.						⊕			+					+								
2.	Reese W.									+	+									⊕			
3.	Myrtle R.									⊕					+						+		
4.	Lynn F.						+	+														⊕	
5.	Bob W.												+			+							⊕
6.	Kate M.	⊕								⊕												⊕	
7.	Ed P.						+		⊕		+												
8.	Dave P.							⊕				⊕	⊕										
9.	Mary P.			⊕			⊕								+								
10.	Ray B.								⊕			⊕		⊕									
11.	Jim E.								⊕		⊕			⊕									
12.	Bill F.										+					⊕					⊕		
13.	Mike P.										⊕	⊕						⊕					
14.	Libby S.												+			+					⊕		
15.	Gil S.				+								⊕								⊕		
16.	Marylan J.		+													+		⊕					
17.	Harriet N.	+			+											+							
18.	Jan A.															+	⊕			+			
19.	Len K.		⊕								+			⊕									
20.	Ann F.												⊕		⊕	⊕							
21.	Betty H.				⊕		⊕	+															
22.	Benton J.				⊕					+						+							
Number of Times Chosen		2	2	1	3	1	5	2	4	4	8	3	4	3	4	8	1	0	1	3	4	2	1
Number of Mutual Choices		1	1	1	1	1	3	1	3	2	3	3	2	3	1	2	1	0	1	2	3	2	1
Number of Choices by Same Sex		2	1	1	2	1	4	1	3	3	8	3	2	3	4	3	1	0	1	2	2	2	1
Number of Choices by Opposite Sex		0	1	0	1	0	1	1	1	1	0	0	2	0	0	5	0	0	0	1	2	0	1

FIGURE 16.2.   Choice Matrix of 22 Students Asked to Identify 3 Classmates with Whom They Would Like to Work on a Project

Source: Adapted with the permission of the publishers from K. M. Evans, *Sociometry and education* (New York: Humanities Press; London: Routledge and Kegan Paul, 1962).

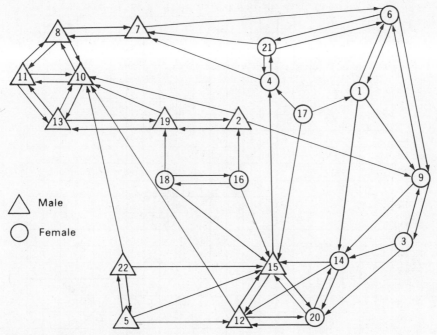

FIGURE 16.3. Sociogram of Data in Figure 16.2

Source: Adapted with the permission of the publishers from K. M. Evans, *Sociometry and education* (New York: Humanities Press; London: Routledge and Kegan Paul, 1962).

Additional subgroups are constructed in the same way, beginning with two individuals who make a positive mutual choice and are not included in the first subgroup. Thus a series of subgroups is identified, as are a number of individuals who do not belong to any subgroup.

The data in Figure 16.2 have been rearranged into a sociomatrix in Figure 16.4. In addition to the differentiation of groups on the basis of the common desire to work together on a project, several different kinds of groups are evident in Figure 16.4. In the upper left-hand corner we note an all-male group, in this case bound by common recreational interests. The next subgroup of two females has musical interests in common. Students 5 and 22 enjoy tennis. The fourth subgroup interacts socially. The final subgroup shares common academic concerns. Definite social cleavage is apparent in the class, as is the presence of several cliques.

Teacher Activities Suggested by Sociometric Data

Fox, Luszki, and Schmuck (1966) have suggested several directions for remedial action based on a teacher's study of sociometric data.

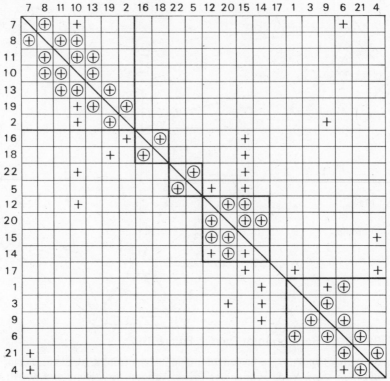

FIGURE 16.4. Sociomatrix of Data in Figure 16.2

Source: Adapted with the permission of the publishers from K. M. Evans, *Sociometry and education* (New York: Humanities Press; London: Routledge and Kegan Paul, 1962).

Obviously, the rejected and neglected students need to be worked with directly. Interaction between the student, teacher(s), parents, and perhaps counselors might be in order. It might be justifiable to explain to the student in confidence the general basis of his rejection. After a mutually respectful relationship between the neglected or rejected student and the teacher is established, it may be gradually expanded to include more and more students, until a reasonable degree of integration is accomplished.

Role-playing is a particularly useful technique aimed at heightening an individual's awareness of the feelings of others.

Restrained healthy competition might be one approach to reducing social cleavage. Assigning members of initially antagonistic subgroups to a project of mutual interest can also promote mutual respect. Assignment to specific projects can do much to change patterns of interrelationships.

It is probably wise for the teacher at some point to take a "general human resources inventory" of the group to demonstrate that everyone in the class has some valuable skill, strength, and knowledge. The class needs the opportunity to perceive the variety of individual differences contained within the classroom.

Another suggestion is to assign "peer helpers"—individuals who are perceived as successful, influential, well-liked, or cooperative—to work with the "low-status" students. Students with whom the teacher has difficulty communicating may be effectively influenced by peers.

Barclay (1968) has suggested an interesting combined use of student-student and teacher-student data. He proposes gathering sociometric data from students on a variable such as "cooperativeness," and having the teacher rate the students on the same variable. A scatter diagram is plotted for the sociometric and teacher ratings, and then arbitrarily simplified to four quadrants like that represented below:

High Socio- metric	QUADRANT I High Sociometric Low Teacher Rating	QUADRANT II High Sociometric High Teacher Rating
Low Socio- metric	QUADRANT III Low Sociometric Low Teacher Rating	QUADRANT IV Low Sociometric High Teacher Rating
	Low Teacher Rating	High Teacher Rating

Barclay's research suggests that males in Quadrant I tend to be impulsive, and intent upon entertaining the class but harassing the teacher. Quadrant IV boys tend to be well-liked by the teacher but disliked by their peers—the stereotypical teacher's pets. Members of this group tend to talk and act like adults, and yet not be truly exceptional culturally or intellectually. In many cases, they present a façade for the teacher. A large number of dropouts, particularly female, come from Quadrant III. The comparison of data in this manner can elicit many insights into individual and group behavior.

STUDENT OBSERVATION AND EVALUATION OF TEACHERS

The movement toward "accountability" in education, particularly higher education, places heavy demands on administrators and educational evaluators to provide data useful in assessing teaching effectiveness (Miller 1972). Student evaluations of teaching effectiveness, though insufficient in themselves, can serve as useful inputs to the assessment system. Costin, Greenough, and Menges (1971) reviewed a considerable body of literature indicating that objective ratings of faculty by students can be a valid index of teaching effectiveness, particularly if such data are accumulated over time.

A useful scale for student evaluations of teacher performance has been developed by Lyle Schoenfeldt of the University of Georgia. After an extensive survey of commercially available instruments and those used at schools,, colleges, and universities throughout the country, Schoenfeldt selected 38 items representing the primary dimensions of teacher performance reported by Deshpande, Webb, and Marks (1970). A Likert-type rating scale was applied to 36 of the items to indicate frequency of occurrence. The remaining two items require summary judgments of the course and instructor respectively. A copy of the University of Georgia Faculty-Course Evaluation Form is presented in Table 16.5.

TABLE 16.5   University of Georgia Faculty-Course Evaluation Form

This questionnaire gives you an opportunity to express anonymously your views of this course and the way it has been taught. The purpose of obtaining the information is to assist in the improvement of instruction. It will serve this purpose best if you answer the items carefully and honestly. Proceed as follows:

A. Indicate the course and instructor at the top of the answer sheet.

B. Read each statement carefully and indicate your response by blackening the appropriate square with a soft lead pencil.

C. In rare cases where you believe the statement does not apply or where you feel you do not have sufficient information to make an estimate, leave the statement blank.

D. Note that you must proceed *across* and not down the answer sheet.

E. The instructor will designate a student to collect the answer sheets and return them to the departmental secretary.

1. What is your sex?   1. Male   2. Female

2. What is your class standing?   1. Fresh   2. Soph   3. Jr   4. Sr   5. Grad

3. Which one of the following was your most important reason for selecting this course?
   1. It was required   2. Advisor's recommendation   3. Subject was of interest
   4. Teacher's excellent reputation   5. Thought I could make a good grade

4. What is your present grade point average?
   1. less than 2.0   2. 2.0–2.49   3. 2.5–2.99   4. 3.0–3.49   5. 3.5–4.0

5. What grade do you expect to get in this course?   1. A   2. B   3. C   4. D   5. F

In the items below, estimate how frequently you feel the following occurred.
   1. Almost *never*   2. *Infrequently*   3. *Occasionally*   4. *Often*   5. Almost *always*

6. The instructor was willing to give individual assistance.

TABLE 16.5 *(Continued)*

7. The instructor encouraged students to think for themselves.
8. The instructor gave tests that were reasonable in length.
9. The instructor repeated materials students did not understand.
10. The instructor spent time on unimportant and irrelevant materials.
11. The instructor gave helpful demonstrations of principles being discussed.
12. The instructor pitched the presentation above the heads of the students.
13. The instructor encouraged students to ask questions.
14. The instructor tried to get you to see beyond the limits of the course.
15. The instructor used teaching aids such as chalkboards, slides, films, and models, to advantage.
16. The instructor was well prepared each day.
17. The instructor found and reported answers to questions he could not answer immediately.
18. The instructor clearly described the grading procedures.
19. Test content was representative of assigned material.
20. The instructor took time to help students after class.
21. The instructor was fair in grading.
22. The instructor stimulated the intellectual curiosity of the students.
23. The instructor was enthusiastic about the subject.
24. The instructor was confused about basic principles.
25. The instructor clearly indicated what material tests would cover.
26. The instructor kept the course moving at a steady pace.
27. The instructor supplemented the text with materials from other sources.
28. The instructor tried to stimulate creative abilities.
29. The instructor gave advice on how to study for the course.
30. The instructor assigned a lot of burdensome busy work.
31. The instructor gave presentations that were logically arranged.
32. The instructor tried to increase the interest of class members in the subject.
33. The instructor's information seemed out of date.
34. The instructor used illustrations based on practical experience.
35. In this class I felt free to express my opinions.
36. The instructor could not explain text materials that were confusing to students.
37. The instructor demanded an unreasonable amount of work.
38. The instructor seemed well informed about the material presented.
39. The instructor was friendly.
40. The instructor explained how much each test would count toward the final grade.
41. The instructor recognized students' limitations in understanding new material.

For the final two items use the following scale. 1. Poor 2. Fair 3. Good 4. Very Good 5. Superior

42. How would you rate the over-all value of this course?
43. How would you rate your instructor in general (all-round) teaching ability?

Source: Developed by Dr. Lyle F. Schoenfeldt. Copyright © 1972 by the University of Georgia. Reprinted by permission of the author.

The instrument was refined on the basis of responses from approximately 5,000 undergraduate and graduate students on the performances of 222 instructors. A factor analysis yielded five factors judged to be most relevant to the evaluation of teaching effectiveness. These factors, found to be moderately related to each other, are summarized in Table 16.6. Initial feedback included (1) item means and standard deviations for each department (e.g., English, Psychology, History), (2) item means and standard deviations for each instructor's class(es), (3) the instructor's score on the five dimensions of teaching effectiveness, and (4) a total score. The total score is a weighted average of the several scales, the weights having been determined by a survey of faculty judgments. Each faculty member was asked to distribute 100 points among the five dimensions in such a way as to reflect his opinion on the relative importance of each dimension. The resulting average weights were: Subject Organization—35, Motivation-Stimulation—30, Instructor Relations—16, Work Load—10, and Grading—9. The last two types

TABLE 16.6   Major Correlated Dimensions of University of Georgia Faculty-Course Evaluation Form

Dimension Label	Content Emphasis	Items Making Primary Contribution to Dimension*
1. Subject Organization and Competence	Instructor preparation and information, clarity and logic of presentations.	10(−), 16, 17, 23, 24(−), 26 31, 36(−), 38, 42, 43
2. Motivation-Stimulation	Instructor's encouragement of students to ask questions, think and see beyond limits of course content.	7, 11, 13, 14, 22, 28, 32, 34, 35
3. Instructor-Student Relations	Provision for individual assistance to students, friendliness, and willingness to repeat material.	6, 9, 20, 39
4. Reasonable Work Load and Tests	Reasonable amount of homework was not "busy work", and use of tests which were fair, relevant and appropriate.	8, 12(−), 19, 30(−), 37(−)
5. Clearness of Grading Procedures	Specific grade requirements are spelled out, weights of tests and other contributions are described, and study habits suggested.	18, 29, 40

Source: Developed by Dr. Lyle F. Schoenfeldt. Copyright © 1972 by the University of Georgia. Reprinted by permission of the author.

* Note: See Figure 16.8 for specific items. All items load positively unless otherwise indicated by a minus sign (−). For negatively weighted items, the scoring weights should be reversed, i.e., Almost Never = 5, Infrequently = 4, etc. Items 15, 21, 25, 27, 33, and 41 did not logically or empirically load sufficiently high on any dimensions.

of scores (dimensions and total) are reported in standard score form, with a mean of 500 and a standard deviation of 100. It is possible, then, for an instructor to examine his ratings relative to departmental, college, school, or university averages, and to keep track of his performance over several quarters or semesters. The development of institutional norms would also provide valuable data.

Although developed for use with university faculties, the Faculty-Course Evaluation Form can easily be adapted for use in the public schools.

OBSERVING AND RECORDING LEARNING PERFORMANCES, PROCEDURES, PROCESSES, AND SKILLS

A great deal of instructional time, particularly in the early grades, is devoted to the development of specific performance skills. Examples are laboratory work, handwriting, physical skills, speaking, social skills, music, artistic and dramatic skills, writing, and a variety of vocational skills. We are, of course, interested in the products of learning, but we are also concerned with *how* the student arrives at his product. Often the development of a technique or skill can be considered an end in itself or so intimately tied to the product as to be inseparable.

The key to performance measurement is *simulation*; most paper-and-pencil devices suffer from artificiality. Developmental situations in which an individual can exhibit real-life behaviors will generally increase the relevance and accuracy of the assessment. In educational settings, one must consider practical limitations, and the development of a simulation test therefore involves compromises. Fitzpatrick and Morrison (1971) note that in making these compromises one must:

1. Determine through careful analysis the critical aspects of the criterion situation it is desired to simulate in view of the purpose of the simulation.
2. Determine the minimum fidelity needed for each aspect and estimate the worth of increasing fidelity beyond the minimum.
3. Develop a scheme for representing a reasonably comprehensive set of aspects, within the limits of available resources.
4. Adjust comprehensiveness and fidelity, compromising as necessary to achieve a balancing of considerations but with primary attention to the aspects shown by analysis to be most critical for the purpose at hand.

The most important step in developing a simulation exercise is identifying the criterion, which usually involves a task analysis. Some major aspects of a task analysis are:

1. Developing a simulation that represents the entire performance as accurately as possible.

2. Specifying those elements in the task that are of greatest relevance to the quality of performance. Some of these elements might be (Bradfield and Moredock 1957):

    a. Speed of performance.

    b. Accuracy of performance.

    c. Number and seriousness of procedural errors.

    d. Errors in following instructions.

    e. Discrimination in selecting appropriate tools or equipment.

    f. Economy of effort (amount of "lost motion").

    g. Timing (in the use of machinery or physical performances such as gymnastics).

    h. Intensity or force (in sports).

    i. Coherence and appropriateness of the sequence of steps followed.

3. Selecting elements for observation in proportion to their emphasis in instruction or training.

4. Evaluating these elements in light of the conditions necessary for accurate measurability.

5. Selecting those elements that require minimal time and expense.

The task analysis, then, basically involves identifying those elements that are to be measured and scored.

There are many types of simulation tests. Fitzpatrick and Morrison (1971) have identified four major types:

Type	Characteristics
Situation Tests	Examinee role-plays in lifelike setting, which may be social or involve apparatus.
In-Basket Tests	Examinee is presented data, e.g., letters, records, or memoranda, and asked to simulate decision-making or administrative behavior. Simulates on-the-job performance.
Work-Sample Tests	A standardized job-relevant task is presented, and performance is observed. Task is usually a duplicate of actual criterion performance, e.g., operating a key-punch or typing.
Problem-Solving Games	Such games are frequently used in business, industry, and the military to assess problem-solving skills. Competition with a standard is usually involved.

In summary, the development of a performance simulation test is similar to that of any test, and includes the following steps:

1.   Analysis of the desired performance.

2.   Identification of crucial and representative elements for observation.

3.   Selection of an appropriate simulation situation.

4.   Specification of the sequence of tasks that incorporate these crucial elements.

5.   Specification of the materials needed by the examinee to accomplish the tasks.

6.   Preparation of directions for examinee.

7.   Development of methods for recording results of simulation.

Following are four examples of performance tests in a variety of subject areas:

Skill in Using a Microscope

In this classic performance test, developed many years ago by Ralph Tyler, the instructor uses a checklist (see Table 16.7) to observe the sequence of actions required for proper identification of a specimen. The teacher is able to note not only what the student does correctly, but also the kinds of errors he makes. Such data have diagnostic implications, and can be used to correct the student's actions.

TABLE 16.7   Checklist of Student Reactions to an Object Under the Microscope

STUDENT'S ACTIONS	Sequence of Actions	STUDENT'S ACTIONS (Continued)	Sequence of Actions
a. Takes slide	1	m. Adjusts cover with finger	
b. Wipes slide with lens paper	2	n. Wipes off surplus fluid	
		o. Places slide on stage	6
c. Wipes slide with cloth		p. Looks through eyepiece with right eye	
d. Wipes slide with finger			
e. Moves bottle of culture along the table		q. Looks through eyepiece with left eye	7
f. Places drop or two of culture on slide	3	r. Turns to objective of lowest power	9
g. Adds more culture		s. Turns to low-power objective	21
h. Adds few drops of water			
i. Hunts for cover glasses	4	t. Turns to high-power objective	
j. Wipes cover glass with lens paper	5	u. Holds one eye closed	8
k. Wipes cover with cloth		v. Looks for light	
l. Wipes cover with finger		w. Adjusts concave mirror	

Source: R. W. Tyler, A test of skill in using a microscope. *Educational Research Bulletin* 9 (1930): 493–496. Reprinted by permission of the author.

	STUDENT'S ACTIONS (Continued)	Sequence of Actions
x.	Adjusts plane mirror	___
y.	Adjusts diaphragm	___
z.	Does not touch diaphragm	_10_
aa.	With eye at eyepiece turns down coarse adjustment	_11_
ab.	Breaks cover glass	_12_
ac.	Breaks slide	___
ad.	With eye away from eyepiece turns down coarse adjustment	___
ae.	Turns up coarse adjustment a great distance	_13, 22_
af.	With eye at eyepiece turns down fine adjustment a great distance	_14, 23_
ag.	With eye away from eyepiece turns down fine adjustment a great distance	_15_
ah.	Turns up fine adjustment screw a great distance	___
ai.	Turns fine adjustment screw a few turns	___
aj.	Removes slide from stage	_16_
ak.	Wipes objective with lens paper	___
al.	Wipes objective with cloth	___
am.	Wipes objective with finger	_17_
an.	Wipes eyepiece with lens paper	___
ao.	Wipes eyepiece with cloth	___
ap.	Wipes eyepiece with finger	_18_
aq.	Makes another mount	___
ar.	Takes another microscope	___
as.	Finds object	___
at.	Pauses for an interval	___
au.	Asks, "What do you want me to do?"	___
av.	Asks whether to use high power	___
aw.	Says, "I'm satisfied"	___
ax.	Says that the mount is all right for his eye	___
ay.	Says he cannot do it	_19, 24_
az.	Told to start new mount	___
aaa.	Directed to find object under low power	_20_

	STUDENT'S ACTIONS (Continued)	Sequence of Actions
aab.	Directed to find object under high power	___

	NOTICEABLE CHARACTERISTICS OF STUDENT'S BEHAVIOR	Sequence of Actions
a.	Awkward in movements	___
b.	Obviously dexterous in movements	___
c.	Slow and deliberate	_X_
d.	Very rapid	___
e.	Fingers tremble	___
f.	Obviously perturbed	___
g.	Obviously angry	___
h.	Does not take work seriously	___
i.	Unable to work without specific directions	_X_
j.	Obviously satisfied with his unsuccessful efforts	_X_

	SKILLS IN WHICH STUDENT NEEDS FURTHER TRAINING	Sequence of Actions
a.	In cleaning objective	_X_
b.	In cleaning eyepiece	_X_
c.	In focusing low power	_X_
d.	In focusing high power	_X_
e.	In adjusting mirror	_X_
f.	In using diaphragm	_X_
g.	In keeping both eyes open	_X_
h.	In protecting slide and objective from breaking by careless focusing	_X_

	CHARACTERIZATION OF THE STUDENT'S MOUNT	Sequence of Actions
a.	Poor light	_X_
b.	Poor focus	___
c.	Excellent mount	___
d.	Good mount	___
e.	Fair mount	___
f.	Poor mount	___
g.	Very poor mount	___
h.	Nothing in view but a thread in his eyepiece	___
i.	Something on objective	___
j.	Smeared lens	_X_
k.	Unable to find object	_X_

Skill in Driving an Automobile

It is one thing to be able to answer a series of paper-and-pencil questions about the operation of an automobile, and quite another to accomplish the task. Many psychomotor behaviors and skills require actual demonstration. The checklist in Table 16.8 is one approach to the description of driving performance.

TABLE 16.8   Checklist for Driving Performance

Aspect observed	Classifications of effectiveness		
Student posture			
Seat adjustment made	Yes	Questionable	No
Mirror adjustment made	Yes	Questionable	No
Foot position (dimmer switch and accelerator)	Correct	Par. Correct	Incorrect
Hand position (10 and 12 o'clock)	Correct	Par. Correct	Incorrect
Posture (erect and behind wheel)	Correct	Par. Correct	Incorrect
Putting automobile in motion			
Releases handbrake	Yes	Questionable	No
Starts auto forward	Smoothly	Unevenly	Jerkily
Shifts gears (low to second)	Quietly	Some Noise	Grinding
Shifts gears (second to high)	Quietly	Some Noise	Grinding
Steering in road	Direct	Weaving	Assistance Required
Bringing automobile to a stop			
Puts hand out and down	Precise	Understand-able	Unidenti-fiable
Slows car down	Smoothly	Unevenly	Jerkily
Brakes to a stop	Smoothly	Unevenly	Jerkily
Sets hand brake	Yes	Questionable	No
Parks car off pavement	Yes	Questionable	No
Showing consideration for others			
When pulling out from curb	Yes	Questionable	No
When stopping	Yes	Questionable	No
Shows respect for rights of others	Yes	Questionable	No
When in question as to others' rights, relinquishes his	Yes	Questionable	No
Response to other drivers' signals and tolerant of their errors	Yes	Questionable	No

Source: J. M. Bradfield and H. S. Moredock, *Measurement and evaluation in education* (New York: Macmillan, 1957), p. 346. Reprinted by permission of J. M. Bradfield.

Skill in Softball Batting

Many skills developed in physical education classes lend themselves to direct observation. A method of evaluating one of these skills is presented in Table 16.9. The use of such a checklist by an experienced observer can yield efficient and accurate results.

TABLE 16.9 Sample Checklist for Softball Batting Form

| Date | Rater's initials | Player's name _____ |
| | | Captain's name _____ |

Instructions: Rate the player each time he bats. Place a tally mark in the space which precedes the best description of player's form in each of six categories. Indicate your observation of errors in the right-hand half of the page, again with a tally mark. Write in any additional errors and add comments below.

1. *Grip*   Errors
   _____ good   _____ Hands too far apart
   _____ fair   _____ Wrong hand on top
   _____ poor   _____ Hands too far from end of bat

2. *Preliminary stance*
   _____ good   _____ Stands too near plate
   _____ fair   _____ Stands too far away
   _____ poor   _____ Rear foot closer to plate than
                                                                          forward foot
                                                  _____ Stands too far forward
                                                  _____ Stands too far backward
                                                  _____ Bat not in readiness position

3. *Stride or footwork*
   _____ good   _____ Fails to step forward
   _____ fair   _____ Fails to transfer weight
   _____ poor   _____ Lifts back foot from ground

4. *Pivot or body twist*
   _____ good   _____ Fails to twist body
   _____ fair   _____ Fails to wind up
   _____ poor   _____ Has less than 90° of pivot

5. *Arm movement or swing*
   _____ good   _____ Arms held too close to body
   _____ fair   _____ Rear elbow held too far up
   _____ poor   _____ Bat not held parallel to ground

6. *General* (Eyes on ball, judgment of pitcher, etc.)
   _____ good   _____ Jerky action
   _____ fair   _____ Tries too hard
   _____ poor   _____ Poor selection of bat
                                                  _____ Lacks confidence

Source: M. G. Scott and E. French, *Better teaching through testing* (New York: A. S. Barnes, 1945). Reprinted by permission of the publisher.

Skill in Public Speaking

It is often the case that some raters are more accurate than others, but we frequently do not know their identities. One method of offsetting this potential source of error is consensus rating, which involves the use of a standard set of observation scales and several raters. A scale like that in Table 16.10 might be used. After all individual ratings have been recorded, they are collected and pooled. Mean ratings for each scale or a total may be used for each speaker.

TABLE 16.10   Sample Scale for Evaluating a Speaking Performance

Directions: Evaluate the speaker by circling the number which most nearly represents his performance on each of the specific aspects listed below. For superior performance circle 4, above-average performance 3, average performance 2, below-average performance 1, and unsatisfactory performance 0.

	Item	*Rating*				
1.	Rapport with audience	4	3	2	1	0
2.	Enthusiastic, interesting presentation	4	3	2	1	0
3.	Effective organization of material	4	3	2	1	0
4.	Clarity of presentation	4	3	2	1	0
5.	Correct grammar usage	4	3	2	1	0
6.	Good word choice	4	3	2	1	0
7.	Adequate knowledge of subject	4	3	2	1	0
8.	Significance of material presented	4	3	2	1	0
9.	Good stage presence	4	3	2	1	0
10.	Appropriate gestures	4	3	2	1	0

Total effectiveness of presentation (Sum of all ratings)

Source: Fig. 6.1, Scale for evaluating a speaking performance (p. 79). From *Teacher-made tests* by John A. Green (Harper & Row, 1963). Reprinted by permission of the publisher.

ASSESSING PRODUCTS

Many of the difficulties encountered in assessing interpersonal relationships and performances are also met when attempting to measure the quality of student products. Such factors as the physical effort required to construct measures, complexity, administrative difficulties, and questions of validity and scoring are among the more prominent considerations. Although many products have physical dimensions that may be measured (e.g., size, weight, number of errors, color), a number of more qualitative dimensions also need to be assessed. Such dimensions might be the flavor of a cake, the composition of a painting, or the neatness of handwriting. There is no doubt that aesthetic properties are more difficult to assess than physical attributes.

Process and product are intimately related, as was noted previously. The decision to focus on product or process, or a combination of both, rests on the answers to the following questions:

1. Are the steps involved in arriving at the product either indeterminate or covert?

2. Are the important characteristics of the product apparent, and can they be measured objectively and accurately?

3. Is the effectiveness of the performance to be discerned in the product itself?

4. Is evaluation of the procedures leading to the product impractical?

If the answer to each of these four questions is "yes," the teacher may wish to focus his assessment efforts on product evaluation.

Products can be readily assessed by the careful application of rating scales and checklists. (The reader is urged to review pages 379–384 on the development of these recording methods.) The usefulness of any product assessment will depend on the accuracy with which its distinctive features have been delineated and defined. Assuming that the critical elements have been identified and appropriately weighted, observational scales like the following three may be used to collect data.

TABLE 16.11 Rating Scale for Evaluating Freehand Art Drawing

	D	C	B	A
1. *Drawing*				
a. Accuracy of proportion *or* Suitability of distortion				
b. Relationship of proportions				
c. Stability of subjects				
d. Ease of interpretation				
2. *Composition*				
a. Balance				
b. Rhythm				
c. Spatial relations				
d. Textural interest				
3. *Feel for Medium*				
a. Line quality				
b. Tone quality				
4. *Subject Matter*				
a. Interest				
b. Arrangement				

Key to Variations

D—Drawing shows no regard for aspect being judged.
C—Aspect not well utilized.
B—Aspect noteworthy, but room for improvement at this grade level.
A—Aspect adds materially to the excellence of the picture.

Source: J. M. Bradfield and H. S. Moredock, *Measurement and evaluation in education* (New York: Macmillan, 1957), p. 345. Reprinted by permission of J. M. Bradfield.

Assessing the Quality of an Artistic Product

Assessment in the artistic and aesthetic areas of human activity is difficult at best and nonexistent at worst. The problem posed by the wide variety of relevant variables is compounded by the basically subjective nature of aesthetic standards. The assessment task can, however, be approached systematically and directly. One direct approach is illustrated by the rating chart in Table 16.11.

This chart might be used to assess a high-school freehand drawing using pencil and charcoal. The number of elements and the number and specificity of the quality categories might be expanded, but an excellent start has been made.

TABLE 16.12 Sample Rating Scales for Nail-Fastening

(1) *Straightness*	1 2 3 4 5 6 7 8 9 10
	Are nails driven straight, heads square with wood, no evidence of bending?
(2) *Hammer marks*	1 2 3 4 5 6 7 8 9 10
	Is wood free of hammer marks around nails?
(3) *Splitting*	1 2 3 4 5 6 7 8 9 10
	Is wood free of splits radiating from nail holes?
(4) *Depth*	1 2 3 4 5 6 7 8 9 10
	Are depths of nails uniform and of pleasing appearance?
(5) *Spacing*	1 2 3 4 5 6 7 8 9 10
	Are nails spaced too close or too far apart?
(6) *Utility*	1 2 3 4 5 6 7 8 9 10
	Will the nails hold?

Source: Dorothy C. Adkins, *Construction and analysis of achievement tests* (Washington: Government Printing Office, 1947), p. 231. Reprinted by permission of the author.

Assessing Woodshop Products

A variety of mechanical devices is available for measuring the quality of shop products, including gauges, rulers, T-squares, and calipers. However, mechanical devices alone cannot measure all significant product characteristics. Almost any metal, plastic, or wood product has many qualitative dimensions. A rating scale useful in assessing the adequacy of nail fastenings has been developed by Dorothy C. Adkins and is presented in Table 16.12. The use of ten categories may require overly fine discriminations, but the general analytic approach to rating this fairly simple skill has much to recommend it.

Assessing Food Products

An efficient scale for evaluating a specific food product, namely waffles, is presented in Table 16.13. Note that both physical and aesthetic qualities are rated. The systematic summary of such data should be useful both for assessment and for teaching purposes.

TABLE 16.13   Food Score Card for Waffles

[Rate on scale from 1 to 3]	1	2	3	Score
1. Appearance	Irregular shape	Regular shape		1. _____
2. Color	Dark brown or pale	Uniform, golden brown		2. _____
3. Moisture Content	Soggy interior or too dry	Slightly moist interior		3. _____
4. Lightness	Heavy	Light		4. _____
5. Tenderness	Tough or hard	Tender; crisp crust		5. _____
6. Taste and Flavor	Too sweet or flat or taste of leavening agent or fat	Pleasing flavor		6. _____
			Total Score	_____

Source: Clara M. Brown, *Food score cards: Waffles,* no. 53 (Minneapolis: University of Minnesota Press, 1940).

SUGGESTED READINGS

Ahmann, J. S., and Glock, M. D. *Evaluating pupil growth: Principles of tests and measurements,* 4th ed. Boston: Allyn and Bacon, 1971. Chapter 7, on judging procedures and products, contains illustrations from a variety of subject-matter areas. Such topics as sociometric techniques, anecdotal records, rating scales, and observational methods are considered in Chapter 13.

Almy, Millie, and Cunningham, Ruth. *Ways of studying children.* New York: Teachers College Press, 1959. This manual on systematic independent child study is a particularly good reference on the application of informal observational methods and the meaning of the resulting data.

Amidon, E. J., and Hough, J. B. *Interaction analysis: Theory, research and application.* Reading, Mass.: Addison-Wesley, 1967. This collection of 30 articles deals with one of the most significant methodological breakthroughs to occur in educational research and evaluation during the last half-century.

Bonney, M. E., and Hampleman, R. S. *Personal-social evaluation techniques.* New York: Center for Applied Research in Education, 1962. Such topics as observational methods, informal self-expression techniques, sociometric techniques, personality ratings, and the evaluation of class attitudes are covered in this very readable book. The section on observational technique and anecdotal records is particularly strong.

Fitzpatrick, R., and Morrison, E. J. Performance and product evaluation. In *Educational Measurement,* ed. R. L. Thorndike. Washington: American Council on Education, 1970. Chapter 9 presents illustrations of methods that can be employed in measuring achievement performance tests. Suggestions for the development and scoring of such tests are also summarized.

Fox, R.; Luszki, Margaret B.; and Schmuck, R. *Diagnosing classroom learning environments.* Chicago: Science Research Associates, 1966. Describes a series of 23 diagnostic tools for gathering reliable classroom data that will assist the teacher in changing the learning environment.

Guilford, J. P. *Psychometric methods,* 2nd ed. New York: McGraw-Hill, 1954. Chapter 11 is one of the most comprehensive descriptions of rating methods available, and surveys the relevant research findings.

Gronlund, N. E. *Measurement and evaluation in teaching,* 2nd ed. New York: Macmillan, 1971. Chapters 16 and 17, "Evaluating Learning and Development: Observational Techniques," and "Evaluating Learning and Development: Peer Appraisal and Self-Report," of this excellent text contain some very useful suggestions and summaries of guidelines and principles. The section of Chapter 16 on anecdotal records is particularly informative.

Green, J. A. *Introduction to measurement and evaluation.* New York: Dodd, Mead, 1970. An introduction to the assessment of the social factors that influence learning can be found in Chapter 8, and some fine illustrations of methods of evaluating learning products and procedures are discussed in Chapter 12.

Gronlund, N. E. *Sociometry in the classroom.* New York: Harper and Row, 1959. A comprehensive integration and interpretation of the sociometric literature and its meaning for education, this book has a definite how-to-do-it flavor.

Helmstadter, G. C. *Principles of psychological measurement.* New York: Appleton-Century-Crofts, 1969. Chapter 8 is a very understandable introduction to the types, development, and application of rating scales.

Horrocks, J. E., and Schoonover, Thelma. *Measurement for teachers.* Columbus, Ohio: Charles Merrill, 1968. Chapter 20, "The Measurement of Social Behaviors," describes some of the standardized measures of social behavior available from commercial publishers.

Long, N. J. *Direct help to the classroom teacher.* Washington: School Research Program of the Washington School of Psychiatry, 1962. This introduction to an assessment system aimed at classroom behavior has immediate implications for classroom management.

Medley, D. M., and Mitzel, H. E. Measuring classroom behavior by systematic observation. In *Handbook of Research on Teaching*, ed. N. L. Gage. Chicago: Rand McNally, 1963. Chapter 6 surveys the historical development of observational methods, reviews relevant research, and presents excerpts from representative instruments.

Moreno, J. L. *et al. The sociometry reader*. Glencoe, Ill.: The Free Press, 1960. This collection of 64 articles touches on the theory and application of sociometry in a variety of settings.

Remmers, H. H. Rating methods in research on teaching. In *Handbook of Research on Teaching*, ed. N. L. Gage. Chicago: Rand McNally, 1963. Chapter 7 is a survey of contemporary thinking and methods, with many good examples.

Remmers, H. H.; Gage, N. L.; and Rummel, J. F. *A practical introduction to measurement and evaluation*, 2nd ed. New York: Harper and Row, 1965. Chapter 11 contains a brief survey of methods useful in assessing emotional and social adjustment. Informal observational and sociometric techniques are covered.

Ryans, D. G., and Frederiksen, N. Performance tests of educational achievement. In *Educational Measurement*, ed. E. F. Lindquist. Washington: American Council on Education, 1951. This excellent reference on performance measures, particularly apparatus tests, emphasizes seven steps in the development of performance tests.

Sawin, E. I. *Evaluation and the work of the teacher*. Belmont, Cal.: Wadsworth, 1969. A straightforward discussion of the purposes, problems, and products of direct observation is presented in Chapter 5. Chapter 6 describes a content analysis of free-response material generated by interviews or questionnaires.

Simon, Anita, and Boyer, E. Gil. *Mirrors for behavior II*. Philadelphia: Research for Better Schools, 1970. A two-volume anthology of abstracts and copies of 79 observation instruments.

Thorndike, R. L., and Hagen, Elizabeth. *Measurement and evaluation in psychology and education*, 3rd ed. New York: John Wiley, 1969. Chapter 13 contains descriptions of a variety of data-gathering techniques, including a good summary of rating methods.

Webb, E. J. *et al. Unobtrusive measures: Nonreactive research in the social sciences*. Chicago: Rand McNally, 1966. This fascinating collection of methods is presented in a most appealing and understandable form.

Wright, H. F. *Recording and analyzing child behavior*. New York: Harper and Row, 1967. An integrated description of the ecological study of individual behavior in naturally occurring situations.

17
USING ASSESSMENT DATA IN REPORTING AND MARKING

SUMMARY PREVIEW STATEMENTS

1. Students have a need and a right to be apprised of their progress in school.

2. It is the responsibility of every teacher to develop valid and informative marking and reporting procedures.

3. The advent of individualized instruction and mastery learning programs intensifies demand for the development of viable reporting systems.

4. Marking and reporting systems should be based on sound and integrated philosophies of education, and on defensible technical procedures.

5. Marking and reporting programs serve the broad purposes of:
   a. Communicating to students and parents.
   b. Communicating to present and future school personnel.
   c. Motivating student learning.
   d. Guiding future instruction.

6. Recent developments in reporting procedures can be characterized as increasingly concerned with:
   a. Student behavior.
   b. Affective outcomes.
   c. Student needs at various levels.
   d. Student achievement relative to ability.
   e. Free-response instruction questions.
   f. The involvement of all those concerned with students in developing the reporting system.
   g. Computer processing of reports, allowing for more, and more detailed, information to be communicated.

7. A goal card, listing instructional objectives, can be used effectively as part of the reporting system.

8. Decisions about marking procedures focus on the issues of:
   a. Absolute versus relative standards.
   b. Level of achievement versus effort.
   c. Growth versus status.
   d. Letter versus numerical marks.

9. It is generally recommended that a relative-standard system of marks, using a limited number of categories and relying on an individual's level of achievement, be applied.

10. Marks lack meaning unless reasonable procedural uniformity is achieved within and across classes, departments, and schools.

11. A mark should reflect a variety of areas of achievement, e.g., test scores, class contributions, homework, projects, and similar data.

12. The weight of each component in a composite mark is determined by the variability of the separate component scores.

13. The "inspection model" of marking relies on the instructor to identify naturally occurring breaks in the distribution of composite scores.

14. The "normal curve model" of marking defines fixed percentages for marks, and assumes a normal distribution of achievement that rarely occurs.

15. Ebel has defined a system for assigning marks within a class that adjusts distribution according to the average ability level of the group.

16. Marks represent an integral, fallible, potentially meaningful, though perhaps irritating, element in the educational process.

The need for informative reporting and marking procedures may be more acute today than at any time in the history of our nation's schools. Increased experimentation with innovative teaching methods and organizational systems is accompanied by a demand for effective communication among those engaged in the educational enterprise. Obviously, students need to be apprised of their progress. In addition, data are needed to help teachers plan for effective instructional experiences. This need takes on increasing importance as more and more schools implement individualized instruction and mastery learning programs, which require the continuous monitoring and feedback of progress information. Parents, too, are taking an increased interest in the schools. Their need to be informed should be met with the best techniques available.

PURPOSES OF MARKING AND REPORTING

A noticeable degree of tension is exhibited by students and teachers, and to some extent by parents, as marking time rolls around. This tension is especially characteristic of beginning teachers, and can generally be attributed to their lack of experience in assigning marks and reporting student progress. The summation of complex human behavior into a simple index, in the form of a letter or number mark, may be presumptuous. If, in addition, marks are *not* based on a rational philosophy of education and a set of operational definitions of expected learning outcomes, their meaning will be obscure and ambiguous, and their purpose(s) will be subverted.

Four broad purposes of marking and reporting can be identified:

Communicating to Students and Parents

Marks provide useful and efficient data that can be used to communicate with students and their parents. Marking and reporting are essentially information-processing activities, and might be likened to elements in a communications network (DiVesta and Meyer 1963). Marks are merely the means by which a teacher communicates his evaluations of the progress each student has made toward a specified set of educational goals. As in any communications system, the message, i.e., information about achievement, may be incorrectly transmitted to the receiver because of faulty encoding or decoding or because of the presence of "noise" or "static" in the network.

Students have a right and a need to learn about their progress. In addition to achievement data in the forms of rank in class, grade equivalents, standard scores, and percentile ranks, students seem to desire more "subjective" and criterion-referenced evaluations of their performances. They want to know if their work is outstanding, good, acceptable, or unacceptable. The teacher is probably in a better position than anyone else to integrate the many factors in learning and achievement, and to communicate his summary to the student.

Parents, too, have a right and need to learn of the educational progress of their progeny. Marks are sensible summarizing appraisals which parents can use to counsel their child about his school work and future educational and vocational plans.

Communicating to Present and Future School Personnel

Just as the results of standardized achievement tests can be used to evaluate the overall progress of a particular instructional program and school, so can distributions of marks indicate trends related to progress. Such data are useful in making decisions about promotion, graduation, transfer, and future education.

Indices of past achievement are probably the best single indication of future achievement. College admissions personnel, therefore, view marks as generally indicative of the level of performance to be achieved by individual students admitted to their institution. Marks serve as academic currency in the college marketplace, although their exchange and conversion properties are limited.

Promotional decisions should, of course, never be made on the basis of marks alone. In fact, Coffield and Blommers (1956) have shown that requiring a student to repeat a grade results in very little improvement in achievement.

Motivating Student Learning

The research literature reveals evidence that marks may function to reinforce or inhibit learning. Although we would ideally like learning to result from intrinsic motivation, the gross extrinsic force exerted by marks must be acknowledged.

In considering the motivational function of marks, it is important to define the basis on which marks are assigned. If a mark simply indicates status at a particular point in time, it is doubtful that most students will feel challenged to work for higher marks. If, however, marks reflect improvement or achievement relative to ability, students may be spurred to greater efforts.

Guiding Future Instruction

It is well known that past achievement is the best predictor and prognosticator of future achievement. Information on skills and knowledge already acquired and developed, then, is immensely helpful in designing future educational programs for individual students, groups, or classes. Data on important affective educational outcomes can also serve as a basis for planning meaningful student experiences. The data from criterion-referenced assessment and "goal cards," to be discussed later in this chapter, can be extremely helpful if carefully examined.

CHANGES IN MARKING AND REPORTING PROCEDURES

Thomas (1954) has noted that the traditional *report card* is gradually being replaced by a *progress report*. The development of the progress report has been characterized by several changes in substance and format over the last several decades, among which Thomas notes the following:

Traditional practice	Innovation
1. Listing only broad subject fields, in each of which a student receives a single mark.	Explaining in terms of student behavior the activities that compose each subject-matter field, as well as character traits, making the progress report more detailed and specific.
2. Listing only school *subjects* and perhaps a single category labeled *character* or *deportment*.	Including numerous objectives under such labels as *social adjustment, personal development,* and *work habits.*
3. Using a single report form for the entire school.	Developing forms specifically suited to the goals of individual grades or levels.
4. Comparing all children with an abstract standard or with their classmates.	Comparing each student's progress with his own apparent ability (especially in the lower grades) or with himself and others.
5. Using percentage or letter grades, sometimes defined as *excellent, good, fair,* and *failure.*	Developing additional symbols or statements (such as "needs more time and help") reflecting a more advanced understanding of child development.
6. Using a relatively small card, printed in black on white.	Using a larger folder, printed in color with a new typographical design, friendly explanations for parents, and perhaps pictures or cartoons at the primary level.
7. Providing one line for the teacher's comment and one line for the parent's signature.	Providing more space for comments from both teacher and parent.
8. Assigning the central supervisory staff to develop the report card, possibly with suggestions from a few teachers.	Organizing committees of teachers, supervisors, parents, and students to improve reporting practices.

A few schools prefer informal letters to parents or parent-teacher conferences to report cards. These two techniques can provide more individualized descriptions of a child's behavior but demand considerably more teacher time.

Some of the innovations described above are reflected in the sample elementary report form in Figure 17.1. Note in particular the kinds of

LANGUAGE ARTS	First Quarter			Second Quarter			Third Quarter			Fourth Quarter		
	Excellent Achievement	Satisfactory	Work is Needed Improvement	Excellent Achievement	Satisfactory	Work is Needed Improvement	Excellent Achievement	Satisfactory	Work is Needed Improvement	Excellent Achievement	Satisfactory	Work is Needed Improvement

READING

Working in readiness activities												
Shows growth in vocabulary												
Reads with understanding												
Uses word attack skills												
Reads orally with expression and meaning												
Reads for enjoyment												
READING												

PENMANSHIP

Manuscript _____ Cursive _____												
Working in readiness activities												
Forms letters correctly												
Spaces properly												
Writes neatly												
PENMANSHIP												

ENGLISH

Applies basic rules of grammar												
Spells correctly in written work												
Shows growth in creative expression												
ENGLISH												

SPEAKING AND LISTENING

Speaks clearly and distinctly												
Expresses ideas well												
Listens attentively												
Recalls with accuracy												

MATHEMATICS

Working in readiness activities												
Forms numerals correctly												
Understands the meanings of numbers												
Counts and writes in more than one sequence												
Uses symbols and terms correctly												
Reads, writes, and solves equations												
Reasons well in solving problems												
Knows and understands number facts												
MATHEMATICS												

SCIENCE

Shows curiosity												
Applies observation techniques												
Demonstrates understanding and makes application												
Bases conclusions on facts and experiences												
SCIENCE												

FIGURE 17.1. Representative Elementary School Report Form

	First Quarter				Second Quarter				Third Quarter				Fourth Quarter			
	Excellent Achievement	Satisfactory	Work is Needed	Improvement	Excellent Achievement	Satisfactory	Work is Needed	Improvement	Excellent Achievement	Satisfactory	Work is Needed	Improvement	Excellent Achievement	Satisfactory	Work is Needed	Improvement

SOCIAL STUDIES

Contributes to activities and discussions																
Has interest in current events																
Shows growth in understanding of people																
Understands charts, maps, and graphs																
Reports information accurately and effectively																
SOCIAL STUDIES																

ACHIEVEMENT IN SUBJECT AREAS:

A - Excellent
B - Good
C - Fair
D - Poor

MUSIC AND ART

Participates in music																
Participates in art																

HEALTH AND PHYSICAL EDUCATION

Practices good health habits																
Participates in organized games and free play																

WORK AND STUDY HABITS

Works independently · uses time wisely																
Uses materials wisely																
Works well with the group																
Takes pride in work																
Follows directions																

PERSONAL GROWTH

Accepts responsibilities																
Practices self-discipline																
Practices good sportsmanship																
Respects the rights and property of others																
Shows courtesy and consideration																
Shows growth in self-confidence																

ATTENDANCE

	First Quarter	Second Quarter	Third Quarter	Fourth Quarter
Date of Report				
Days Present				
Days Absent				
Days Tardy				

Winnetka Public Schools

MATHEMATICS GOAL RECORD CARD 1

Pupil _____ Teacher _____ Year _____

	Check
Can count 10 objects...	
Can read and write numerals to 10...............................	
Recognizes number groups up to 5	
Recognizes patterns of objects to 10	
Can read and write numerals to 20..............................	
Can count objects to 100	
Recognizes numbers to 100.....................................	
Can read and write numerals to 50..............................	
Recognizes addition and subtraction symbols	
*Understands meaning of the inequality signs....................	
Can count objects:	
by 2's to 20	
by 5's to 100	
by 10's to 100	
Recognizes geometric figures:	
triangle...	
circle	
quadrilateral	
Recognizes coins (1¢, 5¢, 10¢, 25¢).............................	
Knows addition combinations 10 and under using objects	
Knows subtraction combinations 10 and under using objects	
Recognizes addition and subtraction vertically and horizontally ...	
*Can construct simple plane figures with straight edge and compass	
Shows understanding of numbers and number combinations (check one)	
1. Using concrete objects	
2. Beginning to visualize and abstract................	
3. Makes automatic responses without concrete objects	
*Can tell time	
1. Hour	
2. Half hour	
*(Goals starred are not essential for all students)	
Comments:	

FIGURE 17.2. Sample Grade 1 Mathematics Goal Card

activities being evaluated. The form is flexible, allowing for a traditional grade as well as the specification of factors contributing to that grade. In addition to cognitive outcomes, some attention is given to student's affective development.

Goal Cards

Bauernfeind (1967) has described a reporting procedure in keeping with the behavioral objectives movement described in Chapter Two. A

Winnetka Public Schools
MATHEMATICS GOAL RECORD CARD 2

Pupil _____ Teacher _____ Year _____

	Check
Addition combinations 10 and under (automatic response)	
Subtraction combinations 10 and under (automatic response)	
Can count to 200	
Can understand zero as a number	
Can understand place value to tens	
Can read and write numerals to 200.......................................	
Can read and write numeral words to 10	
Can read and write number words to 20...................................	
Use facts in 2-digit column addition (no carrying)	
Roman numerals to XII	
Can tell time:	
Half hour...	
Quarter hour	
Calendar (months, days of week, dates)	
Coins and their equivalent value to 25¢...................................	
Recognition of 50¢ coin and $1.00	
Recognize and use $1/2$, $1/4$, $1/3$ of a whole	
Addition facts to 18 (aim for mastery)	
Subtraction facts to 18 (aim for mastery)	
*Can identify simple plane figures:	
Quadrilateral..	
Pentagon	
Hexagon	
Octagon	
*Can use compass to bisect line segment, construct triangles, and	
construct perpendiculars	
Word problems: (check one)	
1. Can set the problem up	
2. Can understand process involved	
3. Can notate word problems	
(Goals starred are not essential for all students)	
Comments:	

FIGURE 17.3. Sample Grade 2 Mathematics Goal Card

given teacher's instructional objectives are communicated through the use of a "goal card," which is simply a list of specified educational objectives in clear and appropriate language. Both teacher and student have copies of the goal card, which ordinarily lists the minimal objectives to be obtained and can be used to monitor progress and report to parents. Sample goal cards are illustrated in Figures 17.2 and 17.3. Figure 17.2 lists basic goals for Grade 1 mathematics and Figure 17.3 presents goals for Grade 2. These cards were described by Bauernfeind (1967) and used in the Winnetka, Illinois, Public Schools. A given student may progress quickly through one set of objectives and into another, and goals may be tailored to a student's ability and progress. Bauernfeind (1967) has noted six major advantages of using goal cards:

1. Goal cards help the student "see" his progress as he acquires information and develops skills.

2. Goal cards help the teacher specify objectives and arrange them in a logical way.

3. Goal cards are an effective way to communicate with parents and the general public. They serve as an excellent basis for a parent-teacher conference.

4. Goal cards can contribute to planning for instruction, particularly if individualized programs are desired.

5. Goal cards facilitate communication among educators, e.g., the Grade 1 arithmetic teacher with Grade 2 teachers, or the regular teacher with a substitute teacher.

6. Because they emphasize important objectives, preferably specified in behavioral terms, goal cards can serve as a sound basis for classroom assessment.

MARKING PROCEDURES

Despite tremendous technical and theoretical advances in education and psychology during the past century, particularly in regard to quantitative methods, we are still unable to recommend a perfectly viable system for assigning marks that will satisfy the majority of educators. This is true partly because most people consider marking a philosophical decision-making process, rather than a statistical one. This view leads to the treatment of marks as "evaluations" representing value judgments about students' learning and achievement. Others resolve the problem by considering grades as "measurements." Information about a student's progress toward a specified set of instructional objectives is gathered, combined in appropriate ways, and summarized as a mark, usually a letter (A through E) or number (1 through 100). Such marks are viewed as summarizations of data, rather than value judgments. This view of marking has some intrinsic appeal because it seems to relieve the teacher of the burden of making subjective judgments. He can say, "Look, I'm just reporting how well my students achieved. I'm not making judgments about them." Despite the psychological comfort that may be derived from such a philosophy, the problem has really not been resolved. The teacher continually makes value judgments about what to teach, how to teach, and the like, and how "measurement" will be reported unavoidably rests on a subjective decision by the teacher.

DECISION POINTS IN ESTABLISHING MARKING SYSTEMS

Failure on the part of an instructor, department, school, or school system to specify the basis upon which marks are assigned can only result in chaos. Look, for example, at interschool differences in marking practices. A recent survey of 129 high schools completed by Educational Testing Service (Terwilliger 1971), indicates the diversity of marking policies and practices in effect: (1) 22 percent of the schools in the survey had no fixed policy governing the assignment of marks; (2) 27 percent reported that an absolute standard of achievement was used; (3) 29 percent marked students on achievement in relation to ability; and (4) 16 percent said that marks represented achievement with respect to others in the class. Apparently marks mean different things to different people. The purpose of assigning marks is obviously obscured if uniform policies are not adopted. Among the more important decisions that must be confronted in developing policy statements on marking are the following:

Should an Absolute or Relative Standard Be Used?

Because most of the data of education and psychology do *not* conform to the requirement of a ratio scale—i.e., a zero score has an absolute meaning—the use of an absolute scale to assign grades is probably not justified. Because a student responds correctly to every item on a test does not mean that he knows all there is to know about a particular subject. Such a score does not represent 100 percent comprehension. Tests are only samples of behavior, and the use of a percentage of the total number of items on a test, or of the raw total number of points it is possible to obtain over a semester's work, is not a legitimate basis upon which to assign marks.

An allied problem is that a fixed method of marking is frequently imposed by school administrators and boards of education. The usual method requires specification of a fixed percentage, e.g., 65 percent, as a passing grade. Furthermore, an instructor is frequently limited in the percentage of certain grades he may assign. Such limitations actually require the instructor to predict the difficulty level of the items on his tests and predetermine the shape of the final distribution of scores, so that a specified number of students will fall into each achievement category. Such a task is almost impossible, even for the most highly trained professional test developer. Such an imposition of fixed percentages requires the teacher to play "catch-up" at the end of the semester. He may provide bonus points for projects or construct very difficult or very easy tests (without considering what they are supposed to measure) until the "correct" number of marks has been achieved.

The ability levels of classes as a whole do vary, and it would therefore seem reasonable to allow the performance of the class to determine the distribution of marks. A reference point, however, is needed. One might use a measure of central tendency—either the mean or the median—as a starting point for assigning marks. The former, however, being an arithmetic average, is unduly affected by extreme scores, and because classroom tests frequently yield asymmetrical distributions, the mean is probably an unwise choice. The median is generally considered the most representative measure of central tendency of all the scores in a distribution, and its selection makes sense, at least from a logical standpoint. If one assigns marks on a relative basis, a more logical starting point than the mean or median is needed. Such a starting point could be derived from the table of specifications and list of objectives for the course. Minimal requirements and competencies to be achieved could be identified, translated into expected scores, and then used to assign marks. Additional points to consider in marking on a relative scale will be discussed on pages 429–432.

Should Level of Achievement or Effort Form the Basis of Marks?

Even under the most ideal conditions, marks are ambiguous. It would seem, then, that expanding the content base of a mark to include such variables as effort, perseverance, and assiduousness could only serve to further cloud already murky waters. Is it reasonable for us to assign a higher mark to a student who "tried harder" but attained the same level of achievement as several of his peers? Probably not. Effort should be rewarded, both formally and informally. The teacher can positively reinforce a student's efforts to learn. That a student is working hard should be communicated to his parents. A marking and reporting system that treats achievement and effort separately is recommended.

Should Growth or Status at a Particular Point Form the Basis for Marks?

Assigning marks on the basis of improvement over the semester has great intrinsic appeal, and intuitively appears to be a fair and unbiased approach. Consider, for example, two students, X and Y. Both have shown a growth of 35 points, according to a pre- and post-test, in a course in American history. Student X, however, was below Q_1 to begin with, while student Y was above Q_3. Does the growth of these two students represent the same thing? Obviously not, either relative to content and skills resulting from instruction as measured on the tests, or in terms of final level achieved.

Marking on the basis of final status, particularly when measured by a comprehensive terminal examination, has much to recommend it. A final-status index is responsive to individual differences in learning rate and is more reliable than growth scores, as Manning and DuBois (1958) have demonstrated.

Should a Letter or Number Marking System Be Used?

Both letter and number systems of marking have enjoyed wide popularity, and each has its strengths and weaknesses. The letter system, which usually uses the symbols A through E, theoretically emphasizes the distinction between marks as measurements and as evaluations. The letter grade represents a translation from a number base, resulting from a combination of test scores, ratings, and the like, and it is assumed that the degree of excellence achieved is better represented by a letter. Letter marks have a common meaning for most people, and for this reason should probably be retained. One disadvantage of letter marks is that they must be converted to numbers if they are to be added or averaged. In addition, the use of only five categories of marks, to some extent masks individual differences. The Bs received by five different students may not mean the same thing, either in terms of level (there are high and low Bs) or of content and proficiencies.

The number system of marking has great appeal for many people. It allows for a greater range of marks than is provided by five letters. One possible source of interpretive error is that the number system implies a greater degree of precision in measuring educational achievement than is warranted by the data. Does the use of a wide range of number marks really mean that fine discriminations among individuals are possible? No! We can probably do a reasonably good job of ranking individuals in the class, but differences of two or three points are not very meaningful.

COMBINING AND WEIGHTING DATA

In order to assign marks, it is generally desirable to derive a composite score distribution weighting individual measurements obtained over, for example, a semester's work, in the appropriate proportions. There are a number of problems related to the combination of separate measures into a single composite measure for each individual student (Dunnette and Hoggatt 1957 and Horst 1936), not the least of which is the fact that test scores tend to weight by their variabilities. For example, if an instructor wishes to combine scores on the midterm exam with those on the final exam to form a composite, he is more than likely simply to add the two scores. Let us further assume that he wants each exam to contribute 50 percent to the composite score. If, however, the standard deviation of the final exam is 20, and that of the midterm 10, the final exam contributes *twice* as much as the midterm to the composite. An allied problem is a logical dilemma: are we justified in combining scores from a number of different sources, representing different learning outcomes, into a composite? Strong arguments can be made pro and con. Assuming an underlying variable called "achievement in such and such a course," we are probably justified in ranking students in terms of overall performance. On the other hand, most of the methods of combining data assume that the measures to be combined are independent of each other—a tenuous assumption at best. If for no other reason than the practical exigencies of the educational assessment situation, deriving composite scores is justified.

Two methods of deriving composite scores will be described in this section. Many methods have been investigated (Lawshe and Schucker 1959), and it has been found that all yield similar results. Keep in mind that the pooled appraisal of competence represented by the composite is a *relative* measurement, not an absolute one. It permits comparisons among individuals and judgments involving "more" or "less." But the real or absolute meaning of the scores is often obscured in a composite score.

Weighting with Standard Scores

A relatively straightforward method of combining scores is through the use of standard scores. The reader will recall from Chapter Nine that the use of standard scores is advocated because it allows a legitimate comparison of an individual's scores on different tests. This is an acceptable procedure because the use of a standard transformation puts all tests on a common score base. The standard score system suggested here is the Z transformation, and can be expressed as follows:

$$Z = 10\left(\frac{X - \overline{X}}{S}\right) + 50, \qquad \text{(Equation 9.11)}$$

where
X = is an individual's raw score
$\overline{X}$ = the raw score mean and
S = the raw score standard deviation.

The mean of the Z scores is 50, and the standard deviation is 10. Converting all the measures that one wishes to combine into standard scores will equate their means to an arbitrary value of 50, but, more important, it will adjust the individual scores in terms of the standard deviation. It should be reemphasized at this point that deriving composite score requires that we work with the variabilities of the distributions, as weights are proportional to the variabilities. In this regard, the means are irrelevant in obtaining weighted scores.

How are these standard scores used to obtain composite scores? Refer to the data in Table 17.1. Assume that an instructor wishes to combine two quizzes and a final exam. In addition, he wishes to weight the final three times as heavily as the two quizzes. The first step is to determine the means and standard deviations for the three sets of scores. (See columns 1, 2, and 3 of Table 17.1.) Both the actual and estimated standard deviations are presented in Table 17.1. It can be seen that the standard deviations ($\hat{S}$) derived from the scores of the high- and low-scoring one-sixth of the distribution are very good estimates of the actual standard deviations. Next, Equation 9.11 is used to determine Z-scores for every student on every test (see columns 4, 5, and 6 of Table 17.1). Finally, after applying the appropriate weight to Z_F, the composite scores are determined by addition. At this point, any

TABLE 17.1 Hypothetical Test Data Illustrating Derivation of Composite Scores Using Standard Scores

	Raw Scores			Standard Scores			Composite[1]	Rank of Composite
Student	Quiz 1	Quiz 2	Final Exam	Z_1	Z_2	Z_F	Z_c	
S_1	38	48	93	69	62	65	326	2
S_2	36	53	98	66	68	68	338	1
S_3	34	47	94	62	61	65	318	3
S_4	33	53	89	61	68	62	315	4
S_5	32	42	82	59	56	56	283	6
S_6	31	45	85	57	59	59	293	5
S_7	30	38	77	55	52	53	266	8
S_8	29	40	74	53	54	50	257	9
S_9	27	43	79	50	57	54	269	7
S_{10}	26	34	72	48	48	49	243	11
S_{11}	26	35	72	48	49	49	244	10
S_{12}	26	34	69	48	48	46	234	12
S_{13}	25	32	70	46	46	47	233	13
S_{14}	25	30	68	46	44	46	228	14
S_{15}	24	29	65	44	42	43	215	15
S_{16}	23	26	60	43	39	40	202	17
S_{17}	22	28	63	41	41	42	208	16
S_{18}	20	22	61	37	35	40	192	18
S_{19}	19	24	55	36	37	36	181	19
S_{20}	16	22	48	30	35	31	158	20
$\overline{X}$ =	27.1	36.2	73.7					
S =	5.6	9.6	13.2					
$\hat{S}^2$ =	5.7	9.3	13.2					

[1] Composite obtained with following expression, $Z_c = Z_1 + Z_2 + 3(Z_F)$.

[2] $\hat{S}$ = Sum of scores for the highest scoring one-sixth of the distribution, minus the sum of the scores for the lowest scoring one-sixth of the distribution, divided by one-half the number of students.

of the marking procedures described in the next section may be applied. It should again be noted that in addition to providing a convenient method of eventually combining scores, standard scores themselves may be useful in test interpretation.

Weighting with Adjusted Raw Scores

An efficient method of equating the standard deviations of a number of measures is to divide each raw score in a particular distribution by its own standard deviation. Such a procedure automatically adjusts each raw score in relation to the variability of the total distribution. The adjusted raw scores for the three exams represented in Table 17.1 are summarized in Table 17.2.

TABLE 17.2 Derivation of Composite Scores Through Use of Adjusted Raw Scores (Based on Actual Raw Scores and Standard Deviations of Table 17.1)

	Adjusted Raw Scores ($\frac{X}{S}$)			Composite[2]	Rank of Composite	Mark[3]
Student	(1) Quiz 1	(2) Quiz 2	(3) Final Exam[1]	(4)	(5)	(6)
S_1	6.79	5.00	21.13	32.92	2	A
S_2	6.43	5.52	22.27	34.22	1	A
S_3	6.07	4.90	21.36	32.33	3	A
S_4	5.89	5.52	20.22	31.63	4	B
S_5	5.71	4.38	18.63	28.72	6	B
S_6	5.54	4.69	19.31	29.54	5	B
S_7	5.36	3.96	17.49	26.81	8	B
S_8	5.18	4.17	16.81	26.16	9	C
S_9	4.82	4.48	17.95	27.27	7	B
S_{10}	4.64	3.54	16.36	24.54	11	C
S_{11}	4.64	3.65	16.36	24.65	10	C
S_{12}	4.64	3.54	15.68	23.86	12	C
S_{13}	4.46	3.33	15.90	23.69	13	C
S_{14}	4.46	3.13	15.45	23.04	14	C
S_{15}	4.29	3.02	14.77	22.08	15	C
S_{16}	4.11	2.71	13.63	20.45	17	D
S_{17}	3.93	2.92	14.31	21.16	16	C
S_{18}	3.57	2.29	13.86	19.72	18	D
S_{19}	3.39	2.50	12.50	18.39	19	D
S_{20}	2.86	2.29	10.91	16.06	20	F

[1] Final exam adjusted raw obtained by dividing each raw score by the standard deviation, and multiplying by 3.

[2] Composite obtained by summing entries across columns.

[3] Mark determined by procedure described by Ebel (1965, pp. 426–435).

The mere fact that the "adjusted raw score" procedure bypasses computation of the raw-score mean and standard scores may be enough to recommend it. The results obtained through the use of standard scores or adjusted raw scores yield the identical ranking of students.

THREE REPRESENTATIVE MARKING MODELS

Before discussing the assignment of marks, several words of caution are in order. First, the use of quantitative procedures does not eliminate the human factor from marking. Marking decisions are still basically philosophical. Second, the meaning ascribed to marks, be they letters or numbers, really rests on arbitrary conventions. The measures we use to assign marks must have meaning with respect to expected behavioral changes in students if the resulting marks are to have any meaning.

The Inspection Model

A method of assigning grades that is widely used but rarely acknowledged is the inspection method. It generally involves examining the distribution of composite scores in hopes of finding "natural breaks" or "cutoff points," and represents the zenith of marking on a relative curve. The distribution of scores, then, in a sense determines the percentage of marks to be assigned. Some experts have argued that these "natural breaks" in distribution are unreliable. This is to some extent true, but if the data upon which the marks are based are reliable, confidence can be placed in the results.

To avoid being completely arbitrary about the distribution of marks, some reference-point is needed. It has been suggested that the objectives of the course and summary tables of specification be perused to determine a minimal level of performance. Such a procedure, used in conjunction with "inspection," allows for either a high or low percentage of high or low marks. Such a state of affairs would appear to have some basis in reality, since any given class during any given grading period may display relatively high or low performance. Other methods may be used to determine minimal standards. A teacher may determine what chance performance would have been on all exams, relate this to the composite distribution of scores, and use it as a starting-point to evaluate the overall performance of the group. Some instructors like to use Q_1-level and Q_3-level performance on all measures as reference-points to gauge the performance of the group. Ideally, one would like to have normative data from past groups to use in assessing present class performance.

The "Normal Curve" Model

In using the so-called normal curve as a model for assigning marks, several assumptions of varying degrees of credibility are involved. First, this curve assumes that achievement is normally distributed and that if the resulting distribution is nonnormal, it is a result of sampling error. Second, it is assumed the sample means and standard deviations are the best estimates of the means and standard deviations of the population of which this particular class represents a sample. These assumptions involve about as much subjective judgment as any a teacher must make in order to mark.

A typical "normal curve" distribution of marks is presented in Figure 17.4. There are at least two ways that this curve may be used to

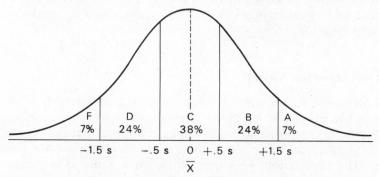

FIGURE 17.4. Selected Hypothetical Distribution of Marks Based on Standard Deviations

assign marks. First, the instructor may mark off appropriate standard deviation units along the score scale, and assign the appropriate marks to them. Second, the percentage of marks dictated by the normal curve may be assigned the class. Will either procedure insure that the normal curve assumptions have been met? Yes, if and only if the underlying class distribution is normally distributed. Despite this restriction, the actual and theoretical percentages of marks come fairly close together.

The Ability-Adjusted Mark Distribution Model

Homogeneous grouping in the schools, particularly if organized on the basis of academic aptitude, poses additional marking dilemmas. A teacher, principal, parent, or student might well ask if, given two classes in the same subject taught by the same instructor and using the same syllabus, the same distributions of marks should be applied to both? The answer to such a question must be negative. A related question posed by a student in a low-ability track might be, "Am I to be discriminated against, markwise, because I do not possess high academic aptitude?" Some compromise that enables a student at the lowest ability level to achieve an A comparable in meaning to that received by a high-ability student is needed. Such a procedure has been described by Dr. Robert Ebel.[1] Basically, the model provides for an adjustment of the distribution of marks, depending on the ability level of the group. Central to the model are the relationships between average class ability levels and theoretical distributions of marks. These relationships are summarized in Table 17.3. Several features of this

TABLE 17.3   Letter-Mark Distribution Statistics for Classes at Seven Levels of Ability

Ability Level	Ability Measures		Lower Limit Factor	Percent of Marks				
	GPA	Percentile		A	B	C	D	F
Exceptional	2.80	79	0.7	24	38	29	8	1
Superior	2.60	73	0.9	18	36	32	12	2
Good	2.40	66	1.1	14	32	36	15	3
Fair	2.20	58	1.3	10	29	37	20	4
Average	2.00	50	1.5	7	24	38	24	7
Weak	1.80	42	1.7	4	20	37	29	10
Poor	1.60	34	1.9	3	15	36	32	14

Source: Robert L. Ebel, *Measuring educational achievement,* © 1965, p. 428. By permission of Prentice-Hall, Inc.

table deserve comment. First, either an ability test or grade-point average (GPA) may be used to identify appropriate distribution of grades. One feature of Ebel's method is its flexibility. It lends itself well to adoption by a school or school system, thereby increasing the uniformity of marking practices among instructors, and ideally resulting in greater comparability of marks. To maintain uniformity, it would be highly desirable to use the same ability measure with all groups. Perhaps a standardized intelligence test could be used to determine the ability levels of the classes. Ebel suggests that the percentile ranks or scores on the ability measure of individual students could be averaged to determine the appropriate ability category for the class. Another approach is to determine the raw-score or standard-score median for the class, and to convert this to a percentile rank by reference to either local or national norms tables. It is also obvious from Table 17.3 that there exists a significant overlap in the distribution of grades, again

[1] The technique to be described was originally developed by Dr. Ebel in cooperation with Dean Dewey B. Stuit at the State University of Iowa. It was described in Technical Bulletin No. 8 of the University Examination Service, published in November 1954. (See also Robert L. Ebel, *Measuring educational achievement* (Englewood Cliffs, N.J.: Prentice-Hall, 1965), pp. 426–435.)

emphasizing that with this system it is possible for an exceptional student to obtain an F and a poor student to obtain an A. An illustration of the procedure will now be described.

Let us refer back to the composite scores in Table 17.2, derived from the adjusted raw-score procedure, to illustrate Ebel's marking model. After the appropriate distribution of marks has been selected (we have assumed an average level of ability here), and a median and standard deviation computed (the estimated standard deviation is quite appropriate here), the score limits for the various mark categories are calculated using the appropriate lower-limit factor from Table 17.3. These lower-limit values show how far the lower limit of the score interval for A marks lies above the median in standard-deviation units. We have determined the median of our hypothetical distribution of composite scores to be 24.60, and estimated the standard deviation to be 4.84. The lower limit of the A marks is determined as follows:

$$\text{Lower Limit of A's} = \text{Median} - 1.5\,(\hat{S})$$

Substituting in the expression for the lower limit of A, and determining subsequent limits by successively subtracting the standard deviation from the lower limit of the A's, we can assign marks as follows:

Average Ability Group

Marks	Lower Limits	Invervals	f	Actual Percent	Expected Percent
A	$24.60 + 1.5 \times 4.84 = 31.86$	32–	3	15	7
B	$31.86 - 4.84 = 27.02$	27–31	5	25	24
C	$27.02 - 4.84 = 22.18$	22–26	8	40	38
D	$22.18 - 4.84 = 17.34$	17–21	3	15	24
F		–16	1	5	7

Although the actual and expected percentages of marks do not exactly coincide, because of a small sample and nonnormal distribution, they are in general agreement. The overall rationale for using the procedure (i.e., adjusting for ability level of classes) is perhaps sufficient justification for its use.

DISHONEST WAYS OF MARKING

We cannot leave the topic of marking without pointing out some of the pitfalls that await the unwary, unthinking, or unmotivated grader. Palmer (1962) has provided us with seven danger signs that need to be heeded if we are to grade successfully.

Do not fall victim to grading by:

1. *Abdication,* i.e., don't, because of overwork or lack of effort, tailor

courses to tests or rely on tests developed by other teachers or textbook publishers.

2.   *Employing the carrots and clubbing system,* i.e., don't add bonus credit for good behavior or avoidance of the prejudices of the teacher.

3.   *Default,* i.e., don't, because of a deep-seated hatred of grading and testing, base a final grade on a single exam in which a single misstep could spell disaster.

4.   *Becoming a zealot,* i.e., do not set the student racing with a vengeance and make the course an ordeal, endurance contest, or problem in survival in which you measure everything short of classroom posture.

5.   *Changing rules in midgame,* i.e., don't strew the line of march with booby traps and obstacles aimed at tightening up the standards after the game has started.

6.   *Becoming a psychic grader,* i.e., don't believe you have powers inaccessible to ordinary man, allowing only you to "see" how much a student has learned without using any measurements.

7.   *Anchoring everyone in a system of impossible perfection,* i.e., don't overlook the fallibility of man-as-student or set yourself up as guardian of standards.

In short, don't fall victim, as the Dean did in the following limerick, to basing marks on irrelevancies:

> There was a young girl at McMaster
> Whose head was alfalfa and plaster
> But she looked like a queen
> And she smiled at the dean
> So he graded her paper—and passed her.

ON THE PHILOSOPHY OF MARKING

It is incumbent upon every teacher, at every level of instruction, to spell out for his students the basis upon which marks will be assigned. It must be assumed that the practice of marking, despite the problems of accuracy and reliability, will continue for many years to come. Despite a particular instructor's disagreement with the whole notion of marking, he has an obligation to assign the most valid and reliable marks he can. The many and important decisions that are made about students every day, and throughout their educational and occupational careers, dictate such a recommendation. An instructor who pursues a "no-grade" philosophy abrogates his responsibility as an educator to communicate with the student about his progress.

There is no solution to the marking problem that would prove to be satisfactory to all concerned. Suffice it to say that the assignment of marks constitutes a powerful system of reward and punishment, which can be used to bring about some highly desirable behavioral changes. Such a point of view implies the expenditure of a significant amount of time and effort in arriving at student marks. But preoccupation with marks, on the part of either teacher or student, must be considered unhealthy. Keeping in mind the limitations of marks, the basis of their assignment, and the fact that many significant outcomes of education are neither subject to marking nor markable (e.g., attitudes, values, interests) should lead to a proper perspective. Marks represent an integral, fallible, potentially meaningful, though perhaps irritating, element in the educational process.

SUGGESTED READINGS

Brodinsky, B., ed. *Grading and reporting.* Arlington, Va.: National School Public Relations Association, 1972. This survey of current trends in school policies and programs contains some good illustrations of new types of report cards from kindergarten through the secondary school.

Cureton, Louise W. The history of grading practices. *Measurement in Education* 2 (May 1971): 8. A fascinating, engaging, and scholarly description of trends in grading and marking.

Davis, F. B. *Educational measurements and their interpretation.* Belmont, Cal.: Wadsworth, 1964. Chapter 13, "School Marketing Procedures," considers, in addition to the usual topics, effort ratings, the reliability and validity of teacher marks, and comparability of marks across teachers and schools.

Ebel, R. L. *Essentials of educational measurement.* Englewood Cliffs, N.J.: Prentice-Hall, 1972. The issues involved in assigning marks and establishing marking systems are treated in a very informative and readable way in Chapter 12 of this excellent text.

Terwilliger, J. S. *Assigning grades to students.* Glenview, Ill., 1971. An excellent overview of both practical and technical issues in the marking process.

Thomas, R. M. *Judging student progress,* 2nd ed. New York: David McKay, 1960. Chapters 13 and 14 are concerned respectively with marking and reporting student progress.

Thorndike, R. L., and Hagen, Elizabeth. *Measurement and evaluation in psychology and education,* 2nd ed. New York: John Wiley and Sons, 1961. Chapter 17, "Marking and Reporting," contains an extensive discussion of the philosophical and technical aspects of marking and reporting.

Wrinkle, W. L. *Improving marking and reporting practices in elementary and secondary schools.* New York: Holt, Rinehart and Winston, 1956. This textbook is probably the most comprehensive treatment of the problems and methods of reporting and marking available.

18

TESTING AND THE CONCERNS OF INDIVIDUALS AND SOCIETY

SUMMARY PREVIEW STATEMENTS

1. The testing profession is continually subject to criticism, some of which is justified and most of which is not.

2. Many of the criticisms leveled at tests and testing would be more appropriate if aimed at the users of tests.

3. Criticisms of testing revolve around the issues of:
   a. Discrimination against minority and disadvantaged groups.
   b. Imperfect predictability.
   c. Inflexible classification of individuals.
   d. Implied measurement of innate characteristics.
   e. Potentially harmful social, educational, and psychological effects.
   f. Potential dangers in controlling curricula.
   g. Invasion of privacy.

4. The majority of the problems posed by the use of educational and psychological tests can be overcome with common sense, intelligent application, establishment of standards, and education.

5. Recent court decisions have required that educational and psychological tests, particularly those bearing on employment, be of proven validity.

6. Ideally, the use of validated tests should work to reduce discrimination in employment and educational situations.

7. Through the development of guidelines, codes, and ethical standards, professional organizations are making great strides toward eliminating the unethical practices associated with test use.

8. College admission and scholarship testing programs have been criticized for their:
   a. Duplication.
   b. Lack of demonstrated relevance.

    c. Cost.

    d. Susceptibility to coaching.

    e. Susceptibility to invidious interschool comparisons.

    f. Possible adverse psychological effects on examinees.

9. Most of the criticisms of external tests can be stilled by the cooperative efforts of the testing profession, school administrators, college faculties, test publishers, and admissions officers.

10. Common misapprehensions about tests rest on the false beliefs that:

    a. Tests are perfectly reliable.

    b. Test norms constitute standards.

    c. Intelligence and achievement are separable.

    d. Tests measure only recall of specific facts.

11. The National Assessment of Educational Progress (NAEP) is an attempt to provide censuslike survey data on the growth of knowledge, skills, understanding, and attitudes among certain subgroups of American students.

12. NAEP is concerned with performance differences in ten subject areas, four age groups, various geographic regions and community sizes, three community types, and other demographic variables.

13. Individuals involved in test administration should maintain a respectful attitude toward test instruments, individuals, and the setting in which the tests are to be applied.

14. The intelligent use of tests constitutes one of the most powerful, fair, comprehensive, and democratic methods of improving the quality of life for individuals and society.

    A considerable volume of intense critical comment on educational and psychological testing is published each year. Illustrative is the flood of magazine and newspaper articles on testing problems, as well as such books as *The Brain Watchers* (Gross 1962), *The Tyranny of Testing* (Hoffmann 1962), and *They Shall Not Pass* (Black 1962). These publications reflect public antipathy, uneasiness, distrust, and ignorance about tests and testing. They are written by professionals and laymen alike, and occasionally by hack journalists. Many of the criticisms are justified; most are not. As is often the case with observations on technical or social phenomena—particularly those related to education

—intended for public consumption, the views expressed are often narrowly defined and biased. It is therefore hoped that the final chapter of this book will provide the reader with a balanced view of the present state of the art and science of testing.

Two initial comments are in order. First, the critics of testing are saying nothing new. They offer no unique words of wisdom or new insights. They have not exposed long-forgotten or suppressed psychometric skeletons in the testers' closets. Secondly, criticism focuses on an unethical, or at least ignorant, minority of the psychological profession—the self-appointed testers trying to make a quick profit. Unfortunately, the public is likely to assume that these criticisms apply to tests and testers in general.

What can be said in support of the critics? The potential positive effects of their judgments can readily be discerned. First, they reemphasize the inadequacy of certain testing practices. Second, their comments should serve to caution both professionals and laymen against the misuse of tests. Third, they have joined with professional testers in demanding better training for those who administer, interpret, and use tests. Lastly, they have made a significant contribution by identifying issues in need of research. The latter contribution is, however, directly related to a distinctly negative outcome: the critics, both directly by influencing professional educators and indirectly through parents, may tend to deter schools from participating in the much-needed research in testing. Furthermore, the brunt of criticism falls on the tests, instruments, methods, or devices themselves, when all too often the users are at fault.

Most observers would agree that the need for improving communications between the testing profession and the public is being acknowledged. Publications by Chauncey and Dobbin (1963), Hawes (1964), and the American Psychological Association (1965) attest to this fact. Continued vigilance is necessary on the part of professional and lay groups to expose quacks and incompetents, and to press for higher standards in the test-publishing industry and more intensive preservice and in-service training in measurement.

RESPONSES TO SPECIFIC CRITICISMS OF TESTING

Criticisms and controversies periodically draw attention to the many problems associated with standardized educational and psychological tests (Goslin 1968). Some of these are long-standing, while others have arisen out of changes in society. Following is a list of ten criticisms of testing summarized by Holmen and Docter (1972). Each criticism is followed by a response that might typically be made by a representative of the testing profession.

1. CRITICISM: *Tests discriminate against some individuals.*

RESPONSE: A growing body of literature suggests that this may be the case in particular situations. However, an extensive survey by Kirkpatrick and others (1968) of test and criterion data on some 1200 persons—including whites, blacks, and Puerto Ricans—indicates that many of the tests perform equally well in different ethnic groups. In some cases, given tests work best in particular groups. It is argued by some that it is not the test but the unresponsive society that discriminates. It will be argued by all testing professionals that the use of any test that has no demonstrable job-related validity is inexcusable. There is evidence that certain tests do discriminate between selected groups, particularly in employment situations. If such discrimination can be shown to be a function of the relationship between test content and criterion performance, there are no grounds for objection. Such a test distinguishes between those who have and have not achieved, and between those who are and are not likely to be successful. If, on the other hand, the test discriminates on the basis of variables unrelated to validity, it should not be used. Cultural factors can operate to decrease the validity of any test. Some of the issues central to this problem have been highlighted by Cole (1972), Darlington (1971), Thorndike (1971), and Cleary (1968).

Very few instruments have been developed specifically for use with the disadvantaged. However, one prototype instrument has been developed by the Psychological Corporation. The *Fundamental Achievement Series* (FAS) consists of two 30-minute tests, FAS–Verbal and FAS–Numerical, which cover the ability range from basic literacy to slightly above the eighth-grade level. The tests are administered orally, using tape recordings, to enable examinees with limited reading skills to demonstrate their true capabilities. Items in the *Fundamental Achievement Series* are based on everyday experiences and simulate real-life situations and demands. Can the applicant tell which bus will take him to work? Can he determine how much his lunch will cost? Does he understand safety signs? Thus, the FAS measures knowledge and competencies that are relevant for predicting success in training and on the job. More such tests need to be developed and validated in real-life and on-the-job situations.

2. CRITICISM: *Tests predict imperfectly.*

RESPONSE: Agreed. All instruments are fallible. In many instances, however, the use of test data is preferable to reliance on subjective judgment alone. In combination with other kinds of information, tests can do a very creditable job. The fallibility of tests can in part be traced to the fact that humans are fallible. They are inconsistent in responding to tests. In addition, the criteria we use for test validation are less than perfect. It is no wonder that we fall somewhat short of perfection.

3. CRITICISM: *Tests rigidly classify individuals.*

RESPONSE: This criticism would be more appropriate if applied to the users of tests. The classification of individuals into broad categories is useful, efficient, and enhances our understanding of people and their behavior. The failure to recognize that (1) people are ever-changing and that (2) test results are only approximations of human characteristics smacks of ignorance. The use of test scores to label individuals permanently is indefensible.

4. • CRITICISM: *Tests imply the measurement of innate characteristics.*

RESPONSE: The author does not know of a single educational or psychological test publisher who would claim that his tests measure innate human characteristics. Some individual users ignorant of the concepts of validity and reliability may make this claim, but such beliefs in "fixed scores" and the capacity of tests to measure native intelligence are naive, scientifically unsound, and socially detrimental.

5. CRITICISM: *Tests provide the basis for self-fulfilling prophecies.*

RESPONSE: There is no doubt that expectations play an important role in the relationship between teacher and student. Test scores help mold those expectations because they describe important dimensions of a student's ability, proficiency, accomplishments, and personality. When test scores act to rigidify a teacher's thinking about a student and predetermine evaluations of his performance, serious problems can result. We need to know more about the factors that shape teacher expectations.

6. CRITICISM: *Tests have a harmful effect on a student's cognitive style.*

RESPONSE: There is little or no evidence that exposure to particular kinds of tests, e.g., multiple-choice or true-false, adversely affects the development of an individual's style of thinking or problem solving.

7. CRITICISM: *Tests shape school curricula and inhibit educational change.*

RESPONSE: There is a real danger that this can happen. However, such an occurrence reflects a misuse of tests, rather than a shortcoming of the tests themselves. The critical question is whether or not the teachers' objectives are the same as those of the test items. If they are, there is no problem. If, however, the content of the test becomes the determining criterion, serious distortion of the educational process can result.

8.   CRITICISM: *Tests distort student self-concept and level of aspiration.*

RESPONSE: It can be argued that, quite to the contrary, tests help the individual to see himself, his capacities, and his accomplishments more realistically. We must assume that the tests provide fair and valid results, which are communicated by a trained professional skilled in test interpretation. This is an area in which school guidance and counseling personnel can make a significant contribution.

9.   CRITICISM: *Tests select homogeneous educational groups.*

RESPONSE: This criticism should perhaps more accurately be leveled at the practices of grouping and ability-tracking, rather than at tests. If tests were not used to select groups, other measures—grades, teacher ratings, and the like—would probably be substituted. In any event, research does not support effectiveness of grouping as an organizational scheme.

10.   CRITICISM: *Tests invade privacy.*

RESPONSE: This criticism is aimed primarily at measures of personality, values, and attitudes. If these kinds of measures have little relevance to a meaningful criterion, e.g., school performance or job success, they should not be used. But if such information can be shown to be useful to the institution and the individual, it can legitimately be gathered.

INVASION OF PRIVACY—LEGAL AND ETHICAL CONSIDERATIONS

The right to privacy is the precious birthright of all members of a free democratic society. There must be a compelling justification for tests to invade that privacy.

Congressional hearings were held in 1965 to investigate the possible misapplication of a specific test (the *Minnesota Multiphasic Personality Inventory*) in situations relating to federal employment. Gallagher (1965) has presented a summary of the charges.

1. Some federal job applicants were compelled to take personality tests as part of the employment screening process.

2. No effective appeal procedure was available.

3. Personality testing represented a form of "searching the minds of federal employees and job applicants."

4. Tests improperly excluded desirable people from jobs they deserved to hold.

5. The reliability and validity of score patterns on the personality tests used was an "unsettled controversy."

6. Personality-test questions inquired into highly personal and intimate matters.

7. The tests were utilized by personnel workers who were unqualified to do so.

8. Test reports were retained; they tended to follow a person through his career.

9. Test records were not kept confidential, as promised.

10. Personality tests raised questions about applicants that tended to cause personnel decisions to be made against them.

11. Personality testing was required of many federal job applicants in some agencies, but was not required of top-level federal employees.

Obviously, the implications of these charges transcend the application of personality tests in federal employment. The invasion-of-privacy issue touches a number of fields in which tests are used. Messick (1965) notes that inasmuch as tests are used extensively in (1) diagnosis and guidance, (2) academic selection and employment, and (3) human research, potential dangers may arise from the misapplication of tests in a variety of settings.

Misapplication of any test can result in legal action. Two recent court cases illustrate this point. It was charged in Griggs *vs.* Duke Power Company, and United States *et al. vs.* Georgia Power Company, that tests were used in discriminatory ways. Title VII of the 1964 Civil Rights Act, which requires employers to hire individuals without regard to their race, religion, national origin, or sex, led to the establishment of the Equal Employment Opportunity Commission. EEOC has established guidelines for testing and other selection procedures. In writing the Supreme Court's unanimous opinion in Griggs *vs.* Duke Power Company, Chief Justice Burger noted that

> The Act proscribes not only overt discrimination but also practices that are fair in form, but discriminatory in operation. The touchstone is business necessity. If an employment practice which operates to exclude Negroes cannot be shown to be related to job performance, the practice is prohibited. . . . Nothing in the Act precludes the use of testing or measuring procedures; obviously they are useful. What Congress has forbidden is giving these devices and mechanisms controlling force unless they are demonstrably a reasonable measure of job performance. Congress has not commanded that the less qualified be preferred over the better qualified simply because of minority origins. Far from disparaging job qualifications as such, Congress has made such qualifications the controlling factor, so that race, religion, nationality and sex become

irrelevant. . . . Congress has placed on the employer the burden of showing that any given requirement must have a manifest relationship to the employment in question.

The reader is referred to Deutsch *et al.* (1969) for a set of guidelines for testing the disadvantaged.

What procedures are available for curbing the misuses of educational and psychological tests? There is, of course, now a legal precedent requiring proof of validity for tests used for selection purposes. Tightening state licensing and certification laws is another avenue for improvement. Voluntary restrictions on the sale and distribution of tests by test publishers is yet another possibility. Perhaps the most powerful pressure for improved testing practices can be exerted within the profession. Pre- and in-service training programs should be expanded and updated. Greater adherence to the recommendations of state and national professional organizations must be secured. The kinds of ethical responsibilities that need to be assumed by those engaged in testing are illustrated by the following principles, excerpted from the American Psychological Association's *Ethical Standards of Psychologists*:[1]

Principle 13. *Test Security.* Psychological tests and other assessment devices, the value of which depends in part on the naiveté of the subject, are not reproduced or described in popular publications in ways that might invalidate the techniques. Access to such devices is limited to persons with professional interests who will safeguard their use.

   a. Sample items made up to resemble those of tests being discussed may be reproduced in popular articles and elsewhere, but scorable tests and actual test items are not reproduced except in professional publications.

   b. The psychologist is responsible for the control of psychological tests and other devices and procedures used for instruction when their value might be damaged by revealing to the general public their specific contents or underlying principles.

Principle 14. *Test Interpretation.* Test scores, like test materials, are released only to persons who are qualified to interpret and use them properly.

   a. Materials for reporting test scores to parents, or which are designed for self-appraisal purposes in schools, social agencies, or industry are closely supervised by qualified psychologists or counselors with provisions for referring and counseling individuals when needed.

---

[1] American Psychological Association, Ethical standards of psychologists. *American Psychologist* 18 (1963): 56–60. Reprinted by permission of the American Psychological Association.

    b. Test results or other assessment data used for evaluation or classification are communicated to employers, relatives or other appropriate persons in such a manner as to guard against misinterpretations or misuse. In the usual case, an interpretation of the test result rather than the score is communicated.

    c. When test results are communicated directly to parents and students, they are accompanied by adequate interpretive aids or advice.

Principle 15. *Test Publication.* Psychological tests are offered for commercial publication only to publishers who present their tests in a professional way and distribute them only to qualified users.

    a. A test manual, technical handbook, or other suitable report on the test is provided which describes the method of constructing and standardizing the test, and summarizes the validation research.

    b. The populations for which the test has been developed and the purposes for which it is recommended are stated in the manual. Limitations upon the test's dependability, and aspects of its validity on which research is lacking or incomplete, are clearly stated. In particular, the manual contains a warning regarding interpretations likely to be made which have not yet been substantiated by research.

    c. The catalog and manual indicate the training or professional qualifications required for sound interpretation of the test.

    d. The test manual and supporting documents take into account the principles enunciated in the *Standards for Educational and Psychological Tests and Manuals* (American Psychological Association 1966).

    e. Test advertisements are factual and descriptive rather than emotional and persuasive.

These three principles and the position statement on pages 449–453 should serve as an excellent basis for a code of ethics for testers.

EXTERNAL TESTING PROGRAMS

Within the last few decades the number of external tests administered to high-school students has spiraled dramatically. Explanations of this phenomenon are varied, but primarily involve college admissions and the granting of scholarships. Objections to external tests are voiced by many local school administrators, because the burden of proving the legitimacy and validity of such programs frequently falls on their shoulders. External tests are characterized by three distinctive features: 1) their results are used primarily by an institution or organization other than the high school; 2) the local school is unable to choose whether or not their students take such tests; and 3) responsibility for security of the tests is assumed by the test publisher. Three tests widely used for selection purposes are the College Entrance Examination Board's Scholastic Aptitude and Achievement Tests; the American College Testing Program tests; and the College Qualification Test. The National Merit Scholarship Qualifying Test and the Preliminary Scholastic Aptitude Test are used to select recipients of scholarships. In addition, some states have their own selection testing programs.

The administration of these tests to hundreds of thousands of students each year has generated considerable controversy. Ebel (1962) and Womer (1961) have listed the major criticisms of external testing programs and suggested rebuttals or solutions to each:

Criticism of External Testing	*Response or Possible Solution*
1. Not all important outcomes are measured.	1. Those variables of primary importance to college work are assessed. If important variables are ignored they may not have been defined clearly enough.
2. Only facts and knowledge are measured.	2. Within the last several years external tests have stressed the ability to use information. Command of useful knowledge is important.
3. External tests are unfair to some students.	3. Measuring instruments are fallible. Common essential outcomes are emphasized.
4. The use of objective (e.g., multiple-choice) items is discriminatory.	4. If these items are relevant to the criterion of college success, they are valid. Choice making is an aspect of all human activities.
5. External tests adversely influence curriculum innovation and educational change.	5. There is a danger that this will be the case. Test developers work *with* curriculum experts and educators in establishing objectives.
6. Tests do not predict perfectly.	6. Tests, as well as individuals, are fallible. Successful predictions far outnumber mispredictions. It is impossible to assess all relevant variables in advance.
7. There is too much duplication of testing.	7. Development of general-purpose equivalency tables would help.

8. Too much time and money are expended for tests.

8. Considering the potential payoff and the importance of the decisions to be made, the investment is minimal.

9. The advantaged can secure coaching that helps insure success on tests.

9. Research indicates that coaching does on the whole have an effect. If coaching also improves school performance, so much the better. The validity of the test is not undermined. As well, the opportunity for coaching should be made available to all.

10. The use of external tests invites invidious comparisons between schools.

10. Scores should be reported only to target institutions and individual students.

11. Exposure to external testing situations adversely affects students' emotional stability and mental health.

11. There is little or no evidence that this is true.

12. External test scores determine college entrance.

12. Nothing could be further from the truth. An entrance decision is made on the basis of a collection of relevant data, *never* on a single test score.

The overall positive contribution of external testing programs is evident. In addition to the potential advantages to the individual, society benefits by identifying and training the students best qualified to make contributions. The voluntary nature of the testing system is another point in its favor. It promotes initiative. Problems within the system should be worked out cooperatively by test specialists, college faculties and admissions officers, test publishers, and school administrators.

SOME MISUSES AND MISINTERPRETATIONS OF STANDARDIZED TESTS

As we have seen, the testing profession has recently come under attack from many quarters (Black 1963; Gross 1962; and Hoffmann 1962).

Our intent here is not to rebut such charges (this has already been adequately accomplished by, for example, Chauncey and Dobbin 1963, and Hawes 1964), but to (1) emphasize that criticisms should generally be aimed at test *users* rather than the instruments themselves, and (2) highlight some of the mistakes that users can make. Ideas expressed by Dyer (1961) and Womer (1961) have significantly influenced the author's thinking about the following misconceptions:

The Belief that Standardized Tests Are Perfectly Reliable

Educational and psychological tests are fallible devices, subject to many sources of error. Considering the vast number of possible sources of error, it is astonishing that we do as good a job as we do. The people who take tests are also unpredictable and subject to error. Human beings are inconsistent and ever-changing. The combination of these two types of variability must of necessity lead to an imperfect degree of measurement consistency. Regarding tests as perfectly reliable increases the danger of categorizing a student at a certain level of achievement or mental capacity. The assignment to each student of a formal or implicit "ability level" that persists throughout his school life is a practice to be avoided at all costs. Such a use of test scores can only be described as highly unprofessional. In any event, one must ask, "If tests are fallible, would students, employers, employees, and society be better served if test results were ignored?" The answer must be no. What are the alternatives?

The Belief that Test Norms Are Standards

Some uninformed users of standardized tests regard the distributions of scores derived from nationwide population samplings as goals to be achieved by each of their students. National norms may serve a useful function by providing "benchmarks" to judge students' overall progress, but they should *never* serve as the sole criterion of program effectiveness or pupil progress. Failure to take into account the educational philosophy of local teachers, administrators, and the community, and the socioeconomic and ability level of the school population, can lead to gross misevaluations. A related danger is that the tests may begin to determine the nature of the instructional program. A school and its teachers should not be evaluated exclusively on the basis of students' performances on standardized achievement tests. Nor should standards for a local school district be determined by blind consultation of norms tables. Furthermore, a standardized achievement test should never be the sole source of data for marking or promotional decisions.

The Belief that Achievement and Intelligence Are Distinct

In a very real sense, intelligence and achievement tests measure the same thing: the ability to perform selected tasks at a specified point in time. Although achievement tests measure abilities acquired under relatively controlled conditions, and intelligence tests measure abilities acquired under relatively uncontrolled conditions, a cursory review of standardized achievement and intelligence tests will reveal significant overlap. The content of the two types of tests is quite similar, and the correlations between scores are usually in the .50s and above. The tests do differ, however, in the ways in which results are used. We tend to use achievement tests to measure past performance or describe how well certain learning tasks have been accomplished, and intelligence tests to predict future performance. In schools and colleges today, however, achievement tests are playing an increasingly important role in prediction.

The Belief that Standardized Achievement Tests Measure Only Recall of Facts

Most standardized achievement tests do emphasize recall, but it can legitimately be argued that one must have a large fund of information at his command in order to reason, argue, solve problems, or function effectively in society. And, as we have said, most reputable achievement tests do measure such higher-order abilities such as comprehension, application, and problem solving. The user must remember that even the highest-quality achievement test cannot measure an entire subject-matter area. Such tests can only sample types of learning. Similarly, users should be very cautious in interpreting the multiscore profiles that many survey batteries provide. Test experts have demonstrated that, because of the high degree of relationship between subtests, the differences reflected in such profiles are highly unreliable.

NATIONAL ASSESSMENT OF EDUCATIONAL PROGRESS

The ever-increasing cost of public education is a matter of growing concern to professional educators, laymen, and government personnel. As was noted in Chapter One, the concept of accountability is being implemented in a variety of ways to make the educational process more effective and efficient. And efficiency, of course, influences cost. Billions of dollars are spent in the United States each year on buildings, salaries, and curricula, with minimal attention to the effectiveness of these expenditures. The purpose of the National Assessment of Educational Progress is to collect information that can be used in rational decisionmaking about our schools. The resulting data would have implications both for curricula and for the allocation of funds.

The NAEP is a censuslike survey of the knowledge, skills, understandings, and attitudes of certain groups of young Americans. It focuses on growth and decline in selected educational attainments of young Americans. Ten subject areas—citizenship, science, writing, music, mathematics, literature, social studies, reading, art, and career and occupational development—are examined cyclically. The first assessment cycle began in 1969, with coverage of science, writing, and citizenship. These areas will again be assessed during the last portion of first cycle, which ends in August 1975. Repeated assessments will reveal whether change has occurred. During the first year of data gathering, approximately 90,000 people participated. Extreme care is exercised to avoid identifying any individual, student, school, city, or state. A given student will respond to only a portion of the exercises.

Approximately half of the exercises administered during any given year are reported. Results are reported as percentages of various groups that respond correctly (and incorrectly) to the exercises. The groups are made up of individuals representing various combinations of the following categories:

1. Age—9-, 13-, and 17-year-olds, and young adults (between ages of 26 and 35).

2. Geographic region—Northeast, Southeast, Central, and West.

3. Size of community—big cities, urban fringes, medium-size cities, and less populated places.

4. Type of community—impoverished inner cities, affluent suburbs, and rural areas.

5. Sex.

6. Color—black, nonblack, and total.

7. Socioeducational background.

NAEP is currently under the control of the Education Commission of the States (ECS). This quasipublic, quasipolitical organization is currently composed of representatives of 43 states and territories whose purpose is to consider mutual educational problems and to act together to achieve educational goals. Since its membership includes governors, state school officials, legislators, and lay people, National Assessment is legally responsible to the public.

Extensive effort was expended by scholars, school personnel, and representatives of the public to identify the most relevant objectives of American education. The resulting objectives were then translated, mostly under contract with commercial test developers, into a variety of tasks—some paper-and-pencil, some group activities, and a variety of other formats.

The interested reader is referred to articles by Merwin and Womer (1969), Tyler (1969), Finley (1971), and Womer (1970) for descriptions of the background, initial readouts, and implications of NAEP.

THE RESPONSIBLE USE OF TESTS: A POSITION PAPER BY THE PROFESSION[2]

Tests and testing programs have been challenged by those who see them as operating to the disadvantage, in effect, of one or more minority groups. What position should concerned, conscientious test makers and test users take to insure that tests are given, and examinees are treated, fairly and wisely?

What Testing Is

Testing is not a policy nor a set of beliefs or principles. Testing is a technique for obtaining information. Its special virtue is that this information is provided in organized form, and that the technology of testing also provides methods for determining how dependable or undependable the information is.[3]

As a technique, testing itself is neutral. It is a tool that serves the ends of the user. The better he understands the technology of testing, the better it meets his needs. The less well he grasps this technology, the greater the risk that inadvertently (and perhaps unknowingly) he may work at cross-purposes to his own goals.

---

[2] At the 1970 convention in New Orleans, the American Personnel and Guidance Association (APGA) Senate adopted a resolution expressing concern over certain effects of tests and testing on minority groups in education and industry. Among steps taken in implementing this resolution was one charging one of the APGA divisions, the Association for Measurement and Evaluation in Guidance (AMEG), to prepare a statement of position on the use of tests. This task was undertaken by the Past President, President, and President-Elect, who solicited the help of the heads of other measurement associations and prepared a draft submitted to the APGA Board of Directors and Senate at the 1971 meeting in Atlantic City. After revision in the light of comments and criticisms from both inside and outside APGA, the paper presented here was adopted as an official position of APGA by its Board of Directors and of the National Council on Measurement in Education by its Board at their Chicago conventions in March and April, 1972.

Abridged from The responsible use of tests: A position paper of AMEG, APGA, and NCME. *Measurement and Evaluation in Guidance* 5, No. 2 (July 1972): 385–388, by permission of APGA. Copyright © 1972 by American Personnel and Guidance Association.

[3] In this position paper, we are concerned with the testing of knowledge and abilities, not with clinical testing as used in helping persons who have mental or emotional problems.

In schools and colleges, the principal needs served by testing include the providing of information (a) to teachers, as an aid to the improvement of instruction; (b) to students and, in the case of younger students, to their parents, as an aid to self-understanding and to both educational and vocational planning; and (c) to administrators, as a basis for planning, decisionmaking, and evaluating the effectiveness of programs and operations.

In business, industry, government service, and other walks of life, the general goal of testing is that of improving the match between persons and jobs, whether they be manual or managerial, personal contact or professional. Tests serve either to verify claimed knowledge or competency (e.g., a typing test) or to appraise readiness to master the training needed in order to perform the job. They may be used either competitively (to aid in selecting the best qualified and to avoid political or racial favoritisms), or as a standard (to avoid placing on the job persons whose work would likely be unsafe or uneconomic). Not every job nor every selection situation is equally likely to benefit from the use of tests, of course.

In these terms, testing as such would seem hard to criticize and quite unlikely to arouse antagonism or draw complaints from anyone. Yet it has been the target of bitter attacks, by members of some minority groups and by others in their behalf. The attacks usually result from one, or from a combination of two, of these three factors:

1.   The use of tests, more or less competently, by administrators, and others with whose goals and values the attackers disagree.

2.   Side effects of testing, unintended results obtained when tests are used incompetently or without due regard for their technological strengths and limitations.

3.   Misunderstandings of the role played by testing—the tendency to attribute to the tool shortcomings of its user, often accompanied by the simplistic assumption that if use of the tool is forbidden, things will somehow get better if not be entirely all right.

The Role of APGA and the Measurement Societies

In the first case, the intentional use of tests to accomplish a questionable purpose, the remedy—whatever the contribution of testing may be—lies with the courts, boards of education, civil service commissions, and other public bodies. Professional associations, including the measurement societies, do not have the authority to control intentional discrimination against particular groups, though individual members acting in accordance with their own consciences may bring to bear such powers as their positions afford them.

There are distinct and positive roles for measurement societies, on the other hand, in connection with the second and third causes of distress. Continuing education, publication, and such other forms of communications as speaking before concerned groups can do much to alleviate the misunderstandings that give rise to the third phenomenon. But it is in the effects of the second that the most legitimate complaints about testing are rooted, and it is in reducing this set of causes and in coping with these effects that the professional associations devoted to tests and measurements find their deepest obligations and their greatest opportunities.

The Respectful Use of Tests

Those who work well at any trade or art hold in deep respect the concepts, tools, and materials with which they accomplish their tasks. For the producers and users of test information, the important elements are the people who are tested, the tests that are used, and the situations or purposes in or for which the work is done. Good testing is marked by

I. *Respect for the Individual.* In educational and clinical testing, all the work is undertaken for the benefit ultimately of those who are tested, not of the institutions and agencies doing the testing.

In employment testing, the primary benefit may be the employer's—but in the long run no selection program can be of genuine value to the employer if it is not so designed and conducted as to benefit also the employees and the applicants.

II. *Respect for the Instrument.* It is an abuse of the instrument, as well as disrespectful of the individual's needs and rights, to use a test for a purpose inappropriate to those characteristics and limits that make it a test. Test directions, stimulus material, verbal or other content, time limit, and supporting data, all must be considered in the decision to use a particular measure with particular individuals for a particular purpose under particular circumstances. When the application of the instrument is inappropriate, neither the characteristics of those tested nor the accuracy and utility of the instrument can be determined from the data obtained.

Decisions of this kind may be quite clear and easy to make, but often are neither; frequently the *purpose* is the crucial consideration. It may, for example, be both fair and useful to give an individual examination in English to a child or adult whose native language is another, when the purpose is simply to appraise his readiness to profit from lectures given in English; yet the same activity clearly is indefensible if the test score is to be used as an estimate of his all-round intellectual capability.

III. *Respect for the Setting.* Use of a test or battery that is appropriate for a given purpose, with individuals whom it might well benefit, may still be frustrating, discouraging, or worse if the setting is one that does not afford the options or opportunities needed for effective use of the information obtained from the testing. An understaffed guidance department or very limited alternatives in the curriculum or on the job can render test results essentially useless except for fattening files.

The castigations of tests and testing by those who are deeply concerned with the status and opportunities of minority groups have increased markedly in the recent past. While some complaints merely reflect misunderstandings, others no doubt are justified—though not all will agree on which cases are which. What, then, is to be done to remedy the faulty applications of testing and make their recurrence less likely? Write rules? Fix the tools? Ban testing? Provide for review and remedy?

Write rules? To the extent that the problems arise from inadequate respect for, or attention to, the elements listed in the first section, can a code be formulated, adherence to which would keep us from going wrong?

In the light of the thousands of pages that already exist treating these matters, the answer almost certainly is no, not in any form concise enough to be of practical use. And those who go wrong even now cannot be said to do so for lack of the pointing out of good practice by others. There remains a challenge to professionals to see that understandings and rules of good practice are more widely disseminated and observed.

Fix the tools? It is very tempting to think that if only better, "fairer," more nearly perfect tests were made, all will be well. But better tests will not solve the social ills they reflect. Indeed, as John W. Gardner pointed out ten years ago in *Excellence* (Gardner 1961), the more adequately tests do what they are supposed to do, the *more, not the less,* will they provide disturbing information when the underlying social, economic, and educational conditions are not those of equality.

Better tests can and will be made—but while seeking perfection, we cannot wait for its realization. Even though imperfect and incomplete, the information tests provide is essential to realistic handling of our educational and personnel problems—whether they be those of learning or of reading, of hiring a worker or of getting a job.

Ban testing? The role of measurement is too central, too fundamental to the conduct and improvement of education and to sound personnel practices in business and industry for this to be a realistic alternative. For some years it was illegal to request information as to race on applications for admission or employment; forbidding the recording of such information was thought to work toward the abolition of discrimination. Now the trend is reversed; organizations are required by law to obtain and report the very information that they once were forbidden to ask. What vanished under the ban was not discrimination, but the ability to tell whether and to what extent colleges or employers were doing what nearly all now agree they should do. The same cycle may be predicted if we try to deal with the present problem by doing away with tests; the ostrich approach does not lead to the effective solution of problems. Organizations and persons committed to changing educational or social systems, no less than those seeking to preserve a system, will need the information that measurement provides.

Provide, then, for review and remedy. This, we believe, is the process to which the measurement societies and their parent association can best contribute, and in which their contribution is most needed.

People depend on the laws of the land and on many arts to meet their needs and protect their rights. Courts build policy and practice by judging not only points of law but also the applications and effects of arts and technologies. Case by case, tediously perhaps, but always with reference to a concrete happening, positions and rules of practice can be formed and established. The measurement societies must help.

It can be seen, then, that the profession is concerned about the many issues surrounding the development and use of tests in all areas of human endeavor. And despite the shortcomings of some tests and users, tests have proven to be valuable educational tools. As Angoff and Anderson (1963) have noted:

> For both human and practical reasons, the standardized test is a necessary outcome of the philosophy of a modern democratic society in which large masses of individuals, competing for educational awards or simply seeking better self-understanding, assemble for an objective, unbiased evaluation of their abilities. No other method that we know of today can provide measurement for the tremendous numbers of individuals who demand objective consideration of their talents. Certainly no other method that we know of today can accomplish this measurement as equitably as the standardized test.

SUGGESTED READINGS

American Psychological Association. *Standards for educational and psychological tests and manuals*. Washington: APA, 1966. A set of three-level standards (Essential, Very Desirable, and Desirable) aimed at influencing test development, reporting, and selection.

Anastasi, Anne. *Psychological testing*, 3rd ed. New York: Macmillan, 1968. Chapter 21, "Social Implications of Psychological Testing," contains an excellent survey of such major issues as invasion of privacy and testing of the culturally disadvantaged.

Barclay, J. R. *Controversial issues in testing.* Boston: Houghton Mifflin, 1968. A readable overview of the issues involved in the anti-test revolt and problems related to test interpretation in a variety of settings.

College Entrance Examination Board. *Report of the Commission on Tests. I. Righting the balance, and II. Briefs.* New York: CEEB, 1970. This two-volume report and collection of position papers on CEEB activities by the Commission on Tests is an example of internal policing by the largest external testing organization in the country. Proposed changes and recommendations are offered.

Findley, W. G. *The impact and improvement of school testing programs* (62nd Yearbook of the National Society for the Study of Education, Part II). Chicago: University of Chicago Press, 1963. Particularly recommended are Chapter 4, "The Impact of Testing on School Organization"; Chapter 6, "Effects of Testing Programs on the Attitudes of Students, Teachers, Parents and Community"; and Chapter 9, "The Impact of External Testing Programs."

Goslin, D. A. *The search for ability: Standardized testing in social perspective.* New York: John Wiley, 1966. An extensive survey and study of the potential social, legal, and emotional impact of standardized testing on society, the groups and organizations that make use of tests, and the individuals who are directly affected by the results.

————. *Teachers and testing.* New York: Russell Sage Foundation, 1967. An examination of teachers' opinions and practices with regard to tests and a discussion of their implications for educational policy.

Holmen, M. G., and Docter, R. F. *Educational and psychological testing: A study of the industry and its practices.* New York: Russell Sage Foundation, 1972. An investigative report on the capabilities of different kinds of companies to meet established standards of test development and an examination of how these organizations actually function.

Lennon, R. T. *Testimony of Dr. Roger T. Lennon as expert witness on psychological testing.* New York: Harcourt Brace Jovanovich, 1966. This absorbing brief paperback summarizes the courtroom testimony of Dr. Lennon in the case of Hobson *et al. vs.* Hansen *et al.* and the Washington D. C. Board of Education. The charge under investigation was the alleged discriminatory use of psychological tests in ability-tracking.

Tyler, R. W., and Wolf, R. M., eds. *Crucial issues in testing.* Berkeley, California: McCutchan Publishing Corporation, 1974.

REFERENCES

Adams, Georgia S. *Measurement and evaluation in education, psychology, and guidance.* New York: Holt, Rinehart and Winston, 1964.

Ahmann, J. S., and Glock, M. D. *Evaluating pupil growth,* 2nd ed. Boston: Allyn and Bacon, 1963.

Alkin, M. C. Accountability defined. *Evaluation Comment 3,* no. 3 (May 1972): 1–5. Published by the University of California at Los Angeles Center for the Study of Evaluation.

Alkin, M. C. Evaluating net cost-effectiveness of instructional programs. In *The evaluation of instruction: Issues and problems,* ed. M. Wittrock and D. Wiley, pp. 221–255. New York: Holt, Rinehart and Winston, 1970.

Allen, R. M. *Personality assessment procedures,* New York: Harper & Row, 1958.

Allport, G. W. *The use of personal documents in psychological science.* New York: Social Science Research Council, 1942.

Allport, G. W.; Vernon, P. E.; and Lindzey, G. *A study of values,* 3rd ed. Boston: Houghton Mifflin, 1960.

American Council on Education. *A design for general education.* Washington: ACE, 1944.

American Psychological Association. *Standards for educational and psychological tests and manuals.* Washington: 1973. Testing and public policy (special issue). *American Psychologist* 20 (1965): 857–993.

Amidon, E., and Flanders, N. *The role of the teacher in the classroom.* Minneapolis: Paul S. Amidon and Associates, 1963.

Amidon, E. J., and Hough, J. B., eds. *Interaction analysis: Theory, research and application.* Reading, Mass.: Addison-Wesley, 1967.

Angoff, W. H., and Anderson, Scarvia B. The standardization of educational and psychological tests. *Illinois Journal of Education* (February 1963): 19–23.

Atkin, J. M. Behavioral objectives in curriculum design: A cautionary note. *The Science Teacher* 35 (May 1968): 27–39.

Atkinson, J. W. Towards experimental analysis of human motivation in terms of motives, expectancies, and incentives. In *Motives in fantasy, action, and society,* ed. J. W. Atkinson, pp. 288–305. Princeton, N.J.: D. Van Nostrand, 1958.

Ayers, J. D. Justification of Bloom's taxonomy by factor analysis. Paper presented at the annual meeting of the American Educational Research Association, February 1966, in Chicago.

Bahrick, H. P. Retention curves: Facts or artifacts? *Psychological Bulletin* 61 (1964): 188–194.

Balch, J. The influence of the evaluating instrument on student's learning. *American Educational Research Journal* 1, no. 3 (May 1964): 169–182.

Barclay, J. R. *Controversial issues in testing.* Boston: Houghton Mifflin, 1968.

Barker, R. G., and Wright, H. F. *Midwest and its children, the psychological ecology of an American town.* New York: Harper and Row, 1954.

Barro, S. M. An approach to developing accountability measures for the public schools. *Phi Delta Kappan* 52 (December 1970): 196–205.

Bass, B. M., and Berg, I. A. *Objective approaches to personality assessment.* Princeton, N.J.: Van Nostrand, 1959.

Bassham, H.; Murphy, M.; and Murphy, Katherine. Attitude and achievement in arithmetic. *The Arithmetic Teacher* 11 (1964): pp. 66–72.

Bauernfeind, R. F. Goal cards and future developments in achievement testing. *Proceedings of the 1966 Invitational Conference on Testing Problems.* Princeton, N.J.: Educational Testing Service, 1967.

Beatty, Walter H., ed. *Improving educational assessment and an inventory of measures of affective behavior.* Washington: Association for Supervision and Curriculum Development, 1969.

Black, H. *They shall not pass.* New York: William Morrow, 1963.

Bledsoe, J. C. *Essentials of educational research,* 2nd ed. Athens, Ga.: Optima House, 1972.

Block, J. H. Criterion-referenced measurements: Potential. *School Review* 79, no. 2 (1971): 289–297.

Block, J. *The challenge of response sets.* New York: Appleton-Century-Crofts, 1965.

Blommers, P., and Lindquist, E. F. *Elementary statistical methods in psychology and education.* Boston: Houghton Mifflin, 1960.

Bloom, B. S. Toward a theory of testing which includes measurement-evaluation-assessment. In *The evaluation of instruction: Issues and problems,* ed. M. C. Wittrock and D. E. Wiley. New York: Holt, Rinehart and Winston, 1970.

Bloom, B., *et al. Taxonomy of educational objectives. Handbook I: The cognitive domain.* New York: David McKay, 1956.

Bloom, B. S.; Hastings, J. T.; and Madaus, G. F. *Handbook on formative and summative evaluation of student learning.* New York: McGraw-Hill, 1971.

Bonney, M. E., and Hampleman, R. S. *Personal-social evaluation techniques.* Washington: Center for Applied Research in Education, 1962.

Bradfield, J. M., and Moredock, H. S. *Measurement and evaluation in education,* New York: Macmillan, 1957.

Breer, P. E., and Locke, E. A. *Task experience as a source of attitudes.* Homewood, Ill.: Dorsey Press, 1965.

Bronfenbrenner, U. *The measurement of sociometric status, structure and development. Sociometry Monographs,* No. 6. New York: Beacon House, 1945.

Broudy, H. S. Can research escape the dogma of behavioral objectives? *School Review* 79 (November 1970): 43–56.

Brownell, W. A. The evaluation of learning under different systems of instruction. *Educational Psychologist* 3 (1965): 5–7.

Buros, O. K., ed. *The seventh mental measurements yearbook.* Highland Park, N.J.: Gryphon Press, 1972.

———. *Personality tests and reviews.* Highland Park, N.J.: Gryphon Press, 1970.

———. *Reading tests and reviews.* Highland Park, N.J.: Gryphon Press, 1969.

———. *The sixth mental measurements yearbook.* Highland Park. N.J.: Gryphon Press, 1965.

———. *The mental measurements yearbooks.* Highland Park, N.J.: Gryphon Press, (Sixth) 1965, (Fifth) 1959, (Fourth) 1953, and (Third) 1949.

Campbell, D. T. The indirect assessment of social attitudes. *Psychological Bulletin* 47, no. 1 (January 1950): 15–38.

Campbell, D. T., and Fiske, D. W. Convergent and discriminant validation by the multitrait-multimethod matrix. *Psychological Bulletin* 56 (1959): 81–105.

Campbell, D. T., and Stanley, J. C. *Experimental and quasi-experimental designs.* Chicago: Rand McNally, 1963.

Cattell, R. B.; Heist, A. B.; and Stewart, R. G. The objective measurement of dynamic traits. *Educational and Psychological Measurement* 10 (1950): 224–248.

Charters, Margaret. *A study of the congruence between curriculum intent and evaluation objectives using two strategies for stating curriculum objectives.* Unpublished doctoral dissertation, Syracuse University, 1970.

Chauncey, H., and Dobbin, J. E. *Testing: Its place in education today.* New York: Harper & Row, 1963.

Churchman, C. W. Why measure? In *Measurement definitions and theories* ed. C. W. Churchman and P. Ratoosh. New York: John Wiley and Sons, 1959.

Cleary, T. Anne. Test bias: Prediction of grades of Negro and white students in integrated colleges. *Journal of Educational Measurement* 5 (1968): 115–124.

Coffield, W. H., and Blommers, P. Effects of non-promotion on educational achievement in elementary school. *Journal of Educational Psychology* 47 (1956): 235–250.

Cole, Marilyn; Fletcher, F. M.; and Pressey, S. L. Forty-year changes in college student attitudes. *Journal of Counseling Psychology* 10 (1963): 53–55.

Cole, Nancy. *Bias in selection.* ACT Research Report no. 51, May 1972. Iowa City: American College Testing Program, Research and Development Division.

Cook, D. L. *Program evaluation and review technique: Applications in education.* U.S. Department of Health, Education, and Welfare Cooperative Research Monograph no. 17. Washington: U.S. Government Printing Office, 1966.

Cook, W. W. The functions of measurement in the facilitation of learning. In *Educational measurement,* ed. E. F. Lindquist. Washington: American Council on Education, 1951.

Corey, S. M. Measuring attitudes in the classroom. *Elementary School Journal* 43 (1943): 437–461.

———. Professed attitudes and actual behavior. *Journal of Educational Psychology* 38 (1937): 271–280.

Costin, F.; Greenough, W. T.; and Menges, R. J. Student ratings of college teaching: reliability, validity, and usefulness. *Review of Educational Research* 41 (1971): 511–535.

Cottle, W. C. *Interest and personality inventories.* Boston: Houghton Mifflin, 1968.

Cox, R. C. Evaluative aspects of criterion-references measures. In *Criterion-referenced measurement: An introduction,* ed. W. J. Popham. Englewood Cliffs, N.J.: Educational Technology Publications, 1971.

Cox, R. C., and Graham, G. T. The development of sequentially scaled achievement tests. *Journal of Educational Measurement* 3 (1966): 147–150.

Cox, R. C., and Vargas, Julie S. A comparison of item selection techniques for norm-referenced and criterion-referenced tests. Paper read at annual meeting of the National Council on Measurement in Education, February 1966, in Chicago. ERIC Microfilm ED010517, 1966.

Cox, R. C., and Wildemann, Carole E. *Taxonomy of educational objectives: Cognitive domain—An annotated bibliography.* University of Pittsburgh Learning Research and Development Center monograph no. 1. Pittsburgh: 1970.

Crane, P., and Abt, C. C. A model for curriculum evaluation. *Educational Technology* 9 (1969): 17–25.

Cronbach, L. J. *Essentials of psychological testing,* 3rd ed. New York: Harper & Row, 1970.

———. *Essentials of psychological testing,* 2nd ed. New York: Harper & Row, 1960.

———. *Educational psychology,* 2nd ed. New York: Harcourt Brace Jovanovich, 1963a.

———. Course improvement through evaluation. *Teachers College Record* 64 (1963b): 276–268.

———. Coefficient alpha and the internal structure of tests. *Psychometrika* 16 (1951): 297–334.

———. Further evidence on response sets and test design. *Educational and Psychological Measurement* 10 (1950): 3–31.

————. Response sets and test validity. *Educational and Psychological Measurement* 6 (1946): 475–494.

————. Test validation. In *Educational measurement,* 2nd ed., ed. R. L. Thorndike, pp. 443–507. Washington: American Council on Education, 1971.

Cronbach, L. J.; Gleser, G. C.; Nanda, H.; and Rajaratnam, N. *The dependability of behavioral measurements.* New York: Wiley, 1970.

Cronbach, L. J., and Meehl, P. E. Construct validity in psychological tests, *Psychological Bulletin* 52 (1955): 281–302.

Cronbach, L. J.; Rajaratnam, N.; and Gleser, G. C. Theory of generalizability: A liberalization of reliability theory. *British Journal of Statistical Psychology* 15 (1963): 137–163.

Crowne, D. P., and Marlowe, D. *The approval motive.* New York: John Wiley and Sons, 1964.

————. A new scale of social desirability independent of psychopathology. *Journal of Consulting Psychology* 24 (1960): 349–354.

Cureton, E. E. Kuder-Richardson reliabilities of classroom tests. *Educational and Psychological Measurement* 26 (1966): 13–14.

————. The rearrangement test. *Educational and Psychological Measurement* 20 (1960): 31–35.

Cureton, E. E.; Cook, J. A.; Fischer, R. T.; Laser, S. A.; Rockwell, N. J.; and Simmons, J. W. Jr. Length of test and standard error of measurement. *Educational and Psychological Measurement* 33 (1973): 63–68.

Darlington, R. B. Another look at "culture fairness." *Journal of Educational Measurement* 8 (1971): 71–82.

Dave, R. H. Psychomotor levels. In *Developing and writing behavioral objectives,* ed. B. J. Armstrong *et al.* Tucson, Ariz.: Educational Innovators Press, 1970.

Davis, F. B. Item analysis in relation to educational and psychological testing. *Psychological Bulletin* 49 (1952): 97–121.

Davis, F. B. Item selection techniques. In *Educational measurement,* ed. E. F. Lindquist, pp. 266–328. Washington: American Council on Education, 1951.

de Sala Pool, I., ed. *Trends in content analysis.* Urbana, Ill.: University of Illinois Press, 1959.

Deri, S. *et al.* Techniques for the diagnosis and measurement of intergroup behavior. *Psychological Bulletin* 45 (1948): 248–271.

Deshpande, A. S.; Webb, S. C.; and Marks, E. Student perceptions of engineering instructor behaviors and their relationships to the evaluation of instructors and courses. *American Educational Research Journal* 7 (1970): 289–305.

Deutsch, M., *et al.* Guidelines for testing minority-group children. *Journal of Social Issues* 20 (1964): 129–145.

Diederich, P. B. *Short-cut statistics for teacher-made tests,* 2nd ed. Evaluation and

Advisory Service Series, Pamphlet no. 5. Princeton, N.J.: Educational Testing Service, 1964.

DiVesta, F. J., and Meyer, D. L. The grading system as a communication process: Related variables and implications for research. March 1963. Prepared under the auspices of the New York Department of Education, Division of Research. Albany, N.Y.: 1963. Mimeographed.

Domino, G. Interactive effects of achievement orientation and teaching style on academic achievement. *Journal of Educational Psychology* 62 (October 1971): 427–431.

Dressel, P. L. Evaluation as instruction. In *Proceedings of the 1953 invitational conference on testing problems.* Princeton, N.J.: Educational Testing Service, 1954.

———. Measurement and evaluation of instructional objectives. In *Seventeenth Yearbook of the National Council on Measurements Used in Education,* pp. 1–6. New York: NCME, 1960.

Dunnette, M. D., and Hoggatt, A. C. Deriving a composite from several measures of the same attribute. *Educational and Psychological Measurement* 17 (1957): 423–434.

Dyer, H. S. The discovery and development of educational goals. In *Proceedings of the 1966 Invitational Conference on Testing Problems,* pp. 12–24. Princeton, N.J.: Educational Testing Service, 1967.

———. Is testing a menace to education? *New York State Education* 49 (1961): 16–19.

Ebel, R. L. Criterion-referenced measurements: Limitations. *School Review* 79, no. 2 (1971): 282–288.

———. *Measuring educational achievement.* Englewood Cliffs, N.J.: Prentice-Hall, 1965a.

———. Confidence weighting and test reliability. *Journal of Educational Measurement* 2 (1965b): 49–57.

———. External testing: Response to challenge. *Teachers College Record* 64 (1962): 190–198.

———. Obtaining and reporting evidence on content validity. *Educational and Psychological Measurement* 16 (1956): 269–282.

Educational Policies Commission. *The central purpose of American education.* Washington: National Education Association and American Association of School Administrators, 1961.

———. *The purpose of education in American democracy.* Washington: National Education Association and American Association of School Administrators, 1938.

Edwards, A. L. *The social desirability variable in personality assessment and research.* New York: Dryden, 1957a.

———. *Techniques of attitude scale construction.* New York: Appleton-Century-Crofts, 1957b.

Eisner, E. W. Educational objectives: Help or hindrance? *School Review* 75, no. 3 (Autumn 1967): 250–260.

English, H. B., and English, Ava Champney. *A comprehensive dictionary of psychological and psychoanalytical terms.* New York: Longmans Green, 1958.

Farquhar, W. W., and Payne, D. A. Factors in the academic-occupational motivations of eleventh grade under- and over-achievers. *Personnel and Guidance Journal* 42, no. 3 (November 1963): 245–251.

Ferguson, G. A. *Statistical analysis in psychology and education,* 2nd ed. New York: McGraw-Hill, 1966.

Finley, Carmen J. National assessment reports and implications for school districts. *The National Elementary Principal* 50, no. 3 (1971): 25–32.

Fitzpatrick, R., and Morrison, E. J. Performance and product evaluation. In *Educational measurement,* 2nd ed., ed. E. L. Thorndike, pp. 237–270. Washington: American Council on Education, 1971.

Flanagan, J. C. A proposed procedure for increasing the efficiency of objective tests. *Journal of Educational Psychology* 28 (1937): 17–21.

———. Units, scores, and norms. In *Educational measurement,* ed. E. F. Lindquist, pp. 695–763. Washington: American Council on Education, 1951.

Flanders, N. A. *Interaction analysis in the classroom: A manual for observers,* rev. ed. Ann Arbor: University of Michigan School of Education, 1964

Forehand, G. A. Curriculum evaluation as decision-making process. *Teachers College Record* 72 (May 1971): 577–591.

Forsyth, E., and Katz, I. A matrix approach to the analysis of sociometric data: Preliminary report. *Sociometry* 9 (1946): 340–347.

Fox, R.; Luszki, Margaret B.; and Schmuck, R. *Diagnosing classroom learning environments.* Chicago: Science Research Associates, 1966.

French, J. W., *et al. Behavioral goals of general education in high school.* New York: Russell Sage Foundation, 1957.

Gagné, R. M. Curriculum research and the promotion of learning. In *Perspectives of curriculum evaluation,* ed. R. W. Tyler, *et. al.,* pp. 19–38. AERA Monograph No. 1. Chicago: Rand McNally, 1967.

———. *The conditions of learning.* New York: Holt, Rinehart and Winston, 1965.

Gallagher, C. E. Why house hearings on invasion of privacy? *American Psychologist* 20, no. 11 (November 1965): 881–882.

Gardner, E. F., and Thompson, G. G. *Investigation and measurement of the social values governing interpersonal relations among adolescent youth and their teachers.* U.S. Office of Education Cooperative Research Project 259A (8418), 1963.

Gardner, J. *Excellence.* New York: Harper & Row, 1961.

Ghiselli, E. E. *Theory of psychological measurement.* New York: McGraw-Hill, 1964.

Glassey, W. The attitude of grammar school pupils and their parents to education, religion, and sport. *British Journal of Educational Psychology* 15 (1945): 101–104.

Gnagey, W. J. Effects on classmates of a deviant student's powers and response to a teacher-exerted control technique. *Journal of Educational Psychology* 51 (1960): 1–8.

Goldman, L. *Using tests in counseling.* New York: Appleton-Century-Crofts, 1961.

Goodwin, W. L. Review of the *School Interest Inventory. Journal of Educational Measurement,* 6, no. 3 (1969): 200–201.

Gordon, I. J. Affect and cognition (A reciprocal relationship). *Educational Leadership* 27 (1970): 661–664.

Gorow, F. F. *Better classroom testing.* San Francisco: Chandler, 1966.

Goslin, D. A. Standardized ability tests and testing. *Science* 159 (February 1968): 851–855.

Green, J. A. *Introduction to measurement and evaluation.* New York: Dodd, Mead, 1970.

Gronlund, N. E. *Measurement and evaluation in teaching,* 2nd ed. New York: Macmillan, 1971.

———. *Measurement and evaluation in teaching.* New York: Macmillan, 1965.

———. *Sociometry in the classroom.* New York: Harper & Row, 1959.

Gross, M. L. *The brain watchers.* New York: Random House, 1962.

Guba, E. G. Significant differences. *Educational Researcher* 20, no. 3 (1969): 4–5.

Guilford, J. P. *Psychometric methods,* 2nd ed. New York: McGraw-Hill, 1954.

Guion, R. M. *Personnel testing.* New York: McGraw-Hill, 1965.

Hand, T.; Hoppock, R.; and Zlatchin, P. J. Job satisfaction: Researches of 1944 and 1945. *Occupations* 26 (1948): 425–431.

Harrow, Anita J. *A taxonomy of the psychomotor domain.* New York: David McKay, 1972.

Hartley, H. J. *Educational planning-programming-budgeting: A systems approach.* Englewood Cliffs, N.J.: Prentice-Hall, 1968.

Havighurst, R. J. *Human development and education.* New York: David McKay, 1953.

Hawes, G. R. Twelve sound ways to announce test results. *Nation's Schools* 89, no. 4 (April 1972): 45–52.

———. *Educational testing for the millions.* New York: McGraw-Hill, 1964.

Hayward, Priscilla. Evaluating diagnostic reading tests. *The Reading Teacher* 21, no. 6 (March 1968): 523–528.

Heath, D. H. Affective education: Aesthetics and discipline. *School Review,* 80, no. 3 (May 1972): 353–371.

Heath, R. W. Curriculum evaluation. In *Encyclopedia of educational research,* 4th ed., ed. R. L. Ebel, pp. 280–283. New York: Macmillan, 1969.

Helmstadter, G. C. *Principles of psychological measurement.* New York: Appleton-Century-Crofts, 1964.

Hemphill, J. K. The relationship between research and evaluation studies. In *Educational evaluation: New roles, new means,* ed. Ralph W. Tyler, pp. 189–220. Sixty-Eighth Yearbook of the National Society for the Study of Education. Chicago: University of Chicago Press, 1969.

Hively, W. II; Patterson, H. S.; and Page, Sara H. A universe-defined system of arithmetic achievement tests. *Journal of Educational Measurement* 5, no. 4 (Winter 1968): 275–290.

Hoffmann, B. *The tyranny of testing.* New York: Crowell-Collier, 1962.

Holmen, M. G., and Docter, R. F. *Educational and psychological testing: A study of the industry and its practices.* New York: Russell Sage Foundation, 1972.

Horst, P. Obtaining a composite measure from a number of different measures of the same attribute. *Psychometrika* 1 (1936): 53–60.

———. *Personality: Measurement of dimensions.* San Francisco: Jossey-Bass, 1968.

Jackson, P. W., and Getzels, J. W. Psychological health and classroom functioning: A study of dissatisfaction with school among adolescents. *Journal of Educational Psychology* 50 (1959): 295–300.

Jarvie, L. L., and Ellingson, M. *A handbook on the Anecdotal Behavior Journal.* Chicago: University of Chicago Press, 1940.

Johnson, S. R. Relationships among cognitive and affective outcomes of instruction. Unpublished doctoral dissertation, University of California at Los Angeles, 1966.

Kahl, J. A. Some measurements of achievement orientation. *American Journal of Sociology* 4 (1965): 669–681.

Kearney, N. C. *Elementary school objectives.* New York: Russell Sage Foundation, 1953.

Kelley, T. L. The selection of upper and lower groups for the validation of test items. *Journal of Educational Psychology* 30 (1939): 17–24.

Kelley, T. L.; Madden, R. L.; Gardner, E. F.; Rudman, H. C.; Merwin, J. C.; and Callis, R. *Stanford Achievement Tests.* New York: Harcourt Brace and Jovanovich, 1964 and 1965.

Kelly, E. L. Consistency of the adult personality. *American Psychologist* 10 (1955): 659–681.

Kibler, R. J.; Barker, L. L.; and Miles, D. T. *Behavioral objectives and instruction.* Boston: Allyn and Bacon, 1970.

Kirkpatrick, J. et al. *Testing and fair employment.* New York: New York University Press, 1968.

Klein, S.; Fenstermacher, G.; and Alkin, M. C. The Center's changing evaluation model. *Evaluation Comment* 2 (January 1971): 9–12. Center for the Study of Evaluation, University of California, Los Angeles.

Kleinmuntz, B. *Personality measurement: An introduction.* Homewood, Ill.: Dorsey, 1967.

Krathwohl, D. R. The taxonomy of educational objectives: Its use in curriculum building. In *Defining educational objectives,* ed. C. M. Lindvall. Pittsburgh: University of Pittsburgh Press, 1964.

Krathwohl, D. R.; Bloom, B. S.; and Masia, B. B. *Taxonomy of educational objectives. Handbook II: The affective domain.* New York: David McKay, 1964.

Krathwohl, D. R., and Payne, D. A. Defining and assessing educational objectives. In *Educational measurement* (2nd ed.), ed. R. L. Thorndike, pp. 17–45. Washington, D.C.: American Council on Education, 1971.

Krech, D., and Crutchfield, R. S. *Theory and problems of social psychology.* New York: McGraw-Hill, 1948.

Kropp, R. P.; Stoker, H. W.; and Bashaw, W. L. The validation of the taxonomy of educational objectives. *Journal of Experimental Education* 34 (1968): 69–76.

Krouskopf, C. J. A construct validation of a classroom test. *Journal of Educational Measurement* 2 (1964): 131–133.

Kuder, G. F., and Richardson, M. W. The theory of estimation of test reliability. *Psychometrika* 2 (1937): 151–160.

LaPiere, R. T. Attitudes *vs.* actions. *Social Forces* 14 (1934): 230–237.

Lathrop, R. L. A quick but accurate approximation to the standard deviation of a distribution. *Journal of Experimental Education* 29 (1961): 319–321.

Lawshe, C. H., and Schucker, R. E. The relative efficiency of four test weighting methods in multiple-prediction. *Educational and Psychological Measurement* 19 (1959): 103–114.

Lehmann, I. J. Learning: III. Attitudes and values. *Review of Educational Research* 28, no. 5 (December 1958): 468–474.

Lennon, R. T. Testing: Bond or barrier between pupil and teacher. *Education* 75 (September 1954): 38–42.

Light, R. J., and Smith, P. V. Choosing a future: Strategies for designing and evaluating new programs. *Harvard Educational Review* 40 (Winter 1970): 1–28.

Likert, R. A technique for the measurement of attitudes. *Archives of Psychology* no. 140 (1932).

Lindvall, C. M., and Cox, R. C. The role of evaluation in programs for individualized instruction. In *Educational evaluation: New roles, new means,* ed. Ralph W. Tyler, pp. 156–188. Sixty-Eighth Yearbook of the National Society for the Study of Education. Chicago: University of Chicago Press, 1969.

Lord, F. M. Estimating norms by item-sampling. *Educational and Psychological Measurement* 22 (1962): 259–267.

———. Tests of the same length do have the same standard error of measurement. *Educational and Psychological Measurement* 19 (1959): 233–239.

Macdonald, J. B., and Walfron, Bernice J. A case against behavioral objectives. *Elementary School Journal* 71 (1970): 119–128.

Mager, R. F. *Preparing objectives for programed instruction.* San Francisco: Fearon, 1962.

Manning, W. H., and DuBois, P. Gain in proficiency as a criterion in test validation. *Journal of Applied Psychology* 42 (1958): 191–194.

Marshall, J. C., and Powers, J. M. Writing neatness, composition errors, and essay grades. *Journal of Educational Measurement* 6 (1969): 97–101.

Mayhew, Lewis B. Measurement of noncognitive objectives in the social sciences. In *Evaluation in social studies,* ed. Harry D. Berg. Thirty-Fifth Yearbook of the National Council on Social Studies. Washington: NCSS, 1965.

Mayo, S. T. Mastery learning and mastery testing. *Measurement in Education* 1, no. 3 (March 1970): 1–4.

McGuire, C. A process approach to the construction and analysis of medical examinations. *Journal of Medical Education* 1 (1963): 556–563.

McMorris, R. F. Evidence on the quality of several approximations for commonly used measurement statistics. *Journal of Educational Measurement* 9, no. 2 (Summer 1972): 113–122.

McMorris, R. F.; Brown, J. A.; Snyder, G. W.; and Pruzek, R. M. Effects of violating item construction principles. *Journal of Educational Measurement* 9, no. 4 (Winter 1972): 287–295.

McNemar, Q. *Psychological statistics,* 3rd ed. New York: John Wiley and Sons, 1962.

Medley, D. M., and Mitzel, H. E. Measuring classroom behavior by systematic observation. In *Handbook for research on teaching,* ed. N. L. Gage, pp. 247–328. Chicago: Rand McNally, 1963.

Mehrens, W. A., and Lehmann, I. J. *Standardized tests in education.* New York: Holt, Rinehart and Winston, 1969.

Merwin, J. C. Historical review of changing concepts of evaluation. In *Educational evaluation: New roles, new means,* ed. Ralph W. Tyler, pp. 6–25. Sixty-Eighth Yearbook of the National Society for the Study of Education. Chicago: University of Chicago Press, 1969.

Merwin, J. C., and Womer, F. B. Evaluation in assessing the progress of education to provide bases of public understanding and public policy. In *Educational evaluation: New roles, new means,* ed. Ralph W. Tyler, pp. 305–334. Sixty-Eighth Yearbook of the National Society for the Study of Education. Chicago: University of Chicago Press, 1969.

Messick, S. Personality measurement and the ethics of assessment. *American Psychologist* 20, no. 2 (February 1965): 136–142.

Metfessel, N. S., and Michael, W. B. A paradigm involving multiple criterion measures for the evaluation of the effectiveness of school programs. *Educational and Psychological Measurement* 20 (Winter 1967): 931–943.

Metfessel, W. S.; Michael, W. B.; and Kirsner, D. A. Instrumentation of

Bloom's and Krathwohl's taxonomies for the writing of educational objectives. *Psychology in the Schools* 6 (1969): 227–231.

Meyer, D. L. *Educational statistics.* New York: Center for Applied Research in Education, 1967.

Meyering, R. A. *Uses of test data in counseling.* Boston: Houghton Mifflin, 1968.

Miller, A. T. *Levels of cognitive behavior measured in a controlled teaching situation.* Unpublished master's thesis, Cornell University, 1965.

Miller, R. I. *Evaluating faculty performance.* San Francisco: Jossey-Bass, 1972.

Michaels, W. J., and Karnes, M. R. *Measuring educational achievement.* New York: McGraw-Hill, 1950.

Moore, R. W., and Sutman, F. X. The development, field test and validation of an inventory of scientific attitudes. *Journal of Research in Science Teaching* 7 (1970): 85–94.

Murray, C. K., ed. Systematic observation. *Journal of Research and Development in Education* 4 (1970): entire issue.

Myers, A. E.; McConville, Carolyn; and Coffman, W. E. Simplex structure in the grading of essay tests. *Educational and Psychological Measurement* 26 (1966): 41–54.

National Study of Secondary School Evaluation. *Evaluative criteria—1960 edition.* Washington: NSSSE, 1960.

Nelson, C. H. *Nelson biology test,* rev. ed. New York: Harcourt, Brace and World, 1965.

Niehaus, S. W. The anatomy of evaluation. *The Clearing House* 42 (February 1968): 332–336.

Oppenheim, A. N. *Questionnaire design and attitude measurement.* New York: Basic Books, 1966.

Osgood, C. E.; Suci, G. J.; and Tannenbaum, P. H. *The measurement of meaning.* Urbana, Ill.: University of Illinois Press, 1957.

OSS (Office of Strategic Services) Assessment Staff. *Assessment of men.* New York: Holt, Rinehart and Winston, 1948.

Page, E. B. Grading essays by computer. *Phi Delta Kappan* 47 (1966): 238–243.

Palmer, O. Seven classic ways of grading dishonestly. *The English Journal* 51 (October 1962): 464–467.

Payne, D. A., ed. *Curriculum evaluation: Commentaries on purpose-process-product.* Lexington, Mass.: D. C. Heath, 1974.

———. Some old and new wives tales concerning curriculum evaluation. *Educational Leadership* 30 (January 1973): 343–347.

———. *Evaluation of the State of Georgia's Governor's honors program.* Athens, Ga.: University of Georgia Department of Curriculum and Supervision, October 1972. Mimeographed.

————. *The specification and measurement of learning outcomes.* Lexington, Mass.: Blaisdell, 1968.

————. A note on skewness and internal consistency reliability estimates. *Journal of Experimental Education* 32 (1963): 43–46.

Payne, S. L. *The art of asking questions.* Princeton, N.J.: Princeton University Press, 1951.

Popham, W. J. Indices of adequacy for criterion-referenced test items. In *Criterion-referenced measurement: An introduction,* ed. W. J. Popham, pp. 79–98. Englewood Cliffs, N.J.: Educational Technology Publications, 1971.

————. Objectives and instruction. In *Instructional Objectives,* ed. W. J. Popham, pp. 32–52. Chicago: Rand McNally, 1969.

Popham, W. J., and Husek, T. R. Implications of criterion-referenced measurement. *Journal of Educational Measurement* 6 (Spring 1969): 1–9.

Postman, L., and Rau, L. Retention as a function of the method of measurement. *University of California Publications in Psychology* 8 (1957): 217–270.

Prescott, D. A. *The child in the educative process.* New York: McGraw-Hill, 1957.

Provus, M. *Discrepancy evaluation.* Berkeley, Cal.: McCutchan, 1971.

Ragsdale, C. E. How children learn motor types of activities. In Forty-Ninth Yearbook of the National Society for the Study of Education, pp. 69–91. Chicago: University of Chicago Press, 1950.

Randall, J. A. The anecdotal behavior journal. *Progressive Education* 13 (1936): 21–26.

Raths, L. E. Evaluating the program of a school. *Educational Research Bulletin* 17 (1938): 57–84.

Remmers, H. H.; Gage, N. L.; and Rummel, J. F. *A practical introduction to measurement and evaluation,* 2nd ed. New York: Harper & Row, 1965.

Remmers, H. H., and Silance, Ella B. Generalized attitude scales. *Journal of Social Psychology* 5 (1934): 298–311.

Richardson, M. W., and Kuder, G. F. The calculation of test reliability coefficients based on the method of rational equivalence. *Journal of Educational Psychology* 30 (1939): 681–687.

Ricks, J. H. Jr. *How accurate is a test score?* Test Service Bulletin no. 50. New York: Psychological Corporation, 1956.

Ripple, R. E. Affective factors influence classroom learning. *Educational Leadership* 22, no. 7 (April 1965): 476–480.

Rokeach, M. *Beliefs, attitudes, and values: A theory of organization and change.* San Francisco: Jossey-Bass, 1968.

Ryans, D. G. Research designs for the empirical validation of tests and inventories. *Educational and Psychological Measurement* 17, no. 2 (Summer 1957): 175–184.

Saupe, J. L. Some useful estimates of the Kuder-Richardson Formula Number 20 reliability coefficient. *Educational and Psychological Measurement* 21 (1961): 63–71.

Sawin, E. I. *Evaluation and the work of the teacher.* Belmont, Cal.: Wadsworth, 1969.

Scannell, D. P., and Stellwagen, W. R. Teaching and testing for degrees of understanding. *California Journal of Instructional Improvement* 3, no. 1 (1960): 8–14.

Scriven, M. The methodology of evaluation. *Perspectives of Curriculum Evaluation* Monograph No. 1 (Chicago: Rand McNally, 1967).

————. Student values as educational objectives. In *Proceedings of the 1965 Invitational Conference on Testing Problems*, pp. 33–49. Princeton, N.J.: Educational Testing Service, 1966.

Shaw, M. E., and Wright, J. M. *Scales for the measurement of attitudes.* New York: McGraw-Hill, 1967.

Simon, Anita, and Boyer, E. H. *Mirrors for behavior: An anthology of observation instruments.* Philadelphia: Research for Better Schools, 1970.

Simon, G. B. Comments on "Implications of criterion-referenced measurement." *Journal of Educational Measurement* 6, no. 4 (Winter 1969): 259-260.

Simpson, E. J. The classification of educational objectives: Psychomotor domain. *Illinois Teacher of Home Economics* 10 (1966): 110–144.

Simpson, R. H. The specific meanings of certain terms indicating different degrees of frequency. *Quarterly Journal of Speech* 30 (1944): 328–330.

Sims, V. M. The essay examination is a projective technique. *Educational and Psychological Measurement* 8 (1948): 15–31.

Smith, B. O. Teaching and testing values. In *Proceedings of the 1965 Invitational Conference on Testing Problems*, pp. 50–59. Princeton, N.J.: Educational Testing Service, 1966.

Smith, E. R.; Tyler, R. W.; et al. *Appraising and recording student progress.* New York: Harper & Brothers, 1942.

Spache, G. D. *Diagnostic reading scales.* Monterey, Cal.: California Test Bureau, 1963.

Stanley, J. C. *Measurement in today's schools* (4th ed.). Englewood Cliffs, N.J.: Prentice-Hall, 1964.

Stanley, J. C., and Hopkins, K. D. *Educational and psychological measurement and evaluation.* Englewood Cliffs, N.J.: Prentice-Hall, 1971.

Stake, R. E. Testing hazards in performance contracting. *Phi Delta Kappan* 52 (June 1971): 583–589.

————. Objectives, priorities, and other judgment data. *Review of Educational Research* 40 (April 1970): 181–212.

————. The countenance of educational evaluation. *Teachers College Record* 68, no. 7 (1967): 523–540.

Stake, R. E., and Gooler, D. Measuring educational priorities. *Educational Technology* 11 (September 1971): 44–48.

Starch, D., and Elliott, E. C. Reliability of grading work in history. *School Review* 21 (1913a): 676–681.

————. Reliability of grading work in mathematics. *School Review* 21 (1913b): 254–257.

————. Reliability of grading high school work in English. *School Review* 20 (1912): 442–457.

Stufflebeam, D. L. Toward a science of educational evaluation. *Educational Technology* 8 (1968): 5–12.

Stufflebeam, D. L. *et al. Educational evaluation and decision making.* Itasca, Ill.: Peacock Publishers, 1971.

Suchman, E. A. *Evaluative research.* New York: Russell Sage Foundation, 1967.

Taylor, P. A., and Maguire, T. O. A theoretical evaluation model. *Manitoba Journal of Educational Research* 1 (1966): 11–18.

Terwilliger, J. S. *Assigning grades to students.* Glenview, Ill.: Scott, Foresman, 1971.

Thomas, J. A. Cost-benefit analysis and the evaluation of educational systems. In *Proceedings of the 1968 Invitational Conference on Testing Problems,* pp. 89–100. Princeton, N.J.: Educational Testing Service, 1969.

Thomas, R. N. *Judging student progress,* 2nd ed. New York: David McKay, 1960.

Thorndike, R. L. Concepts of culture-fairness. *Journal of Educational Measurement* 8 (1971): 63–70.

————. *Personnel selection.* New York: John Wiley and Sons, 1949.

Thorndike, R. L., and Hagen, Elizabeth. *Measurement and evaluation in psychology and education,* 2nd ed. New York: John Wiley, 1961.

Thurstone, L. L. A law of comparative judgment. *Psychological Review* 34 (1927a): 273–286.

————. The method of paired comparison for social values. *Journal of Abnormal and Social Psychology* 27 (1927b): 384–400.

Thurstone, L. L., and Chave, E. J. *The measurement of attitude.* Chicago: University of Chicago Press, 1929.

Traub, R. E.; Hambleton, R. K.; and Singh, B. Effects of promised reward and theoretical penalty on performance of a multiple-choice vocabulary test. Unpublished manuscript, The Ontario Institute for Studies in Education, Ontario, Canada, 1968.

Travers, R. M. W. A critical review of the validity and rationale of the forced-choice technique. *Psychological Bulletin* 48 (1951): 62–70.

Traxler, A. E. Administering and scoring the objective test. In *Educational measurement*, ed. E. F. Lindquist; pp. 329–416. Washington: American Council on Education, 1951.

―――. Fifteen criteria of a testing program. *The Clearing House* 25 (1950): pp. 3–7.

Traxler, A. E., and Anderson, H. A. The reliability of an essay examination in English. *School Review* 43 (1935): 534–539.

Tversky, A. On the optimal number of alternatives at a choice point. *Journal of Mathematical Psychology* 1 (1964): 386–391.

Tyler, R. W. Assessing educational achievement in the affective domain. *Measurement in Education* 4, no. 3 (1973): 1–8.

―――. National assessment—some valuable by-products for schools. *The National Elementary Principal* 48, no. 6 (May 1969): 42–48.

―――. Some persistent questions on the defining of objectives. In *Defining educational objectives*, ed. C. M. Lindvall, pp. 77–83. Pittsburgh: University of Pittsburgh Press, 1964.

―――. General statement on evaluation. *Journal of Educational Research* 35 (March 1942): 492–501.

―――. Permanence of learning. *Journal of Higher Education* 4 (1933): 203–204.

U.S. Office of Education. *Cardinal principles of secondary education.* Bulletin no. 35, 1918.

Walbesser, H. H. An evaluation model and its application. Washington: American Association for the Advancement of Science, 1965.

Wall, Janet, and Summerlin, L. Choosing the right test. *The Science Teacher* 39 (November 1972): 32–36.

Wang, C. K. A. Suggested criteria for writing attitude statements. *Journal of Social Psychology* 3 (August 1932): 367–373.

Wang, Marilyn W., and Stanley, J. C. Differentiated weighting: A review of methods and empirical studies. *Review of Educational Research* 40, no. 5 (December 1970): 663–705.

Webb, E. J. *et al. Unobtrusive measures: Nonreactive research in the social sciences.* Chicago: Rand McNally, 1966.

Welch, W. W., and Walberg, H. J. A design for curriculum evaluation. *Science Education* 52 (February 1968): 10–16.

Womer, F. B. National assessment says. *Measurement in Education* 2, no. 1 (October 1970): 1–8.

―――. Pros and cons of external testing programs. *North Central Association Quarterly* 36 (1961): 201–210.

―――. Testing programs—misconceptions, misuse, overuse. *Michigan Journal of Secondary Education* (Spring 1961).

Wylie, Ruth C. *The self-concept.* Lincoln: University of Nebraska Press, 1961.

Wynn, C. Pros and cons of behavioral objectives. *Georgia Educator* 3, no. 3 (January 1973): 12–14.

Yelon, S. L., and Scott, R. O. *A strategy for writing objectives.* Dubuque, Iowa: Kendall/Hunt, 1970.

Zavala, A. Development of the forced-choice rating scale technique. *Psychological Bulletin* 63 (1965): 117–124.

APPENDICES

APPENDIX A. Normal Deviates (z) Corresponding to Proportions (p) and Products pq of a Dichotomized Unit Normal Distribution

Proportion (p)*	Deviate (z)	pq	Proportion (p)*	Deviate (z)	pq
.99	2.326	.0099	.49	− .025	.2499
.98	2.054	.0196	.48	− .050	.2496
.97	1.881	.0291	.47	− .075	.2491
.96	1.751	.0384	.46	− .100	.2484
.95	1.645	.0977	.45	− .126	.2475
.94	1.555	.0564	.44	− .151	.2464
.93	1.476	.0651	.43	− .176	.2451
.92	1.405	.0736	.42	− .202	.2436
.91	1.341	.0819	.41	− .228	.2419
.90	1.282	.0900	.40	− .253	.2400
.89	1.227	.0979	.39	− .279	.2379
.88	1.175	.1056	.38	− .305	.2356
.87	1.126	.1131	.37	− .332	.2331
.86	1.080	.1204	.36	− .358	.2304
.85	1.036	.1275	.35	− .385	.2275
.84	.994	.1344	.34	− .412	.2244
.83	.954	.1411	.33	− .440	.2211
.82	.915	.1476	.32	− .468	.2176
.81	.878	.1539	.31	− .496	.2139
.80	.842	.1600	.30	− .524	.2100
.79	.806	.1659	.29	− .553	.2059
.78	.772	.1716	.28	− .583	.2016
.77	.739	.1771	.27	− .613	.1971
.76	.706	.1824	.26	− .643	.1924
.75	.674	.1875	.25	− .674	.1875
.74	.643	.1924	.24	− .706	.1824
.73	.613	.1971	.23	− .739	.1771
.72	.583	.2016	.22	− .772	.1716
.71	.553	.2059	.21	− .806	.1659
.70	.524	.2100	.20	− .842	.1600
.69	.496	.2139	.19	− .878	.1539
.68	.468	.2176	.18	− .915	.1476
.67	.440	.2211	.17	− .954	.1411
.66	.412	.2244	.16	− .994	.1344
.65	.385	.2275	.15	−1.036	.1275
.64	.358	.2304	.14	−1.080	.1204
.63	.332	.2331	.13	−1.126	.1131
.62	.305	.2356	.12	−1.175	.1056
.61	.279	.2379	.11	−1.227	.0979
.60	.253	.2400	.10	−1.282	.0900
.59	.228	.2419	.09	−1.341	.0819
.58	.202	.2436	.08	−1.405	.0736
.57	.176	.2451	.07	−1.476	.0651
.56	.151	.2464	.06	−1.555	.0564
.55	.126	.2475	.05	−1.645	.0475
.54	.100	.2484	.04	−1.751	.0384
.53	.075	.2491	.03	−1.881	.0291
.52	.050	.2496	.02	−2.054	.0196
.51	.025	.2499	.01	−2.326	.0096
.50	.000	.2500	.00	0.000	.0000

* Can also be read as q, where q = 1 − p.

APPENDIX B. Squares and Square Roots of the Numbers from 1 to 1,000

Number	Square	Square Root	Number	Square	Square Root
1	1	1.000	51	26 01	7.141
2	4	1.414	52	27 04	7.211
3	9	1.732	53	28 09	7.280
4	16	2.000	54	29 16	7.348
5	25	2.236	55	30 25	7.416
6	36	2.449	56	31 36	7.483
7	49	2.646	57	32 49	7.550
8	64	2.828	58	33 64	7.616
9	81	3.000	59	34 81	7.681
10	1 00	3.162	60	36 00	7.746
11	1 21	3.317	61	37 21	7.810
12	1 44	3.464	62	38 44	7.874
13	1 69	3.606	63	39 69	7.937
14	1 96	3.742	64	40 96	8.000
15	2 25	3.873	65	42 25	8.062
16	2 56	4.000	66	43 56	8.124
17	2 89	4.123	67	44 89	8.185
18	3 24	4.243	68	46 24	8.246
19	3 61	4.359	69	47 61	8.307
20	4 00	4.472	70	49 00	8.367
21	4 41	4.583	71	50 41	8.426
22	4 84	4.690	72	51 84	8.485
23	5 29	4.796	73	53 29	8.544
24	5 76	4.899	74	54 76	8.602
25	6 25	5.000	75	56 25	8.660
26	6 76	5.099	76	57 76	8.718
27	7 29	5.196	77	59 29	8.775
28	7 84	5.292	78	60 84	8.832
29	8 41	5.385	79	62 41	8.888
30	9 00	5.477	80	64 00	8.944
31	9 61	5.568	81	65 61	9.000
32	10 24	5.657	82	67 24	9.055
33	10 89	5.745	83	68 89	9.110
34	11 56	5.831	84	70 56	9.165
35	12 25	5.916	85	72 25	9.220
36	12 96	6.000	86	73 96	9.274
37	13 69	6.083	87	75 69	9.327
38	14 44	6.164	88	77 44	9.381
39	15 21	6.245	89	79 21	9.434
40	16 00	6.325	90	81 00	9.487
41	16 81	6.403	91	82 81	9.539
42	17 64	6.481	92	84 64	9.592
43	18 49	6.557	93	86 49	9.644
44	19 36	6.633	94	88 36	9.695
45	20 25	6.708	95	90 25	9.747
46	21 16	6.782	96	92 16	9.798
47	22 09	6.856	97	94 09	9.849
48	23 04	6.928	98	96 04	9.899
49	24 01	7.000	99	98 01	9.950
50	25 00	7.071	100	1 00 00	10.000

Number	Square	Square Root	Number	Square	Square Root
101	1 02 01	10.050	151	2 28 01	12.288
102	1 04 04	10.100	152	2 31 04	12.329
103	1 06 09	10.149	153	2 34 09	12.369
104	1 08 16	10.198	154	2 37 16	12.410
105	1 10 25	10.247	155	2 40 25	12.450
106	1 12 36	10.296	156	2 43 36	12.490
107	1 14 49	10.344	157	2 46 49	12.530
108	1 16 64	10.392	158	2 49 64	12.570
109	1 18 81	10.440	159	2 52 81	12.610
110	1 21 00	10.488	160	2 56 00	12.649
111	1 23 21	10.536	161	2 59 21	12.689
112	1 25 44	10.583	162	2 62 44	12.728
113	1 27 69	10.630	163	2 65 69	12.767
114	1 29 96	10.677	164	2 68 96	12.806
115	1 32 25	10.724	165	2 72 25	12.845
116	1 34 56	10.770	166	2 75 56	12.884
117	1 36 89	10.817	167	2 78 89	12.923
118	1 39 24	10.863	168	2 82 24	12.961
119	1 41 61	10.909	169	2 85 61	13.000
120	1 44 00	10.954	170	2 89 00	13.038
121	1 46 41	11.000	171	2 92 41	13.077
122	1 48 84	11.045	172	2 95 84	13.115
123	1 51 29	11.091	173	2 99 29	13.153
124	1 53 76	11.136	174	3 02 76	13.191
125	1 56 25	11.180	175	3 06 25	13.229
126	1 58 76	11.225	176	3 09 76	13.266
127	1 61 29	11.269	177	3 13 29	13.304
128	1 63 84	11.314	178	3 16 84	13.342
129	1 66 41	11.358	179	3 20 41	13.379
130	1 69 00	11.402	180	3 24 00	13.416
131	1 71 61	11.446	181	3 27 61	13.454
132	1 74 24	11.489	182	3 31 24	13.491
133	1 76 89	11.533	183	3 34 89	13.528
134	1 79 56	11.576	184	3 38 56	13.565
135	1 82 25	11.619	185	3 42 25	13.601
136	1 84 96	11.662	186	3 45 96	13.638
137	1 87 69	11.705	187	3 49 69	13.675
138	1 90 44	11.747	188	3 53 44	13.711
139	1 93 21	11.790	189	3 57 21	13.748
140	1 96 00	11.832	190	3 61 00	13.784
141	1 98 81	11.874	191	3 64 81	13.820
142	2 01 64	11.916	192	3 68 64	13.856
143	2 04 49	11.958	193	3 72 49	13.892
144	2 07 36	12.000	194	3 76 36	13.928
145	2 10 25	12.042	195	3 80 25	13.964
146	2 13 16	12.083	196	3 84 16	14.000
147	2 16 09	12.124	197	3 88 09	14.036
148	2 19 04	12.166	198	3 92 04	14.071
149	2 22 01	12.207	199	3 96 01	14.107
150	2 25 00	12.247	200	4 00 00	14.142

Number	Square	Square Root	Number	Square	Square Root
201	4 04 01	14.177	251	6 30 01	15.843
202	4 08 04	14.213	252	6 35 04	15.875
203	4 12 09	14.248	253	6 40 09	15.906
204	4 16 16	14.283	254	6 45 16	15.937
205	4 20 25	14.318	255	6 50 25	15.969
206	4 24 36	14.353	256	6 55 36	16.000
207	4 28 49	14.387	257	6 60 49	16.031
208	4 32 64	14.422	258	6 65 64	16.062
209	4 36 81	14.457	259	6 70 81	16.093
210	4 41 00	14.491	260	6 76 00	16.125
211	4 45 21	14.526	261	6 81 21	16.155
212	4 49 44	14.560	262	6 86 44	16.186
213	4 53 69	14.595	263	6 91 69	16.217
214	4 57 96	14.629	264	6 96 96	16.248
215	4 62 25	14.663	265	7 02 25	16.279
216	4 66 56	14.697	266	7 07 56	16.310
217	4 70 89	14.731	267	7 12 89	16.340
218	4 75 24	14.765	268	7 18 24	16.371
219	4 79 61	14.799	269	7 23 61	16.401
220	4 84 00	14.832	270	7 29 00	16.432
221	4 88 41	14.866	271	7 34 41	16.462
222	4 92 84	14.900	272	7 39 84	16.492
223	4 97 29	14.933	273	7 45 29	16.523
224	5 01 76	14.967	274	7 50 76	16.553
225	5 06 25	15.000	275	7 56 25	16.583
226	5 10 76	15.033	276	7 61 76	16.613
227	5 15 29	15.067	277	7 67 29	16.643
228	5 19 84	15.100	278	7 72 84	16.673
229	5 24 41	15.133	279	7 78 41	16.703
230	5 29 00	15.166	280	7 84 00	16.733
231	5 33 61	15.199	281	7 89 61	16.763
232	5 38 24	15.232	282	7 95 24	16.793
233	5 42 89	15.264	283	8 00 89	16.823
234	5 47 56	15.297	284	8 06 56	16.852
235	5 52 25	15.330	285	8 12 25	16.882
236	5 56 96	15.362	286	8 17 96	16.912
237	5 61 69	15.395	287	8 23 69	16.941
238	5 66 44	15.427	288	8 29 44	16.971
239	5 71 21	15.460	289	8 35 21	17.000
240	5 76 00	15.492	290	8 41 00	17.029
241	5 80 81	15.524	291	8 46 81	17.059
242	5 85 64	15.556	292	8 52 64	17.088
243	5 90 49	15.588	293	8 58 49	17.117
244	5 95 36	15.620	294	8 64 36	17.146
245	6 00 25	15.652	295	8 70 25	17.176
246	6 05 16	15.684	296	8 76 16	17.205
247	6 10 09	15.716	297	8 82 09	17.234
248	6 15 04	15.748	298	8 88 04	17.263
249	6 20 01	15.780	299	8 94 01	17.292
250	6 25 00	15.811	300	9 00 00	17.321

Number	Square	Square Root	Number	Square	Square Root
301	9 06 01	17.349	351	12 32 01	18.735
302	9 12 04	17.378	352	12 39 04	18.762
303	9 18 09	17.407	353	12 46 09	18.788
304	9 24 16	17.436	354	12 53 16	18.815
305	9 30 25	17.464	355	12 60 25	18.841
306	9 36 36	17.493	356	12 67 36	18.868
307	9 42 49	17.521	357	12 74 49	18.894
308	9 48 64	17.550	358	12 81 64	18.921
309	9 54 81	17.578	359	12 88 81	18.947
310	9 61 00	17.607	360	12 96 00	18.974
311	9 67 21	17.635	361	13 03 21	19.000
312	9 73 44	17.664	362	13 10 44	19.026
313	9 79 69	17.692	363	13 17 69	19.053
314	9 85 96	17.720	364	13 24 96	19.079
315	9 92 25	17.748	365	13 32 25	19.105
316	9 98 56	17.776	366	13 39 56	19.131
317	10 04 89	17.804	367	13 46 89	19.157
318	10 11 24	17.833	368	13 54 24	19.183
319	10 17 61	17.861	369	13 61 61	19.209
320	10 24 00	17.889	370	13 69 00	19.235
321	10 30 41	17.916	371	13 76 41	19.261
322	10 36 84	17.944	372	13 83 84	19.287
323	10 43 29	17.972	373	13 91 29	19.313
324	10 49 76	18.000	374	13 98 76	19.339
325	10 56 25	18.028	375	14 06 25	19.363
326	10 62 76	18.055	376	14 13 76	19.391
327	10 69 29	18.083	377	14 21 29	19.416
328	10 75 84	18.111	378	14 28 84	19.442
329	10 82 41	18.138	379	14 36 41	19.468
330	10 89 00	18.166	380	14 44 00	19.494
331	10 95 61	18.193	381	14 51 61	19.519
332	11 02 24	18.221	382	14 59 24	19.545
333	11 08 89	18.248	383	14 66 89	19.570
334	11 15 56	18.276	384	14 74 56	19.596
335	11 22 25	18.303	385	14 82 25	19.621
336	11 28 96	18.330	386	14 89 96	19.647
337	11 35 69	18.358	387	14 97 69	19.672
338	11 42 44	18.385	388	15 05 44	19.698
339	11 49 21	18.412	389	15 13 21	19.723
340	11 56 00	18.439	390	15 21 00	19.748
341	11 62 81	18.466	391	15 28 81	19.774
342	11 69 64	18.493	392	15 36 64	19.799
343	11 76 49	18.520	393	15 44 49	19.824
344	11 83 36	18.547	394	15 52 36	19.849
345	11 90 25	18.574	395	15 60 25	19.875
346	11 97 16	18.601	396	15 68 16	19.900
347	12 04 09	18.628	397	15 76 09	19.925
348	12 11 04	18.655	398	15 84 04	19.950
349	12 18 01	18.682	399	15 92 01	19.975
350	12 25 00	18.708	400	16 00 00	20.000

Number	Square	Square Root	Number	Square	Square Root
401	16 08 01	20.025	451	20 34 01	21.237
402	16 16 04	20.050	452	20 43 04	21.260
403	16 24 09	20.075	453	20 52 09	21.284
404	16 32 16	20.100	454	20 61 16	21.307
405	16 40 25	20.125	455	20 70 25	21.331
406	16 48 36	20.149	456	20 79 36	21.354
407	16 56 49	20.174	457	20 88 49	21.378
408	16 64 64	20.199	458	20 97 64	21.401
409	16 72 81	20.224	459	21 06 81	21.424
410	16 81 00	20.248	460	21 16 00	21.448
411	16 89 21	20.273	461	21 25 21	21.471
412	16 97 44	20.298	462	21 34 44	21.494
413	17 05 69	20.322	463	21 43 69	21.517
414	17 13 96	20.347	464	21 52 96	21.541
415	17 22 25	20.372	465	21 62 25	21.564
416	17 30 56	20.396	466	21 71 56	21.587
417	17 38 89	20.421	467	21 80 89	21.610
418	17 47 24	20.445	468	21 90 24	21.633
419	17 55 61	20.469	469	21 99 61	21.656
420	17 64 00	20.494	470	22 09 00	21.679
421	17 72 41	20.518	471	22 18 41	21.703
422	17 80 84	20.543	472	22 27 84	21.726
423	17 89 29	20.567	473	22 37 29	21.749
424	17 97 76	20.591	474	22 46 76	21.772
425	18 06 25	20.616	475	22 56 25	21.794
426	18 14 76	20.640	476	22 65 76	21.817
427	18 23 29	20.664	477	22 75 29	21.840
428	18 31 84	20.688	478	22 84 84	21.863
429	18 40 41	20.712	479	22 94 41	21.886
430	18 49 00	20.736	480	23 04 00	21.909
431	18 57 61	20.761	481	23 13 61	21.932
432	18 66 24	20.785	482	23 23 24	21.954
433	18 74 89	20.809	483	23 32 89	21.977
434	18 83 56	20.833	484	23 42 56	22.000
435	18 92 25	20.857	485	23 52 25	22.023
436	19 00 96	20.881	486	23 61 96	22.045
437	19 09 69	20.905	487	23 71 69	22.068
438	19 18 44	20.928	488	23 81 44	22.091
439	19 27 21	20.952	489	23 91 21	22.113
440	19 36 00	20.976	490	24 01 00	22.136
441	19 44 81	21.000	491	24 10 81	22.159
442	19 53 64	21.024	492	24 20 64	22.181
443	19 62 49	21.048	493	24 30 49	22.204
444	19 71 36	21.071	494	24 40 36	22.226
445	19 80 25	21.095	495	24 50 25	22.249
446	19 89 16	21.119	496	24 60 16	22.271
447	19 98 09	21.142	497	24 70 09	22.293
448	20 07 04	21.166	498	24 80 04	22.316
449	20 16 01	21.190	499	24 90 01	22.338
450	20 25 00	21.213	500	25 00 00	22.361

Number	Square	Square Root	Number	Square	Square Root
501	25 10 01	22.383	551	30 36 01	23.473
502	25 20 04	22.405	552	30 47 04	23.495
503	25 30 09	22.428	553	30 58 09	23.516
504	25 40 16	22.450	554	30 69 16	23.537
505	25 50 25	22.472	555	30 80 25	23.558
506	25 60 36	22.494	556	30 91 36	23.580
507	25 70 49	22.517	557	31 02 49	23.601
508	25 80 64	22.539	558	31 13 64	23.622
509	25 90 81	22.561	559	31 24 81	23.643
510	26 01 00	22.583	560	31 36 00	23.664
511	26 11 21	22.605	561	31 47 21	23.685
512	26 21 44	22.627	562	31 58 44	23.707
513	26 31 69	22.650	563	31 69 69	23.728
514	26 41 96	22.672	564	31 80 96	23.749
515	26 52 25	22.694	565	31 92 25	23.770
516	26 62 56	22.716	566	32 03 56	23.791
517	26 72 89	22.738	567	32 14 89	23.812
518	26 83 24	22.760	568	32 26 24	23.833
519	26 93 61	22.782	569	32 37 61	23.854
520	27 04 00	22.804	570	32 49 00	23.875
521	27 14 41	22.825	571	32 60 41	23.896
522	27 24 84	22.847	572	32 71 84	23.917
523	27 35 29	22.869	573	32 83 29	23.937
524	27 45 76	22.891	574	32 94 76	23.958
525	27 56 25	22.913	575	33 06 25	23.979
526	27 66 76	22.935	576	33 17 76	24.000
527	27 77 29	22.956	577	33 29 29	24.021
528	27 87 84	22.978	578	33 40 84	24.042
529	27 98 41	23.000	579	33 52 41	24.062
530	28 09 00	23.022	580	33 64 00	24.083
531	28 19 61	23.043	581	33 75 61	24.104
532	28 30 24	23.065	582	33 87 24	24.125
533	28 40 89	23.087	583	33 98 89	24.145
534	28 51 56	23.108	584	34 10 56	24.166
535	28 62 25	23.130	585	34 22 25	24.187
536	28 72 96	23.152	586	34 33 96	24.207
537	28 83 69	23.173	587	34 45 69	24.228
538	28 94 44	23.195	588	34 57 44	24.249
539	29 05 21	23.216	589	34 69 21	24.269
540	29 16 00	23.238	590	34 81 00	24.290
541	29 26 81	23.259	591	34 92 81	24.310
542	29 37 64	23.281	592	35 04 64	24.331
543	29 48 49	23.302	593	35 16 49	24.352
544	29 59 36	23.324	594	35 28 36	24.372
545	29 70 25	23.345	595	35 40 25	24.393
546	29 81 16	23.367	596	35 52 16	24.413
547	29 92 09	23.388	597	35 64 09	24.434
548	30 03 04	23.409	598	35 76 04	24.454
549	30 14 01	23.431	599	35 88 01	24.474
550	30 25 00	23.452	600	36 00 00	24.495

Number	Square	Square Root	Number	Square	Square Root
601	36 12 01	24.515	651	42 38 01	25.515
602	36 24 04	24.536	652	42 51 04	25.534
603	36 36 09	24.556	653	42 64 09	25.554
604	36 48 16	24.576	654	42 77 16	25.573
605	36 60 25	24.597	655	42 90 25	25.593
606	36 72 36	24.617	656	43 03 36	25.612
607	36 84 49	24.637	657	43 16 49	25.632
608	36 96 64	24.658	658	43 29 64	25.652
609	37 08 81	24.678	659	43 42 81	25.671
610	37 21 00	24.698	660	43 56 00	25.690
611	37 33 21	24.718	661	43 69 21	25.710
612	37 45 44	24.739	662	43 82 44	25.729
613	37 57 69	24.759	663	43 95 69	25.749
614	37 69 96	24.779	664	44 08 96	25.768
615	37 82 25	24.799	665	44 22 25	25.788
616	37 94 56	24.819	666	44 35 56	25.807
617	38 06 89	24.839	667	44 48 89	25.826
618	38 19 24	24.860	668	44 62 24	25.846
619	38 31 61	24.880	669	44 75 61	25.865
620	38 44 00	24.900	670	44 89 00	25.884
621	38 56 41	24.920	671	45 02 41	25.904
622	38 68 84	24.940	672	45 15 84	25.923
623	38 81 29	24.960	673	45 29 29	25.942
624	38 93 76	24.980	674	45 42 76	25.962
625	39 06 25	25.000	675	45 56 25	25.981
626	39 18 76	25.020	676	45 69 76	26.000
627	39 31 29	25.040	677	45 83 29	26.019
628	39 43 84	25.060	678	45 96 84	26.038
629	39 56 41	25.080	679	46 10 41	26.058
630	39 69 00	25.100	680	46 24 00	26.077
631	39 81 61	25.120	681	46 37 61	26.096
632	39 94 24	25.140	682	46 51 24	26.115
633	40 06 89	25.159	683	46 64 89	26.134
634	40 19 56	25.179	684	46 78 56	26.153
635	40 32 25	25.199	685	46 92 25	26.173
636	40 44 96	25.219	686	47 05 96	26.192
637	40 57 69	25.239	687	47 19 69	26.211
638	40 70 44	25.259	688	47 33 44	26.230
639	40 83 21	25.278	689	47 47 21	26.249
640	40 96 00	25.298	690	47 61 00	26.268
641	41 08 81	25.318	691	47 74 81	26.287
642	41 21 64	25.338	692	47 88 64	26.306
643	41 34 49	25.357	693	48 02 49	26.325
644	41 47 36	25.377	694	48 16 36	26.344
645	41 60 25	25.397	695	48 30 25	26.363
646	41 73 16	25.417	696	48 44 16	26.382
647	41 86 09	25.436	697	48 58 09	26.401
648	41 99 04	25.456	698	48 72 04	26.420
649	42 12 01	25.475	699	48 86 01	26.439
650	42 25 00	25.495	700	49 00 00	26.458

Number	Square	Square Root	Number	Square	Square Root
701	49 14 01	26.476	751	56 40 01	27.404
702	49 28 04	26.495	752	56 55 04	27.423
703	49 42 09	26.514	753	56 70 09	27.441
704	49 56 16	26.533	754	56 85 16	27.459
705	49 70 25	26.552	755	57 00 25	27.477
706	49 84 36	26.571	756	57 15 36	27.495
707	49 98 49	26.589	757	57 30 49	27.514
708	50 12 64	26.608	758	57 45 64	27.532
709	50 26 81	26.627	759	57 60 81	27.550
710	50 41 00	26.646	760	57 76 00	27.568
711	50 55 21	26.665	761	57 91 21	27.586
712	50 69 44	26.683	762	58 06 44	27.604
713	50 83 69	26.702	763	58 21 69	27.622
714	50 97 96	26.721	764	58 36 96	27.641
715	51 12 25	26.739	765	58 52 25	27.659
716	51 26 56	26.758	766	58 67 56	27.677
717	51 40 89	26.777	767	58 82 89	27.695
718	51 55 24	26.796	768	58 98 24	27.713
719	51 69 61	26.814	769	59 13 61	27.731
720	51 84 00	26.833	770	59 29 00	27.749
721	51 98 41	26.851	771	59 44 41	27.767
722	52 12 84	26.870	772	59 59 84	27.785
723	52 27 29	26.889	773	59 75 29	27.803
724	52 41 76	26.907	774	59 90 76	27.821
725	52 56 25	26.926	775	60 06 25	27.839
726	52 70 76	26.944	776	60 21 76	27.857
727	52 85 29	26.963	777	60 37 29	27.875
728	52 99 84	26.981	778	60 52 84	27.893
729	53 14 41	27.000	779	60 68 41	27.911
730	53 29 00	27.019	780	60 84 00	27.928
731	53 43 61	27.037	781	60 99 61	27.946
732	53 58 24	27.055	782	61 15 24	27.964
733	53 72 89	27.074	783	61 30 89	27.982
734	53 87 56	27.092	784	61 46 56	28.000
735	54 02 25	27.111	785	61 62 25	28.018
736	54 16 96	27.129	786	61 77 96	28.036
737	54 31 69	27.148	787	61 93 69	28.054
738	54 46 44	27.166	788	62 09 44	28.071
739	54 61 21	27.185	789	62 25 21	28.089
740	54 76 00	27.203	790	62 41 00	28.107
741	54 90 81	27.221	791	62 56 81	28.125
742	55 05 64	27.240	792	62 72 64	28.142
743	55 20 49	27.258	793	62 88 49	28.160
744	55 35 36	27.276	794	63 04 36	28.178
745	55 50 25	27.295	795	63 20 25	28.196
746	55 65 16	27.313	796	63 36 16	28.213
747	55 80 09	27.331	797	63 52 09	28.231
748	55 95 04	27.350	798	63 68 04	28.249
749	56 10 01	27.368	799	63 84 01	28.267
750	56 25 00	27.386	800	64 00 00	28.284

Number	Square	Square Root	Number	Square	Square Root
801	64 16 01	28.302	851	72 42 01	29.172
802	64 32 04	28.320	852	72 59 04	29.189
803	64 48 09	28.337	853	72 76 09	29.206
804	64 64 16	28.355	854	72 93 16	29.223
805	64 80 25	28.373	855	73 10 25	29.240
806	64 96 36	28.390	856	73 27 36	29.257
807	65 12 49	28.408	857	73 44 49	29.275
808	65 28 64	28.425	858	73 61 64	29.292
809	65 44 81	28.443	859	73 78 81	29.309
810	65 61 00	28.460	860	73 96 00	29.326
811	65 77 21	28.478	861	74 13 21	29.343
812	65 93 44	28.496	862	74 30 44	29.360
813	66 09 69	28.513	863	74 47 69	29.377
814	66 25 96	28.531	864	74 64 96	29.394
815	66 42 25	28.548	865	74 82 25	29.411
816	66 58 56	28.566	866	74 99 56	29.428
817	66 74 89	28.583	867	75 16 89	29.445
818	66 91 24	28.601	868	75 34 24	29.462
819	67 07 61	28.618	869	75 51 61	29.479
820	67 24 00	28.636	870	75 69 00	29.496
821	67 40 41	28.653	871	75 86 41	29.513
822	67 56 84	28.671	872	76 03 84	29.530
823	67 73 29	28.688	873	76 21 29	29.547
824	67 89 76	28.705	874	76 38 76	29.563
825	68 06 25	28.723	875	76 56 25	29.580
826	68 22 76	28.740	876	76 73 76	29.597
827	68 39 29	28.758	877	76 91 29	29.614
828	68 55 84	28.775	878	77 08 84	29.631
829	68 72 41	28.792	879	77 26 41	29.648
830	68 89 00	28.810	880	77 44 00	29.665
831	69 05 61	28.827	881	77 61 61	29.682
832	69 22 24	28.844	882	77 79 24	29.698
833	69 38 89	28.862	883	77 96 89	29.715
834	69 55 56	28.879	884	78 14 56	29.732
835	69 72 25	28.896	885	78 32 25	29.749
836	69 88 96	28.914	886	78 49 96	29.766
837	70 05 69	28.931	887	78 67 69	29.783
838	70 22 44	28.948	888	78 85 44	29.799
839	70 39 21	28.965	889	79 03 21	29.816
840	70 56 00	28.983	890	79 21 00	29.833
841	70 72 81	29.000	891	79 38 81	29.850
842	70 89 64	29.017	892	79 56 64	29.866
843	71 06 49	29.034	893	79 74 49	29.883
844	71 23 36	29.052	894	79 92 36	29.900
845	71 40 25	29.069	895	80 10 25	29.916
846	71 57 16	29.086	896	80 28 16	29.933
847	71 74 09	29.103	897	80 46 09	29.950
848	71 91 04	29.120	898	80 64 04	29.967
849	72 08 01	29.138	899	80 82 01	29.983
850	72 25 00	29.155	900	81 00 00	30.000

Number	Square	Square Root	Number	Square	Square Root
901	81 18 01	30.017	951	90 44 01	30.838
902	81 36 04	30.033	952	90 63 04	30.854
903	81 54 09	30.050	953	90 82 09	30.871
904	81 72 16	30.067	954	91 01 16	30.887
905	81 90 25	30.083	955	91 20 25	30.903
906	82 08 36	30.100	956	91 39 36	30.919
907	82 26 49	30.116	957	91 58 49	30.935
908	82 44 64	30.133	958	91 77 64	30.952
909	82 62 81	30.150	959	91 96 81	30.968
910	82 81 00	30.166	960	92 16 00	30.984
911	82 99 21	30.183	961	92 35 21	31.000
912	83 17 44	30.199	962	92 54 44	31.016
913	83 35 69	30.216	963	92 73 69	31.032
914	83 53 96	30.232	964	92 92 96	31.048
915	83 72 25	30.249	965	93 12 25	31.064
916	83 90 56	30.265	966	93 31 56	31.081
917	84 08 89	30.282	967	93 50 89	31.097
918	84 27 24	30.299	968	93 70 24	31.113
919	84 45 61	30.315	969	93 89 61	31.129
920	84 64 00	30.332	970	94 09 00	31.145
921	84 82 41	30.348	971	94 28 41	31.161
922	85 00 84	30.364	972	94 47 84	31.177
923	85 19 29	30.381	973	94 67 29	31.193
924	85 37 76	30.397	974	94 86 76	31.209
925	85 56 25	30.414	975	95 06 25	31.225
926	85 74 76	30.430	976	95 25 76	31.241
927	85 93 29	30.447	977	95 45 29	31.257
928	86 11 84	30.463	978	95 64 84	31.273
929	86 30 41	30.480	979	95 84 41	31.289
930	86 49 00	30.496	980	96 04 00	31.305
931	86 67 61	30.512	981	96 23 61	31.321
932	86 86 24	30.529	982	96 43 24	31.337
933	87 04 89	30.545	983	96 62 89	31.353
934	87 23 56	30.561	984	96 82 56	31.369
935	87 42 25	30.578	985	97 02 25	31.385
936	87 60 96	30.594	986	97 21 96	31.401
937	87 79 69	30.610	987	97 41 69	31.417
938	87 98 44	30.627	988	97 61 44	31.432
939	88 17 21	30.643	989	97 81 21	31.448
940	88 36 00	30.659	990	98 01 00	31.464
941	88 54 81	30.676	991	98 20 81	31.480
942	88 73 64	30.692	992	98 40 64	31.496
943	88 92 49	30.708	993	98 60 49	31.512
944	89 11 36	30.725	994	98 80 36	31.528
945	89 30 25	30.741	995	99 00 25	31.544
946	89 49 16	30.757	996	99 20 16	31.559
947	89 68 09	30.773	997	99 40 09	31.575
948	89 87 04	30.790	998	99 60 04	31.591
949	90 06 01	30.806	999	99 80 01	31.607
950	90 25 00	30.822	1000	100 00 00	31.623

APPENDIX C. Relationships Among T scores, z scores, and Percentile Ranks When Raw Scores are Normally Distributed

z Score	T Score	Percentile Rank	z Score	T Score	Percentile Rank
3.0	80	99.9	−3.0	20	0.1
2.9	79	99.8	−2.9	21	0.2
2.8	78	99.7	−2.8	22	0.3
2.7	77	99.6	−2.7	23	0.4
2.6	76	99.5	−2.6	24	0.5
2.5	75	99.4	−2.5	25	0.6
2.4	74	99.2	−2.4	26	0.8
2.3	73	99	−2.3	27	1
2.2	72	99	−2.2	28	1
2.1	71	98	−2.1	29	2
2.0	70	98	−2.0	30	2
1.9	69	97	−1.9	31	3
1.8	68	96	−1.8	32	4
1.7	67	96	−1.7	33	4
1.6	66	95	−1.6	34	5
.15	65	93	−1.5	35	7
1.4	64	92	−1.4	36	8
1.3	63	90	−1.3	37	10
1.2	62	88	−1.2	38	12
1.1	61	86	−1.1	39	14
1.0	60	84	−1.0	40	16
0.9	59	82	−0.9	41	18
0.8	58	79	−0.8	42	21
0.7	57	76	−0.7	43	24
0.6	56	73	−0.6	44	27
0.5	55	69	−0.5	45	31
0.4	54	66	−0.4	46	34
0.3	53	62	−0.3	47	38
0.2	52	58	−0.2	48	42
0.1	51	54	−0.1	49	46
0.0	50	50	0.0	50	50

APPENDIX D. SELECTED LIST OF TEST PUBLISHERS

American College Testing Program, P.O. Box 168, Iowa City, Iowa 52240

American Guidance Service, 720 Washington Avenue, S. E., Minneapolis, Minnesota 55414

The Bobbs-Merrill Company, 4300 East 62nd Street, Indianapolis, Indiana 46206

Bureau of Educational Measurements, Kansas State Teachers College, Emporia, Kansas 66801

Bureau of Educational Research and Service, University of Iowa, Iowa City, Iowa 52240

California Test Bureau/McGraw-Hill, Del Monte Research Park, Monterey, California 93940

Combined Motivation Education Systems, 6300 River Road, Rosemont, Illinois 60018

Committee on Diagnostic Reading Tests, Mountain Home, North Carolina 28758

Consulting Psychologists Press, 577 College Avenue, Palo Alto, California 94306

Cooperative Test Division, Educational Testing Service, Princeton, New Jersey 08540

Educational Guidance, P.O. Box 511, Main Station, Dearborn, Michigan 48120

Educational and Industrial Testing Service, P.O. Box 7234, San Diego, California 92107

Harcourt Brace Jovanovich, 757 Third Avenue, New York, N.Y. 10017

Houghton Mifflin Company, 110 Tremont Street, Boston, Massachusetts 02107

Institute for Personality and Ability Testing, 1862 Coronado Drive, Champaign, Illinois 61822

Personal Growth Press, 653 Longfellow Drive, Berea, Ohio 44017

Personnel Press, 20 Nassau Street, Princeton, New Jersey 08540

The Psychological Corporation, 304 East 45th Street, New York, N.Y. 10017

Psychometric Affiliates, 1743 Monterey, Chicago, Illinois 60643

Scholastic Testing Service, 480 Meyer Road, Bensenville, Illinois 60106

Science Research Associates, 259 East Erie Street, Chicago, Illinois 60611

Scott, Foresman and Company, 433 East Erie Street, Chicago, Illinois 60025

Sheridan Supply Company, P.O. Box 837, Beverly Hills, California 90213

Springer Publishing Company, 200 Park Avenue South, New York, N.Y. 10003

Stanford University Press, Stanford, California 94305

C. H. Stoelting Company, 424 North Homan Avenue, Chicago, Illinois 60624

Teachers College Press, Teachers College, Columbia University, 502 West 121st Street, New York, N.Y. 10027

Western Psychological Services, Box 775, Beverly Hills, California 90213

GLOSSARY OF MEASUREMENT, EVALUATION, AND TESTING TERMS[1]

ACADEMIC APTITUDE
: The combination of native and acquired abilities needed for schoolwork.

ACCOUNTABILITY
: Responsibility for bringing about certain educational changes or levels of performance.

ACHIEVEMENT TEST
: A test that measures the extent to which an individual has "achieved" something—acquired certain information or mastered certain skills—usually as a result of specific instruction or general schooling.

AGE EQUIVALENT
: The age for which a given score is the real or estimated average score.

AGE–GRADE TABLE
: A table illustrating the relationship between the chronological ages of pupils and the school grade in which they are classified.

AGE NORM
: Values or scores representing typical or average performance of individuals classified according to chronological age.

ADJUSTMENT INVENTORY
: An instrument used to identify personal and social adjustment problems, usually on a self-report basis. Sometimes used synonymously with *personality test, mental-health analysis,* and *temperament test.*

ALTERNATE–FORM RELIABILITY
: A measure of the extent to which two equivalent or parallel forms of a test correlate in measuring whatever they measure.

ALTERNATIVE
: See *distractor.*

APTITUDE
: A combination of abilities and other characteristics, native or acquired, known or believed to be indicative of an individual's ability to learn in a given particular area. Thus, "musical aptitude" refers to that combination of physical and mental characteristics, motivational factors, knowledge, and other characteristics that is conducive to the achievement of proficiency

---

[1] Reproduced in part from *A glossary of 100 measurement terms (Test Service Notebook,* No. 13). Distributed by Harcourt Brace Jovanovich, Inc. Reproduced by special permission.

Also reproduced in part from *A glossary of measurement terms,* copyright © 1959 by McGraw-Hill. Reprinted by permission of the publisher, CTB/McGraw-Hill, Monterey, California.

in the field of music. Motivational factors, including interests, are sometimes distinguished from aptitude, but the more comprehensive definition seems preferable.

ARITHMETIC MEAN
The sum of a set of scores divided by the number of scores (commonly called *average* or *mean*).

ARTICULATED TESTS
A series of tests that provides different levels for different ages or grades, constructed and standardized so that the same or comparable elements or objectives are measured at all levels. Well-articulated tests are characterized by considerable interlevel overlap in order to test the wide ranges of abilities and achievements in any given grade or class. On a well-articulated series of test batteries, a given grade group achieves the same derived scores whether a lower or higher level of the test is used.

AUDITING
The independent examination of an educational effort or performance contract to verify results; check on processes, personnel, and progress; and report to an interested external agency.

AVERAGE
A general term applied to measures of central tendency. The three most widely used averages are the *arithmetic mean,* the *median,* and the *mode.*

BALANCE
The degree to which the proportion of items measuring particular outcomes corresponds to the "ideal" test or to that suggested by the table of specifications.

BATTERY
A group of tests standardized on the same population, so that results on the several tests are comparable (integrated norms). Sometimes loosely applied to any group of tests administered together.

BEHAVIORAL OBJECTIVES
Statements of intended educational outcomes defined in terms of criteria for student performance, sometimes specifying the conditions under which the behavior is to be observed. Akin to "performance" and "competence" objectives.

CEILING
The upper limit of ability that can be measured by a test. Individuals are said to have reached

the ceiling of a test when their abilities exceed the highest performance level at which the test can make reliable discriminations.

CENTILE

A value on the scoring scale below which a given percentage of cases is located. The synonym *percentile* is regarded by some statisticians as superfluous. (See *percentile*.)

CLASS INTERVAL

The divisions of a frequency distribution bounded by upper and lower score values. (See *frequency distribution*.)

COMPLETION ITEM

A test question calling for the completion of a phrase or sentence one or more parts of which have been omitted; a question for which the examinee must supply (rather than select) the correct response.

CONCURRENT VALIDITY

See *criterion-related validity*.

CONFIDENCE INTERVAL

A set of numbers believed to include the numerical value of that which is being estimated. For example, given a 68 percent confidence interval for a true score, one could assert with 68 percent confidence that the true score falls within the interval. The probability may be considered as representing the degree of belief that the value actually falls in the interval, or the percentage of correct assertions if the procedure is repeated.

CONSTRUCT VALIDITY

The degree to which a test measures given psychological qualities. By both logical and empirical methods the theory underlying the test is validated. Arguments for construct validity must be based on theory and empirical evidence. Examples of such methods are correlations of the test score with other test scores, factor analysis, study of the effect of speed on test scores.

CONTENT VALIDITY

The degree to which the content of the test samples the subject matter, behaviors, or situations about which conclusions are to be drawn. Content validity is especially important in an achievement test, and is determined with reference to the table of specifications and objectives. Examples of procedures to measure content validity are textbook analysis, description of the universe of items, judgment of the adequacy of the sample, review of representative illustrations of test content, intercorrelations of subscores, and solicitation of the opinions of a jury of experts.

CORRECTION FOR
GUESSING

A reduction in score for wrong answers, sometimes applied in scoring true-false or multiple-choice questions. Many doubt the validity or usefulness of this device, which is intended to discourage guessing and yield more accurate measures of examinees' true knowledge. It is assumed that if an examinee guesses on an objective test, the number of resulting wrong answers will be proportional to the number of alternate responses to each item.

CORRELATION

The relationship or "going-togetherness" between two sets of scores or measures; the tendency of scores on one variable to vary concomitantly with those on another, e.g., the tendency of students with high IQs to be above average in reading ability. The existence of a strong relationship—that is, a high correlation—between two variables does not necessarily indicate a causal relationship. (See *correlation coefficient.*)

CORRELATION
COEFFICIENT (*r*)

The most commonly used measure of relationship between paired facts or numbers, indicating the tendency of two or more variables or attributes to rank themselves, or individuals measured on them, in the same way. A correlation coefficient (*r*) may range in value from −1.00 for a perfect negative relationship through 0.00 for none or pure chance to +1.00 for a perfect positive relationship, and summarizes the degree and direction of the relationship.

CRITERION

A standard by which a test may be judged or evaluated; a set of scores or ratings that a test is designed to correlate with or to predict. (See *validity.*)

CRITERION-
REFERENCED TEST

A test whose items are tied to specific objectives. Usually used when mastery learning is involved. Variability of scores is of little consequence. Emphasis is on an individual's performance relative to an absolute rather than a normative standard, i.e., and individual's performance is compared with an *a priori* criterion instead of with the performance of other people.

CRITERION–RELATED VALIDITY

The degree to which test scores correlate with measures of criterion performance. Measures of criteria may be gathered concurrently (*concurrent validity*)—for example, correlation of the distribution of scores for men in a given occupation with those for men-in-general, correlation of personality test scores with estimates of adjustments made in counseling interviews, or correlation of end-of-course achievement or ability test scores with school marks—or at a later time—for example, correlation of intelligence test scores with course grades, or correlation of test scores obtained at beginning of the year with marks earned at the end of the year.

CROSS–VALIDATION

The process of determining whether a decision derived from one set of data is truly effective by applying the decision process (or strategy) to an independent but relevant set of data.

CURRICULUM EVALUATION

The process of collecting and processing data for decisionmaking about an educational program. Such data may include (1) objective descriptions of goals, environments, personnel, methods, content, and results, and (2) recorded personal judgments of the quality and appropriateness of goals, inputs, and outcomes. (See *evaluation program*.)

DECILE

Any of the nine percentile points (scores) in a distribution that divide it into ten equal parts; every tenth percentile. The first decile is the 10th percentile, the ninth decile the 90th percentile, and so on.

DERIVED SCORE

A score that has been converted from a qualitative or quantitative mark on one scale into the units of another scale (e.g., standard score, percentile rank, intelligence quotient).

DEVIATION

The amount by which a score differs from some reference value, such as the mean, norm, or score on another test.

DEVIATION I.Q.

A measure of intelligence based on the extent to which an individual's score deviates from a score that is typical for the individual's age. (See *intelligence quotient*.)

DIAGNOSTIC TEST

A test used to identify specific areas of weakness or strength and to determine the nature of deficiencies; it yields measures of the components of larger areas of knowledge and skills. Diagnostic achievement tests are most commonly developed for the skill subjects —reading, arithmetic, and spelling.

DIFFICULTY INDEX

The percentage of some specified group, such as students of a given age or grade, who answer an item correctly or score in a particular direction.

DISCRIMINATION INDEX

The ability of a test item to differentiate between individuals who possess a given characteristic (skill, knowledge, attitude) in abundance, and those who possess little of it.

DISTRACTOR

Any of the plausible but incorrect choices provided in a multiple-choice or matching item. Sometimes called a *foil, alternative,* or *option*. The choice is "distracting" and appears attractive to the less knowledgeable or skillful examinee, thereby reducing the efficacy of guessing.

DISTRIBUTION

An ordered tabulation of scores showing the number of individuals who obtain each score or fall within each score interval. (See *frequency distribution.*)

DUAL STANDARDIZATION

The procedure of norming or standardizing two tests, e.g., a group intelligence test and an achievement battery, simultaneously on one sample, thereby integrating the two instruments.

ERROR OF ESTIMATE

See *standard error of estimate*.

EQUIVALENT FORMS

Any of two or more forms of a test whose content and difficulty are similar, and that yield very similar average scores and measures of variability for a given group.

EVALUATION

The process by which quantitative and qualitative data are processed to arrive at a judgment of value, worth, or effectiveness.

EVALUATION PROGRAM

The process of testing, measuring, and appraising adjustment, status, growth, and/or achievement by means of tests and nontest instruments and techniques. Such a program tends to involve the identification and formulation of a comprehensive set of objectives for a curriculum, their definition in terms of pupil behavior, and the selection and construction of valid, reliable, and practical instruments for appraising specified phases of pupil behavior. Evaluation includes the interpretation and integration of evidence about behavior stability and behavior changes into a multifaceted description of an individual or educational situation. An adequate educational evaluation program is (1) comprehensive and well-balanced in terms of the learner and the curriculum; (2) continuous and well-articulated from the first grade through the secondary grades; (3) functional and practical for those using it; and (4) integrated and based on scientific measuring instruments and techniques. *Evaluation* and *measurement* are not synonymous. Measurement emphasizes single aspects of subject-matter achievement or specific skills and abilities; evaluation focuses on broad personality changes and the objectives of the educational program. (See *curriculum evaluation*.)

EXPECTANCY TABLE

Usually a two-way grid or bivariate table expressing the relationship between two (or more) variables by stating the probability that individuals who belong to each of a set of subgroups defined on the basis of one (or more) variables will belong to each of a set of subgroups defined on the basis of another variable. A method of expressing the validity of a test, if one of the variables is the predictor and the other the criterion.

EXTRAPOLATION

As applied to test norms, the process of extending a norm line beyond the limits of the data in order to permit interpretation of extreme scores. This extension may be accomplished mathematically by fitting a curve to the obtained data or by less rigorous graphic methods.

FACE VALIDITY

The acceptability of the test and test situation by the examinee and, to some extent, the user in light of the apparent uses to which the test is to be put. A test has face validity when it appears to measure the variable it purports to test.

FACTOR

A hypothetical trait, ability, or component of ability that underlies and influences performance on two or more tests, and hence causes scores on the tests to be correlated. Strictly defined, the term *factor* refers to a theoretical variable derived by a process of factor analysis from a table of intercorrelations among tests, but it is also commonly used to denote the psychological interpretation given to the variable—i.e., the mental trait assumed to be represented by the variable, such as verbal or numerical ability. (See *factor analysis*.)

FACTOR ANALYSIS

A set of methods for analyzing the intercorrelations among a set of variables, such as test scores. Using factor analysis we may attempt to account for such interrelationships in terms of underlying factors, preferably fewer in number than the original variables. Factor analysis reveals how much of the variation in each of the original measures is associated with each of the hypothetical factors.

FOIL

See *distractor*.

FORCED–CHOICE ITEM

Broadly, any multiple-choice item that requires the examinee to select one or more of the given choices. The term is best used to denote a special type of multiple-choice item in which the options are (1) of equal "preference value"—i.e., chosen equally often by a typical group—but (2) of differential discriminating ability—i.e., such that one and only one of the options discriminates between persons high and low on the factor that this option measures.

FORMATIVE EVALUATION

The use of evaluation data to modify, revise, and generally improve an educational program during its developmental stages. (See *summative evaluation*.)

FREQUENCY DISTRIBUTION

An ordered tabulation of scores showing the number of individuals who obtain each score or fall within each score interval.

GRADE EQUIVALENT

The grade level for which a given score is the real or estimated average. A grade equivalent of 6.4 is theoretically the average score obtained by students in the fourth month of the sixth grade. Grade equivalent score units are subject to much distortion due to variations in curriculum, individual aptitude, and learning.

GRAPHIC RATING SCALE

A scale that presents the rater with a continuum of phrases describing degrees of a particular trait. The rater makes a judgment about an individual or object with reference to the trait and indicates his opinion by placing a mark on a line.

GROUP TEST

A test that may be administered to a number of individuals simultaneously by a single examiner.

GUESSING

See *correction for guessing*.

INCREMENTAL VALIDITY

The increase in relationship between the predictor(s) and the criterion measure when another predictor is added to the set.

INDIVIDUAL TEST

A test that may be administered to only one person at a time.

INTELLIGENCE QUOTIENT

A now-outmoded index representing the ratio of a person's mental age to his chronological age (MA/CA) or, more precisely, especially for older persons, the ratio of mental age to the mental age typical of chronological age (in both cases multiplied by 100 to eliminate the decimal). More generally, IQ is a measure of "brightness" that takes into account both the score on an intelligence test and age. A *deviation IQ* is such a measure of "brightness," based on the difference or deviation between a person's obtained score and the score that is typical for his age. Usually expressed as a type of standard score. (See *deviation IQ*.)

INTERNAL CONSISTENCY

The extent to which items on a test are correlated with each other, implying the measurement of a common content skill, behavior, or other factor.

INTERPOLATION

In general, any process of estimating intermediate values between two known points. As applied to test norms, the term usually refers to the procedure used in assigning values (e.g., grade or age equivalents) to scores between the successive average scores actually obtained in the standardization process. In reading norm tables, it is necessary to interpolate to obtain a norm value for a score between the scores given in a table.

INVENTORY TEST

As applied to achievement tests, a test that attempts to cover rather thoroughly a relatively small unit of specific instruction or training. The purpose of an inventory test, as its name suggests, is more to "take stock" of an individual's knowledge or skill than to measure in the usual sense. The term sometimes denotes a type of test used to measure achievement status prior to instruction, or general mental health or personality status.

ITEM

A single question or exercise in a test.

ITEM ANALYSIS

Any of several methods used in test development and refinement to determine how well a given test item discriminates among individuals differing in some characteristic. The effectiveness of a test item depends upon three factors: (1) the validity of the item with regard to an outside criterion, curriculum content, or educational objective; (2) the discriminating power of the item with regard to validity and internal consistency; and (3) the difficulty of the item.

ITEM SAMPLING

A procedure used in standardization of tests and curriculum evaluation. Instead of requiring all individuals to respond to all items, subgroups take subsets of items. For example, instead of requiring 100 individuals to answer 70 items, 10 groups of 10 individuals each answer 7 items.

KUDER–RICHARDSON FORMULA(S)

Formulas for estimating the reliability —specifically, the internal consistency—of a test from (1) information about the individual items in the test, or (2) the mean score, standard deviation, and number of items in the test. Because the Kuder-Richardson formulas permit estimation of reliability from a single administration of a test, without dividing the test into halves, their use has become common in test development. The Kuder-Richardson formulas are not appropriate for estimating the reliability of speeded tests.

MASTERY TEST

A test of the extent to which a student has mastered a specified set of objectives or met minimum requirements set by a teacher or examining agency. Usually a criterion-referenced measure. (See *criterion-referenced measure*.)

MATCHING ITEM

A test item calling for the correct association of each entry in one list with an entry in a second list.

MEAN

The sum of a set of scores divided by the number of scores.

MEASUREMENT

The process of quantifying according to a standard. The assignment of numerals to represent objects, individuals, or phenomena.

MEDIAN

The 50th percentile; the point that divides a group into two equal parts. Half of a group of scores falls below the median and half above it.

MENTAL AGE (MA)

The age for which a given score on an intelligence test is average or normal. If a score of 55 on an intelligence test corresponds to a mental age of 6 years 10 months, 55 is presumed to be the average score that would be achieved by an unselected group of children 6 years 10 months of age.

MODE

The score or value that occurs most frequently in a distribution.

MULTIPLE–CHOICE ITEM

A test item in which the examinee's task is to choose the correct or best answer from several given options.

MULTIPLE CORRELATION

The relationship between one variable and the weighted sum of two or more other variables.

MULTIPLE REGRESSION

A method of combining two or more predictors to estimate a single criterion measure. For example, freshman grade point average may be predicted from a combination of high-school rank, intelligence test score, and interest inventory scores.

MULTIPLE–RESPONSE ITEM

A type of multiple-choice item in which two or more of the given choices may be correct.

N

The symbol commonly used to represent the number of cases in a distribution, study, or other sampling. The sum of the frequencies = N.

NORMAL DISTRIBUTION

A derived curve based on the assumption that variations from the mean occur by chance. The curve is bell-shaped, and is accepted as a representational model because of its repeated recurrence in measurements of human characteristics in psychology and education. It has many useful mathematical properties. In a normal distribution curve, scores are distributed symmetrically about the mean, thickly concentrated near it and decreasing in frequency as the distance from it increases. One cannot tell if a particular distribution is "normal" simply by looking at it, but must determine whether the data fit a particular mathematical function.

NORMALIZED
STANDARDIZED SCORE

Usually called T scores, normalized standard scores are made to conform to standard score values of a normal distribution curve by use of percentile equivalents for the normal curve. Most frequently expressed with a mean equated to 50 and a standard deviation equated to 10. (See *stanine*.)

NORM–REFERENCED
MEASURE

A measure used to distinguish among members of a group by comparing an individual's performance with the performance of others in the group.

NORMS

Statistics that describe the test performance of specified subgroups, such as pupils of various ages or grades, in the standardization group for a test. Norms are often assumed to be representative of some larger population, such as pupils in the country as a whole. Norms are descriptive of average or typical performance; they are not to be regarded as standards or desirable levels of attainment. Grade, age, percentile, and standard score are the most common types of norms.

OBJECTIVITY

Consistency in scoring. Objectivity is a characteristic of a test that precludes difference of opinion among scorers as to whether responses are to be scored right or wrong. Such a test is contrasted with a "subjective" test—e.g., the usual essay examination to which different scorers may assign different scores, ratings, or grades. Objectivity is a characteristic of the scoring of the test, not its form. An objective test is one in which the method of gathering data does not distort the phenomenon being measured.

OMNIBUS TEST

A test (1) in which items measuring a variety of mental operations are combined into a single sequence rather than grouped together by type of operation, and (2) from which only a single score is derived. Omnibus tests make for simplicity of administration: one set of directions and one overall time limit usually suffice.

OPTION

See *distractor*.

PERCENTILE

One of the 99 point scores that divide a ranked distribution into groups each of which is composed of 1/100 of the scores. Also, a point below which a certain percentage of the scores fall. For example, the median (the 50th percentile) is the point in a distribution below which 50 percent of the scores fall.

PERCENTILE RANK

The percentage of scores in a distribution equal to or lower than the score in question. If a person obtains a percentile rank of 70, his standing is regarded as equaling or surpassing that of 70 percent of the normative group on which the test was standardized.

PERFORMANCE CONTRACT

Agreement to bring about specified changes in individuals or groups. Criteria are detailed, and level of payment is tied to performance.

PERFORMANCE TEST

A test usually requiring motor or manual response on the examinee's part, and generally but not always involving manipulation of concrete equipment or materials, as contrasted with a paper-and-pencil test. The term is also used to denote a work-sample test, which simulates the behavior about which information is desired. A work-sample instrument may use paper and pencil to test skills such as accounting, shorthand, and proofreading.

PERSONALITY TEST

A test intended to measure one or more nonintellective variables. Personality tests include: so-called *personality inventories* or *adjustment inventories,* which seek to measure a person's status on such traits as dominance, sociability, and introversion by means of self-descriptive responses to a series of questions; *rating scales,* which call for self- or other-administered rating of the extent to which a subject possesses certain characteristics; situation tests, in which the individual's behavior in simulated lifelike situations is observed and evaluated, with reference to various personality traits, by one or more judges; and opinion or attitude inventories. Some writers also classify interest inventories as personality tests.

PLACEMENT

The classification of an individual into one of two or more treatments, programs, or groups. (See *selection*.)

POWER TEST

A test intended to measure level of performance and to sample the range of an examinee's capacity, rather than the speed of response; hence a power test has either no time limit or a very generous one.

PRACTICE EFFECT

The influence of previous experience with a test on a later administration of the same or a similar test, usually resulting in an increase in score. Practice effect is greatest when the time interval between testings is small, the content of the two tests is very similar, and the initial test administration represents a relatively novel experience for the subject.

PREDICTIVE VALIDITY

See *criterion-related validity*.

PRODUCT–MOMENT COEFFICIENT

See *coefficient of correlation*.

PROFILE

A graphic representation of an individual's or group's scores on several tests, expressed in uniform or comparable terms. This method of presentation permits easy identification of areas of strength or weakness.

PROJECTIVE TECHNIQUE (PROJECTIVE METHOD)

A method of personality study in which the subject responds as he chooses to a series of ambiguous stimuli such as inkblots, pictures, or unfinished sentences. So-called because of the assumption that the subject "projects" into his responses manifestations of personality characteristics and organization that can be scored and interpreted by suitable methods to yield a description of his basic personality structure. The *Rorschach* (inkblot) *Technique* and the *Murray Thematic Apperception Test* are the most commonly used examples of this technique.

Q–SORT

A technique used to measure personality, requiring the subject to sort a large number of statements into piles representing the degrees to which they apply to him.

QUARTILE

One of three points that divide the cases in a distribution into four equal groups. The first quartile is the 25th percentile, the second quartile is the 50th percentile or median, and the third quartile is the 75th percentile.

RANDOM SAMPLE

A sample of a population drawn in such a way that every member has an equal chance of being included. That is, the sample is drawn in a way that precludes the operation of bias in selection. One goal of such a sample is, of course, that it be representative of the total population, so that sample findings may be generalized to that population. (However, a random sample may still be atypical and unrepresentative of the population.) A great advantage of random samples is that formulas are available for estimating the expected variation of the sample statistics from their true values in the total population; in other words, we know how precise an estimate of the population is represented by a random sample of any given size.

RANGE

The difference between the highest and lowest scores, plus one, obtained on a test by a particular group.

RATING SCALE

A data-gathering method involving the use of numerals or phrases in conjunction with points along a continuum. A given instrument may include several such scales.

RAW SCORE

The first quantitative result obtained in scoring a test. Usually the number of right answers, the time required for performance, the number of errors, or a similar direct, unconverted, uninterpreted measure.

READINESS TEST

A test that measures the extent to which an individual has achieved the degree of maturity or acquired the skills or information necessary to undertake some new learning activity successfully. Thus a *reading readiness test* indicates the extent to which a child has reached the appropriate developmental stage and acquired the prerequisite skills to profitably begin a formal instructional program in reading.

RECALL ITEM

An item that requires the examinee to supply the correct answer from his own memory, as contrasted with a *recognition item*, which requires him to select or identify the correct answer.

RECOGNITION ITEM

An item requiring the examinee to recognize or select the correct answer from among two or more given answers.

REGRESSION EFFECT

The tendency for a predicted score to be relatively nearer the mean of its series than is the score from which it was predicted to the mean of its series. For example, if we predict school marks from an intelligence test, we will find that the mean of the predicted school marks for all pupils who have IQs two standard deviations above the mean will be less than two standard deviations from the mean of the school marks. There is a regression effect whenever the correlation between two measures is less than perfect.

RELEVANCE

The extent to which specific items are in fact measures of specific objectives. In a real sense, relevance is a function of item validity.

RELIABILITY

The extent to which a test is accurate or consistent in measuring whatever it measures; dependability, stability, and relative freedom from errors of measurement. Estimation of reliability generally involves examination of internal consistency, equivalence of forms, or stability of scores over time.

RELIABILITY OF A DIFFERENCE

The extent to which a difference between scores is consistent, e.g., the extent to which differences between pre- and post-test scores on one form of a test are related to pre- and post-differences on another form of the test.

REPRESENTATIVE SAMPLE

A sample that accurately represents the population from which it is selected with respect to characteristics relevant to the issue under investigation—e.g., in an achievement-test norm sample, representation might be according to pupils from each state, various regions, segregated and nonsegregated schools, and so on.

SCALED SCORE

A unit in a system of equated scores corresponding to the raw scores of a test in such a way that the scaled score values may be interpreted as representative of the mean performance of certain reference groups. The intervals between any pair of scaled scores may be interpreted as differences in terms of the characteristics of the reference group.

SCALED TEST

A test in which the items are arranged in order of increasing difficulty or on some other basis. The term may also refer to a test whose items are assigned weights or values according to the difficulty. Scaled tests are used in evaluating individualized learning programs.

SCHOLASTIC APTITUDE

See *academic aptitude*.

SELECTION

The decision to accept or reject an individual for a treatment, program, school, or other undertaking. (See *placement*.)

SEMANTIC DIFFERENTIAL TECHNIQUE

A method requiring individuals to express their feelings about a concept by rating it on a series of bipolar adjectives, e.g., good-bad, strong-weak, and fast-slow. The format is usually a seven-interval scale, and three major dimensions are generally measured: evaluation, potency, and activity.

SKEWNESS

The tendency of a distribution to depart from symmetry or balance around the mean. For example, a negatively skewed distribution may have more extreme low scores than high scores, causing the mean to be lower than the median.

SOCIOMETRY

Measurement of the interpersonal relationships prevailing among the members of a group by means of sociometric devices, e.g., the *sociogram*. An attempt is made to discover the patterns of choice and rejection, identify the individuals most often chosen as friends or leaders ("stars") or rejected by others ("isolates"), and determine how the group subdivides into clusters or cliques.

SPEARMAN–BROWN FORMULA

A formula giving the relationship between the reliability of a test and its length. The formula permits estimation of the changes in reliability that will occur and the known reliability if a test of specified length is lengthened or shortened by any amount. The formula is most commonly applied to estimate the reliability of an entire test from the correlation between two halves of the test, an estimate of internal consistency.

SPECIFICITY

The extent to which items on a test represent course-specific learnings. Experts should receive near-perfect scores, and testwise but course-naive students near-chance scores.

SPEED TEST

A test in which performance is measured by the number of tasks performed correctly in a given time. All items are on a similar level of difficulty, generally easy.

SPLIT–HALF COEFFICIENT

A set of methods for estimating the internal-consistency reliability of a power test by splitting it into comparable halves (usually odd- and even-numbered items). The most common method involves correlating the scores of the two halves and applying the Spearman-Brown prophecy formula to estimate the correlation.

STABILITY

As applied to the examination of reliability, the method involves administering the same test to the same group on two different occasions, and correlating the scores. (See *reliability*.)

STANDARD DEVIATION

A measure of the variability of dispersion of a set of scores. The more the scores cluster around the mean, the smaller the standard deviation.

STANDARD ERROR OF ESTIMATE

An expression of the degree to which predictions or estimates of criterion scores are likely to correspond to actual values (standard deviation of the criterion times the square root of the quantity, one minus the correlation coefficient squared). A method of expressing the validity of the test. All other things being equal, the smaller the standard error the better the validity.

STANDARD ERROR OF MEASUREMENT

A measure of the estimated difference between the observed test score and the hypothetical "true score," i.e., errorless score (standard deviation of the test times the square root of one minus the reliability coefficient). A method of expressing the reliability of a test. All other things being equal, the smaller the error of measurement the higher the reliability. Used in estimating the true score.

STANDARD SCORE

A general term referring to any of a variety of "transformed" scores in terms of which raw scores may be expressed for reasons of convenience, comparability, ease of interpretation, and the like. The simplest type of standard score expresses the deviation of an individual's raw score from the average score of his group in relation to the standard deviation of the scores of the group. Thus:

$$\text{Standard score } (z) = \frac{\text{raw score } (X) - \text{mean } (\overline{X})}{\text{standard deviations } (S)}$$

Standard scores do not affect the relative standing of the individuals in the group or change the shape of the original distribution. More complicated types of standard scores may yield distributions differing in shape from the original distribution; in fact, they are sometimes used for precisely this purpose.

STANDARDIZATION SAMPLE

The reference sample of those individuals, schools, or other units selected for use in norming a test. This sample should be representative of the target population in essential characteristics such as geographical representation, age, and grade.

STANDARDIZED TEST

A systematic sample of performance obtained under prescribed conditions, scored according to definite rules, and capable of evaluation by reference to normative information. Some writers restrict the term to tests possessing the above properties whose items have been experimentally evaluated and/or for which evidence of validity and reliability is provided.

STANINES

A unit that divides the norm population into nine groups. Except for Stanines 1 and 9, the groups are spaced in half-sigma units, with the mean at Stanine 5 and those scoring the highest at Stanine 9. Stanines are usually normalized standard scores.

Stanine	1	2	3	4	5	6	7	8	9
% in Stanine	4	7	12	17	20	17	12	7	4

STENCIL KEY

A scoring key which, when positioned over an examinee's responses in a test booklet or on an answer sheet, permits rapid identification and tabulation of correct answers. Stencil keys may be perforated in positions corresponding to those of the correct answers, so that only correct answers show through, or they may be transparent, with the positions of the correct answers identified by circles or boxes printed on the key.

STRIP KEY

A scoring key on which the answers to items on any page or column of the test appear in a strip or column that may be placed beside the examinee's responses.

SUBTEST

A collection of items in a battery or test that have distinct similar characteristics or functions. A separate score is usually provided.

SUMMATIVE
EVALUATION

The use of evaluation data to determine the effectiveness of a unit, course, or program after it has been completed. (See *formative evaluation*.)

SURVEY TEST

A test that measures general achievement in a given subject or area, usually with the understanding that the test is intended to measure group, rather than individual, status.

T SCORE

A derived (normalized standard) score based on the equivalence of percentile values to standard scores, thus avoiding the effects of skewed distributions, and usually having a mean equated to 50 and a standard deviation equated to 10.

TABLE OF
SPECIFICATIONS

Usually a two-way grid summarizing the behavioral outcomes and content of a course or unit of instruction. Percentages in the cells of the table indicate the importance of subtopics dictated by value judgments, instructional time spent, and the like. Used to guide achievement test development and selection. The specifications may also call for particular types of item, behaviors, and the like. Tables of specification are also used in the development of tests other than proficiency measures.

TEST

A systematic procedure for gathering data to make intra- or inter-individual comparisons.

TEST–RETEST
COEFFICIENT

A type of reliability coefficient obtained by administering a test to the same sample a second time after an interval and correlating the two sets of scores. (See *stability*.)

TRUE SCORE

The average score on an infinite series of administrations of the same or exactly equivalent tests, assuming no practice effect or change in the examinee during the testings. A score for which errors of measurement have been averaged.

VALIDITY

The extent to which a test does the job for which it is used. Thus defined, validity has different connotations for various kinds of tests and, accordingly, different kinds of evidence are appropriate. (1) The validity of an achievement test is the extent to which the content of the test represents a balanced and adequate sampling of the outcomes of the course or instructional program in question (content, face, or curricular validity). It is best determined by a comparison of the test content with courses of study, instructional materials, and statements of instructional goals, and by critical analysis of the processes required to respond to the items. (2) The validity of an aptitude, prognostic, or readiness test is the extent to which it accurately indicates future learning success in the area in question. It is manifested by correlations between test scores and measures of later success. (3) The validity of a personality test is the extent to which the test yields an accurate description of an individual's personality traits or personality organization. It may be manifested by agreement between test results and other types of evaluation, such as ratings or clinical classification, but only to the extent that such criteria are themselves valid. The traditional definition of validity —"the extent to which a test measures what it is supposed to measure"—fails to acknowledge that validity is always specific to the purposes for which the test is used, that different kinds of evidence are appropriate to different types of tests, and that final responsibility for validation rests with the test interpreter and user. (See *content, construct,* and *criterion-related validity*.)

WORK–LIMIT TEST

A test that allows sufficient time for all or nearly all pupils to complete their work. (See *power test*.)

WORK SAMPLE TEST

A high-relevance performance test that provides for an actual tryout of examinees' behavior in a realistic setting.

INDEXES

SUBJECT AND TEST INDEX

NAME INDEX